An Introduction to Distributed Algorithms

An Introduction to Distributed Algorithms

Valmir C. Barbosa

The MIT Press
Cambridge, Massachusetts
London, England

This book was set in TEX by the author and was printed and bound in the United States of America.

Library of Congress Cataloging-in-Publication Data

Barbosa, Valmir C.
    An introduction to distributed algorithms / Valmir C. Barbosa.
      p.   cm.
    Includes bibliographical references and index.
    ISBN 0-262-02412-8 (hc: alk. paper)
    1. Electronic data processing—Distributed processing. 2. Computer algorithms.
    I. Title.
QA76.9.D5B36   1996
005.2—dc20   96-13747
                                                      CIP

To my children, my wife, and my parents

Contents

Preface

This book presents an introduction to some of the main problems, techniques, and algorithms underlying the programming of distributed-memory systems, such as computer networks, networks of workstations, and multiprocessors. It is intended mainly as a textbook for advanced undergraduates or first-year graduate students in computer science and requires no specific background beyond some familiarity with basic graph theory, although prior exposure to the main issues in concurrent programming and computer networks may also be helpful. In addition, researchers and practitioners working on distributed computing will also find it useful as a general reference on some of the most important issues in the field.

The material is organized into ten chapters covering a variety of topics, such as models of distributed computation, information propagation, leader election, distributed snapshots, network synchronization, self-stability, termination detection, deadlock detection, graph algorithms, mutual exclusion, program debugging, and simulation. Because I have chosen to write the book from the broader perspective of distributed-memory systems in general, the topics that I treat fail to coincide exactly with those normally taught in a more orthodox course on distributed algorithms. What this amounts to is that I have included topics that normally would not be touched (as algorithms for maximum flow, program debugging, and simulation) and, on the other hand, have left some topics out (as agreement in the presence of faults).

All the algorithms that I discuss in the book are given for a "target" system that is represented by a connected graph, whose nodes are message-driven entities and whose edges indicate the possibilities of point-to-point communication. This allows the algorithms to be presented in a very simple format by specifying, for each node, the actions to be taken to initiate participating in the algorithm and upon the receipt of a message from one of the nodes connected to it in the graph. In describing the main ideas and algorithms, I have sought a balance between intuition and formal rigor, so that most are preceded by a general intuitive discussion and followed by formal statements regarding correctness, complexity, or other properties.

The book's ten chapters are grouped into two parts. Part 1 is devoted to the basics in the field of distributed algorithms, while Part 2 contains more advanced techniques or applications that build on top of techniques discussed previously.

Part 1 comprises Chapters 1 through 5. Chapters 1 and 2 are introductory chapters, although in two different ways. While Chapter 1 contains a discussion of various issues related to message-passing systems that in the end lead to the adoption of the generic message-driven system I mentioned earlier, Chapter 2 is devoted to a discussion of constraints that are inherent to distributed-memory systems, chiefly those related to a system's asynchronism or synchronism, and the anonymity of its constituents. The remaining three chapters of Part 1 are each dedicated to a group of fundamental ideas and techniques, as follows. Chapter 3 contains models of computation and complexity measures, while Chapter 4 contains some fundamental algorithms (for information propagation and some simple graph problems) and Chapter 5 is devoted to fundamental techniques (as leader election, distributed snapshots, and network synchronization).

The chapters that constitute Part 2 are Chapters 6 through 10. Chapter 6 brings forth the subject of stable properties, both from the perspective of self-stability and of stability detection (for termination and deadlock detection). Chapter 7 contains graph algorithms for minimum spanning trees and maximum flows. Chapter 8 contains algorithms for resource sharing under the requirement of mutual exclusion in a variety of circumstances, including generalizations of the paradigmatic dining philosophers problem. Chapters 9 and 10 are, respectively, dedicated to the topics of program debugging and simulation. Chapter 9 includes techniques for program re-execution and for breakpoint detection. Chapter 10 deals with time-stepped simulation, conservative event-driven simulation, and optimistic event-driven simulation.

Every chapter is complemented by a section with exercises for the reader and another with bibliographic notes. Of the exercises, many are intended to bring the reader one step further in the treatment of some topic discussed in the chapter.

When this is the case, an indication is given, during the discussion of the topic, of the exercise that may be pursued to expand the treatment of that particular topic. I have attempted to collect a fairly comprehensive set of bibliographic references, and the sections with bibliographic notes are intended to provide the reader with the source references for the main issues treated in the chapters, as well as to indicate how to proceed further.

I believe the book is sized reasonably for a one-term course on distributed algorithms. Shorter syllabi are also possible, though, for example by omitting Chapters 1 and 2 (except for Sections 1.4 and 2.1), then covering Chapters 3 through 6 completely, and then selecting as many chapters as one sees fit from Chapters 7 through 10 (the only interdependence that exists among these chapters is of Section 10.2 upon some of Section 8.3).

Notation

The notation $\log^k n$ is used to indicate $(\log n)^k$. All of the remaining notation in the book is standard.

Acknowledgments

This book is based on material I have used to teach at the Federal University of Rio de Janeiro for a number of years and was prepared during my stay as a visiting scientist at the International Computer Science Institute in Berkeley. Many people at these two institutions, including colleagues and students, have been most helpful in a variety of ways, such as improving my understanding of some of the topics I treat in the book, participating in research related to some of those topics, reviewing some of the book's chapters, and helping in the preparation of the manuscript. I am especially thankful to Cláudio Amorim, Maria Cristina Boeres, Eliseu Chaves, Felipe Cucker, Raul Donangelo, Lúcia Drummond, Jerry Feldman, Edil Fernandes, Felipe França, Lélio Freitas, Astrid Hellmuth, Hung Huang, Priscila Lima, Nahri Moreano, Luiz Felipe Perrone, Claudia Portella, Stella Porto, Luis Carlos Quintela, and Roseli Wedemann.

Finally, I acknowledge the support that I have received along the years from CNPq and CAPES, Brazil's agencies for research funding.

V.C.B.
Berkeley, California
December 1995

An Introduction to Distributed Algorithms

Part 1

Fundamentals

This first part of the book is dedicated to some of the fundamentals in the field of distributed algorithms. It comprises five chapters, in which motivation, some limitations, models, basic algorithms, and basic techniques are discussed.

Chapter 1 opens with a discussion of the distributed-memory systems that provide the motivation for the study of distributed algorithms. These include computer networks, networks of workstations, and multiprocessors. In this context, we discuss some of the issues that relate to the study of those systems, such as routing and flow control, message buffering, and processor allocation. The chapter also contains the description of a generic template to write distributed algorithms, to be used throughout the book.

Chapter 2 begins with a discussion of full asynchronism and full synchronism in the context of distributed algorithms. This discussion includes the introduction of the asynchronous and synchronous models of distributed computation to be used in the remainder of the book, and the presentation of details on how the template introduced in Chapter 1 unfolds in each of the two models. We then turn to a discussion of intrinsic limitations in the context of anonymous systems, followed by a brief discussion of the notions of knowledge in distributed computations.

The computation models introduced in Chapter 2 (especially the asynchronous model) are in Chapter 3 expanded to provide a detailed view in terms of events, orders, and global states. This view is necessary for the proper treatment of timing issues in distributed computations, and also allows the introduction of the complexity measures to be employed throughout. The chapter closes with a first discussion (to be resumed later in Chapter 5) of how the asynchronous and synchronous models relate to each other.

Chapters 4 and 5 open the systematic presentation of distributed algorithms, and of their properties, that constitutes the remainder of the book. Both chapters are devoted to basic material. Chapter 4, in particular, contains basic algorithms in the context of information propagation and of some simple graph problems.

In Chapter 5, three fundamental techniques for the development of distributed algorithms are introduced. These are the techniques of leader election (presented only for some types of systems, as the topic is considered again in Part 2, Chapter 7), distributed snapshots, and network synchronization. The latter two techniques draw heavily on material introduced earlier in Chapter 3, and constitute some of the essential building blocks to be occasionally used in later chapters.

1

Message-Passing Systems

The purpose of this chapter is twofold. First we intend to provide an overall picture of various real-world sources of motivation to study message-passing systems, and in doing so to provide the reader with a feeling for the several characteristics that most of those systems share. This is the topic of Section 1.1, in which we seek to bring under a same framework seemingly disparate systems as multiprocessors, networks of workstations, and computer networks in the broader sense.

Our second main purpose in this chapter is to provide the reader with a fairly rigorous, if not always realizable, methodology to approach the development of message-passing programs. Providing this methodology is a means of demonstrating that the characteristics of real-world computing systems and the main assumptions of the abstract model we will use throughout the remainder of the book can be reconciled. This model, to be described timely, is graph-theoretic in nature and encompasses such apparently unrealistic assumptions as the existence of infinitely many buffers to hold the messages that flow on the system's communication channels (thence the reason why reconciling the two extremes must at all be considered).

This methodology is presented as a collection of interrelated aspects in Sections 1.2 through 1.7. It can also be viewed as a means to abstract our thinking about message-passing systems from various of the peculiarities of such systems in the real world by concentrating on the few aspects that they all share and which constitute the source of the core difficulties in the design and analysis of distributed algorithms.

Sections 1.2 and 1.3 are mutually complementary, and address respectively the topics of communication processors and of routing and flow control in message-passing systems. Section 1.4 is devoted to the presentation of a template to be used for the development of message-passing programs. Among other things, it is here that the assumption of infinite-capacity channels appears. Handling such an assumption in realistic situations is the topic of Section 1.5. Section 1.6 contains a treatment of various aspects surrounding the question of processor allocation, and completes the chapter's presentation of methodological issues. Some remarks on some of the material presented in previous sections comes in Section 1.7.

Exercises and bibliographic notes follow respectively in Sections 1.8 and 1.9.

1.1. Distributed-memory systems

Message passing and distributed memory are two concepts intimately related to each other. In this section, our aim is to go on a brief tour of various distributed-memory systems and to demonstrate that in such systems message passing plays a chief role at various levels of abstraction, necessarily at the processor level but often at higher levels as well.

Distributed-memory systems comprise a collection of processors interconnected in some fashion by a network of communication links. Depending on the system one is considering, such a network may consist of point-to-point connections, in which case each communication link handles the communication traffic between two processors exclusively, or it may comprise broadcast channels that accommodate the traffic among the processors in a larger cluster. Processors do not physically share any memory, and then the exchange of information among them must necessarily be accomplished by message passing over the network of communication links.

The other relevant abstraction level in this overall panorama is the level of the programs that run on the distributed-memory systems. One such program can be thought of as comprising a collection of sequential-code entities, each running on a processor, maybe more than one per processor. Depending on peculiarities well beyond the intended scope of this book, such entities have been called tasks, processes, or threads, to name some of the denominations they have received. Because the latter two forms often acquire context-dependent meanings (e.g., within a specific operating system or a specific programming language), in this book we choose to refer to each of those entities as a *task*, although this denomination too may at times have controversial connotations.

While at the processor level in a distributed-memory system there is no choice but to rely on message passing for communication, at the task level there are plenty of options. For example, tasks that run on the same processor may communicate with each other either through the explicit use of that processor's memory or by means of message passing in a very natural way. Tasks that run on different processors also have essentially these two possibilities. They may communicate by message passing by relying on the message-passing mechanisms that provide interprocessor communication, or they may employ those mechanisms to emulate the sharing of memory across processor boundaries. In addition, a myriad of hybrid approaches can be devised, including for example the use of memory for communication by tasks that run on the same processor and the use of message passing among tasks that do not.

Some of the earliest distributed-memory systems to be realized in practice were long-haul computer networks, i.e., networks interconnecting processors geographically separated by considerable distances. Although originally employed for remote terminal access and somewhat later for electronic-mail purposes, such networks progressively grew to encompass an immense variety of data-communication services, including facilities for remote file transfer and for maintaining work sessions on remote processors. A complex hierarchy of protocols is used to provide this variety of services, employing at its various levels message passing on point-to-point connections. Recent advances in the technology of these protocols are rapidly leading to fundamental improvements that promise to allow the coexistence of several different types of traffic in addition to data, as for example voice, image, and video. The protocols underlying these advances are generally known as Asynchronous Transfer Mode (ATM) protocols, in a way underlining the aim of providing satisfactory service for various different traffic demands. ATM connections, although frequently of the point-to-point type, can for many applications benefit from efficient broadcast capabilities, as for example in the case of teleconferencing.

Another notorious example of distributed-memory systems comes from the field of parallel processing, in which an ensemble of interconnected processors (a multiprocessor) is employed in the solution of a single problem. Application areas in need of such computational potential are rather abundant, and come from various of the scientific and engineering fields. The early approaches to the construction of parallel processing systems concentrated on the design of shared-memory systems, that is, systems in which the processors share all the memory banks as well as the entire address space. Although this approach had some success for a limited number of processors, clearly it could not support any significant growth in that number, because the physical mechanisms used to provide the sharing of memory cells would soon saturate during the attempt at scaling.

The interest in providing massive parallelism for some applications (i.e., the parallelism of very large, and scalable, numbers of processors) quickly led to the introduction of distributed-memory systems built with point-to-point interprocessor connections. These systems have dominated the scene completely ever since. Multiprocessors of this type were for many years used with a great variety of programming languages endowed with the capability of performing message passing as explicitly directed by the programmer. One problem with this approach to parallel programming is that in many application areas it appears to be more natural to provide a unique address space to the programmer, so that, in essence, the parallelization of preexisting sequential programs can be carried out in a more straightforward fashion. With this aim, distributed-memory multiprocessors have recently appeared whose message-passing hardware is capable of providing the task level with a single address space, so that at this level message passing can be done away with. The message-passing character of the hardware is fundamental, though, as it seems that this is one of the key issues in providing good scalability properties along with a shared-memory programming model. To provide this programming model on top of a message-passing hardware, such multiprocessors have relied on sophisticated cache techniques.

The latest trend in multiprocessor design emerged from a re-consideration of the importance of message passing at the task level, which appears to provide the most natural programming model in various situations. Current multiprocessor designers are then attempting to build, on top of the message-passing hardware, facilities for both message-passing and scalable shared-memory programming.

As our last example of important classes of distributed-memory systems, we comment on networks of workstations. These networks share a lot of characteristics with the long-haul networks we discussed earlier, but unlike those they tend to be concentrated within a much narrower geographic region, and so frequently employ broadcast connections as their chief medium for interprocessor communication (point-to-point connections dominate at the task level, though). Also because of the circumstances that come from the more limited geographic dispersal, networks of workstations are capable of supporting many services other than those already available in the long-haul case, as for example the sharing of file systems. In fact, networks of workstations provide unprecedented computational and storage power in the form, respectively, of idling processors and unused storage capacity, and because of the facilitated sharing of resources that they provide they are already beginning to be looked at as a potential source of inexpensive, massive parallelism.

As it appears from the examples we described in the three classes of distributed-memory systems we have been discussing (computer networks, multiprocessors, and networks of workstations), message-passing computations over point-to-point connections constitute some sort of a pervasive paradigm. Frequently, however, it comes in the company of various other approaches, which emerge when the computations that take place on those distributed-memory systems are looked at from different perspectives and at different levels of abstraction.

The remainder of the book is devoted exclusively to message-passing computations over point-to-point connections. Such computations will be described at the task level, which clearly can be regarded as encompassing message-passing computations at the processor level as well. This is so because the latter can be regarded as message-passing computations at the task level when there is exactly one task per processor and two tasks only communicate with each other if they run on processors directly interconnected by a communication link. However, before leaving aside the processor level completely, we find it convenient to have some understanding of how a group of processors interconnected by point-to-point connections can support intertask message passing even among tasks that run on processors not directly connected by a communication link. This is the subject of the following two sections.

1.2. Communication processors

When two tasks that need to communicate with each other run on processors which are not directly interconnected by a communication link, there is no option to perform that intertask communication but to somehow rely on processors other than the two running the tasks to relay the communication traffic as needed. Clearly, then, each processor in the system must, in addition to executing the tasks that run on it, also act as a relayer of the communication traffic that does not originate from (or is destined to) any of the tasks that run on it. Performing this additional function is quite burdensome, so it appears natural to somehow provide the processor with specific capabilities that allow it to do the relaying of communication traffic without interfering with its local computation. In this way, each processor in the system can be viewed as actually a pair of processors that run independently of each other. One of them is the processor that runs the tasks (called the *host processor*) and the other is the *communication processor*. Unless confusion may arise, the denomination simply as a processor will in the remainder of the book be used to indicate either the host processor or, as it has been so far, the pair comprising the host processor and the communication processor.

In the context of computer networks (and in a similar fashion networks of workstations as well), the importance of communication processors was recognized at the very beginning, not only by the performance-related reasons we indicated, but mainly because, by the very nature of the services provided by such networks, each communication processor was to provide services to various users at its site. The first generation of distributed-memory multiprocessors, however, was conceived without any concern for this issue, but very soon afterwards it became clear that the communication traffic would be an unsurmountable bottleneck unless special hardware was provided to handle that traffic. The use of communication processors has been the rule since.

There is a great variety of approaches to the design of a communication processor, and that depends of course on the programming model to be provided at the task level. If message passing is all that needs to be provided, then the communication processor has to at least be able to function as an efficient communication relayer. If, on the other hand, a shared-memory programming model is intended, either by itself or in a hybrid form that also allows message passing, then the communication processor must also be able to handle memory-management functions.

Let us concentrate a little more on the message-passing aspects of communication processors. The most essential function to be performed by a communication processor is in this case to handle the reception of messages, which may come either from the host processor attached to it or from another communication processor, and then to decide where to send it next, which again may be the local host processor or another communication processor. This function *per se* involves very complex issues, which are the subject of our discussion in Section 1.3.

Another very important aspect in the design of such communication processors comes from viewing them as processors with an instruction set of their own, and then the additional issue comes up of designing such an instruction set so to provide communication services not only to the local host processor but in general to the entire system. The enhanced flexibility that comes from viewing a communication processor in this way is very attractive indeed, and has motivated a few very interesting approaches to the design of those processors. So, for example, in order to send a message to another (remote) task, a task running on the local host processor has to issue an instruction to the communication processor that will tell it to do so. This instruction is the same that the communication processors exchange among themselves in order to have messages passed on as needed until a destination is reached. In addition to rendering the view of how a communication processor handles the traffic of point-to-point messages a little simpler, regarding the communication processor as an instruction-driven entity has many other advantages. For example, a host processor may direct its associated communication processor to perform complex group communication functions and do something else until that function has been completed system-wide. Some very natural candidate functions are discussed in this book, especially in Chapters 4 and 5 (although algorithms presented elsewhere in the book may also be regarded as such, only at a higher level of complexity).

1.3. Routing and flow control

As we remarked in the previous section, one of the most basic and important functions to be performed by a communication processor is to act as a relayer of the messages it receives by either sending them on to its associated host processor or by passing them along to another communication processor. This function is known as *routing*, and has various important aspects that deserve our attention.

For the remainder of this chapter, we shall let our distributed-memory system be represented by the connected undirected graph $G_P = (N_P, E_P)$, where the set of nodes N_P is the set of processors (each processor viewed as the pair comprising a host processor and a communication processor) and the set E_P of undirected edges is the set of point-to-point bidirectional communication links. A message is normally received at a communication processor as a pair (q, Msg), meaning that Msg is to be delivered to processor q. Here Msg is the message as it is first issued by the task that sends it, and can be regarded as comprising a pair of fields as well, say $Msg = (u, msg)$, where u denotes the task running on processor q to which the message is to be delivered and msg is the message as u must receive it. This implies that at each processor the information of which task runs on which processor must be available, so that intertask messages can be addressed properly when they are first issued. Section 1.6 is devoted to a discussion of how this information can be obtained.

When a processor r receives the message (q, Msg), it checks whether $q = r$ and in the affirmative case forwards Msg to the host processor at r. Otherwise, the message must be destined to another processor, and is then forwarded by the communication processor for eventual delivery to that other processor. At processor r, this forwarding takes place according to the function $next_r(q)$, which indicates the processor directly connected to r to which the message must be sent next for eventual delivery to q (that is, $(r, next_r(q)) \in E_P$). The function $next$ is a *routing function*, and ultimately indicates the set of links a message must traverse in order to be transported between any two processors in the system. For processors p and q, we denote by $R(p, q) \subseteq E_P$ the set of links to be traversed by a message originally sent by a task running on p to a task running on q. Clearly, $R(p, p) = \emptyset$ and in general $R(p, q)$ and $R(q, p)$ are different sets.

Routing can be *fixed* or *adaptive*, depending on how the function *next* is handled. In the fixed case, the function *next* is time-invariant, whereas in the adaptive case it may be time-varying. Routing can also be *deterministic* or *nondeterministic*, depending on how many processors *next* can be chosen from at a processor. In the deterministic case there is only one choice, whereas the nondeterministic case allows multiple choices in the determination of *next*. Pairwise combinations of these types of routing are also allowed, with adaptivity and nondeterminism being usually advocated for increased performance and fault-tolerance. Advantageous as some of these enhancements to routing may be, not many of adaptive or nondeterministic schemes have made it into practice, and the reason is that many difficulties accompany those enhancements at various levels. For example, the FIFO (First In, First Out) order of message delivery at the processor level cannot be trivially guaranteed in the adaptive or nondeterministic cases, and then so cannot at the task level either, that is, messages sent from one task to another may end up delivered in an order different than the order they were sent. For some applications, as we discuss for example in Section 5.2.1, this would complicate the treatment at the task level and most likely do away with whatever improvement in efficiency one might have obtained with the adaptive or nondeterministic approaches to routing. (We return to the question of ensuring FIFO message delivery among tasks in Section 1.6.2, but in a different context.)

Let us then concentrate on fixed, determinist routing for the remainder of the chapter. In this case, and given a destination processor q, the routing function $next_r(q)$ does not lead to any *loops* (i.e., by successively moving from processor to processor as dictated by *next* until q is reached it is not possible to return to an already visited processor). This is so because the existence of such a loop would either require at least two possibilities for the determination of $next_r(q)$ for some r, which is ruled out by the assumption of deterministic routing, or require that *next* be allowed to change with time, which cannot be under the assumption of fixed routing. If routing is deterministic, then another way of arriving at this loop-free property of *next* is to recognize that, for fixed routing, the sets R of links are such that $R(r, q) \subseteq R(p, q)$ for every processor r that can be obtained from p by successively applying *next* given q. The absence of loops comes as a consequence. Under this alternative view, it becomes clear that, by building the sets R to contain shortest paths (i.e., paths with the least possible numbers of links) in the fixed, deterministic case, the containments for those sets appear naturally, and then one immediately obtains a routing function with no loops.

Loops in a routing function refer to one single *end-to-end directed path* (i.e., a sequence of processors obtained by following $next_r(q)$ from $r = p$ for some p and fixed q), and clearly should be avoided. Another related concept, that of a *directed cycle* in a routing function, can also lead to undesirable behavior in some situations (to be discussed shortly), but cannot be altogether avoided. A directed cycle exists in a routing function when two or more end-to-end directed paths share at least two processors (and sometimes links as well), say p and q, in such a way that q can be reached from p by following $next_r(q)$ at the intermediate r's, and so can p from q by following $next_r(p)$. Every routing function contains at least the directed cycles implied by the sharing of processors p and q by the sets $R(p,q)$ and $R(q,p)$ for all $p,q \in N_P$. A routing function containing only these directed cycles does not have any end-to-end directed paths sharing links in the same direction, and is referred to as a *quasi-acyclic* routing function.

Another function that is normally performed by communication processors and goes closely along that of routing is the function of *flow control*. Once the routing function *next* has been established and the system begins to transport messages among the various pairs of processors, the storage and communication resources that the interconnected communication processors possess must be shared not only by the messages already on their way to destination processors but also by other messages that continue to be admitted from the host processors. Flow control strategies aim at optimizing the use of the system's resources under such circumstances. We discuss three such strategies in the remainder of this section.

The first mechanism we investigate for flow control is the *store-and-forward* mechanism. This mechanism requires a message (q, Msg) to be divided into *packets* of fixed size. Each packet carries the same addressing information as the original message (i.e., q), and can therefore be transmitted independently. If these packets cannot be guaranteed to be delivered to q in the FIFO order, then they must also carry a sequence number, to be used at q for the re-assembly of the message. (However, guaranteeing the FIFO order is a straightforward matter under the assumption of fixed, deterministic routing, so long as the communication links themselves are FIFO links.) At intermediate communication processors, packets are stored in buffers for later transmission when the required link becomes available (a queue of packets is kept for each link).

Store-and-forward flow control is prone to the occurrence of deadlocks, as the packets compete for shared resources (buffering space at the communication processors, in this case). One simple situation in which this may happen is the following. Consider a cycle of processors in G_P, and suppose that one task running on each of the processors in the cycle has a message to send to another task running on another processor on the cycle that is more than one link away. Suppose in addition that the routing function *next* is such that all the corresponding communication processors, after having received such messages from their associated host processors, attempt to send them in the same direction (clockwise or counterclockwise) on the cycle of processors. If buffering space is no longer available at any of the communication processors on the cycle, then deadlock is certain to occur.

This type of deadlock can be prevented by employing what is called a *structured buffer pool*. This is a mechanism whereby the buffers at all communication processors are divided into classes, and whenever a packet is sent between two directly interconnected communication processors, it can only be accepted for storage at the receiving processor if there is buffering space in a specific buffer class, which is normally a function of some of the packet's addressing parameters. If this function allows no cyclic dependency to be formed among the various buffer classes, then deadlock is ensured never to occur. Even with this issue of deadlock resolved, the store-and-forward mechanism suffers from two main drawbacks. One of them is the latency for the delivery of messages, as the packets have to be stored at all intermediate communication processors. The other drawback is the need to use memory bandwidth, which seldom can be provided entirely by the communication processor and has then to be shared with the tasks that run on the associated host processor.

The potentially excessive latency of store-and-forward flow control is partially remedied by the second flow-control mechanism we describe. This mechanism is known as *circuit switching*, and requires an end-to-end directed path to be entirely reserved in one direction for a message before it is transmitted. Once all the links on the path have been secured for that particular transmission, the message is then sent and at the intermediate processors incurs no additional delay waiting for links to become available. The reservation process employed by circuit switching is also prone to the occurrence of deadlocks, as links may participate in several paths in the same direction. Portions of those paths may form directed cycles that may in turn deadlock the reservation of links. Circuit switching should, for this reason, be restricted to those routing functions that are quasi-acyclic, which by definition pose no deadlock threat to the reservation process.

Circuit switching is obviously inefficient for the transmission of short messages, as the time for the entire path to be reserved becomes then prominent. Even for long messages, however, its advantages may not be too pronounced, depending primarily on how the message is transmitted once the links are reserved. If the message is divided into packets that have to be stored at the intermediate communication processors, then the gain with circuit switching may be only marginal, as a packet is only sent on the next link after it has been completely received (all that is saved is then the wait time on outgoing packet queues). It is possible, however, to pipeline the transmission of the message so that only very small portions have to be stored at the intermediate processors, as in the third flow-control strategy we describe next.

The last strategy we describe for flow control employs packet blocking (as opposed to packet buffering or link reservation) as one of its basic paradigms. The resulting mechanism is known as *wormhole routing* (a misleading denomination, because it really is a flow-control strategy), and contrasting with the previous two strategies, the basic unit on which flow control is performed is not a packet but a *flit* (*flow-control digit*). A flit contains no routing information, so every flit in a packet must follow the leading flit, where the routing information is kept when the packet is subdivided. With wormhole routing, the inherent latency of store-and-forward flow control due to the constraint that a packet can only be sent forward after it has been received in its entirety is eliminated. All that needs to be stored is a flit, significantly smaller than a packet, so the transmission of the packet is pipelined, as portions of it may be flowing on different links and portions may be stored. When the leading flit needs access to a resource (memory space or link) that it cannot have immediately, the entire packet is blocked and only proceeds when that flit can advance. As with the previous two mechanisms, deadlock can also arise in wormhole routing. The strategy for dealing with this is to break the directed cycles in the routing function (thereby possibly making pairs of processors inaccessible to each other), then add *virtual links* to the already existing links in the network, and then finally fix the routing function by the use of the virtual links. Directed cycles in the routing function then become "spirals," and deadlocks can no longer occur. (Virtual links are in the literature referred to as *virtual channels*, but channels will have in this book a different connotation—cf. Section 1.4.)

In the case of multiprocessors, the use of communication processors employing wormhole routing for flow control tends to be such that the time to transport a message between nodes directly connected by a link in G_P is only marginally smaller than the time spent when no direct connection exists. In such circumstances, G_P can often be regarded as being a complete graph (cf. Section 2.1, where we discuss details of the example given in Section 1.6.2).

To finalize this section, we mention that yet another flow-control strategy has been proposed that can be regarded as a hybrid strategy combining store-and-forward flow control and wormhole routing. It is called *virtual cut-through*, and is characterized by pipelining the transmission of packets as in wormhole routing, and by requiring entire packets to be stored when an outgoing link cannot be immediately used, as in store-and-forward. Virtual cut-through can then be regarded as a variation of wormhole routing in which the pipelining in packet transmission is retained but packet blocking is replaced with packet buffering.

1.4. Reactive message-passing programs

So far in this chapter we have discussed how message-passing systems relate to distributed-memory systems, and have outlined some important characteristics at the processor level that allow tasks to communicate with one another by message passing over point-to-point communication channels. Our goal in this section is to introduce, in the form of a template algorithm, our understanding of what a distributed algorithm is and of how it should be described. This template and some of the notation associated with it will in Section 2.1 evolve into the more compact notation that we use throughout the book.

We represent a *distributed algorithm* by the connected directed graph $G_T = (N_T, D_T)$, where the node set N_T is a set of tasks and the set of directed edges D_T is a set of unidirectional communication channels. (A connected directed graph is a directed graph whose underlying undirected graph is connected.) For a task t, we let $In_t \subseteq D_T$ denote the set of edges directed towards t and $Out_t \subseteq D_T$ the set of edges directed away from t. Channels in In_t are those on which t receives messages and channels in Out_t are those on which t sends messages. We also let $n_t = |In_t|$, that is, n_t denotes the number of channels on which t may receive messages.

A task t is a *reactive* (or *message-driven*) entity, in the sense that normally it only performs computation (including the sending of messages to other tasks) as a response to the receipt of a message from another task. An exception to this rule is that at least one task must be allowed to send messages out "spontaneously" (i.e., not as a response to a message receipt) to other tasks at the beginning of its execution, inasmuch as otherwise the assumed message-driven character of the tasks would imply that every task would idle indefinitely and no computation would take place at all. Also, a task may initially perform computation for initialization purposes.

Algorithm *Task_t*, given next, describes the overall behavior of a generic task t. Although in this algorithm we (for ease of notation) let tasks compute and then send messages out, no such precedence is in fact needed, as computing and sending messages out may constitute intermingled portions of a task's actions.

Algorithm $Task\_t$:

> Do some computation;
> **send** one message on each channel of a (possibly empty) subset of Out_t;
> **repeat**
>> **receive** message on $c_1 \in In_t$ **and** $B_1 \to$
>>> Do some computation;
>>> **send** one message on each channel of a (possibly empty) subset
>>> of Out_t
>>
>> **or**...
>> **or**
>> **receive** message on $c_{n_t} \in In_t$ **and** $B_{n_t} \to$
>>> Do some computation;
>>> **send** one message on each channel of a (possibly empty) subset
>>> of Out_t
>>
> **until** global termination is known to t.

There are many important observations to be made in connection with Algorithm $Task\_t$. The first important observation is in connection with how the computation begins and ends for task t. As we remarked earlier, task t begins by doing some computation and by sending messages to none or more of the tasks to which it is connected in G_T by an edge directed away from it (messages are sent by means of the operation **send**). Then t iterates until a global termination condition is known to it, at which time its computation ends. At each iteration, t does some computation and may send messages. The issue of global termination will be thoroughly discussed in Section 6.2 in a generic setting, and before that in various other chapters it will come up in more particular contexts. For now it suffices to notice that t acquires the information that it may terminate its local computation by means of messages received during its iterations. If designed correctly, what this information signals to t is that no message will ever reach it again, and then it may exit the **repeat**...**until** loop.

The second important observation is on the construction of the **repeat**...**until** loop and on the semantics associated with it. Each iteration of this loop contains n_t guarded commands grouped together by **or** connectives. A *guarded command* is usually denoted by

$$guard \to command,$$

where, in our present context, *guard* is a condition of the form

$$\textbf{receive} \text{ message on } c_k \in In_t \textbf{ and } B_k$$

for some Boolean condition B_k, where $1 \le k \le n_t$. The **receive** appearing in the
description of the *guard* is an operation for a task to receive messages. The *guard*
is said to be *ready* when there is a message available for immediate reception on
channel c_k and furthermore the condition B_k is **true**. This condition may depend
on the message that is available for reception, so that a guard may be ready or
not, for the same channel, depending on what is at the channel to be received.
The overall semantics of the **repeat** ... **until** loop is then the following. At each
iteration, execute the *command* of exactly one guarded command whose *guard* is
ready. If no *guard* is ready, then the task is suspended until one is. If more than
one *guard* is ready, then one of them is selected arbitrarily. As the reader will
verify by our many distributed algorithm examples along the book, this possibility
of nondeterministically selecting guarded commands for execution provides great
design flexibility.

Our final important remark in connection with Algorithm *Task_t* is on the
semantics associated with the **receive** and **send** operations. Although as we have
remarked the use of a **receive** in a *guard* is to be interpreted as an indication that
a message is available for immediate receipt by the task on the channel specified,
when used in other contexts this operation in general has a *blocking* nature. A
blocking **receive** has the effect of suspending the task until a message arrives on
the channel specified, unless a message is already there to be received, in which
case the reception takes place and the task resumes its execution immediately.

The **send** operation too has a semantics of its own, and in general may be
blocking or *nonblocking*. If it is blocking, then the task is suspended until the
message can be delivered directly to the receiving task, unless the receiving task
happens to be already suspended for message reception on the corresponding channel when the **send** is executed. A blocking **send** and a blocking **receive** constitute
what is known as *task rendez-vous*, which is a mechanism for task synchronization. If the **send** operation has a nonblocking nature, then the task transmits
the message and immediately resumes its execution. This nonblocking version of
send requires buffering for the messages that have been sent but not yet received,
that is, messages that are *in transit* on the channel. Blocking and nonblocking
send operations are also sometimes referred to as *synchronous* and *asynchronous*,
respectively, to emphasize the synchronizing effect they have in the former case.
We refrain from using this terminology, however, because in this book the words
synchronous and asynchronous will have other meanings throughout (cf. Section
2.1). When used, as in Algorithm *Task_t*, to transmit messages to more than one
task, the **send** operation is assumed to be able to do all such transmissions in
parallel.

The relation of blocking and nonblocking **send** operations with message buffering requirements raises important questions related to the design of distributed algorithms. If, on the one hand, a blocking **send** requires no message buffering (as the message is passed directly between the synchronized tasks), on the other hand a nonblocking **send** requires the ability of a channel to buffer an unbounded number of messages. The former scenario poses great difficulties to the program designer, as communication deadlocks occur with great ease when the programming is done with the use of blocking operations only. For this reason, however unreal the requirement of infinitely many buffers may seem, it is customary to start the design of a distributed algorithm by assuming nonblocking operations, and then at a later stage performing changes to yield a program that makes use of the operations provided by the language at hand, possibly of a blocking nature or of a nature that lies somewhere in between the two extremes of blocking and nonblocking **send** operations.

The use of nonblocking **send** operations does in general allow the correctness of distributed algorithms to be shown more easily, as well as their properties. We then henceforth assume that, in Algorithm *Task_t*, **send** operations have a nonblocking nature. Because Algorithm *Task_t* is a template for all the algorithms appearing in the book, the assumption of nonblocking **send** operations holds throughout. Another important aspect affecting the design of distributed algorithms is whether the channels in D_T deliver messages in the FIFO order or not. Although as we remarked in Section 1.3 this property may at times be essential, we make no assumptions now, and leave its treatment to be done on a case-by-case basis. We do make the point, however, that in the guards of Algorithm *Task_t* at most one message can be available for immediate reception on a FIFO channel, even if other messages have already arrived on that same channel (the available message is the one to have arrived first and not yet received). If the channel is not FIFO, then any message that has arrived can be regarded as being available for immediate reception.

1.5. Handling infinite-capacity channels

As we saw in Section 1.4, the blocking or nonblocking nature of the **send** operations is closely related to the channels' ability to buffer messages. Specifically, blocking operations require no buffering at all, while nonblocking operations may require an infinite amount of buffers. Between the two extremes, we say that a channel has *capacity* $k \geq 0$ if the number of messages it can buffer before either a message is received by the receiving task or the sending task is suspended upon attempting a transmission is k. The case of $k = 0$ corresponds to a blocking **send**, and the case in which $k \to \infty$ corresponds to a nonblocking **send**.

Although Algorithm *Task_t* of Section 1.4 is written under the assumption of infinite-capacity channels, such an assumption is unreasonable, and must be dealt with somewhere along the programming process. This is in general achieved along two main steps. First, for each channel c a nonnegative integer $b(c)$ must be determined that reflects the number of buffers actually needed by channel c. This number must be selected carefully, as an improper choice may introduce communication deadlocks in the program. Such a deadlock is represented by a directed cycle of tasks, all of which are suspended to send a message on the channel on the cycle, which cannot be done because all channels have been assigned insufficient storage space. Secondly, once the $b(c)$'s have been determined, Algorithm *Task_t* must be changed so that it now employs **send** operations that can deal with the new channel capacities. Depending on the programming language at hand, this can be achieved rather easily. For example, if the programming language offers channels with zero capacity, then each channel c may be replaced with a serial arrangement of $b(c)$ *relay tasks* alternating with $b(c) + 1$ zero-capacity channels. Each relay task has one input channel and one output channel, and has the sole function of sending on its output channel whatever it receives on its input channel. It has, in addition, a storage capacity of exactly one message, so the entire arrangement can be viewed as a $b(c)$-capacity channel.

The real problem is of course to determine values for the $b(c)$'s in such a way that no new deadlock is introduced in the distributed algorithm (put more optimistically, the task is to ensure the deadlock-freedom of an originally deadlock-free program). In the remainder of this section, we describe solutions to this problem which are based on the availability of a bound $r(c)$, provided for each channel c, on the number of messages that may require buffering in c when c has infinite capacity. This number $r(c)$ is the largest number of messages that will ever be in transit on c when the receiving task of c is itself attempting a message transmission, so the messages in transit have to be buffered.

Although determining the $r(c)$'s can be very simple for some distributed algorithms (cf. Sections 5.4 and 8.5), for many others such bounds are either unknown, or known imprecisely, or simply do not exist. In such cases, the value of $r(c)$ should be set to a "large" positive integer M for all channels c whose bounds cannot be determined precisely. Just how large this M has to be, and what the limitations of this approach are, we discuss later in this section.

If the value of $r(c)$ is known precisely for all $c \in D_T$, then obviously the strategy of assigning $b(c) = r(c)$ buffers to every channel c guarantees the introduction of no additional deadlock, as every message ever to be in transit when its destination is engaged in a message transmission will be buffered (there may be more messages in transit, but only when their destination is not engaged in a message transmission, and will therefore be ready for reception within a finite amount of time). The interesting question here is, however, whether it can still be guaranteed that no new deadlock will be introduced if $b(c) < r(c)$ for some channels c. This would be an important strategy to deal with the cases in which $r(c) = M$ for some $c \in D_T$, and to allow (potentially) substantial space savings in the process of buffer assignment. Theorem 1.1 given next concerns this issue.

Theorem 1.1. *Suppose that the distributed algorithm given by Algorithm Task_t for all $t \in N_T$ is deadlock-free. Suppose in addition that G_T contains no directed cycle on which every channel c is such that either $b(c) < r(c)$ or $r(c) = M$. Then the distributed algorithm obtained by replacing each infinite-capacity channel c with a $b(c)$-capacity channel is deadlock-free.*

Proof: A necessary condition for a deadlock to arise is that a directed cycle exists in G_T whose tasks are all suspended on an attempt to send messages on the channels on that cycle. By the hypotheses, however, every directed cycle in G_T has at least one channel c for which $b(c) = r(c) < M$, so at least the tasks t that have such channels in Out_t are never indefinitely suspended upon attempting to send messages on them. ∎

The converse of Theorem 1.1 is also often true, but not in general. Specifically, there may be cases in which $r(c) = M$ for all the channels c of a directed cycle, and yet the resulting algorithm is deadlock-free, as M may be a true upper bound for c (albeit unknown). So setting $b(c) = r(c)$ for this channel does not necessarily mean providing it with insufficient buffering space.

As long as we comply with the sufficient condition given by Theorem 1.1, it is then possible to assign to some channels c fewer buffers than $r(c)$ and still guarantee that the resulting distributed algorithm is deadlock-free if it was deadlock-free to begin with. In the remainder of this section, we discuss two criteria whereby these channels may be selected. Both criteria lead to intractable optimization problems (i.e., *NP*-hard problems), so heuristics need to be devised to approximate solutions to them (some are provided in the literature).

The first criterion attempts to save as much buffering space as possible. It is called the *space-optimal criterion*, and is based on a choice of M such that

$$M > \sum_{c \in D_T - C^+} r(c),$$

where C^+ is the set of channels for which a precise upper bound is not known. This criterion requires a subset of channels $C \subseteq D_T$ to be determined such that every directed cycle in G_T has at least one channel in C, and such that

$$\sum_{c \in C} r(c)$$

is minimum over all such subsets (clearly, C and C^+ are then disjoint, given the value of M, unless C^+ contains the channels of an entire directed cycle from G_T). Then the strategy is to set

$$b(c) = \begin{cases} r(c), & \text{if } c \in C; \\ 0, & \text{otherwise}, \end{cases}$$

which ensures that at least one channel c from every directed cycle in G_T is assigned $b(c) = r(c)$ buffers (Figure 1.1). By Theorem 1.1, this strategy then produces a deadlock-free result if no directed cycle in G_T has all of its channels in the set C^+. That this strategy employs the minimum number of buffers comes from the optimal determination of the set C.

The space-optimal approach to buffer assignment has the drawback that the concurrency in intertask communication may be too low, inasmuch as many channels in D_T may be allocated zero buffers. Extreme situations can happen, as for example the assignment of zero buffers to all the channels of a long directed path in G_T. A scenario might then happen in which all tasks in this path (except the last one) would be suspended to communicate with its successor on the path, and this would only take place for one pair of tasks at a time. When at least one channel c has insufficient buffers (i.e., $b(c) < r(c)$) or is such that $r(c) = M$, a measure of concurrency that attempts to capture the effect we just described is to take the minimum, over all directed paths in G_T whose channels c all have $b(c) < r(c)$ or $r(c) = M$, of the ratio

$$\frac{1}{L+1},$$

where L is the number of channels on the path. Clearly, this measure can be no less than $1/|N_T|$ and no more than $1/2$, as long as the assignment of buffers conforms to the hypotheses of Theorem 1.1. The value of $1/2$, in particular, can only be achieved if no directed path with more than one channel exists comprising channels c such that $b(c) < r(c)$ or $r(c) = M$ only.

Another criterion for buffer assignment to channels is then the *concurrency-optimal criterion*, which also seeks to save buffering space, but not to the point

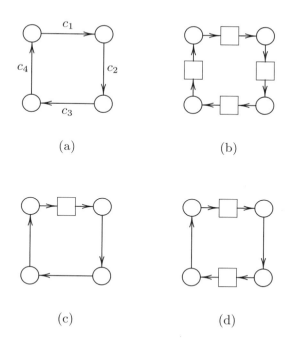

(a)   (b)

(c)   (d)

Figure 1.1. *A graph G_T is shown in part (a). In the graphs of parts (b) through (d), circular nodes are the nodes of G_T, while square nodes represent buffers assigned to the corresponding channel in G_T. If $r(c) = 1$ for all $c \in \{c_1, c_2, c_3, c_4\}$, then parts (b) through (d) represent three distinct buffer assignments, all of which deadlock-free. Part (b) shows the strategy of setting $b(c) = r(c)$ for all $c \in \{c_1, c_2, c_3, c_4\}$. Parts (c) and (d) represent, respectively, the results of the space-optimal and the concurrency-optimal strategies.*

that the concurrency as we defined might be compromised. This criterion looks for buffer assignments that yield a level of concurrency equal to 1/2, and for this reason does not allow any directed path with more than one channel to have all of its channels assigned insufficient buffers. This alone is, however, insufficient for the value of 1/2 to be attained, as for such it is also necessary that no directed path with more than one channel contain channels c with $r(c) = M$ only. Like the space-optimal criterion, the concurrency-optimal criterion utilizes a value of M

such that

$$M > \sum_{c \in D_T - C^+} r(c).$$

This criterion requires a subset of channels $C \subseteq D_T$ to be found such that no directed path with more than one channel exists in G_T comprising channels from C only, and such that

$$\sum_{c \in C} r(c)$$

is maximum over all such subsets (clearly, $C^+ \subseteq C$, given the value of M, unless C^+ contains the channels of an entire directed path from G_T with more than one channel). The strategy is then to set

$$b(c) = \begin{cases} 0, & \text{if } c \in C; \\ r(c), & \text{otherwise,} \end{cases}$$

thereby ensuring that at least one channel c in every directed path with more than one channel in G_T is assigned $b(c) = r(c)$ buffers, and that, as a consequence, at least one channel c from every directed cycle in G_T is assigned $b(c) = r(c)$ buffers as well (Figure 1.1). By Theorem 1.1, this strategy then produces a deadlock-free result if no directed cycle in G_T has all of its channels in the set C^+. The strategy also provides concurrency equal to $1/2$ by our definition, as long as C^+ does not contain all the channels of any directed path in G_T with more than one channel. Given this constraint that optimal concurrency must be achieved (if possible), then the strategy employs the minimum number of buffers, as the set C is optimally determined.

1.6. Processor allocation

When we discussed the routing of messages among processors in Section 1.3 we saw that addressing a message at the task level requires knowledge by the processor running the task originating the message of the processor on which the destination task runs. This information is provided by what is known as an *allocation function*, which is a mapping of the form

$$A : N_T \rightarrow N_P,$$

where N_T and N_P are, as we recall, the node sets of graphs G_T (introduced in Section 1.4) and G_P (introduced in Section 1.3), respectively. The function A is such that $A(t) = p$ if and only if task t runs on processor p.

For many of the systems reviewed in Section 1.1 the allocation function is given naturally by how the various tasks in N_T are distributed throughout the system, as for example computer networks and networks of workstations. However, for multiprocessors and also for networks of workstations when viewed as parallel processing systems, the function A has to be determined during what is called the *processor allocation* step of program design. In these cases, G_T should be viewed not simply as the task graph introduced earlier, but rather as an enlargement of that graph to accommodate the relay tasks discussed in Section 1.5 (or any other tasks with similar functions—cf. Exercise 4).

The determination of the allocation function A is based on a series of attributes associated with both G_T and G_P. Among the attributes associated with G_P is its routing function, which, as we remarked in Section 1.3, can be described by the mapping

$$R : N_P \times N_P \to 2^{E_P}.$$

For all $p, q \in N_P$, $R(p, q)$ is the set of links on the route from processor p to processor q, possibly distinct from $R(q, p)$, and such that $R(p, p) = \emptyset$. Additional attributes of G_P are the relative *processor speed* (in instructions per unit time) of $p \in N_P$, s_p, and the relative *link capacity* (in bits per unit time) of $(p, q) \in E_P$, $c_{(p,q)}$ (the same in both directions). These numbers are such that the ratio s_p/s_q indicates how faster processor p is than processor q; similarly for the communication links.

The attributes of graph G_T are the following. Each task t is represented by a relative *processing demand* (in number of instructions) ψ_t, while each channel $(t \to u)$ is represented by a relative *communication demand* (in number of bits) from task t to task u, $\zeta_{(t \to u)}$, possibly different from $\zeta_{(u \to t)}$. The ratio ψ_t/ψ_u is again indicative of how much more processing task t requires than task u, the same holding for the communication requirements.

The process of processor allocation is generally viewed as one of two main possibilities. It may be *static*, if the allocation function A is determined prior to the beginning of the computation and kept unchanged for its entire duration, or it may be *dynamic*, if A is allowed to change during the course of the computation. The former approach is suitable to cases in which both G_P and G_T, as well as their attributes, vary negligibly with time. The dynamic approach, on the other hand, is more appropriate to cases in which either the graphs or their attributes are time-varying, and then provides opportunities for the allocation function to be revised in the light of such changes. What we discuss in Section 1.6.1 is the static allocation of processors to tasks. The dynamic case is usually much more difficult, as it requires tasks to be migrated among processors, thereby interfering with the ongoing computation. Successful results of such dynamic approaches are for this reason scarce, except for some attempts that can in fact be regarded as a periodic repetition of the calculations for static processor allocation, whose resulting allocation functions are then kept unchanged for the duration of the period. We do nevertheless address the question of task migration in Section 1.6.2 in the context of ensuring the FIFO delivery of messages among tasks under such circumstances.

1.6.1. The static approach

The quality of an allocation function A is normally measured by a function that expresses the time for completion of the entire computation, or some function of this time. This criterion is not accepted as a consensus, but it seems to be consonant with the overall goal of parallel processing systems, namely to compute faster. So obtaining an allocation function by the minimization of such a function is what one should seek. The function we utilize in this book to evaluate the efficacy of an allocation function A is the function $H(A)$ given by

$$H(A) = \alpha H_P(A) + (1 - \alpha)H_C(A),$$

where $H_P(A)$ gives the time spent with computation when A is followed, $H_C(A)$ gives the time spent with communication when A is followed, and α such that $0 < \alpha < 1$ regulates the relative importance of $H_P(A)$ and $H_C(A)$. This parameter α is crucial, for example, in conveying to the processor allocation process some information on how efficient the routing mechanisms for interprocessor communication are (cf. Section 1.3).

The two components of $H(A)$ are given respectively by

$$H_P(A) = \sum_{p \in N_P} \left(\sum_{t \in N_T \mid A(t)=p} \frac{\psi_t}{s_p} + \sum_{t,u \in N_T \mid t \neq u, A(t)=A(u)=p} \frac{\psi_t \psi_u}{s_p} \right)$$

and

$$H_C(A) = \sum_{(p,q) \in E_P} \frac{1}{c_{(p,q)}} \sum_{(t \to u) \in D_T \mid (p,q) \in R\big(A(t),A(u)\big)} \zeta_{(t \to u)}.$$

This definition of $H_P(A)$ has two types of components. One of them, ψ_t/s_p, accounts for the time to execute task t on processor p. The other component, $\psi_t \psi_u/s_p$, is a function of the additional time incurred by processor p when executing both tasks t and u (various other functions can be used here, as long as nonnegative). If an allocation function A is sought by simply minimizing $H_P(A)$, then the first component will tend to lead to an allocation of the fastest processors to run all tasks, while the second component will lead to a dispersion of the tasks among the processors. The definition of $H_C(A)$, in turn, embodies components of the type $\zeta_{(t \to u)}/c_{(p,q)}$, which reflects the time spent in communication from task t to task u on link $(p, q) \in R(A(t), A(u))$. Contrasting with $H_P(A)$, if an allocation function A is sought by simply minimizing $H_C(A)$, then tasks will tend to be concentrated on a few processors. The minimization of the overall $H(A)$ is then an attempt to reconcile conflicting goals, as each of its two components tend to favor different aspects of the final allocation function.

As an example, consider the two-processor system comprising processors p and q. Consider also the two tasks t and u. If the allocation function A_1 assigns p to run t and q to run u, then we have, assuming $\alpha = 1/2$,

$$2H(A_1) = \frac{\psi_t}{s_p} + \frac{\psi_u}{s_q} + \frac{\zeta_{(t \to u)} + \zeta_{(u \to t)}}{c_{(p,q)}}.$$

An allocation function A_2 assigning p to run both t and u yields

$$2H(A_2) = \frac{\psi_t}{s_p} + \frac{\psi_u}{s_p} + \frac{\psi_t \psi_u}{s_p}.$$

Clearly, the choice between A_1 and A_2 depends on how the system's parameters relate to one another. For example, if $s_p = s_q$, then A_1 is preferable if the additional cost of processing the two tasks on p is higher than the cost of communication between them over the link (p, q), that is, if

$$\frac{\psi_t \psi_u}{s_p} > \frac{\zeta_{(t \to u)} + \zeta_{(u \to t)}}{c_{(p,q)}}.$$

Finding an allocation function A that minimizes $H(A)$ is a very difficult problem, NP-hard in fact, as the problems we encountered in Section 1.5. Given this inherent difficulty, all that is left is to resort to heuristics that allow a "satisfactory" allocation function to be found, that is, an allocation function that can be found reasonably fast and that does not lead to a poor performance of the program. The reader should refer to more specialized literature for various such heuristics.

1.6.2. Task migration

As we remarked earlier in Section 1.6, the need to migrate tasks from one processor to another arises when a dynamic processor allocation scheme is adopted. When tasks migrate, the allocation function A has to be updated throughout all those processors running tasks that may send messages, according to the structure of G_T, to the migrating task. While performing such an update may be achieved fairly simply (cf. the algorithms given in Section 4.1), things become more complicated when we add the requirement that messages continue to be delivered in the FIFO order. We are in this section motivated not only by the importance of the FIFO property in some situations, as we mentioned earlier, but also because solving this problem provides an opportunity to introduce a nontrivial, yet simple, distributed algorithm at this stage in the book. Before we proceed, it is very important to make the following observation right away. The distributed algorithm we describe in this section is not described by the graph G_T, but rather uses that graph as some sort of a "data structure" to work on. The graph on which the computation actually takes place is a task graph having exactly one task for each processor and two unidirectional communication channels (one in each direction) for every two processors in the system. It is then a complete undirected graph or node set N_P, and for this reason we describe the algorithm as if it were executed by the processors themselves. Another important observation, now in connection with G_P, is that its links are assumed to deliver interprocessor messages in the FIFO order (otherwise it would be considerably harder to attempt this at the task level). The reader should notice that considering a complete undirected graph is a means of not having to deal with the routing function associated with G_P explicitly, which would be necessary if we described the algorithm for G_P.

The approach we take is based on the following observation. Suppose for a moment and for simplicity that tasks are not allowed to migrate to processors where they have already been, and consider two tasks u and v running respectively on processors p and q. If v migrates to another processor, say q', and p keeps sending to processor q all of task u's messages destined to task v, and in addition processor q forwards to processor q' whatever messages it receives destined to v, then the desired FIFO property is maintained. Likewise, if u migrates to another processor, say p', and every message sent by u is routed through p first, then the FIFO property is maintained as well. If later these tasks migrate to yet other processors, then the same forwarding scheme still suffices to maintain the FIFO order. Clearly, this scheme cannot be expected to support any efficient computation, as messages tend to follow ever longer paths before eventual delivery. However, this observation serves the purpose of highlighting the presence of a line of processors that initially contains two processors (p and q) and increases with the addition of other processors (p' and q' being the first) as u and v migrate. What the algorithm we are about to describe does, while allowing tasks to migrate even to processors where they ran previously, is to shorten this line whenever a task migrates out of a processor by removing that processor from the line. We call such a line a *pipe* to emphasize the FIFO order followed by messages sent along it, and for tasks u and v denote it by $pipe(u, v)$.

This pipe is a sequence of processors sharing the property of running (or having run) at least one of u and v. In addition, u runs on the first processor of the pipe, and v on the last processor. When u or v (or both) migrates to another processor, thereby stretching the pipe, the algorithm we describe in the sequel removes from the pipe the processor (or processors) where the task (or tasks) that migrated ran. Adjacent processors in a pipe are not necessarily connected by a communication link in G_P, and in the beginning of the computation the pipe contains at most two processors.

A processor p maintains, for every task u that runs on it and every other task v such that $(u \rightarrow v) \in Out_u$, a variable $pipe_p(u, v)$ to store its view of $pipe(u, v)$. Initialization of this variable must be consonant with the initial allocation function. In addition, for every task v, at p the value of $A(v)$ is only an indication of the processor on which task v is believed to run, and is therefore denoted more consistently by $A_p(v)$. It is to $A_p(v)$ that messages sent to v by other tasks running on p get sent. Messages destined to v that arrive at p after v has migrated out of p are also sent to $A_p(v)$. A noteworthy relationship at p is the following. If $v \in Out_u$, then $pipe_p(u, v) = \langle p, \ldots, q \rangle$ if and only if $A_p(v) = q$. Messages sent to $A_p(v)$ are then actually being sent on $pipe(u, v)$.

First we informally describe the algorithm for the single pipe $pipe(u, v)$, letting p be the processor on which u runs (i.e., the first processor in the pipe) and q the processor on which v runs (i.e., the last processor in the pipe). The essential idea of the algorithm is the following. When u migrates from p to another processor p', processor p sends a message $flush(u, v, p')$ along $pipe_p(u, v)$. This message is aimed at informing processor q (or processor q', to which task v may have already migrated) that u now runs on p', and also "pushes" every message still in transit from u to v along the pipe (it *flushes* the pipe). When this message arrives at q (or q') the pipe is empty and $A_q(u)$ (or $A_{q'}(u)$) may then be updated. A message $flushed(u, v, q)$ (or $flushed(u, v, q')$) is then sent directly to p', which then updates $A_{p'}(v)$ and its view of the pipe by altering the contents of $pipe_{p'}(u, v)$. Throughout the entire process, task u is suspended, and as such does not compute or migrate.

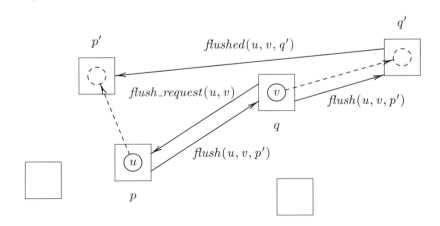

Figure 1.2. *When task u migrates from processor p to processor p' and v from q to q', a flush(u, v, p') message and a flush_request(u, v) message are sent concurrently, respectively by p to q and by q to p. The flush message gets forwarded by q to q', and eventually causes q' to send p' a flushed(u, v, q') message.*

This algorithm may also be initiated by q upon the migration of v to q', and then v must also be suspended. In this case, a message $flush\_request(u, v)$ is sent by q to p, which then engages in the flushing procedure we described after suspending task u. There is also the possibility that both p and q initiate concurrently. This happens when u and v both migrate (to p' and q', respectively) concurrently, i.e., before news of the other task's migration is received. The procedures are exactly the same, with only the need to ensure that $flush(u, v, p')$ is not sent again upon receipt of a $flush\_request(u, v)$, as it must already have been sent (Figure 1.2).

When a task u migrates from p to p', the procedure we just described is executed concurrently for every $pipe(u, v)$ such that $(u \rightarrow v) \in Out_u$ and every $pipe(v, u)$ such that $(v \rightarrow u) \in In_u$. Task u may only resume its execution at p' (and then possibly migrate once again) after all the pipes $pipe(u, v)$ such that $(u \rightarrow v) \in Out_u$ and $pipe(v, u)$ such that $(v \rightarrow u) \in In_u$ have been flushed, and is then said to be *active* (it is *inactive* otherwise, and may not migrate). Task u also becomes inactive upon the receipt of a $flush\_request(u, v)$ when running on p. In this case, only after $pipe_p(u, v)$ is updated can u become once again active.

Later in the book we return to this algorithm, both to provide a more formal description of it (in Section 2.1), and to describe its correctness and complexity properties (in Sections 2.1 and 3.2.1).

1.7. Remarks on program development

The material presented in Sections 1.4 through 1.6 touches various of the fundamental issues involved in the design of message-passing programs, especially in the context of multiprocessors, where the issues of allocating buffers to communication channels and processors to tasks are most relevant. Of course not always does the programmer have full access to or control of such issues, which are sometimes too tightly connected to built-in characteristics of the operating system or the programming language, but some level of awareness of what is really happening can only be beneficial.

Even when full control is possible, the directions provided in the previous two sections should not be taken as much more than that. The problems involved in both sections are, as we mentioned, probably intractable from the standpoint of computational complexity, so that the optima that they require are not really achievable. Also the formulations of those problems can be in many cases troublesome, because they involve parameters whose determination is far from trivial, like for example the upper bound M used in Section 1.5 to indicate our inability in determining tighter values, or the α used in Section 1.6 to weigh the relative importance of computation versus communication in the function H. This function cannot be trusted too blindly either, because there is no assurance that, even if the allocation that optimizes it could be found efficiently, no other allocation would in practice provide better results albeit its higher value for H.

Imprecise and troublesome though they may be, the guidelines given in Sections 1.5 and 1.6 do nevertheless provide a conceptual framework within which one may work given the constraints of the practical situation at hand. In addition, they in a way bridge the abstract description of a distributed algorithm we gave in Section 1.4 to what tends to occur in practice.

1.8. Exercises

1. For $d \geq 0$, a *d-dimensional hypercube* is an undirected graph with 2^d nodes in which every node has exactly d neighbors. If nodes are numbered from 0 to $2^d - 1$, then two nodes are neighbors if and only if the binary representations of their numbers differ by exactly one bit. One routing function that can be used when G_P is a hypercube is based on comparing the number of a message's destination processor, say q, with the number of the processor where the message is, say r. The message is forwarded to the neighbor of r whose number differs from that of r in the least-significant bit at which the numbers of q and r differ. Show that this routing function is quasi-acyclic.

2. In the context of Exercise 1, consider the use of a structured buffer pool to prevent deadlocks when flow control is done by the store-and-forward mechanism. Give details of how the pool is to be employed for deadlock prevention. How many buffer classes are required?

3. In the context of Exercise 1, explain in detail why the reservation of links when doing flow control by circuit switching is deadlock-free.

4. Describe how to obtain channels with positive capacity from zero-capacity channels, under the constraint the exactly two additional tasks are to be employed per channel of G_T.

1.9. Bibliographic notes

Sources in the literature to complement the material of Section 1.1 could hardly be more plentiful. For material on computer networks, the reader is referred to the traditional texts by Bertsekas and Gallager (1987) and by Tanenbaum (1988), as well as to more recent material on the various aspects of ATM networks (Bae and Suda, 1991; Stamoulis, Anagnostou, and Georgantas, 1994). Networks of workstations are also well represented by surveys (e.g., Bernard, Steve, and Simatic, 1993), as well as by more specific material (Blumofe and Park, 1994).

    References on multiprocessors also abound, ranging from reports on early experiences with shared-memory (Gehringer, Siewiorek, and Segall, 1987) and message-passing systems (Hillis, 1985; Seitz, 1985; Arlauskas, 1988; Grunwald and Reed, 1988; Pase and Larrabee, 1988) to the more recent revival of distributed-memory architectures that provide a shared address space (Fernandes, de Amorim, Barbosa, França, and de Souza, 1989; Martonosi and Gupta, 1989; Bell, 1992; Bagheri, Ilin, and Ridgeway Scott, 1994; Reinhardt, Larus, and Wood, 1994; Protić, Tomašević, and Milutinović, 1995). The reader of this book may be particularly interested in the recent recognition that explicit message-passing is often needed, and in the resulting architectural proposals, as for example those of Kranz, Johnson, Agarwal, Kubiatowicz, and Lim (1993), Kuskin, Ofelt, Heinrich, Heinlein, Simoni, Gharachorloo, Chapin, Nakahira, Baxter, Horowitz, Gupta, Rosenblum, and Hennessy

(1994), Heinlein, Gharachorloo, Dresser, and Gupta (1994), Heinrich, Kuskin, Ofelt, Heinlein, Singh, Simoni, Gharachorloo, Baxter, Nakahira, Horowitz, Gupta, Rosenblum, and Hennessy (1994), and Agarwal, Bianchini, Chaiken, Johnson, Kranz, Kubiatowicz, Lim, Mackenzie, and Yeung (1995). Pertinent theoretical insights have also been pursued (Bar-Noy and Dolev, 1993).

The material in Section 1.2 can be expanded by referring to a number of sources in which communication processors are discussed. These include, for example, Dally, Chao, Chien, Hassoun, Horwat, Kaplan, Song, Totty, and Wills (1987), Ramachandran, Solomon, and Vernon (1987), Barbosa and França (1988), and Dally (1990). The material in Barbosa and França (1988) is presented in considerably more detail by Drummond (1990), and, in addition, has pioneered the introduction of messages as instructions to be performed by communication processors. These were later re-introduced under the denomination of active messages (von Eicken, Culler, Goldstein, and Schauser, 1992; Tucker and Mainwaring, 1994).

In addition to the aforementioned classic sources on computer networks, various other references can be looked up to complement the material on routing and flow control discussed in Section 1.3. For example, the original source for virtual cut-through is Kermani and Kleinrock (1979), while Günther (1981) discusses techniques for deadlock prevention in the store-and-forward case and Gerla and Kleinrock (1982) provide a survey of early techniques. The original publication on wormhole routing is Dally and Seitz (1987), and Gaughan and Yalamanchili (1993) should be looked up by those interested in adaptive techniques. Wormhole routing is also surveyed by Ni and McKinley (1993), and Awerbuch, Kutten, and Peleg (1994) return to the subject of deadlock prevention in the store-and-forward case.

The template given by Algorithm *Task_t* of Section 1.4 originates from Barbosa (1990a), and the concept of a guarded command on which it is based dates back to Dijkstra (1975). The reader who wants a deeper understanding of how communication channels of zero and nonzero capacities relate to each other may wish to check Barbosa (1990b), which contains a mathematical treatment of concurrency-related concepts associated with such capacities. What this work does is to start at the intuitive notion that greater channel capacity leads to greater concurrency (present, for example, in Gentleman (1981)), and then employ (rather involved) combinatorial concepts related to the coloring of graph edges (Edmonds, 1965; Fulkerson, 1972; Fiorini and Wilson, 1977; Stahl, 1979) to argue that such a notion may not be correct. The Communicating Sequential Processes (CSP) introduced by Hoare (1978) constitute an example of notation based on zero-capacity communication.

Section 1.5 is based on Barbosa (1990a), where in addition a heuristic is presented to support the concurrency-optimal criterion for buffer assignment to channels. This heuristic employs an algorithm to find maximum matchings in graphs (Sysło, Deo, and Kowalik, 1983).

The reader has many options to complement the material of Section 1.6. References on the intractability of processor allocation (in the sense of *NP*-hardness, as in Karp (1972) and Garey and Johnson (1979)) are Krumme, Venkataraman, and Cybenko (1986) and Ali and El-Rewini (1994). For the static approach, some references are Ma, Lee, and Tsuchiya (1982), Shen and Tsai (1985), Sinclair (1987), Barbosa and Huang (1988)—on which Section 1.6.1 is based, Ali and El-Rewini (1993), and Selvakumar and Siva Ram Murthy (1994). The material in Barbosa and Huang (1988) includes heuristics to overcome intractability that are based on neural networks (as is the work of Fox and Furmanski (1988)) and on the A^* algorithm for heuristic search (Nilsson, 1980; Pearl, 1984). A parallel variation of the latter algorithm (Freitas and Barbosa, 1991) can also be employed. Fox, Kolawa, and Williams (1987) and Nicol and Reynolds (1990) offer treatments of the dynamic type. References on task migration include Theimer, Lantz, and Cheriton (1985), Ousterhout, Cherenson, Douglis, Nelson, and Welch (1988), Ravi and Jefferson (1988), Eskicioğlu and Cabrera (1991), and Barbosa and Porto (1995)—which is the basis for our treatment in Section 1.6.2.

Details on the material discussed in Section 1.7 can be found in Hellmuth (1991), or in the more compact accounts by Barbosa, Drummond, and Hellmuth (1991a; 1991b; 1994).

There are many books covering subjects quite akin to our subject in this book. These are books on concurrent programming, operating systems, parallel programming, and distributed algorithms. Some examples are Ben-Ari (1982), Hoare (1984), Maekawa, Oldehoeft, and Oldehoeft (1987), Perrott (1987), Burns (1988), Chandy and Misra (1988), Fox, Johnson, Lyzenga, Otto, Salmon, and Walker (1988), Raynal (1988), Almasi and Gottlieb (1989), Andrews (1991), Tanenbaum (1992), Fox, Williams, and Messina (1994), Silberschatz, Peterson, and Galvin (1994), and Tel (1994b). There are also surveys (Andrews and Schneider, 1983), sometimes specifically geared toward a particular class of applications (Bertsekas and Tsitsiklis, 1991), and class notes (Lynch and Goldman, 1989).

2

Intrinsic Constraints

This chapter, like Chapter 1, still has the flavor of a chapter on preliminaries, although various distributed algorithms are presented and analyzed in its sections. The reason why it is still in a way a chapter on preliminary concepts is that it deals mostly with constraints on the computations that may be carried out over the model introduced in Section 1.4 for distributed computations by point-to-point message passing.

Initially, in Section 2.1, we return to the graph-theoretic model of Section 1.4 to specify two of the variants that it admits when we consider its timing characteristics. These are the fully asynchronous and fully synchronous variants that will accompany us throughout the book. For each of the two, Section 2.1 contains an algorithm template, which again is used through the remaining chapters. In addition to these templates, in Section 2.1 we return to the problem of ensuring the FIFO delivery of intertask messages when tasks migrate discussed in Section 1.6.2. The algorithm sketched in that section to solve the problem is presented in full in Section 2.1 to illustrate the notational conventions adopted for the book. In addition, once the algorithm is known in detail, some of its properties, including some complexity-related ones, are discussed.

Sections 2.2. and 2.3 are the sections in which some of our model's intrinsic constraints are discussed. The discussion in Section 2.2 is centered on the issue of anonymous systems, and in this context several impossibility results are presented.

Along with these impossibility results, distributed algorithms for the computations
that can be carried out are given and to some extent analyzed.

In Section 2.3 we present a somewhat informal discussion of how various notions of knowledge translate into a distributed algorithm setting, and discuss some
impossibility results as well. Our approach in this section is far less formal and
complete than in the rest of the book because the required background for such
a complete treatment is normally way outside what is expected of this book's intended audience. Nevertheless, the treatment we offer is intended to build up a
certain amount of intuition, and at times in the remaining chapters we return to
the issues considered in Section 2.3.

Exercises and bibliographic notes follow respectively in Sections 2.4 and 2.5.

2.1. Full asynchronism and full synchronism

We start by recalling the graph-theoretic model introduced in Section 1.4, according to which a distributed algorithm is represented by the connected directed graph
$G_T = (N_T, D_T)$. In this graph, N_T is the set of tasks and D_T is the set of unidirectional communication channels. Tasks in N_T are message-driven entities whose
behavior is generically depicted by Algorithm $Task\_t$ (cf. Section 1.4), and the channels in D_T are assumed to have infinite capacity, i.e., no task is ever suspended upon
attempting to send a message on a channel (reconciling this assumption with the
reality of practical situations was our subject in Section 1.5). Channels in D_T are
not generally assumed to be FIFO channels unless explicitly stated.

For the remainder of the book, we simplify our notation for this model in the
following manner. The graph $G_T = (N_T, D_T)$ is henceforth denoted simply by
$G = (N, D)$, with $n = |N|$ and $m = |D|$. For $1 \leq i, j \leq n$, n_i denotes a member
of N, referred to simply as a *node*, and if $j \neq i$ we let $(n_i \rightarrow n_j)$ denote a member
of D, referred to simply as a *directed edge* (or an *edge*, if confusion may not arise).
The set of edges directed away from n_i is denoted by $Out_i \subseteq D$, and the set of
edges directed towards n_i is denoted by $In_i \subseteq D$. Clearly, $(n_i \rightarrow n_j) \in Out_i$ if
and only if $(n_i \rightarrow n_j) \in In_j$. The nodes n_i and n_j are said to be *neighbors* of
each other if and only if either $(n_i \rightarrow n_j) \in D$ or $(n_j \rightarrow n_i) \in D$. The set of n_i's
neighbors is denoted by $Neig_i$, and contains two partitions, I_Neig_i and O_Neig_i,
whose members are respectively n_i's neighbors n_j such that $(n_j \rightarrow n_i) \in D$ and n_j
such that $(n_i \rightarrow n_j) \in D$.

Often G is such that $(n_i \rightarrow n_j) \in D$ if and only if $(n_j \rightarrow n_i) \in D$, and in
this case viewing these two directed edges as the single undirected edge (n_i, n_j) is
more convenient. In this undirected case, G is denoted by $G = (N, E)$, and then

$m = |E|$. Members of E are referred to simply as *edges*. In the undirected case, the set of edges incident to n_i is denoted by $Inc_i \subseteq E$. Two nodes n_i and n_j are neighbors if and only if $(n_i, n_j) \in E$. The set of n_i's neighbors continues to be denoted by $Neig_i$.

Our main concern in this section is to investigate the nature of the computations carried out by G's nodes with respect to their timing characteristics. This investigation will enable us to complete the model of computation given by G with the addition of its timing properties.

The first model we introduce is the *fully asynchronous* (or simply *asynchronous*) *model*, which is characterized by the following two properties.

- Each node is driven by its own, local, independent time basis, referred to as its *local clock*.

- The delay that a message suffers to be delivered between neighbors is finite but unpredictable.

The complete asynchronism assumed in this model makes it very realistic from the standpoint of somehow reflecting some of the characteristics of the systems discussed in Section 1.1. It is this same asynchronism, however, that accounts for most of the difficulties encountered during the design of distributed algorithms under the asynchronous model. For this reason, frequently a far less realistic model is used, one in which G's timing characteristics are pushed to the opposing extreme of complete synchronism. We return to this other model later in this section.

One important fact to notice is that the notation used to describe a node's computation in Algorithm *Task_t* (cf. Section 1.4) is quite well suited to the assumptions of the asynchronous model, because in that algorithm, except possibly initially, computation may only take place at the reception of messages, which are in turn accepted nondeterministically when there is more than one message to choose from. In addition, no explicit use of any timing information is made in Algorithm *Task_t* (although the use of timing information drawn from the node's local clock would be completely legitimate and in accordance with the assumptions of the model).

According to Algorithm *Task_t*, the computation of a node in the asynchronous model can be described by providing the actions to be taken initially (if that node is to start its computation and send messages spontaneously, as opposed to doing it in the wake of the reception of a message) and the actions to be taken upon receiving messages when certain Boolean conditions hold. Such a description is given by Algorithm *A_Template*, which is a template for all the algorithms studied in this book under the asynchronous model, henceforth referred to as *asynchronous algorithms.* Algorithm *A_Template* describes the computation carried out by $n_i \in N$. In this algorithm, and henceforth, we let $N_0 \subseteq N$ denote the nonempty set of nodes that may send messages spontaneously. The prefix *A_* in the algorithm's denomination is meant to indicate that it is asynchronous, and is used in the names of all the asynchronous algorithms in the book.

Algorithm *A_Template* is given for the case in which G is a directed graph. For the undirected case, all that needs to be done to the algorithm is to replace all occurrences of both In_i and Out_i with Inc_i.

Algorithm *A_Template*:

▷ **Variables:**
  Variables used by n_i, and their initial values, are listed here.

▷ **Input:**
  $msg_i = $ **nil**.
  Action if $n_i \in N_0$:   (2.1)
    Do some computation;
    Send one message on each edge of a (possibly empty) subset of Out_i.

▷ **Input:**
  msg_i such that $origin_i(msg_i) = c_k \in In_i$ with $1 \leq k \leq |In_i|$.
  Action when B_k: (2.2)
    Do some computation;
    Send one message on each edge of a (possibly empty) subset of Out_i.

Before we proceed to an example of how a distributed algorithm can be expressed according to this template, there are some important observations to make in connection with Algorithm *A_Template*. The first observation is that the algorithm is given by listing the variables it employs (along with their initial values) and then a series of *input/action pairs*. Each of these pairs, in contrast with Algorithm *Task_t*, is given for a specific message type, and may then correspond to more than one guarded command in Algorithm *Task_t* of Section 1.4, with the input corresponding to the message reception in the *guard* and the action corresponding to the *command* part, to be executed when the Boolean condition expressed in the *guard* is **true**. Conversely, each guarded command in Algorithm *Task_t* may also correspond to more than one input/action pair in Algorithm *A_Template*. In addition, in order to preserve the functioning of Algorithm *Task_t*, namely that a new guarded command is only considered for execution in the next iteration, therefore after the *command* in the currently selected guarded command has been executed to completion, each action in Algorithm *A_Template* is assumed to be an *atomic action*. An atomic action is an action that is allowed to be carried out to completion before any interrupt. All actions are numbered to facilitate the discussion of the algorithm's properties.

Secondly, we make the observation that the message associated with an input, denoted by msg_i, is if $n_i \in N_0$ treated as if $msg_i = $ **nil**, since in such cases no message really exists to trigger n_i's action, as in (2.1). When a message does exist, as in (2.2), we assume that its origin, in the form of the edge on which it was received, is known to n_i. Such an edge is denoted by $origin_i(msg_i) \in In_i$. In many cases, knowing the edge $origin_i(msg_i)$ can be regarded as equivalent to knowing $n_j \in I\_Neig_i$ for $origin_i(msg_i) = (n_j \to n_i)$ (that is, n_j is the node from which msg_i originated). Similarly, sending a message on an edge in Out_i is in many cases equivalent to sending a message to $n_j \in O\_Neig_i$ if that edge is $(n_i \to n_j)$. However, we refrain from stating these as general assumptions because they do not hold in the case of anonymous systems, treated in Section 2.2. When they do hold and G is an undirected graph, then all occurrences of I_Neig_i and of O_Neig_i in the modified Algorithm *A_Template* must be replaced with occurrences of $Neig_i$.

As a final observation, we recall that, as in the case of Algorithm *Task_t*, whenever in Algorithm *A_Template* n_i sends messages on a subset of Out_i containing more than one edge, it is assumed that all such messages may be sent in parallel.

We now turn once again to the material introduced in Section 1.6.2, namely a distributed algorithm to ensure the FIFO order of message delivery among tasks that migrate from processor to processor. As we mentioned in that section, this is an algorithm described on a complete undirected graph that has a node for every processor. So for the discussion of this algorithm G is the undirected graph $G = (N, E)$. We also mentioned in Section 1.6.2 that the directed graph whose nodes represent the migrating tasks and whose edges represent communication channels is in this algorithm used as a data structure. While treating this problem, we then let this latter graph be denoted, as in Section 1.6.2, by $G_T = (N_T, D_T)$, along with the exact same notation used in that section with respect to G_T. Care should be taken to avoid mistaking this graph for the directed version of G introduced at the beginning of this section.

Before introducing the additional notation that we need, let us recall some of the notation introduced in Section 1.6.2. Let A be the initial allocation function. For a node n_i and every task u such that $A(u) = n_i$, a variable $pipe_i(u, v)$ for every task v such that $(u \to v) \in Out_u$ indicates n_i's view of $pipe(u, v)$. Initially,

$pipe_i(u, v) = \langle n_i, A(v) \rangle$. In addition, for every task v a variable $A_i(v)$ is used by n_i to indicate the node where task v is believed to run. This variable is initialized such that $A_i(v) = A(v)$. Messages arriving at n_i destined to v are assumed to be sent to $A_i(v)$ if $A_i(v) \neq n_i$, or to be kept in a FIFO queue, called $queue_v$, otherwise.

Variables employed in connection with task u are the following. The Boolean variable $active_u$ (initially set to **true**) is used to indicate whether task u is active. Two counters, $pending\_in_u$ and $pending\_out_u$, are used to register the number of pipes that need to be flushed before u can once again become active. The former counter refers to pipes $pipe(v, u)$ such that $(v \rightarrow u) \in In_u$ and the latter to pipes $pipe(u, v)$ such that $(u \rightarrow v) \in Out_u$. Initially these counters have value zero. For every v such that $(v \rightarrow u) \in In_u$, the Boolean variable $pending\_in_u(v)$ (initially set to **false**) indicates whether $pipe(v, u)$ is one of the pipes in need of flushing for u to become active. Constants and variables carrying the subscript u in their names may be thought of as being part of task u's "activation record," and do as such migrate along with u whenever it migrates.

Algorithm A_FIFO, given next for node n_i, is an asynchronous algorithm to ensure the FIFO order of message delivery among migrating tasks. When listing the variables for this algorithm, only those carrying the subscript i are presented. The others, which refer to tasks, are omitted from the description. This same practice of only listing variables that refer to G is adopted everywhere in the book.

Algorithm A_FIFO:

    ▷ **Variables:**

        $pipe_i(u, v) = \langle n_i, A(v) \rangle$ for all $(u \rightarrow v) \in D_T$ such that $A(u) = n_i$;
        $A_i(v) = A(v)$ for all $v \in N_T$.

▷ **Input:**

$msg_i = $ **nil**.

Action when $active_u$ **and a decision is made to migrate** u **to** n_j:

$$(2.3)$$

$active_u := $ **false**;

for all $(u \to v) \in Out_u$ **do**

     begin

          Send $flush(u, v, n_j)$ to $A_i(v)$;

          $pending\_out_u := pending\_out_u + 1$

     end;

for all $(v \to u) \in In_u$ **do**

     begin

          Send $flush\_request(v, u)$ to $A_i(v)$;

          $pending\_in_u := pending\_in_u + 1$;

          $pending_in_u(v) := $ **true**

     end;

$A_i(u) := n_j$;

Send u to n_j.

▷ **Input:**

$msg_i = u$.

Action:

$$(2.4)$$

$A_i(u) := n_i$.

▷ **Input:**
$$msg_i = flush(v, u, n_j).$$

Action:

if $A_i(u) = n_i$ **then**

    begin

        $A_i(v) := n_j$;

        Send $flushed(v, u, n_i)$ to n_j;

        if $pending\_in_u(v)$ **then**

            begin

                $pending_in_u(v) := $ **false**;

                $pending\_in_u := pending\_in_u - 1$;

                $active_u$

                      $:= (pending\_in_u = 0)$ **and** $(pending\_out_u = 0)$

            end

    end

else

    Send $flush(v, u, n_j)$ to $A_i(u)$.

▷ **Input:**
$$msg_i = flush\_request(u, v).$$

Action:

if $A_i(u) = n_i$ **then**

    begin

        $active_u := $ **false**;

        Send $flush(u, v, n_i)$ to $A_i(v)$;

        $pending\_out_u := pending\_out_u + 1$

    end.

▷ **Input:**
$$msg_i = flushed(u, v, n_j).$$

Action when $A_i(u) = n_i$**:**

    $A_i(v) := n_j$;

    $pipe_i(u, v) := \langle n_i, n_j \rangle$;

    $pending\_out_u := pending\_out_u - 1$;

    $active_u := (pending\_in_u = 0)$ **and** $(pending\_out_u = 0)$.

Algorithm *A_FIFO* expresses, following the conventions established with Algorithm *A_Template*, the procedure described informally in Section 1.6.2. One important observation about Algorithm *A_FIFO* is that the set N_0 of potential spontaneous senders of messages now comprises the nodes that concurrently decide to send active tasks to run elsewhere (cf. (2.3)), in the sense described in Section 1.6.2, and may then be such that $N_0 = N$. In fact, the way to regard spontaneous initiations in Algorithm A_FIFO is to view every maximal set of nodes concurrently executing (2.3) as an N_0 set for a new execution of the algorithm, provided every such execution operates on data structures and variables that persist (i.e., are not re-initialized) from one execution to another.

For completeness, next we give some of Algorithm A_FIFO's properties related to its correctness and performance.

Theorem 2.1. *For any two tasks u and v such that $(u \to v) \in Out_u$, messages sent by u to v are delivered in the FIFO order.*

Proof: Consider any scenario in which both u and v are active, and in this scenario let n_i be the node on which u runs and n_j the node on which v runs. There are three cases to be analyzed in connection with the possible migrations of u and v out of n_i and n_j, respectively.

In the first case, u migrates to another node, say $n_{i'}$, while v does not concurrently migrate, that is, the $flush(u, v, n_{i'})$ sent by n_i in (2.3) arrives at n_j when $A_j(v) = n_j$. A $flushed(u, v, n_j)$ is then by (2.5) sent to $n_{i'}$, and may upon receipt cause u to become active if it is no longer involved in the flushing of any pipe ($pending\_in_u = 0$ and $pending\_out_u = 0$), by (2.7). Also, $pipe_{i'}(u, v)$ is in (2.7) set to $\langle n_{i'}, n_j \rangle$, and it is on this pipe that u will send all further messages to v once it becomes active. These messages will reach v later than all the messages sent previously to it by u when u still ran on n_i, as by G_P's FIFO property all these messages reached n_j and were added to $queue_v$ before n_j received the $flush(u, v, n_{i'})$.

In the second case, it is v that migrates to another node, say $n_{j'}$, while u does not concurrently migrate, meaning that the $flush\_request(u, v)$ sent by n_j to n_i in (2.3) arrives when $A_i(u) = n_i$. What happens then is that, by (2.6), as $pending\_out_u$ is incremented and u becomes inactive (if already it was not, as $pending\_out_u$ might already be positive), a $flush(u, v, n_i)$ is sent to n_j and, finding $A_j(v) \neq n_j$, by (2.5) gets forwarded by n_j to $n_{j'}$. Upon receipt of this message at $n_{j'}$, a $flushed(u, v, n_{j'})$ is sent to n_i, also by (2.5). This is a chance for v to become active, so long as no further pipe flushings remain in course in which it is involved ($pending\_in_v = 0$ and $pending\_out_v = 0$ in (2.5)). The arrival of that message at n_i causes $pending\_out_u$ to be decremented in (2.7), and possibly u to become active if it is not any longer involved in the flushing of any other pipe ($pending\_in_u = 0$ and $pending\_out_u = 0$). In addition, $pipe_i(u, v)$ is updated to $\langle n_i, n_{j'} \rangle$. Because u remained inactive during the flushing of $pipe(u, v)$, every message it sends to v at $n_{j'}$ when it becomes active will arrive at its destination later than all the messages it had sent previously to v at n_j, as once again G_P's FIFO property implies that all these messages must have reached $n_{j'}$ and been added to $queue_v$ ahead of the $flush(u, v, n_i)$.

The third case corresponds to the situation in which both u and v migrate concurrently, say respectively from n_i to $n_{i'}$ and from n_j to $n_{j'}$. This concurrency implies that the $flush(u, v, n_{i'})$ sent in (2.3) by n_i to n_j finds $A_j(v) \neq n_j$ on its arrival (and is therefore forwarded to $n_{j'}$, by (2.5)), and likewise the $flush\_request(u, v)$ sent in (2.3) by n_j to n_i finds $A_i(u) \neq n_i$ at its destination (which by (2.6) does nothing, as the $flush(u, v, n_{i'})$ it would send as a consequence is already on its way to n_j or $n_{j'}$). A $flushed(u, v, n_{j'})$ is sent by $n_{j'}$ to $n_{i'}$, where by (2.7) it causes the contents of $pipe_{i'}(u, v)$ to be updated to $\langle n_{i'}, n_{j'} \rangle$. The conditions for u and v to become active are entirely analogous to the ones we discussed under the previous two cases. When u does finally become active, any messages it sends to v will arrive later than the messages it sent previously to v when it ran on n_i and v on n_j. This is so because, once again by G_P's FIFO property, such messages must have reached $n_{j'}$ and been added to $queue_v$ ahead of the $flush(u, v, n_{i'})$. ∎

Let $|pipe(u, v)|$ denote the number of nodes in $pipe(u, v)$. Before we state Lemma 2.2, which establishes a property of this quantity, it is important to note that the number of nodes in $pipe(u, v)$ is not to be mistaken for the number of nodes in n_i's view of that pipe if n_i is the node on which u runs. This view, which we have denoted by $pipe_i(u, v)$, clearly contains at most two nodes at all times, by (2.7). The former, on the other hand, does not have a precise meaning in the framework of any node considered individually, but rather should be taken in the context of a consistent global state (cf. Section 3.1).

Lemma 2.2. *For any two tasks u and v such that $(u \to v) \in Out_u$, $|pipe(u, v)| \leq 4$ always holds.*

Proof: It suffices to note that, if u runs on n_i, $|pipe(u, v)|$ is larger than the number of nodes in $pipe_i(u, v)$ by at most two nodes, which happens when both u and v migrate concurrently, as neither of the two tasks is allowed to migrate again before the pipe between them is shortened. The lemma then follows easily from the fact that by (2.7) $pipe_i(u, v)$ contains at most two nodes. ∎

To finalize our discussion of Algorithm *A_FIFO* in this section, we present its complexity. This quantity, which we still have not introduced and will only describe at length in Section 3.2, yields, in the usual worst-case asymptotic sense, a distributed algorithm's "cost" in terms of the number of messages it employs and the time it requires for completion. The *message complexity* is expressed simply as the worst-case asymptotic number of messages that flow among neighbors during the computation ("worst case" here is the maximum over all variations in the structure of G, when applicable, and over all executions of the algorithm— cf. Section 3.2.1). The time-related measures of complexity are conceptually more complex, and an analysis of Algorithm A_FIFO in these terms is postponed until our thorough discussion of complexity measures in Section 3.2.

For a nonempty set $K \subseteq N_T$ of tasks, we henceforth let m_K denote the number of directed edges in D_T of the form $(u \to v)$ or $(v \to u)$ for $u \in K$ and $v \in N_T$. Clearly,

$$m_K \leq \sum_{u \in K} \left(|In_u| + |Out_u| \right) \leq 2m_K.$$

Theorem 2.3. *For the concurrent migration of a set K of tasks, Algorithm A_FIFO employs $O(m_K)$ messages.*

Proof: When a task $u \in K$ migrates from node n_i to node $n_{i'}$, n_i sends $|In_u|$ messages $flush\_request(v, u)$ for $(v \to u) \in In_u$ and $|Out_u|$ messages $flush(u, v, n_{i'})$ for $(u \to v) \in Out_u$. In addition, $n_{i'}$ receives $|In_u|$ messages $flush(v, u, n_j)$ for $(v \to u) \in In_u$ and some appropriate n_j, and $|Out_u|$ messages $flushed(u, v, n_j)$ for $(u \to v) \in Out_u$ and some appropriate n_j. Node $n_{i'}$ also sends $|In_u|$ messages $flushed(v, u, n_{i'})$ for $(v \to u) \in In_u$. Only $flush$ messages traverse pipes, which by Lemma 2.2 contain no more than four nodes or three edges each. Because no other messages involving u are sent or received even if other tasks v such that $(v \to u) \in In_u$ or $(u \to v) \in Out_u$ are members of K as well, except for the receipt by n_i of one innocuous message $flush\_request(u, v)$ for each $v \in K$ such that $(u \to v) \in Out_u$, the concurrent migration of the tasks in K accounts for $O(m_K)$ messages. ∎

The message complexity asserted by Theorem 2.3 refers to messages sent on the edges of G, which is a complete graph. It would also be legitimate, in this context, to consider the number of interprocessor messages actually employed, that is, the number of messages that get sent on the edges of G_P. In the case of fixed, deterministic routing (cf. Section 1.3), a message on G corresponds to no more than $n - 1$ messages on G_P, so by Theorem 2.3 the number of interprocessor messages is $O(nm_K)$. However, recalling our remark in Section 1.3 when we discussed the use of wormhole routing for flow control in multiprocessors, if the transport of interprocessor messages is efficient enough that G_P too can be regarded as a complete graph, then the message complexity given by Theorem 2.3 applies to interprocessor messages as well.

In addition to the asynchronous model we have been discussing so far in this section, another model related to G's timing characteristics is the *fully synchronous* (or simply *synchronous*) *model*, for which the following two properties hold.

- All nodes are driven by a global time basis, referred to as the *global clock*, which generates *time intervals* (or simply *intervals*) of fixed, nonzero duration.

- The delay that a message suffers to be delivered between neighbors is nonzero and strictly less than the duration of an interval of the global clock.

The intervals generated by the global clock do not really need to be of the same duration, so long as the assumption on the delays that messages suffer to be delivered between neighbors takes as bound the minimum of the different durations.

The following is an outline of the functioning of a distributed algorithm, called a *synchronous algorithm*, designed under the assumptions of the synchronous model. The beginning of each interval of the global clock is indicated by a *pulse*. For $s \geq 0$, pulse s indicates the beginning of interval s. At pulse $s = 0$, the nodes in N_0 send messages on some (or possibly none) of the edges directed away from them. At pulse $s > 0$, all the messages sent at pulse $s - 1$ have by assumption arrived, and then the nodes in N may compute and send messages out.

One assumption that we have tacitly made, but which should be very clearly spelled out, is that the computation carried out by nodes during an interval takes no time. Without this assumption, the duration of an interval would not be enough for both the local computations to be carried out and the messages to be delivered, because this delivery may take nearly as long as the entire duration of the interval to happen. Another equivalent way to approach this would have been to say that, for some $d \geq 0$ strictly less than the duration of an interval, local computation takes no more than d time, while messages take strictly less than the duration of an interval minus d to be delivered. What we have done has been to take $d = 0$. We return to issues related to these in Section 3.2.2.

The set N_0 of nodes that may send messages at pulse $s = 0$ has in the synchronous case the same interpretation as a set of potential spontaneous senders of messages it had in the asynchronous case. However, in the synchronous case it does make sense for nodes to compute without receiving any messages, because what drives them is the global clock, not the reception of messages. So a synchronous algorithm does not in principle require any messages at all, and nodes can still go on computing even if $N_0 = \emptyset$. Nevertheless, in order for the overall computation to have any meaning other than the parallelization of n completely independent sequential computations, at least one message has to be sent by at least one node, and for a message that gets sent at the earliest pulse that has to take place at pulse $s = d$ for some $d \geq 0$. What we have done has been once again to make the harmless assumption that $d = 0$, because whatever the nodes did prior to this pulse did not depend on the reception of messages and can therefore be regarded as having been done at this pulse as well. Then the set N_0 has at least the sender of that message as member.

Unrealistic though the synchronous model may seem, it may at times have great appeal in the design of distributed algorithms, not only because it frequently simplifies the design (cf. Section 4.3, for example), but also because there have been cases in which it led to asynchronous algorithms more efficient than the ones available (cf. Section 3.4). One of the chiefest advantages that comes from reasoning under the assumptions of the synchronous model is the following. If for some $d > 0$ a node n_i does not receive any message during interval s for some $s \geq d$, then surely no message that might "causally affect" the behavior of n_i at pulse $s + 1$ was sent at pulses $s - d, \ldots, s$ by any node whose shortest distance to n_i is at least d. The "causally affect" will be made much clearer in Section 3.1 (and before that used freely a few times), but for the moment it suffices to understand that, in the synchronous model, nodes may gain information by just waiting, i.e., counting pulses. When designing synchronous algorithms, this simple observation can be used for many purposes, including the detection of termination in many cases (cf., for example, Sections 2.2.2 and 2.2.3).

It should also be clear that every asynchronous algorithm is also in essence a synchronous algorithm. That is, if an algorithm is designed for the asynchronous model and it works correctly under the assumptions of that model, then it must also work correctly under the assumptions of the synchronous model for an appropriate choice of interval duration (to accommodate nodes' computations). This happens because the conditions under which communication takes place in the synchronous model is only one of the infinitely many possibilities that the asynchronous model allows. We treat this issue in more detail in Section 3.3. The converse of this implication (i.e., that synchronous algorithms run correctly in the asynchronous model) can also be achieved with appropriate algorithm transformation, and is not at all immediate as its counterpart. This transformation lends support to our interest in the synchronous model and is our subject in Section 5.3, after we return to it in Sections 3.3 and 3.4.

Our last topic in this section is the presentation of Algorithm $S\_Template$, which sets the conventions on how to describe a synchronous algorithm and is used as a template throughout the book. The prefix $S\_$, similarly to the asynchronous case discussed earlier, indicates that the algorithm is synchronous, and is used in all synchronous algorithms we present. For $s \geq 0$ and $n_i \in N$, in Algorithm $S\_Template$ $MSG_i(s)$ is either the empty set (if $s = 0$) or denotes the set of messages received by n_i during interval $s - 1$ (if $s > 0$), which may be empty as well. The algorithm for n_i is given next. As with Algorithm $A\_Template$, Algorithm $S\_Template$ too is given for the case in which G is a directed graph. The undirected case is obtained by simply replacing In_i and Out_i with Inc_i throughout the algorithm.

> **Algorithm** $S\_Template$:

>> ▷ **Variables:**
>>>   Variables used by n_i, and their initial values, are listed here.

>> ▷ **Input:**
>>> $s = 0$, $MSG_i(0) = \emptyset$.
>>   **Action if** $n_i \in N_0$:   (2.8)
>>>   Do some computation;
>>>   Send one message on each edge of a (possibly empty) subset of Out_i.

>> ▷ **Input:**
>>> $s > 0$, $MSG_i(1), \ldots, MSG_i(s)$ such that $origin_i(msg) = c_k \in In_i$
>>>   with $1 \leq k \leq |In_i|$ for $msg \in \bigcup_{r=1}^{s} MSG_i(r)$.
>>   **Action:**   (2.9)
>>>   Do some computation;
>>>   Send one message on each edge of a (possibly empty) subset of Out_i.

As in the case of Algorithm $A\_Template$, Algorithm $S\_Template$ is presented as a set of input/action pairs whose actions are numbered for ease of reference ((2.8) corresponds to $s = 0$ and (2.9) to $s > 0$). The inputs now include information from the global clock (in the form of the nonnegative integer s), which is, as we have seen, what really drives the nodes. The atomicity of the actions comes as a consequence of the characteristics of the synchronous model, because no node performs more than one action per interval of the global clock. In fact, it is simple to see that every node performs exactly one action per interval of the global clock, because actions are now unconditional, that is, in describing Algorithm $S\_Template$ we have done away with the Boolean conditions that Algorithm $A\_Template$ inherited from the *guard*'s of Algorithm $Task\_t$ of Section 1.4. The reason why we could do this is that such conditions are in the synchronous case evaluated only at the occurrence of pulses, and this can be treated inside the action itself (through the use of **if**'s, as opposed to the use of **when**'s in the asynchronous case).

Another important observation regarding Algorithm $S\_Template$ is that we allow n_i to have access, during its computation at interval $s > 0$, to all the sets $MSG_i(1), \ldots, MSG_i(s)$. Although normally only $MSG_i(s)$ is needed, the greater generality is useful for our purposes in various situations, as for example in Sections 2.2.3 and 3.3.

2.2. Computations on anonymous systems

The system represented by the graph G is said to be an *anonymous system* when its nodes do not have identifications that they can use in their computations. Of course, we as outside observers can still make use of the identifications $n_1, \ldots, n_n$ in describing the anonymous system, the computations that run on it, and the properties of those computations. The nodes themselves, however, cannot have access to such identifications for use in the algorithm, not even to identify a neighbor as the source or the destination of a message. In an anonymous system, all that is known to a node n_i are the sets In_i and Out_i of edges (Inc_i, in the undirected case), so messages have to be received and sent over these edges without explicit mention to the nodes on the other side, whose identifications are unknown. When receiving a message msg_i, the only information related to the origin of msg_i that n_i can use is the identification of the edge on which the message arrived, and this is denoted by $origin_i(msg_i)$, as we discussed in Section 2.1. The reader should check that Algorithms $A\_Template$ and $S\_Template$ of Section 2.1 were written in this fashion, so they can be used directly to express algorithms on anonymous systems.

The study of computations on anonymous systems is interesting from at least two perspectives. First of all, this study provides an opportunity to investigate the limits of what can be computed distributedly when nodes do not have, and cannot possibly obtain, complete information on the overall structure of G. The second perspective is that of systems that really should be regarded as anonymous, as many systems represented by massively parallel models that in fact can be viewed as performing distributed computations (cf. Section 10.2 for examples).

One of the foremost consequences of assuming that a system is anonymous is that the algorithm describing the computation to be carried out by a node must be the same for all nodes. The reason why this property must hold is that differences in the algorithms performed by the nodes might provide a means to establish identifications that the nodes would then be able to use in their computations, in which case the system would no longer be anonymous.

Our discussion throughout Section 2.2. will be limited to the cases in which G is an undirected graph with one single cycle, that is, an undirected ring. In the case of a ring, Inc_i has exactly two members for all $n_i \in N$, which we let be called $left_i$ and $right_i$. If every edge (n_i, n_j) is such that $(n_i, n_j) = left_i = right_j$, then we say that the ring is *locally oriented*, or, equivalently, that the assignment of denominations to edges locally at the nodes establishes a *local orientation* on the ring. Equivalently, this can be expressed by rephrasing the condition as $(n_i, n_j) = left_j = right_i$ for all $(n_i, n_j) \in E$.

Section 2.2.1 contains a discussion of two impossibility results under the assumption of anonymity. These two results refer to computations of Boolean functions and to the establishment of local orientations under certain assumptions on n, the number of nodes in the ring. The remaining two sections contain algorithms to compute Boolean functions (Section 2.2.2) and to find a local orientation (Sections 2.2.2 and 2.2.3) when the conditions leading to the impossibility results of Section 2.2.1 do not hold.

2.2.1. Some impossibility results

Let f be a Boolean function of the form

$$f : \{\textbf{true}, \textbf{false}\}^n \to \{\textbf{true}, \textbf{false}\}.$$

In this section, we consider algorithms to compute f when the n Booleans that constitute its arguments are initially scattered throughout the nodes, one per node, in such a way that at the end of the algorithm every node has the same value for f (we say that such an algorithm *computes f at all nodes*). Naturally, the assignment of arguments to nodes has to be assumed to be given initially, because an anonymous system cannot possibly perform such an assignment by itself.

The first impossibility result that we discuss is given by Theorem 2.4, and is related to the availability of n to be used by the nodes in their computations.

Theorem 2.4. *No synchronous algorithm exists to compute f at all nodes if n is not known to the nodes.*

Proof: We show that any synchronous algorithm that computes f in the absence of information on n must in some cases fail, that is, we show that such an algorithm does not necessarily compute f at all nodes.

For consider an algorithm to compute f when n is not known to the nodes. This algorithm must function independently of n, therefore for rings with all numbers of

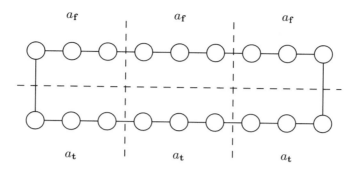

Figure 2.1. *This is the $2\nu(2\lceil T/3 \rceil + 1)$-node ring used in the proof of Theorem 2.4, here shown for $\nu = 3$ and $T = 3$. Each of the three portions in the upper half comprising three contiguous nodes each is assigned f's arguments according to $a_\mathbf{f}$. Similar portions in the lower half of the ring follow assignment $a_\mathbf{t}$.*

nodes. In particular, for a ring with $n = \nu \geq 3$ nodes, let $a_\mathbf{f}$ and $a_\mathbf{t}$ be assignments of f's arguments to nodes, i.e.,

$$a_\mathbf{f}, a_\mathbf{t} : \{n_1, \ldots, n_\nu\} \to \{\mathbf{false}, \mathbf{true}\},$$

such that

$$f\big(a_\mathbf{f}(n_1), \ldots, a_\mathbf{f}(n_\nu)\big) = \mathbf{false}$$

and

$$f\big(a_\mathbf{t}(n_1), \ldots, a_\mathbf{t}(n_\nu)\big) = \mathbf{true}.$$

Furthermore, let $T_\mathbf{f}$ and $T_\mathbf{t}$ be the numbers of pulses that the algorithm spends in computing f for, respectively, assignments $a_\mathbf{f}$ and $a_\mathbf{t}$. Let T be such that

$$T \geq \max\{T_\mathbf{f}, T_\mathbf{t}\}.$$

The next step is to consider a ring with $n = 2\nu(2\lceil T/3 \rceil + 1)$ nodes, for which the algorithm must also work, and to assign arguments to the nodes as follows. Divide the ring into two connected halves, and within each half identify $2\lceil T/3 \rceil + 1$ portions, each with ν contiguous nodes. To each such portion in one of the halves assign arguments as given by $a_\mathbf{f}$. Then use $a_\mathbf{t}$ to do the assignments to each of the portions in the other half (Figure 2.1).

Because the number of portions in each half is odd, we can identify a middle portion in each of the halves. Also, except for the nodes at either end of the two halves, every node is in the larger ring connected as it was in the smaller one (i.e., the Booleans assigned to a node's neighbors are the same in the two rings). In the synchronous model, it takes at least d pulses for a node to causally affect another that is d edges apart on a shortest path, so nodes in the middle portions of both halves cannot be causally affected by any other node in the other half within T pulses of the beginning of the computation. What these considerations imply is that the nodes in the middle portion of the half related to $a_{\mathbf{f}}$ will by pulse T have terminated and proclaimed the value of f to be **false**, because this is what happened by assumption under the same circumstances on the smaller ring. Similarly, nodes in the middle portion of the half related to $a_{\mathbf{t}}$ will have terminated and proclaimed f to have value **true** within T pulses of the beginning of the computation.   ■

Corollary 2.5. *No algorithm exists to compute f at all nodes if n is not known to the nodes.*

Proof: This is a direct consequence of our discussion in Section 2.1, where we mentioned that every asynchronous algorithm easily yields an equivalent synchronous algorithm. So, if an asynchronous algorithm existed to compute f at all nodes in the absence of information on n at the nodes, then the resulting synchronous algorithm would contradict Theorem 2.4.   ■

If n is known to the nodes, then f can be computed at all nodes by a variety of algorithms, as we discuss in Section 2.2.2.

The second impossibility result that we discuss in this section is related to establishing a local orientation on the ring when, for $n_i \in N$, the identifications $left_i$ and $right_i$ are not guaranteed to yield a local orientation initially. This problem is related to the problem of computing f we discussed previously in the following manner. At node n_i, the positioning of $left_i$ and $right_i$ with respect to how its neighbors' edge identifications are positioned can be regarded as constituting a Boolean input. Establishing a local orientation for the ring can then be regarded as computing a function f on these inputs and then switching the denominations of the two edges incident to n_i if the value it computes for f turns out to be, say, **false**. Now, this function is not in general expected to yield the same value at all nodes, and then Corollary 2.5 would not in principle apply to it. However, another Boolean function, call it f', can be computed easily once f has been computed. This function has value **true** if and only if the ring is locally oriented, and this is the value it would be assigned at each node right after that node had computed f and chosen either to perform the switch in edge identifications or not to. Clearly,

f' is expected to be assigned the same value at all nodes, and then by Corollary 2.5 there is no algorithm to compute it at all nodes in the absence of information on n. As a consequence, there is no algorithm to compute f either.

Even when n is known to the nodes, there are cases in which no algorithm can be found to establish a local orientation on the ring. Theorem 2.6 gives the conditions under which this happens.

Theorem 2.6. *No synchronous algorithm exists to establish a local orientation on the ring if n is even.*

Proof: Our argument is to show that any synchronous algorithm to establish a local orientation on the ring fails in some cases if n is even. To do so, we let $n = 2\nu$ for some $\nu \geq 2$, and then consider the following arrangement of $left_i$ and $right_i$ for all $n_i \in N$. For $1 \leq i \leq \nu - 1$, we let

$$right_i = left_{i+1},$$

and for $\nu + 2 \leq i \leq 2\nu$ we let

$$right_i = left_{i-1}.$$

Clearly, this arrangement also implies

$$left_1 = left_{2\nu}$$

and

$$right_\nu = right_{\nu+1},$$

so the ring is not locally oriented.

Now we consider a mapping φ of the form

$$\varphi : \{1, \ldots, 2\nu\} \rightarrow \{1, \ldots, 2\nu\}$$

such that, for $1 \leq i \leq 2\nu$,

$$\varphi(i) = 2\nu + 1 - i,$$

for which it clearly holds that $i = \varphi(\varphi(i))$ (Figure 2.2). This mapping is also such that, for $1 \leq i \leq 2\nu$, if n_i sends a message at a certain pulse (or receives a message during the corresponding interval) on edge $left_i$ or edge $right_i$, then $n_{\varphi(i)}$ does exactly the same at the same pulse, respectively on edge $left_{\varphi(i)}$ or edge $right_{\varphi(i)}$. Consequently, n_i and $n_{\varphi(i)}$ reach the same conclusion on whether they

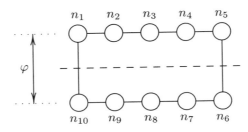

Figure 2.2. *The 2ν-node ring used in the proof of Theorem 2.6 is depicted here for $\nu = 5$. Shown is also the mapping φ, emphasizing the symmetry among the nodes in the ring's upper half and the corresponding nodes in the lower half.*

should switch their incident edges' identifications or not, and the ring continues to be not locally oriented.   ∎

Corollary 2.7. *No algorithm exists to establish a local orientation on the ring if n is even.*

Proof: The proof here is entirely analogous to that of Corollary 2.5.   ∎

If n is known to the nodes and is odd, then a local orientation can be established on the ring. We give algorithms to do this in Sections 2.2.2 and 2.2.3.

2.2.2. Boolean-function computations

When n is known to the nodes, Corollary 2.5 does not apply and the function f introduced in Section 2.2.1 can be computed at all nodes. Also, if such a function is computed with the aim of eventually establishing a local orientation on the ring, then n has to be odd for Corollary 2.7 not to apply.

In this section, we start by presenting Algorithm *A_Compute_f*, which is an asynchronous algorithm to compute f at all nodes when n is known to the nodes. In addition, we present this algorithm in such a way that, if n is odd, then it may be used almost readily to establish a local orientation on the ring as well.

In Algorithm *A_Compute_f*, $b_i \in \{\textbf{false}, \textbf{true}\}$ denotes f's argument corresponding to $n_i \in N$. In order for the algorithm to be also suitable to the determination of a local orientation on the ring, the messages that it employs carry the pair of Booleans comprising one argument of f and a Boolean constant.

So far as computing f goes, the essence of Algorithm $A\_Compute\_f$ is very simple. If $n_i \in N_0$, or upon receiving the first message if $n_i \notin N_0$, n_i sends the pair $(b_i, \textbf{false})$ on $left_i$ and the pair $(b_i, \textbf{true})$ on $right_i$. For each of the $\lfloor n/2 \rfloor$ messages it receives on each of the edges incident to it, n_i records the Booleans contained in the message and sends them onward on the edges opposite to those on which they were received. After all these messages have been received, n_i has the Booleans originally assigned to every node and may then compute f locally.

Node n_i employs two variables to count the numbers of messages received, respectively $count\_left_i$ and $count\_right_i$ for $left_i$ and $right_i$. Initially, these counters have value zero. In addition, n_i employs the n Boolean variables b_i^j to record the values of $b_1, \ldots, b_n$ when they are received in messages (if $j \neq i$) for $1 \leq j \leq n$. Initially, $b_i^1 = b_i$ (the others do not need any initial value to be set). Another variable j_i is used to contain the subscripts to these variables.

Because Algorithm $A\_Compute\_f$ has to be exactly the same for all nodes in N, another Boolean variable, $initiated_i$ (initially set to $\textbf{false}$), is employed by n_i to indicate whether $n_i \in N_0$ or not. This variable is set to $\textbf{true}$ when n_i starts its computation if it is a member of N_0. Nonmembers of N_0 will have this variable equal to $\textbf{false}$ upon receiving the first messages, and will then know that first of all it must send messages out. In the absence of anonymity, sometimes it is simpler to specify an algorithm for $n_i \in N_0$ and another for $n_i \notin N_0$.

Algorithm $A\_Compute\_f$:

▷ **Variables:**

$count\_left_i = 0$;
$count\_right_i = 0$;
$b_i^k \; (= b_i, \text{ if } k = 1) \text{ for } 1 \leq k \leq n$;
$j_i = 1$;
$initiated_i = \textbf{false}$.

▷ **Input:**

$msg_i = \textbf{nil}$.

Action if $n_i \in N_0$:   (2.10)

$initiated_i := \textbf{true}$;
Send $(b_i^1, \textbf{false})$ on $left_i$;
Send $(b_i^1, \textbf{true})$ on $right_i$.

▷ **Input:**
$$msg_i = (b, B).$$

Action: (2.11)

    if not $initiated_i$ **then**

        begin

            $initiated_i :=$ **true**;

            Send $(b_i^1, $ **false**$)$ on $left_i$;

            Send $(b_i^1, $ **true**$)$ on $right_i$

        end;

    if $origin_i(msg_i) = left_i$ **then**

        begin

            $count\_left_i := count\_left_i + 1$;

            $j_i := j_i + 1$;

            if $j_i \leq n$ **then**

                $b_{j_i} := b$;

            if $count\_left_i \leq \lfloor n/2 \rfloor - 1$ **then**

                Send msg_i on $right_i$

        end;

    if $origin_i(msg_i) = right_i$ **then**

        begin

            $count\_right_i := count\_right_i + 1$;

            $j_i := j_i + 1$;

            if $j_i \leq n$ **then**

                $b_{j_i} := b$;

            if $count\_right_i \leq \lfloor n/2 \rfloor - 1$ **then**

                Send msg_i on $left_i$

        end;

    if $count\_left_i + count\_right_i = 2\lfloor n/2 \rfloor$ **then**

        Compute $f(b_i^1, \ldots, b_i^n)$.

An instructive observation at this point is that Algorithm *A_Compute_f* is indeed an algorithm for anonymous rings. Nowhere in the algorithm are the identities of the nodes mentioned, except in the description of (2.10), but this is only for notational consistency with Algorithm *A_Template*, because in any event the set N_0 is determined by an "external agent." In fact, it is because of the system's anonymity that the b's that n_i receives have to placed by (2.11) in the variables $b_i^2, \ldots, b_i^n$ irrespective of their original senders, which would be simpler if the denominations of those senders could be used by the algorithm. In addition, the algorithm does make use of n, as anticipated by Corollary 2.5.

Let us now examine Algorithm $A\_Compute\_f$ carefully. During n_i's computation, it receives the messages originally sent to it by its neighbors by (2.10) or (2.11), and whatever those neighbors forward to it by (2.11). Because by (2.11) a node only forwards to each of its neighbors $\lfloor n/2 \rfloor - 1$ messages, n_i actually receives $2\lfloor n/2 \rfloor$ messages, of which the last two it does not forward. Upon receipt of the last of the $2\lfloor n/2 \rfloor$ messages, n_i has either n (if n is odd) or $n+1$ (if n is even) arguments of f, which it may then compute. Although it may be possible to modify the algorithm a little bit to ensure that exactly n arguments are received if n is even as well (cf. Exercise 1), as presented the last argument received is a repetition and may be dropped (as in (2.11)).

In many cases, it may only be possible to compute f if the information n_i receives is organized more orderly than as in Algorithm $A\_Compute\_f$. In other words, unless f is invariant with respect to the order of its arguments (as in the case of the AND and OR functions, for example), then the variables $b_i^2, \ldots, b_i^n$ have to be replaced with two sets of similar variables, each with $\lfloor n/2 \rfloor$ variables to accommodate the Booleans received from each of n_i's neighbors. In addition, if such an invariance does not hold, then the edges in E have to be assumed to be FIFO. Even so, however, because the system is anonymous f can only be computed if it is invariant under rotations of its arguments.

As we mentioned earlier, Algorithm $A\_Compute\_f$ can also be used to provide the ring with a local orientation, and this is the role of the B's that get sent along with every message. When the algorithm is used with this purpose, then the b's have no role and the B's are treated as follows at the step in which f would be computed in (2.11). A B that n_i receives indicates either that its original sender had its *left* and *right* edges positioned like $left_i$ and $right_i$ (if $B = $ **true** is received on $left_i$ or $B = $ **false** is received on $right_i$) or positioned otherwise (if $B = $ **false** is received on $left_i$ or $B = $ **true** is received on $right_i$). In either case, so long as n is odd (and n has to be odd, by Corollary 2.7), n_i can decide whether its edges are positioned like those of the majority of the nodes, in which case it maintains their positioning, or not, in which case it reverses their positioning. The result of these decisions system-wide is clearly to establish a local orientation on the ring. (Note that in this case Algorithm $A\_Compute\_f$ would have to be modified to treat the B's, not the b's, n_i receives—cf. Exercise 3.)

Because each node receives $2\lfloor n/2 \rfloor$ messages during the computation, the total number of messages employed by the algorithm is $2n\lfloor n/2 \rfloor$, and its message complexity is clearly $O(n^2)$. In Section 3.2.1, we return to Algorithm $A\_Compute\_f$ to discuss its time-related complexity measures.

In the remainder of this section and in Section 2.2.3, we show that synchronous algorithms exist whose message complexities are significantly lower than that of Algorithm $A\_Compute\_f$, so long as the generality of this algorithm can be given up. The synchronous algorithm that we discuss next is specific to computing the AND function, while the one we discuss in Section 2.2.3 is specific to providing the ring with a local orientation.

The key ingredient in obtaining the more efficient synchronous algorithm is that the AND function can be assumed to be **true** unless any of its arguments is **false**. In the synchronous case, this observation can be coupled with the assumptions of the synchronous model as follows. Only nodes with **false** arguments send their argument to neighbors. The others simply wait to receive a **false** or long enough to know that any existing **false** would already have reached them. In either case, computing the AND is a simple matter. Algorithm $S\_Compute\_AND$ embodies this strategy and is given next. In this algorithm, $N_0 = N$ and a Boolean variable f_i (initially set to **true**) is employed by n_i to store the result of evaluating the AND function.

> **Algorithm** $S\_Compute\_AND$:
>
> ▷ **Variables:**
>> $f_i = $ **true**.
>
> ▷ **Input:**
>> $s = 0$, $MSG_i(0) = \emptyset$.
>> **Action if** $n_i \in N_0$:
>>> **if** $b_i = $ **false then**
>>>> **begin**
>>>>> $f_i := $ **false**;
>>>>> Send b_i on $left_i$ and on $right_i$
>>>> **end**.

(2.12)

▷ **Input:**
$$0 < s < \lfloor n/2 \rfloor, \; MSG_i(s).$$
  Action: (2.13)
    if f_i **then**
      if $MSG_i(s) \neq \emptyset$ **then**
        begin
          $f_i :=$ **false**;
          if there exists $msg \in MSG_i(s)$ such that
          $origin_i(msg) = left_i$ **then**
            Send msg on $right_i$;
          if there exists $msg \in MSG_i(s)$ such that
          $origin_i(msg) = right_i$ **then**
            Send msg on $left_i$
      end.

If n_i is not such that $b_i =$ **false**, then the largest number of pulses that can go by before n_i concludes that f_i cannot be changed from its initial value of **true** is $\lfloor n/2 \rfloor$, so that after pulse $s = \lfloor n/2 \rfloor = O(n)$ no further computation has to be performed and the algorithm may terminate.

By (2.12) and (2.13), n_i sends at most two messages during its computation, either initially if $b_i =$ **false**, by (2.12), or upon receiving the first message, if any messages are at all received, by (2.13). Clearly, then, the message complexity of Algorithm *S_Compute_AND* is $O(n)$.

2.2.3. Another algorithm for local orientation

In addition to Algorithm *S_Compute_AND*, another example of how to employ many fewer messages than those required by Algorithm *A_Compute_f* comes from considering a synchronous algorithm tailored specifically to establishing a local orientation on the ring. By Theorem 2.6, such an algorithm may only exist if n is odd, as we assume henceforth in this section.

The basic strategy behind this algorithm employs the following terminology. Say that two nodes n_i and n_j are *segment ends* if $(n_i, n_j) \in E$ and furthermore $(n_i, n_j) = left_i = left_j$. Segment ends delimit *segments*, which are subsets of N inducing connected subgraphs of G with at least two nodes. If n_i and n_j are segment ends and $(n_i, n_j) \in E$, then n_i and n_j belong to different segments, unless the number of segments in the ring is exactly one. Clearly, a locally oriented ring contains no segment ends, while a ring that is not locally oriented contains a nonzero even number of segment ends, and half as many segments. Because n is odd, an odd number of segments must have an odd number of nodes each.

The synchronous algorithm proceeds in iterations, each one comprising two phases. Initially, all nodes are said to be *active*, and the goal of each of the iterations is to reduce the number of active nodes. During an iteration, nodes that are not active function solely as message relays, so that the computation can always be looked at as being carried out on a ring containing the active nodes only, called the *active ring*. Iterations proceed until exactly one active node remains or until an active ring is reached which is locally oriented (in this case with more than one active node). A local orientation can then be established on the entire ring by the last active nodes.

The number of iterations that the algorithm requires depends largely on how active nodes are eliminated from one iteration to the next. In Algorithm *S_Locally_Orient*, given next, this elimination takes place as follows. In the first phase of an iteration, segment ends are identified on the active ring. Then, in the second phase, the nodes, called *center nodes*, occupying the central positions in the segments having an odd number of nodes are identified and selected to be the only active nodes to remain through to the next iteration. By our preceding discussion, the number of center nodes must be odd, and then so must the number of nodes in every active ring, thereby guaranteeing the feasibility of every iteration. The last iteration is characterized by the absence of segment ends among the active nodes. Because at each iteration segments with an even number of nodes do not contribute with any active node to the next iteration, and considering that segments with odd numbers of nodes have at least three nodes each, clearly the number of iterations required is no larger than $\lceil \log_3 n \rceil = O(\log n)$.

Letting $\sigma \geq 0$ indicate the pulses within each of the iterations, the following is how the two aforementioned phases within an iteration are implemented. At pulse $\sigma = 0$, node n_i, if active, sends *token* on edge $right_i$. Active nodes then idle throughout the following $n - 1$ pulses, while nodes that are not active simply relay *token* onward if they at all receive it. An active node n_i that by pulse $\sigma = n$ has not received *token* on $left_i$ is a segment end, and at pulse $\sigma = n$ sends the integer 0 on $right_i$. Throughout the following $n - 1$ pulses (i.e., from pulse $\sigma = n + 1$ through pulse $\sigma = 2n - 1$), active nodes forward the integer $z + 1$ upon receiving integer z, for some $z \geq 0$, while the other nodes continue to function as relays. An active node n_i that by pulse $\sigma = 2n$ has received the same integer over $left_i$ and $right_i$ during the same interval is a center node. This is the last iteration if n_i did not receive any message during intervals n through $2n - 1$, otherwise only center nodes remain active for the next iteration. A message *orient* is sent on, say, $left_i$ by an active node n_i after the last iteration. This message, if received on $left_i$ by a node n_i that is not active, causes $left_i$ and $right_i$ to be interchanged.

The reader should notice that the characteristics of the synchronous model are used profusely in this strategy to establish a local orientation. Indeed, both the determination of segment ends and of center nodes rely heavily on the assumed synchronism, as does the determination of when an iteration is the last one.

In Algorithm $S\_Locally\_Orient$, k identifies the iteration and is then such that $1 \leq k \leq K$, where K is the last iteration, therefore such that $K \leq \lceil \log_3 n \rceil$. Pulses within the kth iteration are numbered $s = 2n(k-1) + \sigma$, that is, from $s = 2n(k-1)$ through $s = 2nk$. After the last iteration, additional $n - 1$ pulses must elapse before termination. The only variable employed by n_i is the Boolean variable $active_i$, initially set to **true**, used to indicate whether n_i is active. Because initially $active_i = $ **true** for all $n_i \in N$, in this algorithm $N_0 = N$. Because K has to be determined as the algorithm progresses, it is assumed to be equal to infinity initially.

Algorithm $S\_Locally\_Orient$:

    ▷ **Variables:**
        $active_i = $ **true**.

    ▷ **Input:**
        $s = 2n(k-1)$, $MSG_i(s) = \emptyset$.
      Action (if $n_i \in N_0$, for $k = 1$):
        if $active_i$ then
            Send $token$ on $right_i$.   (2.14)

    ▷ **Input:**
        $2n(k-1) + 1 \leq s \leq 2nk - n - 1$, $MSG_i(s)$.
      Action: (2.15)
        if **not** $active_i$ then
            begin
                if there exists $token \in MSG_i(s)$ such that $origin_i(token) = left_i$ then
                    Send $token$ on $right_i$;
                if there exists $token \in MSG_i(s)$ such that $origin_i(token) = right_i$ then
                    Send $token$ on $left_i$
          end.

▷ **Input:**

$$s = 2nk - n, \ MSG_i\big(2n(k-1)+1\big), \ldots, MSG_i(2nk - n).$$

Action: (2.16)

    if $active_i$ **then**

        if there does not exist $token \in \bigcup_{r=2n(k-1)+1}^{2nk-n} MSG_i(r)$ such that $origin_i(token) = left_i$ **then**

            Send 0 on $right_i$.

▷ **Input:**

$$2nk - n + 1 \le s \le 2nk - 1, \ MSG_i(s).$$

Action: (2.17)

    if $active_i$ **then**

        begin

            if there exists $z \in MSG_i(s)$ such that $origin_i(z) = left_i$

            then

                Send $z + 1$ on $right_i$;

            if there exists $z \in MSG_i(s)$ such that $origin_i(z) = right_i$

            then

                Send $z + 1$ on $left_i$

        end

    else

        begin

            if there exists $z \in MSG_i(s)$ such that $origin_i(z) = left_i$

            then

                Send z on $right_i$;

            if there exists $z \in MSG_i(s)$ such that $origin_i(z) = right_i$

            then

                Send z on $left_i$

        end.

▷ **Input:**
$$s = 2nk, \; MSG_i(2nk - n + 1), \ldots, MSG_i(2nk).$$

Action: (2.18)

    if $active_i$ **then**

        if $MSG_i(r) = \emptyset$ for all $r \in \{2nk - n, \ldots, 2nk - 1\}$ **then**

            begin

                $K := k;$

                Send $orient$ on $left_i$

            end

    else

        if there do not exist $r \in \{2nk - n, \ldots, 2nk - 1\}$ and $z_1, z_2 \in MSG_i(r)$ with $z_1 = z_2$ such that $origin_i(z_1) = left_i$ and $origin_i(z_2) = right_i$ **then**

            $active_i := $ **false**.

▷ **Input:**
$$2nK + 1 \le s \le 2nK + n - 1, \; MSG_i(s).$$

Action: (2.19)

    if not $active_i$ **then**

        begin

            if there exists $orient \in MSG_i(s)$ such that $origin_i(orient) = left_i$ **then**

                Interchange $left_i$ and $right_i$;

            Send $orient$ on $left_i$

        end.

In Algorithm *S_Locally_Orient*, (2.14) implements the sending of *token* at the beginning of each iteration, while in (2.15) the relaying of *token* by nodes that are not active appears. In (2.16), segment ends are identified and initiate the propagation of integers, which are relayed as appropriate by (2.17). Center nodes are identified in (2.18), which, in the last iteration, also includes the propagation of *orient*, relayed onward by (2.19). In no action does a node send more than two messages, and then the number of messages per iteration is clearly $O(n)$. It follows from our earlier determination of the maximum number of iterations that the message complexity of Algorithm *S_Locally_Orient* is $O(n \log n)$.

2.3. The role of knowledge in distributed computations

The notion of knowledge is a notion of many possible meanings, but even the simplest algorithms we have seen so far in this chapter indicate that much of what distributed computations do is, in some sense, to collectively manipulate the system's knowledge so that at the end of the computation what nodes "know" individually relates in some way to the computation's original goal. During the past decade, various interesting hints at how notions related to knowledge might be used in the design and analysis of distributed algorithms were envisaged. Although today the interest in such an approach has waned somewhat, a few interesting insights were obtained that can be expressed in a particularly simple fashion when viewed from the standpoint of knowledge in the system.

Our goal in this section is to finalize the chapter by presenting some of these insights, which will be referred back to in forthcoming chapters for the sake of illustration within the context of those chapters. The ideal approach to our discussion in this section would be that of a logician, but naturally we refrain from doing that, especially because the necessary background to undertake such an approach intersects what is expected of a reader of this book very narrowly. Rather, we approach the subject quite informally, aiming essentially at conveying some of its intuitive underpinnings.

If $\mathcal{P}$ denotes a sentence (in the logical sense), then we denote the notion that a node n_i knows $\mathcal{P}$ by $K_i\mathcal{P}$, where, loosely, K_i is an operator indicating knowledge by n_i. Normally, only true sentences are assumed to be knowable, that is, in order for $\mathcal{P}$ to be known by n_i it is necessary that $\mathcal{P}$ be true, giving rise to the axiom

$$K_i\mathcal{P} \to \mathcal{P}.$$

(If $\mathcal{A}$ and $\mathcal{B}$ are two formulas, in the usual logical sense, then $\mathcal{A} \to \mathcal{B}$ is equivalent to $\neg\mathcal{A} \vee \mathcal{B}$.) Every distributed algorithm embodies various steps whereby the knowledge status of the nodes evolves. For example, if n_i sends a message containing a true sentence $\mathcal{P}$ to $n_j \in Neig_i$, then $K_i\mathcal{P}$ holds as early as when the message is sent, but $K_j\mathcal{P}$ may happen to hold only from the time of receipt of the message onward, and then $K_jK_i\mathcal{P}$ also holds.

Despite the simplicity of such a notion of knowledge by n_i, it contains not too evident idiosyncrasies that include limits on what n_i may know. This has been illustrated in the literature in the following anecdotic fashion.

> "In a class with daily meetings the teacher announces, by the end
> of a Friday class, that there will be an unexpected exam in the

following week. The students reason over the possibilities during the weekend, and conclude that the exam will not be on Friday, otherwise it would not be unexpected, and inductively that it cannot be on any other day of the week either. As a result, they do not study for the exam and, surely enough, a totally unexpected exam is given on Monday."

If we let $\mathcal{E}$ denote "there will be an exam today," then the flaw in the students' reasoning is that, while it is possible for the sentence $\mathcal{E} \wedge \neg K_i \mathcal{E}$ to be true for a node (student) n_i, the same cannot possibly hold for the sentence $K_i(\mathcal{E} \wedge \neg K_i \mathcal{E})$, so that there are limits to what is knowable to n_i.

In a distributed setting like the one we have been considering in this book, there is interest in generalizing the notion of individual knowledge embodied in the operator K_i to notions of group knowledge, say by all the members of N. Two simple possibilities of generalization in this sense are summarized by the operators S_N and E_N, intended respectively to convey the notions of knowledge by at least one node and by all nodes. In other words,

$$S_N \mathcal{P} \equiv \bigvee_{n_i \in N} K_i \mathcal{P}$$

and

$$E_N \mathcal{P} \equiv \bigwedge_{n_i \in N} K_i \mathcal{P}.$$

Another similar possibility of generalization is that of the notion of *implicit knowledge* by the group N. The meaning of implicit knowledge of $\mathcal{P}$ by N, denoted $I_N \mathcal{P}$, is that $\mathcal{P}$ can be concluded from the individual knowledge that the members of N have. For example, if $\mathcal{Q}$ and $\mathcal{Q} \to \mathcal{P}$ are both true sentences, and moreover both $K_i \mathcal{Q}$ and $K_j(\mathcal{Q} \to \mathcal{P})$ hold for $n_i, n_j \in N$, then $\mathcal{P}$ is also true and $I_N \mathcal{P}$ holds as well.

Associated with this notion of implicit knowledge is a notion of conservation, which states that no communication can change the implicit knowledge of propositional nature that N has. This result, which we do not investigate in any further depth in this book, is to be regarded with care. In particular, the requirement that the conserved implicit knowledge be propositional is crucial, as otherwise the conservation need not hold. For example, if for a true sentence $\mathcal{P}$ it holds that $\neg K_i \mathcal{P}$ and $K_j \mathcal{P}$ for $n_i, n_j \in N$ such that $(n_i, n_j) \in E$, then a message sent by n_j to n_i containing $\mathcal{P}$ suffices for $K_i \mathcal{P}$ to become implicit knowledge, although such was not the case prior to the receipt of the message by n_i. However, the sentence

$K_i \mathcal{P}$ is not propositional, and then no contradiction to the conservation principle is implied by this acquisition of new implicit knowledge.

The next step in generalizing the notion of individual knowledge to broader notions of group knowledge is to consider the notion of *common knowledge* by N. This notion, denoted by $C_N \mathcal{P}$ for a true sentence $\mathcal{P}$, is such that

$$C_N \mathcal{P} \equiv \bigwedge_{k \geq 1} E_N^k \mathcal{P},$$

where $E_N^1 \mathcal{P} = E_N \mathcal{P}$ and, for $k > 1$, $E_N^k \mathcal{P} = E_N E_N^{k-1} \mathcal{P}$. This notion is very hard to grasp intuitively, but nonetheless it should be clear that

$$C_N \mathcal{P} \to K_{i_1} \dots K_{i_z} \mathcal{P}$$

holds for any set of integers $\{i_1, \dots, i_z\} \subseteq \{1, \dots, n\}$ with $z \geq 1$. Another anecdote is usually very helpful in building up some intuition on the notion of common knowledge.

> "A group of boys are playing together and have been advised by their parents that they should not get dirty. However, it does happen that some of them, say $k \geq 1$, get dirty, but only on their foreheads, so that no boy knows whether his own forehead is dirty though he can see the others'. One of the parents then shows up and states, 'At least one of you has a dirty forehead,' thereby expressing a fact already known to all the boys if $k > 1$. The parent then asks repeatedly, 'Can anyone prove that his own forehead is dirty?' If we assume that all the boys are unusually intellectually gifted, and moreover that they all reply simultaneously at each repetition of the parent's question, then every boy replies 'No' to the first $k - 1$ questions, and the boys with dirty foreheads reply 'Yes' to the kth question."

What supports the boys' reasoning in replying to the parent's repeated questions is the following inductive argument. If $k = 1$, then the only boy with a dirty forehead replies "Yes" immediately upon the first question, because he knows that at least one boy has a dirty forehead, and seeing no one else in that condition he must be the one. If we inductively hypothesize that the boys reason correctly for $1 \leq k \leq k'$ with $k' \geq 1$, then for $k = k' + 1$ we have the following. A boy with a dirty forehead sees k' other boys with dirty foreheads, while a boy with a clean forehead sees $k' + 1$ boys with dirty foreheads. By the induction hypothesis, a boy with a dirty forehead must reply "Yes" to the kth question, because if he did not have a dirty forehead the other k' boys with dirty foreheads that he sees would all have replied "Yes" upon hearing the previous question. Because they did not, his own forehead must be dirty.

In the context of this anecdote, the issue of knowledge comes in as follows. If $\mathcal{P}$ represents the parent's statement concerning the existence of boys with dirty foreheads and N is the set of boys, then, before the statement, $E_N^{k-1}\mathcal{P}$ holds but $E_N^k\mathcal{P}$ does not. What the parent's statement does is to establish $C_N\mathcal{P}$, therefore $E_N^k\mathcal{P}$, which is the necessary state of knowledge for the boys' reasoning to be carried out.

The various notions of knowledge we have encountered so far relate to each other hierarchically in such a way that

$$C_N\mathcal{P} \to \cdots \to E_N^{k+1}\mathcal{P} \to \cdots \to E_N\mathcal{P} \to S_N\mathcal{P} \to I_N\mathcal{P} \to \mathcal{P}$$

holds for every $k \geq 1$. While every information that is "built in" the nodes constitutes common knowledge, the acquisition of new common knowledge is far from trivial, unless some sort of "shared memory" can be assumed, as in the case of the anecdote we presented on the dirty-forehead boys (the parent's statement can be regarded as having been "written" into such a shared memory). To see why acquiring new common knowledge may be important, we consider yet another anecdote.

> "Two divisions of an army are camped on the hills surrounding a valley, and in the valley is the enemy army. Both divisions would like to attack the enemy army simultaneously some time the next day, because each division individually is outnumbered by the enemies. Having agreed on no plan beforehand, the divisions' generals are forced to rely on forerunners to convey messages to each other. Forerunners must go through the enemy's camp with their messages, and then do it at night, although the risk of being caught still exists and in addition they may get lost. Given that normally one hour is enough for the trip, and that at this particular night the forerunners travel uneventfully through the enemy's camp and do not get lost, how long does it take for an agreement to be reached between the two generals?"

Clearly, what the two generals seek in this anecdote is common knowledge of an agreement. The reader must quickly realize, though, that such a state of knowledge cannot be attained. Indeed, unless communication is totally reliable (as we have implicitly been assuming) and the model of distributed computation is the synchronous model, no new common knowledge can ever be attained. However, the literature contains examples of how to attain new common knowledge in the asynchronous model with reliable communication by restricting the definition of common knowledge to special global states (cf. Section 3.1).

2.4. Exercises

1. Show that, if the ring is locally oriented, then Algorithm $A\_Compute\_f$ can be modified so that every node receives exactly n arguments of f even if n is even.

2. Describe how to simplify Algorithm $S\_Locally\_Orient$ if the determination of K is not required (that is, if the algorithm is to run for the maximum possible number of iterations).

3. Show how to modify Algorithm $A\_Compute\_f$ so that it can be used to establish a local orientation on the ring (i.e., show how it should be changed to treat the B's instead of the b's).

2.5. Bibliographic notes

Readers in need of references on concepts from graph theory, for use not only in this chapter but throughout the book, may choose from a variety of sources, including some of the classic texts, like Harary (1969), Berge (1976), Bondy and Murty (1976), and Wilson (1979). The asynchronous and synchronous models introduced in Section 2.1 are pretty standard in the field, and can also be found in Lamport and Lynch (1990), for example. Algorithm A_FIFO, used as example in that section, is from Barbosa and Porto (1995).

The material on anonymous systems in Section 2.2 is based on Attiya and Snir (1985), which later appeared in revised form in Attiya, Snir, and Warmuth (1988). Further developments on the theme can be found in Attiya and Snir (1991), Bodlaender, Moran, and Warmuth (1994), Kranakis, Krizanc, and van den Berg (1994), and Lakshman and Wei (1994).

Readers seeking additional information on the notions related to knowledge can look for the survey by Halpern (1986), as well as the guide to the logics involved by Halpern and Moses (1992). The material in Section 2.3 is drawn from a variety of publications, which the reader may seek in order to deepen the treatment of a particular topic. The application of knowledge-related notions to problems in the context of distributed computations dates back to the first version of Halpern and Moses (1990) and to Lehmann (1984). In Halpern and Moses (1990), the reader will also find the definitions of implicit and common knowledge, as well as the argument for the impossibility of attaining common knowledge in the asynchronous model or under unreliable communication. Fischer and Immerman (1986) describe situations in which common knowledge can be attained in the asynchronous model if communication is totally reliable and in addition one is restricted to considering only some special global states. The anecdote involving students and the unexpected exam is from Lehmann (1984). The conservation of implicit knowledge is from Fagin and Vardi (1986). Problems related to the agreement between generals of a same army can be found in Lamport, Shostak, and Pease (1982) and in Dwork and Moses (1990). Additional work on knowledge in distributed systems has appeared by Halpern and Fagin (1989), Fagin, Halpern, and Vardi (1992), Neiger and Toueg (1993), and van der Meyden (1994).

3

Models of Computation

In this chapter, we return to the topic of computation models for distributed algorithms. We start where we stopped at the end of Section 2.1, which was devoted essentially to introducing the asynchronous and synchronous models of distributed computation. In that section, we also introduced, along with examples throughout Chapter 2, Algorithms *A_Template* and *S_Template*, given respectively as templates to write asynchronous and synchronous algorithms.

Our first aim in this chapter is to establish a more detailed model of the distributed computations that occur under the assumption of both the asynchronous and the synchronous model. We do this in Section 3.1, where we introduce an event-based formalism to describe distributed computations. Such a formalism will allow us to be much more precise than we have been so far when referring to global timing issues in the asynchronous case, and will in addition provide us with the necessary terminology to define the time-related complexity measures that we have so far avoided.

This discussion of complexity measures appears in Section 3.2, where the emphasis is on time-related measures for asynchronous algorithms, although we also discuss such measures for synchronous algorithms and return to the issue of message complexity introduced in Section 2.1.

We continue in Section 3.3 by returning to the template algorithms of Section 2.1 to provide details on how asynchronous algorithms can be executed under the assumptions of the synchronous model. In addition, we also indicate, but only superficially in this chapter, how synchronous algorithms can be transformed into equivalent asynchronous algorithms.

Section 3.4 is dedicated to a deeper exploration of the synchronous model, which, as we have indicated previously, although unrealistic possesses some conceptual and practical features of great interest. Some of these are our subject in Section 3.4, as an example of a computation that is strictly more efficient in time-related terms in the synchronous model than in the asynchronous model, and another in which the initial assumption of full synchronism in the process of algorithm design eventually leads to greater overall efficiency with respect to existing solutions to the same problem.

Sections 3.5 and 3.6 contain exercises and bibliographic notes, respectively.

3.1. Events, orders, and global states

So far in the book there have been several occasions in which we had to refer to global characteristics of the algorithms we studied and found ourselves at a loss concerning appropriate conceptual bases and terminology. This has been most pronounced in the case of asynchronous algorithms, and then we have resorted to expressions as "concurrent," "scenario," and "causally affect" to make up for the appropriate terminology and yet convey some of the intuition of what was actually meant. This happened, for example, during our discussion of task migration in Sections 1.6.2 and 2.1, in our introduction of the synchronous model in Section 2.1, and in the proof of Theorem 2.4. As we indicated in Sections 2.1 and 2.3, such imprecisions can be corrected easily once the appropriate concept of a global state has been established. Such a concept lies at the core of our discussion in this section.

The case of synchronous algorithms is clearly much simpler as far as the concepts underlying global temporal issues are concerned. In fact, in describing Algorithms $S\_Compute\_AND$ and $S\_Locally\_Orient$, respectively in Sections 2.2.2 and 2.2.3, we managed without any difficulty to identify the number of pulses that had to elapse for termination of the algorithm at hand. This number, as we will see in Section 3.2.1, essentially gives the algorithm's time-related measure of complexity, which in the asynchronous case we have not even approached.

Our discussion in this section revolves around the concept of an event, and is intended especially to the description of computations taking place in the asynchronous model (that is, executions of asynchronous algorithms). However, as we mentioned in Section 2.1, the conditions under which the synchronous model is defined can be regarded as a particularization of the conditions for the asynchronous model, and then all of our discussion is also applicable in its essence to the synchronous model as well. We shall return to this issue later to be more specific on how the characteristics of the synchronous model can be seen to be present in our event-based formalism.

The concept of an event in our formalism is that of a fundamental unit of a distributed computation, which in turn is an execution of a distributed algorithm. A distributed computation is then viewed simply as a set of events, which we denote by Ξ. An *event* ξ is the 6-tuple

$$\xi = \langle n_i, t, \varphi, \sigma, \sigma', \Phi \rangle,$$

where

- n_i is the node at which the event occurs;

- t is the time, as given by n_i's local clock, at which the event occurs;

- φ is the message, if any, that triggered the event upon its reception by n_i;

- σ is the state of n_i prior to the occurrence of the event;

- σ' is the state of n_i after the occurrence of the event;

- Φ is the set of messages, if any, sent by n_i as a consequence of the occurrence of the event.

This definition of an event is based on the premise that the behavior of each node during the distributed computation can be described as that of a state machine, which seems to be general enough. The computation Ξ then causes every node to have its state evolve as the events occur. We let Σ_i denote the sequence of states n_i goes through as Ξ goes on. The first member of Σ_i is n_i's *initial state*. The last member of Σ_i (which may not exist if Ξ is not finite) is n_i's *final state*.

This definition of an event is also general enough to encompass both the assumed reactive character of our distributed computations (cf. Section 1.4) and to allow the description of *internal events*, i.e., events that happen without any immediate external cause (understood as a message reception or the spontaneous initiation by the nodes in N_0, which ultimately can also be regarded as originating externally). In order to be able to describe internal events and events associated with the spontaneous initiation by the nodes in N_0, we have allowed the input message φ associated with an event to be absent sometimes. The atomic actions that we have associated with asynchronous algorithms (cf. Algorithm *A_Template*) can then be regarded as sequences of events, the first of which triggered by the reception of a message (or corresponding to the spontaneous initial activity of a node in N_0), and the remaining ones being internal events.

For synchronous algorithms, these definitions are essentially valid as well, but a few special characteristics should be spelled out. Specifically, because in the synchronous case it helps to assume that local computation within an interval of the global clock takes zero time (cf. Section 2.1), and because nodes in the synchronous case are in reality driven by the global clock and not by the reception of messages, at each node exactly one event can be assumed to take place at each pulse, with t being a multiple of an interval's duration. Such an event does not have an input message associated with it, because by assumption every message is in the synchronous model delivered in strictly less time than the duration of an interval. In addition to these events, others corresponding solely to the reception of messages may also happen, but then with a different restriction on the value of t, namely that t be something else than a multiple of an interval's duration. Finally, internal events are now meaningless, because every event either has an input message associated with it, or occurs in response to a pulse, having in either case an external cause. The overall picture in the synchronous case is then the following. At the beginning of the first interval (i.e., at the first pulse), an event happens at each of the nodes in N_0. Subsequently, at each new pulse and at each node an event happens corresponding to the computation by that node on the messages (if any) that it received during the preceding interval. Other events may happen between successive pulses, corresponding exclusively to the reception of messages for use at the succeeding pulse. The reader should notice that this description of a synchronous computation is in entire accordance with Algorithm *S_Template*, that is, the events for which t is a multiple of an interval's duration correspond to the actions in that algorithm. The other events do not correspond to any of the algorithm's actions, being responsible for establishing the sets $MSG_i(s)$ for $n_i \in N$ and $s > 0$.

Events in Ξ are strongly interrelated, as messages that a node sends in connection with an event are received by that node's neighbors in connection with other events. While this relationship is already grasped by the definition of an event, it is useful to elaborate a little more on the issue. Let us then define a binary relation, denoted by $\prec$, on the set of events Ξ as follows. If ξ_1 and ξ_2 are events, then $\xi_1 \prec \xi_2$ if and only if one of the following two conditions holds.

(i) Both ξ_1 and ξ_2 occur at the same node, respectively at (local) times t_1 and t_2 such that $t_1 < t_2$. In addition, no other event occurs at the same node at a time t such that $t_1 < t < t_2$.

(ii) Events ξ_1 and ξ_2 occur at neighbor nodes, and a message φ exists that is sent in connection with ξ_1 and received in connection with ξ_2.

It follows from conditions (i) and (ii) that $\prec$ is an acyclic relation. Condition (i) expresses our intuitive understanding of the causality that exists among events that happen at the same node, while condition (ii) gives the basic cause-effect relationship that exists between neighbor nodes.

One interesting way to view the relation $\prec$ defined by these two conditions is to consider the acyclic directed graph $H = (\Xi, \prec)$. The node set of H is the set of events Ξ, and its set of edges is given by the pairs of events in $\prec$. The graph H is a *precedence graph*, and can be pictorially represented by displaying the events associated with a same node along a horizontal line, in the order given by $\prec$. In this representation, horizontal edges correspond to pairs of events that fall into the category of condition (i), while all others are in the category of condition (ii). Equivalently, horizontal edges can be viewed as representing the states of nodes (only initial and final states are not represented), and edges between the horizontal lines of neighbor nodes represent messages sent between those nodes. Viewing the computation Ξ with the aid of this graph will greatly enhance our understanding of some important concepts to be discussed later in this section and in Section 3.2.

The transitive closure of $\prec$, denoted by $\prec^+$, is irreflexive and transitive, and therefore establishes a *partial order* on the set of events Ξ. Two events ξ_1 and ξ_2 unrelated by $\prec^+$, i.e., such that

$$(\xi_1, \xi_2) \in \Xi \times \Xi - \prec^+$$

and

$$(\xi_2, \xi_1) \in \Xi \times \Xi - \prec^+,$$

are said to be *concurrent events*. This denomination, as one readily understands, is meant to convey the notion that two such events are in no way causally related to each other.

In addition to its use in defining this concept of concurrent events, the relation $\prec^+$ can also be used to define other concepts of equally great intuitive appeal, as for example those of an event's *past* and *future*. For an event ξ, we let

$$Past(\xi) = \{\xi' \mid \xi' \in \Xi \text{ and } \xi' \prec^+ \xi\}$$

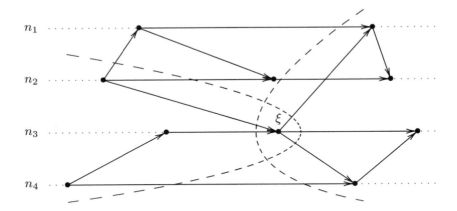

Figure 3.1. *A precedence graph has* Ξ *for node set and the pairs in the partial order* $\prec$ *for edges. It is convenient to draw precedence graphs so that events happening at the same node in* N *are placed on a horizontal line and positioned on this line, from left to right, in increasing order of the local times at which they happen. In this figure, shown for* $n = 4$, *the "conically"-shaped regions delimited by dashed lines around event* ξ *happening at node* n_3 *represent* $\{\xi\} \cup Past(\xi)$ *(the one on the left) and* $\{\xi\} \cup Future(\xi)$ *(the one on the right).*

and

$$Future(\xi) = \{\xi' \mid \xi' \in \Xi \text{ and } \xi \prec^+ \xi'\}.$$

These two sets can be easily seen to induce "conical" regions emanating from ξ in the precedence graph H and contain, respectively, the set of events that causally influence ξ and the set of events that are causally influenced by ξ (Figure 3.1).

We now focus on a closer examination of the issues raised in the beginning of this section with respect to an appropriate conceptual basis and a terminology for the treatment of global timing aspects in a distributed computation. The key notion that we need is that of a *consistent global state*, or simply *global state*, or yet *snapshot*. This notion is based on the formalism we have developed so far in this section, and, among other interesting features, allows several global properties of distributed systems to be referred to properly in the asynchronous model. We will in this section provide two definitions of a global state. While these two definitions are equivalent to each other (cf. Exercise 1), each one has its particular appeal, and is more suitable to a particular situation. Our two definitions are based on the weaker concept of a *system state*, which is simply a collection of n local states, one for each node, and one edge state for each edge. If G is a directed graph, then the number of edge states is m, otherwise it is $2m$ (one edge state for each of the two directions of each of the m edges).

The state of node n_i in a system state is drawn from Σ_i, the sequence of states n_i goes through as the distributed computation progresses, and is denoted by σ_i. Similarly, the state of an edge $(n_i \to n_j)$ is simply a set of messages, representing the messages that are in transit from n_i to n_j in that system state, i.e., messages that have been sent by n_i on edge $(n_i \to n_j)$ but not yet received by n_j. We denote this set by Φ_{ij}. The notion of a system state is very weak, in that it allows absurd global situations to be represented. For example, there is nothing in the definition of a system state that precludes the description of a situation in which a message φ has been sent by n_i on edge $(n_i \to n_j)$, but nevertheless neither has arrived at n_j nor is in transit on $(n_i \to n_j)$.

Our first definition of a global state is based on the partial order $\prec^+$ that exists on the set Ξ of events of the distributed computation, and requires the extension of $\prec^+$ to yield a *total order*, i.e., a partial order that includes exactly one of (ξ_1, ξ_2) or (ξ_2, ξ_1) for all $\xi_1, \xi_2 \in \Xi$. This total order does not contradict $\prec^+$, in the sense that it contains all pairs of events already in $\prec^+$. It is then obtained from $\prec^+$ by the inclusion of pairs of concurrent events, that is, events that do not relate to each other according to $\prec^+$, in such a way that the resulting relation is indeed a partial order. A total order thus obtained is said to be *consistent* with $\prec^+$.

Given any total order $<$ on Ξ, exactly $|\Xi| - 1$ pairs $(\xi_1, \xi_2) \in <$ can be identified such that every event $\xi \neq \xi_1, \xi_2$ is either such that $\xi < \xi_1$ or such that $\xi_2 < \xi$. Events ξ_1 and ξ_2 are in this case said to be *consecutive* in $<$. It is simple to see that, associated with every pair (ξ_1, ξ_2) of consecutive events in $<$, there is a system state, denoted by *system_state*(ξ_1, ξ_2), with the following characteristics.

- For each node n_i, σ_i is the state resulting from the occurrence of the most recent event (i.e., with the greatest time of occurrence) at n_i, say ξ, such that $\xi_1 \nprec \xi$ (this includes the possibility that $\xi = \xi_1$).

- For each edge $(n_i \to n_j)$, Φ_{ij} is the set of messages sent in connection with an event ξ such that $\xi_1 \nprec \xi$ (including the possibility that $\xi = \xi_1$) and received in connection with an event ξ' such that $\xi' \nprec \xi_2$ (including the possibility that $\xi' = \xi_2$).

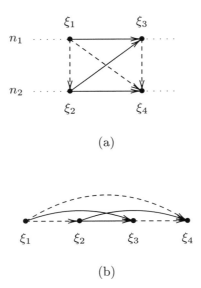

(a)

(b)

Figure 3.2. *Part (a) of this figure shows a precedence graph, represented by solid lines, for $n = 2$. As $\prec$ is already transitive, we have $\prec^+ = \prec$. Members of $\prec^+$ are then represented by solid lines, while the dashed lines are used to represent the pairs of concurrent events, which, when added to $\prec^+$, yield a total order $\prec_t^+$ consistent with $\prec^+$. The same graph is redrawn in part (b) of the figure to emphasize the total order. In this case, $system\_state(\xi_2, \xi_3)$ is such that n_1 is in the state at which it was left by the occurrence of ξ_1, n_2 is in the state at which it was left by the occurrence of ξ_2, and a message sent in connection with ξ_2 is in transit on the edge from n_2 to n_1 to be received in connection with ξ_3. Because $\prec_t^+$ is consistent with $\prec^+$, $system\_state(\xi_2, \xi_3)$ is a global state, by our first definition of global states.*

The first definition we consider for a global state is then the following. A system state Ψ is a global state if and only if either in Ψ all nodes are in their initial states (and then all edges are empty), or in Ψ all nodes are in their final states (and then all edges are empty as well), or there exists a total order $\prec_t^+$, consistent with $\prec^+$, in which a pair (ξ_1, ξ_2) of consecutive events exists such that $\Psi = system\_state(\xi_1, \xi_2)$ (Figure 3.2).

Our second definition of a global state is somewhat simpler, and requires that we consider a partition of the set of events Ξ into two subsets Ξ_1 and Ξ_2. Associated with the pair (Ξ_1, Ξ_2) is the system state, denoted by $system\_state(\Xi_1, \Xi_2)$, in which σ_i is the state in which n_i was left by the most recent event of Ξ_1 occurring at n_i, and Φ_{ij} is the set of messages sent on $(n_i \to n_j)$ in connection with events in Ξ_1 and received in connection with events in Ξ_2.

The second definition is then the following. A system state Ψ is a global state if and only if $\Psi = system\_state(\Xi_1, \Xi_2)$ for some partition (Ξ_1, Ξ_2) of Ξ such that

$$Past(\xi) \subseteq \Xi_1$$

whenever $\xi \in \Xi_1$. (Equivalently, we might have required the existence of a partition (Ξ_1, Ξ_2) such that

$$Future(\xi) \subseteq \Xi_2$$

whenever $\xi \in \Xi_2$.) For simplicity, often we refer to such a partition as the global state itself. Note that there is no need, in this definition, to mention explicitly the cases in which all nodes are either in their initial or final states, as we did in the case of the first definition. These two cases correspond, respectively, to $\Xi_1 = \emptyset$ and $\Xi_2 = \emptyset$.

As we mentioned earlier, these two definitions of a global state are equivalent to each other. The first definition, however, is more suitable to our discussion in Section 5.2.1, particularly within the context of proving Theorem 5.5. The second definition, on the other hand, provides us with a more intuitive understanding of what a global state is. Specifically, the partition (Ξ_1, Ξ_2) involved in this definition can be used in connection with the precedence graph H introduced earlier to yield the following interpretation. The partition (Ξ_1, Ξ_2) induces in H a cut (a set of edges) comprising edges that lead from events in Ξ_1 to events in Ξ_2 and edges from events in Ξ_2 to events in Ξ_1. This cut contains no edges from Ξ_2 to Ξ_1 if and only if $system\_state(\Xi_1, \Xi_2)$ is a global state, and then comprises the edges that represent the local states of all nodes (except those in their initial or final states) in that global state, and the edges that represent messages in transit in that global state (Figure 3.3).

We also mentioned at the beginning of this section that our discussion would apply both under full asynchronism and under full synchronism. In fact, when defining an event we explicitly described how the definition specializes to the case of full synchronism. It should then be noted that the concept of a global state is indeed equally applicable in both the asynchronous and the synchronous models, although it is in the former case that its importance is more greatly felt. In the

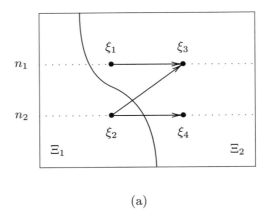

(a)

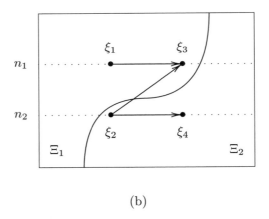

(b)

Figure 3.3. *Parts (a) and (b) show the same precedence graph for $n = 2$. Each of the cuts shown establishes a different partition (Ξ_1, Ξ_2) of Ξ. The cut in part (a) has no edge leading from an event in Ξ_2 to an event in Ξ_1, and then system_state(Ξ_1, Ξ_2) is a global state, by our second definition. In this global state, n_1 is in its initial state, n_2 is in the state at which it was left by the occurrence of ξ_2, and a message is in transit on the edge from n_2 to n_1, sent in connection with ξ_2 and to be received in connection with ξ_3. The cut in part (b), on the other hand, has an edge leading from $\xi_2 \in \Xi_2$ to $\xi_3 \in \Xi_1$, so system_state(Ξ_1, Ξ_2) cannot be a global state.*

synchronous case, many global states can be characterized in association with the value of the global clock, as for example in "the global state at the beginning of pulse $s \geq 0$." However, there is nothing in the definition of a global state that precludes the existence in the synchronous case of global states in which nodes' local states include values of the global clock that differ from node to node.

Having defined a global state, we may then extend the definitions of the past and the future of an event, given earlier in this section, to encompass similar notions with respect to global states. If Ψ is a global state, then we define its *past* and *future* respectively as

$$Past(\Psi) = \bigcup_{\xi \in \Xi_1} \left[\{\xi\} \cup Past(\xi) \right]$$
$$= \Xi_1$$

and

$$Future(\Psi) = \bigcup_{\xi \in \Xi_2} \left[\{\xi\} \cup Future(\xi) \right]$$
$$= \Xi_2,$$

where $\Psi = system\_state(\Xi_1, \Xi_2)$ (this definition demonstrates another situation in which our second definition of a global state is more convenient). Similarly, we say that a global state Ψ_1 comes *earlier* in the computation Ξ than another global state Ψ_2 if and only if $Past(\Psi_1) \subset Past(\Psi_2)$ (or, alternatively, if $Future(\Psi_2) \subset Future(\Psi_1)$). This definition will be of central importance in our discussion of stable properties in Chapter 6. Another related definition, that of an earliest global state with certain characteristics in a computation, can be given likewise. We shall return to it in detail in Section 9.3.1.

In finalizing this section, the reader should return to our discussion at the section's beginning to recognize the importance of the concepts we have introduced in establishing a rigorous and meaningful terminology. In particular, it should be clear that the partial order $\prec^+$ and the notion of a global state suffice to do away with all the ambiguities in our previous use of expressions like "concurrent," "scenario," and "causally affect" when referring to global timing aspects in the asynchronous model.

3.2. The complexity of distributed computations

Analyzing the complexity of any computation is a means of expressing quantitatively how demanding that computation is on the resources that it requires to be carried out. Depending on the type of computation one is considering, such resources may include the number of processor cycles, the number of processors, the number of messages that are sent, and various other quantities that relate to the resources upon which the computation's demands are heaviest. Determining which resources are crucial in this sense is then the fundamental issue when defining the appropriate measures of complexity for a computation. For example, for sequential computations the chiefest resource is time, as given by the number of processor cycles that elapse during the computation, but often the number of memory cells employed is also important.

Another example comes from considering parallel computations. Quite often the study of such computations is concerned with the feasibility of solving a certain problem on more than one processor so that the computation can be solved faster than on one single processor. In such cases, one of the fundamental resources continues to be the number of processor cycles, but now the number of processors is also important, because it is the interplay of these two quantities that establishes the overall efficiency of the resulting algorithm and also how that algorithm relates to its sequential counterpart. Models of parallel computation adopting measures of complexity related to these two types of resource include the PRAM (Parallel Random Access Machine), which is essentially a synchronous model of parallel computation on shared-memory cells, as well as other distributed-memory variants, also synchronous.

Whereas the models of parallel computation we just mentioned are geared towards the so-called data parallelism, the computations we treat in this book relate more closely to what is known as control parallelism, and then the approach to measure complexity needs to be substantially revised. Data parallelism is the parallelism of problem solving, that is, given a problem, the task is to solve it efficiently in parallel, which includes the design of an algorithm and the choice of a number of processors leading to the desired efficiency. Control parallelism, by contrast, is concerned with the computations that have to be carried out on a fixed number of processors, interconnected in a fixed manner, like our graph G. The computations of interest are not so much geared towards problem solving, but mainly towards controlling the sharing of resources, understood in a very broad sense, throughout the system. Very often this also includes the solution of problems very much in the data-parallel sense, but now the problem is stated on G, which is fixed, so that the control-parallel aspects of the computation become far more relevant.

The complexity of distributed algorithms is based on the assumption that communication and time are the resources whose usage should be measured. Given this choice of crucial resources, the measures of complexity are expressed in the usual worst-case, asymptotic fashion, as functions of n and m, respectively the number of nodes and edges in G. However, because G is in this book taken to represent a great variety of real-world systems (cf. Section 1.1) at some level of abstraction, some elaboration is required when establishing the appropriate complexity measures.

A convenient starting point to establish the complexity measures of distributed algorithms is to first consider communication as the predominant resource under demand. This does not mean that time ceases to be a relevant issue, but rather that only the time directly related to communication should be taken into account. This approach takes care of most of our needs in the book, and is our subject in Section 3.2.1. In Section 3.2.2, we relax this assumption that communication takes precedence over time that is not related to communication, and then the time that a node spends computing locally becomes a third resource whose usage is to be measured. The resulting extended definitions of complexity will be of use especially in Section 9.3.3.

3.2.1. Communication and time complexities

If communication is the dominating resource under demand, then the complexity of a distributed algorithm is expressed as two measures. The first measure is the already seen message complexity (cf. Section 2.1), which is given by the number of messages sent between neighbors during the computation in the worst case, that is, the maximum number of messages when variations in the structure of G are considered (when applicable), as well as all possible executions of the algorithm (each yielding a different set of events, in the terminology of Section 3.1). Alternatively, this measure can be substituted by the more accurate *message-bit complexity*, or simply *bit complexity*, which can be useful in conveying relevant differences among algorithms when the messages' lengths depend on n or m (as opposed to being $O(1)$). This is, for example, the case of Algorithm *A_FIFO* of Section 2.1 and of Algorithm *S_Locally_Orient* of Section 2.2.3. In the former case, a message may contain a task's identification and a node's identification (it may also contain a migrating task, but we may assume for our present purposes that such a message does not actually contain the task's code, which would already be present at all nodes, but rather simply the task's identification), and then the algorithm's bit complexity is, by Theorem 2.3, $O\left(m_K\left(\log|N_T| + \log n\right)\right)$. In the latter case, messages are sent containing integers no larger than n (cf. (2.16) and (2.17)), so that the algorithm's bit complexity is $O(n\log^2 n)$. The bit complexity will be sometimes employed for our analyses in the book.

The other measure that contributes to expressing the algorithm's complexity is its *time complexity*, which, in very loose terms, is given by the time spent in communication that elapses during the computation in the worst case (again a maximum over the possible structures of G and over all of the algorithm's executions). Any further elaboration on this definition requires that we consider the asynchronous model and the synchronous model separately.

For the synchronous model, the assumption that the cost of communication dominates all others should come as no surprise, because since the definition of this model in Section 2.1 we have assumed that local computation takes no time (or takes a constant time, which can be assumed to be zero). Although we made this assumption so that the synchronous model could be described without much further elaboration, in this section the assumption comes in handy as well, because it is in full accord with the assumed dominance of communication costs.

The definition of the time complexity in the synchronous model is rather simple, and amounts essentially to counting the number of pulses that elapse during the computation. In essence, then, already in Sections 2.2.2 and 2.2.3 we would have been able to express the time complexities of Algorithms *S_Compute_AND* and *S_Locally_Orient*, respectively. In fact, in Section 2.2.2 we saw that Algorithm *S_Compute_AND* requires $O(n)$ pulses for completion, and that is then its time complexity. Similarly, in Section 2.2.3 the number of iterations required by Algorithm *S_Locally_Orient* was seen to be given by $O(\log n)$, and because each iteration comprises $O(n)$ pulses, the time complexity of that algorithm is $O(n \log n)$.

Defining the time complexity for the synchronous model in this straightforward fashion may seem to the reader not to be in complete agreement with our stated purpose of measuring time solely as it relates to communication. After all, many pulses may elapse without any communication taking place (cf., for example, the synchronous algorithms presented in Sections 2.2.2 and 2.2.3), but such pulses do nevertheless get counted when assessing the algorithm's time complexity. What should be considered to resolve this apparent conflict is that, as we have mentioned more than once already, in the synchronous model messages are as important as their absence. By including in the time complexity intervals during which messages are not sent, we are essentially accounting for the time needed to convey information through the absence of communication as well.

In the asynchronous model, the assumption that the time complexity only takes into account the time to perform communication leads to the following methodology to compute an algorithm's time complexity. First assume, as in the synchronous model, that local computation takes no time, and also that the time to communicate one message to each node in a nonempty subset of a node's set of neighbors is $O(1)$.

The time complexity is then the number of messages in the longest causal chain of the form "receive a message and send a message as a consequence" occurring in all executions of the algorithm and over all applicable variations in the structure of G.

This definition can be made more formal, but before we do that let us consider two important related issues. First of all, it should be clear that the time complexity can never be larger than the message complexity, because every message taken into account to compute the former is also used in the computation of the latter. The usefulness of the time complexity in spite of this relationship with the message complexity is that it only considers messages that happen "sequentially" one after the other, that is, messages that are causally bound to one another. Essentially, then, the time complexity in the asynchronous case can be regarded as being obtained from the message complexity by trimming off all the messages that are "concurrent" to those in the longest receive-send causal chain.

The second issue is that the assumption of $O(1)$ message transmission times for the computation of the time complexity is only completely valid if every message has length $O(1)$ as well. However, we do maintain the assumption to compute the time complexity even otherwise, because taking variable lengths into account would not contribute qualitatively to establishing what the lengthiest causal chain is. In addition, the effect of variable length is already captured by the algorithm's bit complexity, introduced earlier in this section, which should be used when needed.

The way to define the time complexity of an asynchronous algorithm more formally is to resort to the precedence graph H introduced in Section 3.1. This graph summarizes the essential causal dependencies among events in the computation, and allows the definition of the time complexity to be given rather cleanly as follows. Let every edge in H be labeled either with a 1, if it corresponds to a message, or with a 0, otherwise. Clearly, this reflects our assumptions that messages take constant time to be sent between neighbors and that local computation takes no time. The time complexity for fixed G and H (i.e., for a fixed execution of the algorithm) is then the length of the longest directed path in H, with the labels of individual edges taken as their lengths. Taking the maximum over the applicable variations of G and over all the executions of the algorithm (all H's) yields the desired measure.

The reader should now be in position to return to the asynchronous algorithms given previously in the book, and have their time complexities assessed to $O(1)$, in the case of Algorithm A_FIFO, and to $O(n)$, in the case of Algorithm $A\_Compute\_f$.

3.2.2. Local and global measures

Assuming that communication dominates the complexity of a distributed computation, and that in turn local computation takes no time, is reasonable for many of the systems discussed in Section 1.1, especially computer networks and networks of workstations. However, G is intended to model a greater variety of message-passing systems, and for some of these, including the multiprocessors also discussed in Section 1.1, such an assumption may be a bit too strong.

In this section, we consider the impact of facing nonconstant local processing times, and expand our collection of complexity measures to encompass others that may reflect this extended view more appropriately. In the synchronous case, all that would be required would be to let the duration of an interval of the global clock be a function of n and m. This function would then yield a third complexity measure for the synchronous model, and everything else would remain essentially as is. It is interesting to note, however, that under this broader assumption on the duration of an interval the overall picture of a synchronous computation would change a little. Specifically, it would be possible to send messages at any point inside an interval, not only at the interval's beginning. Furthermore, in terms of the event-based formalism of Section 3.1, internal events would exist in the synchronous model as well.

It is important to note, in the synchronous model, that at pulse $s > 0$ a node n_i may need to examine the set of $MSG_i(s)$ of messages received during the previous interval, and the time to do this should continue to be assumed constant even when the time to do local processing is taken to be variable. What this implies, together with the assumption we have made so far that a node may send one message to all of its neighbors in parallel, is that none of the synchronous algorithms we have seen so far requires taking local processing times to be anything else than constant. Even Algorithm *S_Locally_Orient*, in which by (2.16) and (2.18) it would seem that the examination of $O(n)$ sets of messages is required at a single pulse, can be easily written in more detail and then seen to require the examination of only one such set per pulse.

In the context of this book, however, it is in the asynchronous case that nonconstant times for local computation will be most important, although not until Chapter 9. In the asynchronous model, then, we shall let the *local time complexity* refer to the time to perform local computation upon receiving a message. This is then the complexity of an atomic action in Algorithm *A_Template*. Whenever we use this complexity measure in the book, and if confusion may arise, we refer to the algorithm's time complexity as its *global time complexity*.

Algorithm *A_Compute_f* is the only algorithm we have seen so far for which variable local processing times may need to be considered. What leads to this is that the computation of $f(b_i^1, \ldots, b_i^n)$ in (2.11) may require a time to be performed that is a function of n. Considering this algorithm carefully leads us to other situations in which it would be justifiable to assume nonconstant local processing times. As we mentioned earlier in Section 3.2, often a distributed algorithm is designed to solve a problem that is posed on G. Typical examples of such problems are the ones in consider in Sections 4.2 and 4.3 and in Chapter 7, in which we discuss graph algorithms. Clearly, in such cases a possibility would be to have all nodes transmit their local share of information on the structure of G to a previously designated node (a leader—cf. Section 5.1), which would then solve the problem locally and then after that possibly spread the solution to the other nodes. This would be very much in the style of Algorithm *A_Compute_f*, although the assumed anonymity in the case of that algorithm disallows the existence of a leader altogether, as we discuss in Section 5.1. In fact, in the presence of anonymity there is no other choice but to program all nodes to perform the same computation, as we discussed in Section 2.2.

However, if the system is not anonymous, then the alternative of coalescing all the information regarding G into a leader for solution of the problem is a real possibility, and for this possibility it is important to consider the local time complexity of solving the entire problem in one single node. Moreover, concentrating all the relevant information in the leader may have $O(nm)$ message complexity (considering that each message contains a constant number of node identifications) and $O(n)$ time complexity, which, after added to the complexity of electing a leader, should also be compared with the corresponding measures elicited by the fully distributed alternative, in which all nodes participate in the solution of the problem by computing on its share of the problem's input (the structure of G).

3.3. Full asynchronism and full synchronism

Having introduced the complexity measures of relevance for distributed algorithms, in this section we return to the question, first raised in Section 2.1, of the equivalence between the asynchronous and synchronous models. What we do is first to indicate explicitly how Algorithm *S_Template* can be used to express an asynchronous algorithm (originally written over the template given by Algorithm *A_Template*). Then, conversely, we show how to employ Algorithm *A_Template* as a basis to transform a synchronous algorithm (originally written over the template Algorithm *S_Template*) into an asynchronous algorithm.

The first part is simpler, because an asynchronous algorithm runs under all possible variations in the timing of the asynchronous model, in particular in the variation that corresponds to the synchronous model. The only concern we must have when translating Algorithm *A_Template* into Algorithm *S_Template* is that, in the former, atomic actions are in general triggered by the arrival of messages and executed when the corresponding Boolean conditions hold, while in the latter nodes are driven solely by the global clock and operate on the sets of messages received during the preceding intervals. Algorithm *S_Template* makes no provisions to condition the execution of an action upon the validity of a Boolean expression, which must then be treated inside the action itself. What this amounts to in the translation of an asynchronous algorithm into a synchronous one is that, upon the occurrence of pulse $s = 1$, only those messages in $MSG_i(1)$ received by $n_i \in N$ on edges for which the corresponding Boolean conditions in the asynchronous algorithm hold can lead to the execution of the corresponding actions. The others must be held for reconsideration upon the occurrence of pulse $s = 2$. In general, then, at pulse $s > 0$ a node n_i may compute on messages from any of $MSG_i(1), \ldots, MSG_i(s)$, at which occasion those messages are deleted from the set to which they belong so that the remaining ones may be considered in further pulses. This strategy is reflected in Algorithm *A-to-S_Template*, given next.

The message msg_i that in Algorithm *A_Template* triggers n_i's action is in Algorithm *A-to-S_Template* viewed as a variable, initially equal to **nil**.

Algorithm *A-to-S_Template*:

▷ **Variables:**
$msg_i = $ **nil**;
Other variables used by n_i, and their initial values, are listed here.

▷ **Input:**
$s = 0$, $MSG_i(0) = \emptyset$.
Action if $n_i \in N_0$:   (3.1)
Do some computation;
Send one message on each edge of a (possibly empty) subset of Out_i.

▷ **Input:**

$s > 0$, $MSG_i(1), \ldots, MSG_i(s)$ such that $origin_i(msg) = c_k \in In_i$
with $1 \le k \le |In_i|$ for $msg \in \bigcup_{r=1}^{s} MSG_i(r)$.

Action: (3.2)

    while there exist msg, $r \in \{1, \ldots, s\}$, and $k \in \{1, \ldots, |In_i|\}$ such
that $msg \in MSG_i(r)$ with $origin_i(msg) = c_k$ **and** B_k **do**
        begin
            Let r' be the smallest such r and k' any such k;
            $msg_i := msg$;
            Remove msg from $MSG_i(r')$;
            Do some computation;
            Send one message on each edge of a (possibly empty) sub-
            set of Out_i
        end.

In Algorithm *A-to-S_Template*, (3.1) is identical to (2.8) in Algorithm
S_Template, while (3.2) reflects the need to evaluate the appropriate Boolean conditions before the action corresponding to (2.2) in Algorithm *A_Template* can be
executed. What (3.2) does at pulse $s > 0$ is to select from $MSG_i(1), \ldots, MSG_i(s)$
one of the earliest messages (in the synchronous sense) for which the corresponding Boolean condition is **true**, and then to allow the corresponding action of the
asynchronous algorithm to be executed. When edges are FIFO, then (3.2) has to
be worked on a little so that the choice of r' and k' guarantees that msg is, of
the messages to have arrived on $c_{k'}$ but not yet received, the one to have arrived
first. The reason why this might not happen is that $B_{k'}$ might be **false** for the first
message and not for some other arriving on the same edge. If this happened for all
edges, then n_i should simply halt, thereby indicating an error in the design of the
algorithm, just as Algorithm *A_Template* would.

Clearly, this translation of an asynchronous algorithm to run in the synchronous model does not change the algorithm's message complexity. In addition,
the reader should check carefully that the same holds for the time complexity, that
is, the number of pulses that elapse before termination of the resulting synchronous
algorithm is exactly the number of messages in the lengthiest causal chain during
an execution of the asynchronous algorithm. In addition, even if local processing cannot be assumed to be instantaneous, the translation does not increase the
amount of local computation that needs to be carried out, even though it would
seem that the need to check so many sets of messages in (3.2) could require further
local processing. Readily, these sets can be organized as $|In_i|$ queues of messages

at n_i, that is, one per incoming edge. Then the work that has to be done at (3.2) is the same that in Algorithm $S\_Template$ n_i has to do, and this is assumed to take constant time even if local processing cannot be so assumed.

The other direction of transformation, namely to transform a synchronous algorithm into an asynchronous one, is not as immediate, and in this secion we only touch the issue superficially. We return to the subject in Section 5.3 for the complete details. Naturally, the problem in this case is that the resulting asynchronous algorithm must only allow the action of n_i at pulse $s > 0$ to be executed when the set $MSG_i(s)$ is available, and this is not immediate in the asynchronous model. It seems apparent, then, that in the resulting asynchronous algorithms there has to be more communication among the nodes than in the synchronous algorithm, so that these sets of messages can be ensured to contain all the pertinent messages when they are used. This further increase in communication may then lead to a greater time complexity for the asynchronous algorithm when compared to the synchronous algorithm.

A template for the translation of a synchronous algorithm into an asynchronous algorithm is given next as Algorithm $S\text{-}to\text{-}A\_Template$. This algorithm employs an integer variable $s_i \geq 0$ for $n_i \in N$. This variable, initially such that $s_i = 0$, is used to keep track of the pulses of the synchronous algorithm. A Boolean function $\text{DONE}_i(s_i)$ is used to indicate whether n_i is ready to proceed to the execution of the action that the synchronous algorithm would execute at pulse $s_i + 1$ for $s_i \geq 0$ (determining what this function should do is then essentially our subject in Section 5.3). Finally, the sets $MSG_i(s)$ for $s \geq 0$ that Algorithm $S\_Template$ employs are also variables of Algorithm $S\text{-}to\text{-}A\_Template$, initially empty sets.

Algorithm $S\text{-}to\text{-}A\_Template$:

   ▷ **Variables:**
      $s_i = 0$;
      $MSG_i(s) = \emptyset$ for all $s \geq 0$;
      Other variables used by n_i, and their initial values, are listed here.

   ▷ **Input:**
      $msg_i = \textbf{nil}$.
    Action if $n_i \in N_0$:   (3.3)
      Do some computation;
      Send one message on each edge of a (possibly empty) subset of Out_i.

▷ **Input:**

msg_i such that $origin_i(msg_i) = c_k \in In_i$ with $1 \le k \le |In_i|$.
   Action: (3.4)
      if $\mathrm{DONE}_i(s_i)$ **then**
         begin
            $s_i := s_i + 1$;
            Do some computation;
            Send one message on each edge of a (possibly empty) sub-
            set of Out_i
         end
      else
         Add msg_i to $MSG_i(s_i + 1)$ if appropriate.

In Algorithm *S-to-A_Template*, (3.3) is identical to (2.1) in Algorithm *A_Template*, while (3.4) indicates how the function $\mathrm{DONE}_i(s_i)$ is to be used to ensure that s_i can be incremented and that the action that Algorithm *S_Template* would perform at pulse $s_i + 1$ by (2.9) can be executed. When (3.4) is executed and $\mathrm{DONE}_i(s_i)$ turns out to be **false**, then msg_i, the message that triggered the action, is added to $MSG_i(s_i + 1)$ if appropriate (msg_i may be a message unrelated to the synchronous algorithm, that is, one of the messages constituting the additional communication traffic that the transformation requires).

As we remarked earlier, transforming a synchronous algorithm into an asynchronous one may lead to increases in both the message complexity and the time complexity with respect to the synchronous algorithm. On the other hand, as will become apparent from the material in Section 5.3, the complexity that results from assuming nonconstant local processing times remains unchanged.

3.4. The role of synchronism in distributed computations

So far in the book we have stressed more than once that the synchronous model is, in at least one important sense, more "powerful" than the asynchronous model. The justification behind this informal notion has been that, in the synchronous model, the absence of messages conveys information to nodes, while in the asynchronous model nothing like this happens. In fact, in Sections 2.2.2 and 2.2.3 we have given two synchronous algorithms, respectively Algorithms *S_Compute_AND* and *S_Locally_Orient*, whose message complexities are strictly lower than that of Algorithm *A_Compute_f*, which is an asynchronous algorithm that may be used for the same purposes as those two synchronous algorithms. Of course, Algorithms

S_Compute_AND and *S_Locally_Orient* do not have the same generality of Algorithm *A_Compute_f*, and then it might be argued that the improvement in message complexity is a consequence of their single-purpose nature, rather than the result of exploiting the characteristics of the synchronous model. However, it should be simple for the reader to verify that the same particularizations would not lead to any improvements in message complexity under the asynchronous model.

The central question that we address in this section is whether the synchronous model can also yield improvements in the time complexity of some asynchronous algorithms. As we remarked in Section 3.3, designing an algorithm for the synchronous model and then transforming it into an asynchronous algorithm may lead to an increase in both the message and time complexities with respect to the synchronous algorithm. But this does not imply that an asynchronous algorithm designed "from scratch" (i.e., not as the result of a transformation from a synchronous algorithm) would not have better complexities than the synchronous algorithm. In order to address this issue, we discuss a problem for which every asynchronous algorithm must have a strictly greater time complexity than a very straightforward synchronous algorithm that solves the same problem, thereby answering our question affirmatively.

The problem that we discuss is stated in very abstract terms, and is related to synchronization issues in distributed systems, although one will probably not easily find any practical situation to which it may be readily applicable. Stating the problem requires the introduction of the following new terminology. A *port* is a special edge in the graph G, and a *port event* is an event that involves the sending of a message on a port. A node at which a port event may happen (i.e., it may send messages on a port) is called a *port node*. A *session* is informally defined in terms of our terminology of Section 3.1 as a set of events including at least one port event for every port and "delimited" by two global states. More formally, if Ξ is the set of events representing a distributed computation, then $S \subseteq \Xi$ is a session if and only if S includes at least one port event for every port and in addition two global states (Ξ_1, Ξ_2) and (Ξ_3, Ξ_4) exist such that

$$S = \Xi_2 \cap \Xi_3.$$

For integers μ and σ such that $1 \leq \mu \leq m$ and $\sigma \geq 1$, the problem that we consider is called the (μ, σ)-*session problem*, and asks that a graph G with μ ports and a distributed algorithm on G be found such that every execution of the algorithm can be partitioned into at least σ sessions. In addition, the set of events associated with every execution of the algorithm is required to be finite and every port node is required to obtain the information that the σ sessions have occurred.

Solving the (μ, σ)-session problem is in general very simple. For the synchronous model, the problem is solved by choosing G to be any graph with no more than one port per node, and the synchronous algorithm to be such that every port node sends a message on its port at each of the pulses $s = 0, \ldots, \sigma - 1$. The time complexity of this synchronous algorithm is $O(\sigma)$.

In the asynchronous model, we can also solve the problem with the same time complexity, as follows. Choose G as in the synchronous case, except that all port nodes can send messages to one another as well. The asynchronous algorithm is such that every port node performs σ rounds of sending a message on its port and then sending a message to every other port node containing information that it has finished its participation in the current session. The next round is only performed after similar messages have been received from all other port nodes. The reader should verify that the time complexity of this algorithm is $O(\sigma)$ if N_0 contains all port nodes.

The difficulty arises when in G we place a constant bound b on $|Out_i|$ (or $|Inc_i|$, in the undirected case), thereby limiting the number of messages that a node may send in a single action of Algorithm $S\_Template$ or Algorithm $A\_Template$ (G is in this case said to be b-bounded). Clearly, this bound does not affect our proposed synchronous solution to the (μ, σ)-session problem, but the asynchronous solution is no longer feasible within $O(\sigma)$ time, because the broadcast to all port nodes at the end of each round can no longer be achieved within $O(1)$ time. We give in Theorem 3.1 a lower bound on the time required by any asynchronous solution to the problem.

Theorem 3.1. *For $b \geq 1$, every asynchronous solution to the (μ, σ)-session problem in which G is b-bounded must be such that the corresponding asynchronous algorithm has time complexity of at least $(\sigma - 1)\lfloor \log_{b+1} \mu \rfloor - 1$.*

Proof: Let G be b-bounded, and consider an asynchronous solution to the (μ, σ)-session problem consisting of G and of an asynchronous algorithm. Let Ξ be the set of events corresponding to an execution of this algorithm, and label every event ξ with an integer $\tau(\xi)$ obtained inductively as follows. If ξ happens at $n_i \in N$ when n_i is in its initial state, then let $\tau(\xi) = 0$. If not, then let $\tau(\xi) = \tau(\xi') + 1$, where ξ' is the event having the greatest label among the events ξ'' in connection with which at least one message is sent and in addition $\xi'' \prec^+ \xi$. Informally, this labeling of the events in Ξ corresponds to attaching to each event the number of messages on which it depends causally. Because Ξ is finite, every label is finite as well. Let t be the greatest label over Ξ. Clearly, the time complexity of the algorithm is at least

t. Now let

$$K = \left\lceil \frac{t+1}{\lfloor \log_{b+1} \mu \rfloor} \right\rceil,$$

and partition Ξ into the K subsets of events $\Xi_1, \ldots, \Xi_K$, where, for $k = 1, \ldots, K$, $\xi \in \Xi_k$ is such that $(k-1)\lfloor \log_{b+1} \mu \rfloor \leq \tau(\xi) \leq k \lfloor \log_{b+1} \mu \rfloor - 1$. Clearly, then, all of

$$(\Xi_1 \cup \cdots \cup \Xi_\ell, \Xi_{\ell+1} \cup \cdots \cup \Xi_K)$$

for $1 \leq \ell < K$ are global states, because of the way the labels τ were assigned and of the fact that no two sets of $\Xi_1, \ldots, \Xi_K$ have any event with the same value for τ.

The next step is to partition every Ξ_k into the sets Γ_k and Θ_k such that all of

$$(\Gamma_1, \Theta_1 \cup \Xi_2 \cup \cdots \cup \Xi_K),$$

$$(\Xi_1 \cup \cdots \cup \Xi_{\ell-1} \cup \Gamma_\ell, \Theta_\ell \cup \Xi_{\ell+1} \cup \cdots \cup \Xi_K)$$

for $1 < \ell < K$, and

$$(\Xi_1 \cup \cdots \cup \Xi_{K-1} \cup \Gamma_K, \Theta_K)$$

are global states, and furthermore the following two conditions hold for a sequence of ports $e_0, \ldots, e_K$ (this sequence may contain the same port more than once).

(i) Γ_k does not contain any port event involving e_{k-1}.

(ii) Θ_k does not contain any port event involving e_k.

This partitioning can be done for all $k = 1, \ldots, K$ inductively as follows. Pick e_0 to be any arbitrary port, and assume that e_{k-1} has been defined. If a port exists that is not involved in any port event in Ξ_k, then let e_k be that port, $\Gamma_k = \emptyset$, and $\Theta_k = \Xi_k$, thereby satisfying conditions (i) and (ii). If, on the other hand, every port is involved in at least one port event in Ξ_k, then let ξ_1 be the earliest port event involving e_{k-1} in Ξ_k, and consider the number of port events contained in the set

$$F_k = \big(\{\xi_1\} \cup \mathit{Future}(\xi_1)\big) \cap \Xi_k.$$

This set includes ξ_1 and every other port event in Ξ_k that is in the future of ξ_1 (including, of course, every other port event involving e_{k-1} in Ξ_k). Because G is b-bounded, and considering the range of values for τ in Ξ_k, the number of port events that we seek is no larger than the sum of the elements in the geometric progression of rate $b + 1$ starting at 1 and ending at

$$(b+1)^{k\lfloor \log_{b+1} \mu \rfloor - 1 - (k-1)\lfloor \log_{b+1} \mu \rfloor},$$

that is,

$$\frac{(b+1)^{k\lfloor \log_{b+1} \mu \rfloor - 1 - (k-1)\lfloor \log_{b+1} \mu \rfloor + 1} - 1}{b + 1 - 1} = \frac{(b+1)^{\lfloor \log_{b+1} \mu \rfloor} - 1}{b}$$

$$\leq \frac{\mu - 1}{b}$$

$$\leq \mu - 1.$$

What this means is that at least one of the μ ports is not involved in any of the port events in F_k. Taking one of these ports to be e_k, $\Gamma_k = \Xi_k - F_k$, and $\Theta_k = F_k$ clearly satisfies conditions (i) and (ii). It can be easily verified that, in both cases, the resulting Γ_k and Θ_k induce global states, as required (cf. Exercise 5).

By conditions (i) and (ii), the sets Γ_1, $\Theta_{k-1} \cup \Gamma_k$ for $1 < k \leq K$, and Θ_K cannot contain a session, because a session must include at least one port event for every port. What this amounts to is that every session must have a nonempty intersection with both Γ_k and Θ_k for some k such that $1 \leq k \leq K$, meaning that K is the maximum number of sessions in Ξ. Because Ξ contains at least σ sessions, and considering the definition of K, we have

$$\sigma \leq K$$

$$\leq \frac{t+1}{\lfloor \log_{b+1} \mu \rfloor} + 1,$$

and then $t \geq (\sigma - 1)\lfloor \log_{b+1} \mu \rfloor - 1$. ∎

Theorem 3.1 and our discussion earlier in this section indicate that the synchronous model possesses characteristics that allow synchronous algorithms to perform better than asynchronous algorithms with respect to the algorithms' message and time complexities. In practice, however, the main interest in the synchronous model stems from the possibility of eventually obtaining an asynchronous algorithm from an algorithm originally designed for the synchronous model. This is the subject of extensive discussion in Section 5.3, but in this section we wish to highlight the role that this approach has had historically in the development of distributed algorithms.

We consider the problem of establishing a breadth-first numbering on the nodes of G when G is a directed graph. This problem asks that every node n_i be assigned a nonnegative integer d_i equal to the shortest distance from a designated node n_1 to n_i in terms of numbers of edges. Initially, $d_i = \infty$ for all $n_i \in N$, thereby taking care of those nodes to which no directed path exists from n_1. This problem is closely related to the problem of determining the shortest distances between all pairs of nodes when G is undirected (we treat this problem in Section 4.3).

Obtaining a synchronous algorithm to solve this problem is a trivial matter. At pulse $s = 0$, n_1 sets d_1 to zero and sends a message on every edge in Out_1. For $s > 0$, if a node n_i receives at least one message during interval $s - 1$ and at pulse s it still holds that $d_i = \infty$, then it must be that the shortest directed path from n_1 to n_i contains s edges. What n_i does in this case is to set d_i to s and then send a message on each edge in Out_i. Readily, this algorithm requires no more than $n - 1$ pulses for completion and employs no more than m messages. Its time and message complexities are then, respectively, $O(n)$ and $O(m)$.

Historically, this simple synchronous algorithm has accounted for the introduction of an asynchronous algorithm of time complexity $O(n \log n / \log k)$ and message complexity $O(kn^2)$ for arbitrary k such that $2 \le k < n$, while the best asynchronous algorithm available at the time had time complexity $O(n^{2-2\ell})$ and message complexity $O(n^{2+\ell})$ for arbitrary ℓ such that $0 \le \ell \le 0.25$. The reader should experiment with these complexities to verify that, given any ℓ in the appropriate range, there exists a k, also in the appropriate range, such that the algorithm obtained from the synchronous algorithm is strictly better in at least one of the two complexity measures (and no worse in neither).

3.5. Exercises

1. Show that the two definitions of a global state given in Section 3.1 are equivalent to each other.

2. Obtain the time complexity of Algorithm *A_FIFO* when it is viewed as being executed over G_P.

3. Give the details of an algorithm to concentrate upon one single node all the information on the structure of G. The resulting algorithm should have the complexities mentioned in Section 3.2.2.

4. Consider the (μ, σ)-session problem in the asynchronous case, and suppose that a node does its σ port events all before the broadcast. What is wrong with this approach?

5. Consider an event ξ and the sets

$$\Xi_1 = \{\xi\} \cup Past(\xi)$$

and

$$\Xi_2 = \{\xi\} \cup \textit{Future}(\xi).$$

Show that both partitions $(\Xi_1, \Xi - \Xi_1)$ and $(\Xi - \Xi_2, \Xi_2)$ are global states.

6. Consider the synchronous algorithm for breadth-first numbering described in Section 3.4. Express that algorithm in the format given by Algorithm *S_Template*.

3.6. Bibliographic notes

The material in Section 3.1 is based on Lamport (1978) and on Chandy and Lamport (1985), having also benefited from the clearer exposition of the concept of a global state to be found in Bracha and Toueg (1984). Additional insights into the concepts discussed in that section can be found in Yang and Marsland (1993), and in the papers in Zhonghua and Marsland (1994).

Formalisms different from the one introduced in Section 3.1, often with accompanying proof systems, have been proposed by a number of authors. These include temporal logic (Pnueli, 1981; Manna and Pnueli, 1992) and I/O automata combined with various proof techniques (Lynch and Tuttle, 1987; Chou and Gafni, 1988; Welch, Lamport, and Lynch, 1988; Lynch, Merritt, Weihl, and Fekete, 1994). Additional sources on related material are Malka and Rajsbaum (1992) and Moran and Warmuth (1993).

Most of the complexity measures introduced in Section 3.2 are standard in the field, and can also be looked up in Lamport and Lynch (1990). The reader may also find it instructive to check different models and associated complexity measures in the field of parallel and distributed computation. Source publications include Gibbons and Rytter (1988), Akl (1989), Karp and Ramachandran (1990), Feldman and Shapiro (1992), JáJá (1992), and Leighton (1992).

Section 3.3 is related to the discussion in Awerbuch (1985a), while the material in Section 3.4 is based mostly on the work by Arjomandi, Fischer, and Lynch (1983). The comments at the end of the section on the breadth-first numbering of nodes derive from Awerbuch (1985b).

4

Basic Algorithms

Three basic problems are considered in this chapter, namely the problems of propagating information from a group of nodes to all nodes, of providing every node with information on which are the identifications of all the other nodes in G, and of computing the shortest distances (in terms of numbers of edges) between all pairs of nodes. Throughout this chapter, G is an undirected graph.

The first problem is treated in Section 4.1, first in the context of propagating information from a group of nodes to all the nodes in G, and then in the context of propagating information from one single node to all others but with the additional requirement that the node originally possessing the information must upon completion of the algorithm have received news that all other nodes were reached by the propagation. Our discussion in Section 4.1 encompasses both the case of one single instance of the algorithm being executed on G and of multiple concurrent instances initiated one after the other.

Section 4.2 contains material on the detection of G's connectivity by all nodes in the form of providing each node with a list of all the other nodes in G. Although many algorithms can be devised with this end, the one we present builds elegantly on top of one of the algorithms discussed in the previous section, and is for this reason especially instructive.

Computing all-pair shortest distances is our subject in Section 4.3. This is the first graph problem we treat in detail in the book (others can be found in Chapter

7). Our approach in Section 4.3 is that of not only giving a fundamental distributed algorithm, but also providing a nontrivial example to be used to illustrate the relationship between the asynchronous and synchronous models of distributed computation when we further return to that topic in Section 5.3.

Sections 4.4 and 4.5 contain, respectively, exercises and bibliographic notes.

4.1. Information propagation

The problem that we consider in this section is that of propagating a piece of information (generically denoted by *inf*) from the single node (or group of nodes) that originally possesses it to all of G's nodes. We divide our discussion into two parts. The first part is the presentation of algorithms to solve two important variations of the problem, and comes in Section 4.1.1.

The second part is a discussion of how to handle multiple concurrent instances of these algorithms without examining the contents of the message being propagated. This is the subject of Section 4.1.2.

4.1.1. Basic algorithms

The problem of propagating information through the nodes of G is the problem of broadcasting throughout G information originally held by only a subset of G's nodes. In this section, we consider two variations of this problem, known respectively as the *Propagation of Information problem* (or *PI problem*) and the *Propagation of Information with Feedback problem* (or *PIF problem*). In the PI problem, all that is asked is that all nodes in G receive *inf*, whereas in the PIF problem the requirement is that not only all nodes receive *inf* but also that the originating node be informed that all the other nodes possess *inf*. Let us discuss the PI problem first.

The PI problem can be solved by a wide variety of approaches, each one with its own advantages. For example, if n_1 is the node that originally possesses *inf*, then one possible approach is to proceed in two phases. In the first phase, a spanning tree is found in G. In the second phase, the spanning tree is employed to perform the broadcast, as follows. Node n_1 sends *inf* on all the edges of the spanning tree that are incident to it. Every other node, upon receiving *inf*, passes it on by sending it on every edge of the spanning tree that is incident to it and is not the edge on which *inf* arrived. Readily, if the spanning tree can be assumed to be available to begin with, then an asynchronous algorithm based on this strategy has message and time complexities both equal to $O(n)$.

This simple approach can be extended to the case in which *inf* is originally possessed by more than one node. In this case, instead of a spanning tree we need a spanning forest, each of whose trees including exactly one of the nodes having *inf* originally. The broadcast procedure on each tree is then entirely the same as we described for the case of a single initiator.

There are essentially three reasons why this simple and effective approach may be undesirable. The first reason is that the spanning tree (or spanning forest) may not be available to begin with and then has to be determined at the cost of additional message and time complexities. Of course, once the tree (or forest) has been determined, then it may in principle be used indefinitely for many further broadcasts from the same nodes, so that apparently at least the additional cost may be somehow amortized over many executions of the algorithm and then become negligible for most purposes. The second reason for investigating other approaches in spite of this possible amortization of the initial cost comes from considering possible applications of the algorithm. By forcing the broadcast to be carried out on the same edges all the time, we are in essence ignoring the effect the possible variations with time on the delays for message delivery and also ignoring the fact that relying on a single tree (or forest) may be unreliable. Although our models of computation make no provisions for either circumstance to actually be an issue, in practice it may certainly be the case.

The third reason for us to consider a different approach (and really the most important one) is that this other approach, although extremely simple, illustrates interesting principles of distributed algorithm design, and in addition constitutes a sort of foundation for the rest of this chapter and for other sections to come as well (Section 5.2.1, for example).

The solution we describe next to the PI problem does the broadcast by "flooding" the network, and for this reason has a higher message complexity than the one we gave based on a spanning forest. The very simple idea behind this approach is that all nodes possessing *inf* initially send it to all of their neighbors at the beginning (they all start concurrently). Every other node, upon receiving *inf* for the first time, sends it on to all of its neighbors, including the one from which it was received. As a result, a node receives *inf* from all of its neighbors. In this strategy, *inf* is propagated from the nodes that initially possess it as a "wave," and then reaches all nodes as fast as possible and regardless of most edge failures (that is, those that do not disconnect G). This figurative view of how the algorithm proceeds globally is quite helpful to one's understanding of various distributed algorithms, including many that we discuss in this book, most notably in Chapters 5, 6, and 9.

This strategy is reflected in Algorithm A_PI, given next. In this algorithm, The set N_0 comprises the nodes that possess inf initially. A node n_i employs the the Boolean variable $reached_i$ (equal to **false**, initially) to indicate whether n_i has been reached by inf. Node n_i, upon receiving inf from a neighbor, must check this variable before deciding whether inf should be passed on or not.

> **Algorithm A_PI:**

> ▷ **Variables:**
> $reached_i = \textbf{false}$.

> ▷ **Input:**
> $msg_i = \textbf{nil}$.
> **Action if $n_i \in N_0$:**   (4.1)
> $reached_i := \textbf{true}$;
> Send inf to all $n_j \in Neig_i$.

> ▷ **Input:**
> $msg_i = inf$.
> **Action:**   (4.2)
>   **if not** $reached_i$ **then**
>   **begin**
> $reached_i := \textbf{true}$;
>   Send inf to all $n_j \in Neig_i$
>   **end**.

It should be instructive for the reader to briefly return to the interpretation of the functioning of this algorithm as a wave propagation to verify the following. It is impossible for a node n_i for which $reached_i = \textbf{true}$ to tell whether a copy of inf it receives in (4.2) is a response to a message it sent in (4.1) or (4.2), or a copy that was already in transit to it when a message it sent out arrived at its destination. In the latter case, letting n_j be the node from which this copy of inf originated, the edge (n_i, n_j) is one of the edges on which two waves meet, one from each of two members of N_0 (possibly n_i, n_j, or both, depending on whether they belong to N_0).

Because in G there exists at least one path between every node and all the nodes in N_0, it is a trivial matter to see that inf does indeed get broadcast to all nodes by Algorithm A_PI. In addition, by (4.1) and (4.2), it is evident that the message complexity of this algorithm is $O(m)$ (exactly one message traverses each edge in each direction, totaling $2m$ messages) and that its time complexity is $O(n)$.

Let us now consider the PIF problem. Unlike the PI problem, the PIF problem is stated only for the case in which *inf* is initially possessed by a single node. Similarly to the PI problem, a solution based on a spanning tree can also be adopted, having essentially the same advantages and drawbacks as in the case of that problem. In such a solution, n_1, the only node originally possessing *inf*, is viewed as the tree's root, while every other node possesses a special neighbor, called $parent_i$ at node n_i, on the tree path from n_i to n_1. The algorithm initiates with n_1 sending *inf* on all tree edges incident to it. Every other node n_i, upon receiving *inf* from a neighbor for the first time, sets $parent_i$ to be that neighbor and, if not a leaf, forwards *inf* on all tree edges incident to it, except the one leading to $parent_i$. If n_i is a leaf, then it sends *inf* back to $parent_i$ immediately upon receiving it for the first time. Every other node, except n_1, having received *inf* on every tree edge, sends *inf* to $parent_i$. Upon receiving *inf* on all tree edges incident to it, n_1 has the information that *inf* has reached all nodes. Clearly, this solution has both the message and time complexities equal to $O(n)$.

The solution by flooding to the PIF problem that we now describe in detail is an extension of the flooding solution we gave in Algorithm *A_PI* to the PI problem. Similarly to the spanning-tree-based solution we just described, a variable $parent_i$ is employed at each node n_i to indicate one of n_i's neighbors. In contrast with that solution, however, this variable is no longer dependent upon a preestablished spanning tree, but rather is determined dynamically to be any of n_i's neighbors as follows. When n_i receives *inf* for the first time, $parent_i$ is set to point to the neighbor of n_i from which it was received. The algorithm is started by n_1, which sends *inf* to all of its neighbors. Every other node n_i, upon receiving *inf* for the first time, sets $parent_i$ appropriately and forwards *inf* to all of its neighbors, except $parent_i$. Upon receiving a copy of *inf* from each of its neighbors, n_i may then send *inf* to $parent_i$ as well. Node n_1 obtains the information that all nodes possess *inf* upon receiving *inf* from all of its neighbors.

This algorithm is given next as Algorithm *A_PIF*. The variable $parent_i$ is initialized to **nil** for all $n_i \in N$. Node n_i also employs the variable $count_i$, initially equal to zero, to register the number of copies of *inf* received, and the Boolean variable $reached_i$, initially set to **false**, to indicate whether n_i has been reached by *inf*. Note that $count_i = 0$ if $reached_i = $ **false**, but not conversely, because $reached_1$ must become **true** right at the algorithm's onset, at which time $count_1 = 0$. The set N_0 now comprises one single element, namely the node that initially possesses *inf*, so $N_0 = \{n_1\}$.

Algorithm A_PIF:

▷ **Variables:**
$parent_i = $ **nil;**
$count_i = 0;$
$reached_i = $ **false.**

▷ **Input:**
$msg_i = $ **nil.**
Action if $n_i \in N_0$:   (4.3)
$reached_i := $ **true;**
Send inf to all $n_j \in Neig_i$.

▷ **Input:**
$msg_i = inf$ such that $origin_i(msg_i) = (n_i, n_j)$.
Action: (4.4)
$count_i := count_i + 1;$
if not $reached_i$ **then**
begin
$reached_i := $ **true;**
$parent_i := n_j;$
Send inf to every $n_k \in Neig_i$ such that $n_k \neq parent_i$
end;
if $count_i = |Neig_i|$ **then**
if $parent_i \neq$ **nil then**
Send inf to $parent_i$.

It follows easily from (4.3) and (4.4) that the collection of variables $parent_i$ for all $n_i \in N$ establishes on G a spanning tree rooted at n_1 (Figure 4.1). The leaves in this tree are nodes from which no other node receives inf for the first time. The construction of this tree can be viewed, just as in the case of Algorithm A_PI, as a wave of information that propagates outward from n_1 to the farther reaches of G. Clearly, this construction involves

$$|Neig_1| + \sum_{n_i \in N - N_0} \left(|Neig_i| - 1 \right) = 2m - n + 1$$

messages and $O(n)$ time. If it can be shown that every edge on the tree (there are $n - 1$ such edges) carries an additional copy of inf from node $n_i \neq n_1$ to $parent_i$ by time $O(n)$ as well, then the total number of messages involved in Algorithm

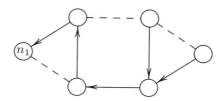

Figure 4.1. *During an execution of Algorithm A_PIF, the variables parent$_i$ for all nodes n_i are set so that a spanning tree is created on G. This spanning tree is rooted at n_1, and its leaves correspond to nodes from which no other node received inf for the first time. In this figure, a directed edge is drawn from n_i to n_j to indicate that parent$_i$ = n_j.*

A_PIF is $2m = O(m)$, while its time complexity is $O(n)$. Theorem 4.1 provides the necessary basis for this argument, with $T_i \subseteq N$ containing the nodes in the subtree rooted at node n_i.

Theorem 4.1. *In Algorithm A_PIF, node $n_i \neq n_1$ sends inf to parent$_i$ within at most 2d time of having received inf for the first time, where d is the number of edges in the longest tree path between n_i and a leaf in T_i. In addition, at the time this message is sent every node in T_i has received inf.*

Proof: The proof proceeds by induction on the subtrees of T_i. The basis is given by T_i's leaves, and then the assertion clearly holds, because no $n_j \in N$ is such that parent$_j$ is a leaf in T_i. Assuming the assertion for all the subtrees of T_i rooted at nodes n_j such that parent$_j = n_i$ leads directly to the theorem, because the induction hypothesis states that every such n_j sends inf to n_i within at most $2(d-1)$ time of having received inf for the first time. The theorem then follows by (4.3) and (4.4). ∎

In addition to helping establish the complexity of Algorithm A_PIF, Theorem 4.1 is also useful in polishing our view of the algorithm's functioning as a wave propagation. What happens then is that a wave is propagated forward from n_1, and then another wave is propagated ("echoed") back to n_1. This second wave is initiated concurrently at all the leaves of the spanning tree and collapses back towards n_1. Notice that the two waves are not really completely separated from each other. In fact, it may happen that the second wave reaches a node before the first wave has reached that node on all possible fronts (i.e., on all possible edges incident to that node).

Corollary 4.2. *In Algorithm A_PIF, node n_1 receives inf from all of its neighbors within time $O(n)$ of having executed (4.3). In addition, at the time the last inf is received every node in N has received inf.*

Proof: Immediate from Theorem 4.1 applied to all nodes n_i such that $parent_i = n_1$ and from (4.4). ∎

Before ending this section, we wish to make one comment that relates the two algorithms we have studied to material we saw previously in Section 2.3. From the perspective of the material discussed in that section, Algorithms A_PI and A_PIF offer good examples of how the knowledge that the nodes have evolve as the algorithms are executed. In the case of Algorithm A_PI, before the algorithm is started it holds that $K_i\mathcal{P}$ for all $n_i \in N_0$, with $\mathcal{P}$ being any sentence that can be deduced from *inf*. When the algorithm is done, then $K_i\mathcal{P}$ holds for all $n_i \in N$.

The situation is quite similar for Algorithm A_PIF, although more can be said. Initially, it holds that $K_1\mathcal{P}$, and after the first wave has reached all nodes it holds that $K_i\mathcal{P}$ for all $n_i \in N$. In addition, by Corollary 4.2, when n_1 has received *inf* from all of its neighbors it also holds that $K_1K_i\mathcal{P}$ for all $n_i \in N$.

4.1.2. Handling multiple concurrent instances

Algorithms for propagating information throughout G like the ones we discussed in the previous section are of fundamental importance in various distributed computations. Together with the three general techniques discussed in Chapter 5 (leader election, distributed snapshots, and network synchronization), these algorithms can be regarded as constituting fundamental building blocks for the design of distributed algorithms in general. In fact, algorithms for propagating information, either through all of G's nodes (as in the previous section) or in a more restricted fashion, are themselves components used widely in the design of the other building blocks we just alluded to. Understandably, then, some of these algorithms have been incorporated in the design of communication processors as built-in instructions to be executed by the nodes of G when this graph represents a network of communication processors (cf. Section 1.2).

It is in this context that the question of how to handle multiple concurrent instances of Algorithms A_PI and A_PIF arises. In the case of Algorithm A_PI, multiple concurrent instances occur when the nodes in N_0 repeatedly broadcast a series of messages, say $inf_1, inf_2, \ldots$. A quick examination of the algorithm reveals that a possibility to handle such a series at a node n_i is to employ a Boolean variable $reached_i^k$ in connection with inf_k, for $k \geq 1$. Upon arrival of a message, its contents indicate which variable to use. However, if G's edges are FIFO, then another alternative can be considered that does not require an unbounded number of Boolean variables to be employed at each node, and furthermore does away with the need to inspect the contents of the messages (as befits a communication processor).

This alternative is based on the simple observation that, under the FIFO assumption, every node receives the stream of messages, on every edge incident to it, in the order the messages were sent by the nodes in N_0. The strategy is to employ $|Neig_i|$ counters at n_i to indicate the number of messages already received on each of the edges in Inc_i. These counters, called $count_i^j$ for $n_j \in Neig_i$, are initially equal to zero and get incremented by 1 upon receipt of a message on the corresponding edge. In order to check whether such a message, when received from $n_\ell \in Neig_i$, is being received at n_i for the first time, it suffices to check whether

$$count_i^\ell > count_i^j$$

for all $n_j \in Neig_i$ such that $j \neq \ell$. In the affirmative case, the message is indeed being received for the first time and should be passed on (cf. Exercise 2).

A similar question arises in the context of Algorithm A_PIF when the stream of messages is sent by node n_1. As in the case of Algorithm A_PI, providing each node n_i with an unbounded number of sets of variables, and then allowing n_i to inspect the contents of incoming messages to decide which set to use, is an approach to solve the problem. Naturally, though, one wonders whether the FIFO assumption on the edges of G can lead to a simplification similar to the one we obtained in the previous case. It should not be hard to realize, however, that the FIFO assumption does not necessarily in this case imply that the stream of messages is received at each node, on every edge incident to it, in the order it was sent by n_1, and then our previous strategy does not carry over (cf. Exercise 3). Nevertheless, the weaker assertion that every node is reached by the stream of messages in the order it was sent does clearly hold under the assumption of FIFO edges, but this does not seem to readily provide a solution that is independent of the messages' contents.

4.2. Graph connectivity

The problem that we treat in this section is the problem of discovery, by each node in N, of the identifications of all the other nodes to which it is connected by a path in G. The relevance of this problem becomes apparent when we consider the myriad of practical situations in which portions of G may fail, possibly disconnecting the graph and thereby making unreachable from each other a pair of nodes that could previously communicate over a path of finite number of edges. The ability to discover the identifications of the nodes that still share a connected component of the system in an environment that is prone to such changes may be crucial in many cases. The algorithm that we present in this section is not really suited to the cases in which G changes dynamically. The treatment of such cases requires techniques that are altogether absent from this book, where we take G to be fixed and connected. The interested reader is referred to the literature for additional information. The algorithm that we present is not the most efficient one, either, but it is the one of our choice because it very elegantly employs techniques for the propagation of information seen in Section 4.1.1.

The algorithm is called Algorithm $A\_Test\_Connectivity$, and its essence is the following. First of all, it may be started by any of the nodes in N, either spontaneously (if the node is in N_0) or upon receipt of the first message (otherwise). In either case, what a node n_i does to initiate its participation in the algorithm is to broadcast its identification, call it id_i, in the manner of Algorithm A_PIF. As we will see, this very simple procedure, coupled with the assumption that the edges in G are FIFO, suffices to ensure that every node in N obtains the identifications of all the other nodes in G.

The set of variables that node n_i employs to participate in Algorithm $A\_Test\_Connectivity$ is essentially an n-fold replication of the set of variables employed in Algorithm A_PIF, because basically what n_i is doing is to participate in as many concurrent instances of Algorithm A_PIF as there are nodes in G (although not in the sense of Section 4.1.2, because now each instance is generated by a different node). So, for $n_j \in N$, $parent_i^j$ (initialized to **nil**) indicates the node in $Neig_i$ from which the first id_j has been received, $count_i^j$ (initially equal to zero) stores the number of times id_j has been received, and the Boolean $reached_i^j$ (equal to **false**, initially) is used to indicate whether id_j has been received at least once. Another Boolean variable, $initiated_i$, initialized to **false**, is employed at n_i to indicate whether $n_i \in N_0$. (Use of this variable is a redundancy, but we keep it for notational simplicity; in fact, $initiated_i = $ **true** if and only if there exists at least one $n_j \in N$ such that $reached_i^j = $ **true**.)

Algorithm $A\_Test\_Connectivity$:

$\triangleright$ **Variables:**

$parent_i^k = $ **nil** for all $n_k \in N$;

$count_i^k = 0$ for all $n_k \in N$;

$reached_i^k = $ **false** for all $n_k \in N$;

$initiated_i = $ **false**.

$\triangleright$ **Input:**

$msg_i = $ **nil**.

Action if $n_i \in N_0$:　　　　　　　　　　　　　　　　　　(4.5)

$initiated_i := $ **true**;

$reached_i^i := $ **true**;

Send id_i to all $n_j \in Neig_i$.

$\triangleright$ **Input:**

$msg_i = id_k$ such that $origin_i(msg_i) = (n_i, n_j)$ for some $n_k \in N$.

Action:　　　　　　　　　　　　　　　　　　　　　　(4.6)

  if not $initiated_i$ **then**

    begin

      $initiated_i := $ **true**;

      $reached_i^i := $ **true**;

      Send id_i to all $n_\ell \in Neig_i$

    end;

  $count_i^k := count_i^k + 1$;

  if not $reached_i^k$ **then**

    begin

      $reached_i^k := $ **true**;

      $parent_i^k := n_j$;

      Send id_k to every $n_\ell \in Neig_i$ such that $n_\ell \neq parent_i^k$

    end;

  if $count_i^k = |Neig_i|$ **then**

    if $parent_i^k \neq $ **nil then**

      Send id_k to $parent_i^k$.

In Algorithm $A\_Test\_Connectivity$, (4.5) and (4.6) should compared respectively with (4.3) and (4.4) of Algorithm A_PIF. What this comparison reveals is that (4.3) and (4.5) are essentially the same, whereas (4.6) is obtained from (4.4) by the addition of the appropriate commands for n_i to initiate its participation in the computation if it is not in N_0.

As we mentioned earlier, this algorithm is based on the assumption that G's edges are FIFO. To see that it works, it is helpful to resort to the pictorial interprepation as propagating waves that we employed in the previous section for the algorithms for information propagation. The wave that node n_i propagates forward with its identification reaches every other node n_j either when $initiated_j = $ **true** or when $initiated_j = $ **false**. By (4.5) and (4.6), and because of the FIFO property of the edges, in either case id_i is only sent along the nodes on the path from n_j to n_i obtained by successively following the *parent* pointers after id_j has been sent on the same path. Therefore, by the time n_i receives id_i from all of its neighbors it has already received id_j at least once (cf. Exercise 4). Because this is valid for all $n_j \in N$, then n_i must by this time know the identifications of all nodes in G.

Algorithm *A_Test_Connectivity* can be regarded as the superposition of n instances of Algorithm *A_PIF*, so its message complexity is n times the message complexity of that algorithm, that is, $O(nm)$ (to be precise, each edge carries exactly n messages in each direction, so the total number of messages is $2nm$). Because the lengths of messages depend upon n, it is in this case appropriate to compute the algorithm's bit complexity as well. If we assume that every node's identification can be expressed in $\lceil \log n \rceil$ bits, then the bit complexity of Algorithm *A_Test_Connectivity* is $O(nm \log n)$. The time complexity of the algorithm is essentially that of Algorithm *A_PIF*, plus the time for a node in N_0 to trigger the initiation of another node as far from it as $n - 1$ edges; in summary, $O(n)$ as well.

4.3. Shortest distances

The last basic problem considered in this chapter is the problem of determining the shortest distances in G between all pairs of nodes. Distances between two nodes are in this section taken to be measured in numbers of edges, so that the problem that we treat is closely related to the problem of breadth-first numbering that we considered briefly at the end of Section 3.4. The problem is now much more general, though, because in that section we concentrated solely on computing the distances from a distinguished node n_1 to the other nodes in N that could be reached from it (G was then a directed graph). In addition, in that section, n_1 was not required to know at the end of the algorithm the numbers that had been assigned to the other nodes.

Another requirement that we add to the algorithm to compute shortest distances is that at the end a node be informed not only of the distance from it to all other nodes, but also of which of its neighbors lies on the corresponding shortest path. Readily, the availability of this information at all nodes provides a means of routing messages from every node to every other node along shortest paths. When G has one node for every processor of some distributed-memory system and its edges reflect the interprocessor connections in that system, this information allows shortest-path routing to be done (cf. Section 1.3).

We approach this problem by first giving a synchronous algorithm that solves it, and then indicating how the corresponding asynchronous algorithm can be obtained. The synchronous algorithm, called Algorithm $S\_Compute\_Distances$, proceeds as follows. At pulse $s = 0$, every node sends its identification to all of its neighbors. At pulse $s = 1$, every node possesses the identifications of all nodes that are no farther from it than one edge (itself and its neighbors). A node then builds a set with the identifications of all those nodes that are exactly one edge away from it and sends this set to its neighbors. At pulse $s = 2$, every node has received the identifications of all nodes located no farther than two edges from it (itself, its neighbors, and its neighbors' neighbors). Because a node knows precisely which nodes are zero or one edge away from it, determining the set of those nodes that are two edges away is a simple matter. What happens then is that, in general, at pulse $s \geq 0$ a node sends to its neighbors a set containing the identifications of all those nodes that are exactly s edges away from it. For $s = 0$, this set comprises the node's own identification only. For $s > 0$, the set comprises every node identification received during interval $s - 1$, except those of nodes which are at most $s - 1$ edges away from itself. Clearly, no more than n pulses are required. The last pulse may be an earlier one, though, specifically pulse S if the set that the node generates at this pulse is empty. Clearly, all further sets the node generated would be empty as well, and then it may cease computing (although innocuous messages may still arrive from some of its neighbors). Naturally, the value of S may differ from node to node. For simplicity, however, in the algorithm that we give next we let all nodes compute through pulse $s = n - 1$ (cf. Exercise 6).

As in Section 4.2, we let id_i denote n_i's identification. Variables used by Algorithm $S\_Compute\_Distances$ are the following. The shortest distance from n_i to $n_j \in N$ is denoted by $dist_i^j$, initially equal to n (unless $j = i$, in which case the initial value is zero). The node in $Neig_i$ on the corresponding shortest path to $n_j \neq n_i$ is denoted by $first_i^j$, initially equal to **nil**. The set of identifications to be sent out to neighbors at each step is denoted by set_i; initially, it contains n_i's identification only. In Algorithm $S\_Compute\_Distances$, $N_0 = N$.

Algorithm *S_Compute_Distances*:

▷ **Variables:**
$dist_i^i = 0$;
$dist_i^k = n$ for all $n_k \in N$ such that $k \neq i$;
$first_i^k = \mathbf{nil}$ for all $n_k \in N$ such that $k \neq i$;
$set_i = \{id_i\}$.

▷ **Input:**
$s = 0$, $MSG_i(0) = \emptyset$.
Action if $n_i \in N_0$:   (4.7)
Send set_i to all $n_j \in Neig_i$.

▷ **Input:**
$0 < s \leq n - 1$, $MSG_i(s)$ such that $origin_i(set_j) = (n_i, n_j)$ for $set_j \in MSG_i(s)$.
Action: (4.8)
$set_i := \emptyset$;
for all $set_j \in MSG_i(s)$ **do**
   for all $id_k \in set_j$ **do**
      if $dist_i^k > s$ **then**
         begin
            $dist_i^k := s$;
            $first_i^k := n_j$;
            $set_i := set_i \cup \{id_k\}$
         end;
Send set_i to all $n_k \in Neig_i$.

Even before the correctness of Algorithm *S_Compute_Distances* is established formally, evaluating its message and time complexities is a simple matter. If the algorithm functions correctly, then every node must receive the identification of every other node, and then by (4.7) and (4.8) every node's identification must traverse every edge in both directions. If we take a node's identification to be a message, then the number of messages employed by Algorithm *S_Compute_Distances* is $2nm$, and its message complexity is then $O(nm)$. As in the case of Algorithm *A_Test_Connectivity*, message lengths are in this case dependent on n. If, as in the case of that algorithm, we assume that node identifications can be expressed in $\lceil \log n \rceil$ bits, then the bit complexity of Algorithm *S_Compute_Distances* is $O(nm \log n)$. By the range of s in (4.8), the time complexity of this algorithm is $O(n)$. What supports these results is Theorem 4.3.

Theorem 4.3. *For $s \geq 0$ in Algorithm S_Compute_Distances, at pulse s every node n_i has received the identifications of exactly those nodes $n_j \in N$ such that the shortest paths between n_i and n_j contain no more than s edges. Furthermore, for $j \neq i$, $dist_i^j$ and $first_i^j$ are, respectively, the number of edges and the neighbor of n_i on one such path.*

Proof: The proof is by induction, and the basis, corresponding to pulse $s = 0$, is trivial. If we inductively assume the theorem's assertion for pulse $s - 1$, then for pulse $s > 0$ we have the following. By the induction hypothesis, n_i has at pulse $s - 1$ received the identifications of all $n_j \in N$ that are at most $s - 1$ edges away from it, and the corresponding $dist_i^j$ and $first_i^j$ have been set correctly. In addition, by the induction hypothesis and by (4.7) and (4.8), during interval $s - 1$ n_i has received from each of its neighbors the identifications of all $n_j \in N$ that are $s - 1$ edges away from that neighbor. A node n_j is s edges away from n_i if and only if it is $s - 1$ edges away from at least one node in $Neig_i$, so at pulse s n_i has received the identifications of all $n_j \in N$ that are no more than s edges away from it. The theorem follows easily from the observation that, by (4.8), the variables $dist_i^j$ and $first_i^j$ for all $n_j \in N$ that are s edges away from n_i are set when n_i first finds in $MSG_i(s)$ the identification of n_j. ∎

Obtaining an asynchronous algorithm from Algorithm S_Compute_Distances goes along the lines of Section 3.3, where Algorithm S-to-A_Template was given just for such purposes. We provide the result of such a transformation next, but only in Section 5.3.2, after we have discussed the general technique of synchronizers, will the reasons why the resulting asynchronous algorithm is correct be given. The asynchronous algorithm that we give to compute all the shortest distances in G is called Algorithm A_Compute_Distances, and requires that all edges in G be FIFO edges (cf. Exercise 7). It is widely used, despite having been displaced by more efficient algorithms of great theoretical interest. In addition to its popularity, good reasons for us to present it in detail are its simplicity and the possibility that it offers of illustrating the synchronization techniques of Section 5.3.2.

In addition to the variables that in Algorithm S_Compute_Distances n_i employs, in Algorithm A_Compute_Distances the following variables are also employed. For each $n_j \in Neig_i$, a variable $level_i^j$ is employed to indicate which sets of node identifications n_i has received from n_j. Specifically, $level_i^j = d$ for some d such that $0 \leq d < n$ if and only if n_i has received from n_j the identifications of those nodes which are d edges away from n_j. Initially, $level_i^j = -1$. Similarly, a variable $state_i$ is employed by n_i with the following meaning. Node n_i has received the identifications of all nodes that are d edges away from it for some d such that $0 \leq d < n$ if and only if $state_i = d$. Initially, $state_i = 0$. Finally, a Boolean variable $initiated_i$, initially set to **false**, is used to indicate whether $n_i \in N_0$.

Algorithm $A\_Compute\_Distances$:

▷ **Variables:**

$dist_i^i = 0$;
$dist_i^k = n$ for all $n_k \in N$ such that $k \neq i$;
$first_i^k = $ **nil** for all $n_k \in N$ such that $k \neq i$;
$set_i = \{id_i\}$;
$level_i^j = -1$ for all $n_j \in Neig_i$;
$state_i = 0$;
$initiated_i = $ **false**.

▷ **Input:**

$msg_i = $ **nil**.

Action if $n_i \in N_0$:   (4.9)

$initiated_i := $ **true**;
Send set_i to all $n_j \in Neig_i$.

▷ **Input:**
$msg_i = set_j$ such that $origin_i(msg_i) = (n_i, n_j)$.
Action:

(4.10)

    if not $initiated_i$ **then**
        begin
            $initiated_i := $ **true**;
            Send set_i to all $n_k \in Neig_i$
        end;
    if $state_i < n - 1$ **then**
        begin
            $level_i^j := level_i^j + 1$;
            for all $id_k \in set_j$ **do**
                if $dist_i^k > level_i^k + 1$ **then**
                    begin
                        $dist_i^k := level_i^k + 1$;
                        $first_i^k := n_j$
                    end;
            if $state_i \leq level_i^j$ for all $n_j \in Neig_i$ **then**
                begin
                    $state_i := state_i + 1$;
                    $set_i := \{id_k \mid n_k \in N$ and $dist_i^k = state_i\}$;
                    Send set_i to all $n_k \in Neig_i$
                end
    end.

In Algorithm *A_Compute_Distances*, (4.9) and the portion of (4.10) that is executed only when $initiated_i = $ **false** are precisely the same as (4.7) in Algorithm *S_Compute_Distances*. The remainder of (4.10) corresponds to the translation of (4.8) into the asynchronous model. Although we relegate most of the discussion on the correctness of Algorithm *A_Compute_Distances* to Section 5.3.2, in this section attention should be given to the fact that, if $initiated_i = $ **true**, then (4.10) is only executed if $state_i < n - 1$. The point to notice is that this is in accord with the intended semantics of $state_i$, because if $state_i = n - 1$ then n_i has already received the identifications of all nodes in N, and is then essentially done with its participation in the algorithm.

Another important point to be discussed right away with respect to Algorithm *A_Compute_Distances* is that the FIFO property of edges, in this case, is essential for the semantics of the *level* variables to be maintained. In (4.10), the distance from n_i to n_k is updated to $level_i^k + 1$ upon receipt of id_k in a set from a neighbor n_j of n_i only because that set is taken to contain the identifications of nodes whose distance to n_j is $level_i^k$. This cannot be taken for granted, though, unless (n_i, n_j) is a FIFO edge.

The complexities of Algorithm $A\_Compute\_Distances$ can also be obtained right away. By (4.9) and (4.10), what node n_i does is to send its identification to all of its neighbors, then the identifications of all of its neighbors get sent, then the identifications of all nodes that are two edges away from it, and so on. Thus n_i sends n messages to each of its neighbors, and the total number of messages employed is then $2nm$, yielding a message complexity of $O(nm)$ and a bit complexity of $O(nm \log n)$ if node identifications can be represented in $\lceil \log n \rceil$ bits. The time complexity comes from considering that a node that is not in N_0 starts executing (4.10) within at most $n - 1$ time of the algorithm's initiation, and that the longest causal dependency involving messages corresponds to sending a node's identification as far as $n - 1$ edges away. The resulting time complexity is then $O(n)$.

Our treatment in Section 5.3 will provide a general methodology for assessing an asynchronous algorithm's complexities from those of the synchronous algorithm from which it originated. As we mentioned in previous occasions, the natural expectation is that higher complexities arise in the asynchronous case, specifically to account for the additional number of messages and time consumed by the function DONE$_i$ appearing in (3.4). However, both the message and time complexities of Algorithm $A\_Compute\_Distances$ are exactly the same as its synchronous originator's. The reason for this intuitively unexpected behavior will become clear in Section 5.3.2.

4.4. Exercises

1. Discuss what happens to Algorithm A_PI if a node refrains from sending inf to the neighbor from which it was received.

2. Write the algorithm that handles multiple concurrent instances of Algorithm A_PI as suggested in Section 4.1.2.

3. Show, by means of an example, that FIFO edges do not suffice to guarantee that messages are received at all nodes in the order sent by node n_1, in the context of multiple concurrent instances of Algorithm A_PIF.

4. Show, by means of an example, that FIFO edges do not suffice to guarantee, in Algorithm $A\_Test\_Connectivity$, that a node receives all the copies of every other node's identification before receiving as many copies of its own identification as it expects.

5. Compare Algorithm *A_Test_Connectivity* with the possibility of solving the problem by a leader (suppose such a leader already exists).

6. Modify Algorithm *S_Compute_Distances* so that it terminates at a node when that node generates an empty list.

7. Show that Algorithm *A_Compute_Distances* can do without the FIFO requirement and without the *level* variables, if lists are sent along with the distances to which they correspond.

4.5. Bibliographic notes

Sections 4.1 through 4.3 are based on Segall (1983) and on Barbosa and França (1988). Additional sources of reference for the problem of determining shortest distances are Awerbuch (1989), Ogier, Rutenburg, and Shacham (1993), Ramarao and Venkatesan (1993), and Haldar (1994).

5

Basic Techniques

This chapter expands considerably on the material of Chapter 4 by presenting three fundamental techniques that can be regarded as building blocks for distributed algorithms in general. These are the techniques of leader election, distributed snapshots, and network synchronization.

The problem of electing a leader in G is treated in Section 5.1, where we discuss various of the problem's characteristics and some of the successful approaches to solve it. Because this problem is intimately related with the problem of establishing a minimum spanning tree on G, treated in Section 7.1, in Section 5.1 we introduce techniques that do not rely on spanning trees to elect a leader. In doing so, we first give an asynchronous algorithm for generic graphs, and then introduce two algorithms (one synchronous and one asynchronous) for the case in which G is a complete graph.

In Section 5.2, we introduce techniques to record, in a distributed fashion, a global state of an ongoing distributed computation. The ability to record global states is fundamental in several cases, and in the remainder of the book there will be several opportunities for us to employ this and related techniques, as for example in Sections 6.2 and 6.3. In Section 5.2, we give a general technique to record global states distributedly and also discuss some centralized variations of interest in some special contexts, as for example in our discussion of some methods of distributed simulation in Chapter 10.

Network synchronization is the subject of Section 5.3, in which we return to material previously covered in Section 3.3 to fill in the details of how to translate a synchronous algorithm into an asynchronous one. Our approach in this section is to provide the principles underlying the transformation, then to present a few techniques exhibiting different communication and time complexities, and then to discuss simplifications that apply in important special cases.

Sections 5.4 and 5.5 contain exercises and bibliographic notes, respectively.

5.1. Leader election

A *leader* is a member of N that all other nodes acknowledge as being distinguished to perform some special task. The *leader election problem* is the problem of choosing a leader from a set of *candidates*, given that initially a node n_i is only aware of its own identification, denoted as previously by id_i. In the spirit of Section 2.2.1, it should be clear after some pondering that the leader election problem is meaningless in the context of anonymous systems. Moreover, even if the system is not anonymous, the leader election problem can only be solved for G if every node's identification is unique in G (cf. Exercise 1), in which case the set of all identifications can be assumed to be totally ordered by $<$.

This assumption is fundamental in the approaches to leader election that take the leader to be the candidate with greatest identification. However, even if this is not the criterion, the ability to compare two candidates' identifications is essential to break ties that may occur with the criterion at hand. (In fact, this is really why unique identifications are needed in the first place. In their absence, any criterion to select a leader from the set of candidates might deadlock for the absence of a tie breaker.) Another assumption that we make on a node's identification is that it can be expressed in $\lceil \log n \rceil$ bits. Also, G is throughout this section assumed to be an undirected graph.

The importance of electing a leader in a distributed environment stems essentially from the occurrence of situations in which some centralized coordination must take place in G, either because a technique to solve the particular problem at hand in a completely distributed fashion is not available, or because the centralized approach offers more attractive performance. Problems for which satisfactory techniques of a completely distributed nature are not available include the many recovery steps that have to be taken after G undergoes a failure (or a topological change, in broader terms). A leader is in this case needed to coordinate, for example, the reestablishment of allocation and routing functions (if G is organized to reflect a distributed-memory system). Although it has been our assumption throughout that G is fixed, all the algorithms that we discuss in this book are also applicable to the cases in which G varies if G is guaranteed to remain constant for "sufficiently long."

Examples to illustrate the importance of electing a leader when the centralized approach to a particular problem proves more efficient than the distributed one come from the area of graph algorithms, treated in Chapter 7 (although in that chapter we concentrate solely on problems for which efficient distributed solutions do exist). As we remarked in Section 3.2.2, such situations are in essence characterized by higher complexities for the distributed approaches than for coalescing into the leader information on the structure of G.

The leader election problem is very closely related to another problem that we treat in Section 7.1, namely the problem of establishing on G a minimum spanning tree (or, as we discuss in that section, the problem of determining any spanning tree on G, which can be reduced to the former). Once a spanning tree has been established on G, a leader can be elected as follows. Every node assumes the role of n_1 in the PIF problem (cf. Section 4.1.1) and propagates a piece of information with feedback on the spanning tree. This piece of information is, if the node is a candidate, its identification. Otherwise, it is simply a token devoid of any special content. The way the n propagations interact with each other is such that a node, before forwarding the information being propagated by any other node, must first ensure that its own information is propagated. If edges are FIFO, then by the time a node receives its own information from all of its neighbors on the tree it has also received the information that all other nodes propagated, and can then select as a leader the candidate with greatest identification. This procedure has message complexity of $O(n^2)$ (bit complexity of $O(n^2 \log n)$) and time complexity of $O(n)$.

Although more efficient approaches exist to elect a leader once a spanning tree has been established on G (cf. Sections 7.1.1), the approach we just described is interesting because it hints immediately at a simple (although not very efficient, either) algorithm to elect a leader on a generic graph with FIFO edges. This algorithm is simply Algorithm $A\_Test\_Connectivity$ of Section 4.2 with N_0 being the set of candidates, slightly modified so that candidates broadcast their identifications, while the remaining nodes broadcast simply a token that serves the purpose of signaling to the node that already it has received every candidate's identification. Upon receiving on all incident edges the information it propagated, a node (be it a candidate or otherwise) is then ready to choose as a leader the candidate with greatest identification. As in Section 4.2, this algorithm's message complexity is $O(nm)$ ($O(nm \log n)$ bit complexity), and its time complexity is $O(n)$.

When G is assumed to be some particular graph, these complexities must be revised accordingly. For example, if G is a ring, then the algorithm's message complexity becomes $O(n^2)$, whereas if it is a complete graph the message complexity is $O(n^3)$. The resulting message complexity for a complete graph is particularly alarming, and it is to the problem of electing a leader on such a graph that we turn our attention now, aiming specifically at providing an algorithm of significantly lower message complexity.

We start with a synchronous algorithm, aiming at illustrating the technique more intuitively, and then provide an asynchronous algorithm. In both algorithms, N_0 is the set of candidates.

The synchronous algorithm that we give is inspired in the following straight-forward synchronous algorithm to elect a leader on a complete graph. At pulse $s = 0$, every candidate sends its identification to all other nodes. At pulse $s = 1$, every node has received every candidate's identification and can then decide on a leader. The message complexity of this algorithm is $O(n^2)$, and its time complexity is $O(1)$. The synchronous algorithm that we derive from this has message complexity of $O(n \log n)$ and time complexity of $O(\log n)$, which have been proved optimal in the literature.

In order to decrease the message complexity from $O(n^2)$ to $O(n \log n)$, a candidate does not send its identification to all of its neighbors at the same pulse, but rather first communicates with one of its neighbors, then with two other neighbors, then with four others, and so on. For $k \geq 1$, the kth set of neighbors with which a candidate communicates has size 2^{k-1}, and then exactly $\lceil \log n \rceil$ such sets have to exist to encompass all of the candidate's $n - 1$ neighbors (that is, $k \leq \lceil \log n \rceil$). When a candidate sends a neighbor a message, it is attempting to "capture" that neighbor, thereby becoming its "owner," so that the candidate that has captured all nodes at the end is the one to be chosen leader. A candidate succeeds in capturing a node if its identification is larger than those of the other candidates that are attempting to capture the same node at the same time, and larger than the identification of the node's current owner. A candidate only proceeds to attempting to capture the next subset of its neighbors if it succeeds in capturing all the neighbors it is currently attempting to capture. Otherwise, it ceases being a candidate.

The resulting synchronous algorithm, called Algorithm $S\_Elect\_Leader\_C$ ("C" for Complete), proceeds as follows. At an even pulse $s \geq 0$, a candidate n_i sends a message $capture(id_i)$ to $2^{s/2}$ of those of its neighbors with which it still has not communicated. At an odd pulse $s > 0$, a node n_i (candidate or otherwise) selects from those nodes that sent it a $capture$ message at pulse $s - 1$ the one with greatest identification. That node is then to become n_i's owner if its identification is greater than n_i's current owner's. If n_i's owner changes, then it sends an *ack* to its new owner. Only a candidate that receives as many *ack*'s as it sent *capture*'s remains being a candidate.

The following are the variables employed by n_i in Algorithm *S_Elect_Leader_C*. A Boolean variable *candidate*$_i$, initially set to **false**, indicates whether n_i is a candidate. For each neighbor n_j of n_i, a Boolean variable *tried*$_i^j$ (equal to **false**, initially) is used to indicate, if n_i is a candidate, whether it has already attempted to capture n_j. Finally, *owner_id*$_i$ contains the identification of n_i's owner. This variable's initial value is **nil** (we assume that **nil** $< id_j$ for all $n_j \in N$).

Algorithm *S_Elect_Leader_C*:

▷ **Variables:**

   candidate$_i$ = **false**;
   tried$_i^j$ = **false** for all $n_j \in Neig_i$;
   owner_id$_i$ = **nil**.

▷ **Input:**

   $s = 0$, $MSG_i(0) = \emptyset$.

Action if $n_i \in N_0$:   (5.1)

   candidate$_i$:= **true**;
   owner$_i$:= id_i;
   Let n_j be a node in $Neig_i$;
   tried$_i^j$:= **true**;
   Send *capture*(id_i) to n_j.

▷ **Input:**

   s odd such that $0 < s \leq 2\lceil \log n \rceil - 1$, $MSG_i(s)$ such that
   origin$_i\big(capture(id_j)\big) = (n_i, n_j)$ for *capture*(id_j) $\in MSG_i(s)$.

Action: (5.2)

   Let $n_k \in Neig_i$ be such that $id_k \geq id_j$ for all *capture*(id_j) $\in$
   $MSG_i(s)$;
   if *owner_id*$_i$ < id_k **then**
      begin
         if *candidate*$_i$ **then**
            candidate$_i$:= **false**;
         owner_id$_i$:= id_k;
         Send *ack* to n_k
      end.

▷ **Input:**
    s even such that $0 < s \leq 2\lceil \log n \rceil$, $MSG_i(s)$.
    Action: (5.3)
        if $candidate_i$ **then**
            if $\left| MSG_i(s) \right| < \min\{2^{(s-2)/2}, n - 2^{(s-2)/2}\}$ **then**
                $candidate_i :=$ **false**
        else
            if $s < 2\lceil \log n \rceil$ **then**
                begin
                    Let $S \subset Neig_i$ be such that $|S| = \min\{2^{s/2}, n - 2^{s/2}\}$ and $tried_i^j =$ **false** for all $n_j \in S$;
                    $tried_i^j :=$ **true** for all $n_j \in S$;
                    Send $capture(id_i)$ to all $n_j \in S$
            end.

In Algorithm *S_Elect_Leader_C*, (5.1) and (5.3) correspond to opportunities that n_i has to capture nodes if it is a candidate. The attempt to capture more nodes in (5.3) is conditioned upon having received as many *ack*'s as needed for the last attempt. In other words, if $s > 0$ is even, then the number of *ack*'s expected to be in $MSG_i(s)$ if n_i is a candidate is $\min\{2^{(s-2)/2}, n - 2^{(s-2)/2}\}$ (this is the number of nodes n_i attempted to capture at the previous even pulse). If $MSG_i(s)$ contains this number of *ack*'s, then n_i sends *capture*'s to other $2^{s/2}$ nodes, unless the number of nodes which it still has not attempted to capture is less than this, in which case it must be $n - 1 - (2^{s/2} - 1)$ (the expression in parentheses is the number of nodes it has captured so far). In (5.2), node n_i decides whether to change its owner or not, regardless of whether it is a candidate. The node that n_i considers to be its owner after all $2\lceil \log n \rceil + 1$ pulses have elapsed (that is, the node whose identification is in $owner\_id_i$ at that time) is the elected leader from n_i's standpoint. By (5.1) and (5.2), n_i's owner is the node with greatest identification, and therefore from every node's standpoint the elected leader is the same.

Algorithm *S_Elect_Leader_C* runs for $2\lceil \log n \rceil + 1$ pulses. Because the number of groups of neighbors that a candidate tries to capture is at most $\lceil \log n \rceil$, the last pulse in (5.3) is only used for a candidate to process the last *ack*'s it has received, if any. The time complexity of Algorithm *S_Elect_Leader_C* is, by (5.3), $O(\log n)$. The following theorem indicates how to assess the algorithm's message complexity.

Theorem 5.1. *For $1 \leq k \leq \lceil \log n \rceil - 1$, the maximum number of nodes to reach pulse $s = 2k$ as candidates in Algorithm S_Elect_Leader_C is $\lfloor n/2^{k-1} \rfloor$.*

Proof: At pulse $s = 2k$, by (5.3) a node must have captured 2^{k-1} nodes to be still a candidate (i.e., it must have received 2^{k-1} ack's). The assertion then follows from the fact that, by (5.2), any of the n nodes may only be captured by at most one candidate at any even pulse.
                                                                                      ■

By Theorem 5.1, at pulse $s = 2\lceil \log n \rceil - 2$ there may still be a number of candidates no greater than

$$\left\lfloor \frac{n}{2^{\lceil \log n \rceil - 2}} \right\rfloor \leq \frac{4n}{2^{\lceil \log n \rceil}}$$

$$\leq \frac{4n}{n}$$

$$= 4,$$

so that the additional even pulse $s = 2\lceil \log n \rceil$ is indeed needed for all but one of them to quit being a candidate.

Corollary 5.2. *Algorithm S_Elect_Leader_C employs at most* $2n\lceil \log n \rceil - n$ *capture messages and at most* $n\lceil \log n \rceil$ *ack messages.*

Proof: The initial number of candidates is at most n, so by (5.1) at pulse $s = 0$ at most n *capture*'s are sent. For $1 \leq k \leq \lceil \log n \rceil - 1$, by (5.3) at pulse $s = 2k$ a candidate sends at most 2^k *capture*'s. By Theorem 5.1, the number of candidates at this pulse is no larger than $\lfloor n/2^{k-1} \rfloor$, and then the total number of *capture*'s is at most

$$n + \sum_{k=1}^{\lceil \log n \rceil - 1} \left\lfloor \frac{n}{2^{k-1}} \right\rfloor 2^k \leq n + 2n(\lceil \log n \rceil - 1)$$

$$= 2n\lceil \log n \rceil - n.$$

By (5.2), a node sends at most one *ack* per odd pulse, so that the total number of *ack*'s is no more than $n\lceil \log n \rceil$, thence the corollary.
                                                                                      ■

It follows from Corollary 5.2 that the message complexity of Algorithm S_Elect_Leader_C is $O(n \log n)$. Also, because a *capture* message carries a node's identification, it follows that the algorithm's bit complexity is $O(n \log^2 n)$. This synchronous algorithm has a better message complexity than the one we devised initially (which had $O(n^2)$ message complexity), but this comes at the cost of an increase in time complexity from $O(1)$ to $O(\log n)$.

What supports the improved message complexity is the technique of comparing a candidate's identification to those of its neighbors in increasingly large groups, so that the number of candidates is guaranteed to decrease steadily from an even pulse to another (cf. Theorem 5.1). When we consider the design of an asynchronous counterpart to Algorithm *S_Elect_Leader_C*, the use of such a technique has to undergo a few modifications, especially because a node cannot in the asynchronous model consider a group of candidate identifications simultaneously as it did in the synchronous model and reply positively to at most one of them. It appears, then, that in the asynchronous model a candidate must attempt to capture one node at a time. However, in order to still be able to benefit from the advantages of capturing nodes in groups of increasing sizes, in the asynchronous algorithm identifications are no longer used as a basis of comparison, but rather only to break ties. Comparisons are instead based on the "level" of each competing candidate, which is the number of groups of nodes a candidate has so far succeeded in capturing. This amounts to simulating the technique employed in the synchronous case, but at the expense of a greater time complexity. As we will see, the resulting algorithm, called Algorithm *A_Elect_Leader_C*, has time complexity $O(n)$ but its message complexity remains as in the synchronous case, that is, $O(n \log n)$.

In order to ensure the correctness of this approach, in the sense that no two candidates must ever be allowed to concurrently remain candidates based on having captured a same node, a candidate must only consider a node as having been captured when (and if) that node's current owner ceases being a candidate. The overall approach is then the following. A candidate attempts to capture nodes one at a time. Its level is at all times given by the number of groups it has succeeded in capturing, in the same sense as in Algorithm *S_Elect_Leader_C*, that is, groups of sizes 1, 2, 4, and so on. If for a candidate n_i we let $level_i$ denote its level and $owns_i$ the number of nodes it has captured, then clearly

$$level_i = \lfloor \log(owns_i + 1) \rfloor.$$

In order to capture a node n_j, n_i sends it a message $capture(level_i, id_i)$. Upon receiving this message, n_j checks whether

$$(level_j, owner\_id_j) < (level_i, id_i)$$

(this comparison is done lexicographically, that is, first the levels are compared and only if they are the same are the identifications compared). If the comparison fails, then n_j sends n_i a *nack* message, and upon receiving it n_i ceases being a candidate (if it still is). If, on the other hand, the comparison succeeds, then $level_j$ is updated to $level_i$. In addition, if n_j is a candidate, then it ceases being so and n_i becomes its owner. Also, n_j sends n_i an *ack*, upon receipt of which n_i proceeds with its node capturing. If n_j is not a candidate, then n_i is marked as n_j's prospective owner.

Before n_i becomes n_j's owner, however, n_i has to ensure that n_j's current owner ceases being a candidate. To this end, n_j sends n_i a message $check(k)$ (assuming that $owner\_id_j = id_k$), and upon receiving this message, n_i, if it still is a candidate, sends a message $eliminate(level_i, id_i)$ to n_k. At n_k, the comparison

$$(level_k, id_k) < (level_i, id_i)$$

is performed and results in one of the following two outcomes. If the comparison fails, then n_k sends n_i a $nack$, thereby causing n_i not to be a candidate any longer (if it still is). If the comparison succeeds, thereby causing n_k to cease being a candidate, or if n_k was no longer a candidate upon receiving the $eliminate$ message, then an $eliminated$ message is sent by n_k to n_i, where it causes n_i, if still a candidate, to try to capture n_j once again by sending it another $capture$ message. If this message, upon arriving at n_j, finds that n_i still is n_j's prospective owner, then n_i becomes n_j's new owner and an ack is sent back to n_i. Otherwise, a $nack$ is sent. Upon receipt of one or the other message, n_i resumes its captures or ceases being a candidate, respectively. Notice that, throughout this entire process, n_k has not yet been captured by n_i, but merely ceased being a candidate.

The variables $level_i$ and $owns_i$, both initially equal to zero, are used by n_i in Algorithm $A\_Elect\_Leader\_C$ in addition to those already used by Algorithm $S\_Elect\_Leader\_C$. Node n_i employs two other variables, both initialized to **nil**, to indicate n_i's prospective owner and the node it is currently attempting to capture. These are, respectively, $p\_owner\_id_i$ and $p\_owned\_id_i$.

Algorithm $A\_Elect\_Leader\_C$:

▷ **Variables:**

$candidate_i = $ **false**;
$tried_i^j = $ **false** for all $n_j \in Neig_i$;
$owner_id_i = $ **nil**;
$level_i = 0$;
$owns_i = 0$;
$p_owner_id_i = $ **nil**;
$p_owned_id_i = $ **nil**.

▷ **Input:**

$msg_i = \textbf{nil}.$

(5.4)

Action if $n_i \in N_0$:

$candidate_i := \textbf{true};$

$owner_i := id_i;$

Let n_j be a node in $Neig_i$;

$tried_i^j := \textbf{true};$

Send $capture(level_i, id_i)$ to n_j.

▷ **Input:**

$msg_i = capture(level_j, id_j)$ such that $origin_i(msg_i) = (n_i, n_j)$.

(5.5)

Action:

if $p\_owner\_id_i = id_j$ **then**

    begin

        $owner\_id_i := id_j;$

        Send ack to n_j

    end

else

    if $(level_i, owner\_id_i) < (level_j, id_j)$ **then**

        begin

            $level_i := level_j;$

            if $candidate_i$ **then**

                begin

                    $candidate_i := \textbf{false};$

                    $owner\_id_i := id_j;$

                    Send ack to n_j

                end

            else

                begin

                    $p\_owner\_id_i := id_j;$

                    Let $n_k \in Neig_i$ be such that $owner\_id_i = id_k;$

                    Send $check(k)$ to n_j

                end

        end

    else

        Send $nack$ to n_j.

▷ **Input:**

$msg_i = nack.$

Action: (5.6)

  if $candidate_i$ **then**

    $candidate_i :=$ **false**.

▷ **Input:**

$msg_i = check(j).$

Action: (5.7)

  if $candidate_i$ **then**

    Send $eliminate(level_i, id_i)$ to n_j.

▷ **Input:**

$msg_i = eliminate(level_j, id_j)$ such that $origin_i(msg_i) = (n_i, n_j).$

Action: (5.8)

  if not $candidate_i$ **then**

    Send $eliminated$ to n_j

  else

    if $(level_i, id_i) < (level_j, id_j)$ **then**

      begin

        $candidate_i :=$ **false**;

        Send $eliminated$ to n_j

      end

    else

      Send $nack$ to n_j.

▷ **Input:**

$msg_i = eliminated.$

Action: (5.9)

  if $candidate_i$ **then**

    begin

      Let $n_j \in Neig_i$ be such that $p\_owned\_id_i = id_j$;

      Send $capture(level_i, id_i)$ to n_j

    end.

▷ **Input:**
$$msg_i = ack.$$

Action: (5.10)

$owns_i := owns_i + 1;$
$level_i := \lfloor \log(owns_i + 1) \rfloor;$
Let $S \subset Neig_i$ be such that $tried_i^j = $ **false** for all $n_j \in S$;
if $S \neq \emptyset$ **then**
    begin
        Let n_j be a node in S;
        $tried_i^j := $ **true**;
        $p\_owned\_id_i := id_j;$
        Send $capture(level_i, id_i)$ to n_j
    end.

In Algorithm $A\_Elect\_Leader\_C$, (5.4) through (5.10) implement the guidelines we gave to employ the technique of Algorithm $S\_Elect\_Leader\_C$ in an asynchronous setting. It should be noted that a candidate n_i becomes a leader when $S = \emptyset$ in (5.10). At this time, it must by (5.5) be the owner of all nodes and its level equal to $\lfloor \log n \rfloor$. Moreover, by (5.4) through (5.9) a candidate may only be the owner of a node if that node's previous owner is no longer a candidate, which leads us to the following counterpart of Theorem 5.1.

Theorem 5.3. *For $1 \leq k \leq \lfloor \log n \rfloor$, the maximum number of candidates of level k in any global state in an execution of Algorithm $A\_Elect\_Leader\_C$ is $\lfloor n/(2^k - 1) \rfloor$.*

Proof: By the definition of level, a candidate n_i at level k must have captured at least $2^k - 1$ of its neighbors, inasmuch as

$$k = \lfloor \log(owns_i + 1) \rfloor$$
$$\leq \log(owns_i + 1).$$

The theorem then follows from the fact that no two candidates can be owners of a same node in any global state.   ∎

Corollary 5.4. *Algorithm $A\_Elect\_Leader\_C$ involves at most $2n\lfloor \log n \rfloor + n$ attempts at capturing a node by a candidate.*

Proof: Before reaching level 1, by (5.4) a candidate attempts to capture exactly one node. For $1 \leq k \leq \lfloor \log n \rfloor$, while at level k a candidate attempts to capture at most 2^k nodes. By Theorem 5.3, the total number of node captures the algorithm involves is then

$$n + \sum_{k=1}^{\lfloor \log n \rfloor} \left\lfloor \frac{n}{2^k - 1} \right\rfloor 2^k \leq n + \sum_{k=1}^{\lfloor \log n \rfloor} \frac{n}{2^{k-1}} 2^k$$
$$= 2n \lfloor \log n \rfloor + n.$$

■

Each node capture by a candidate involves at most six messages (one *capture*, one *check*, one *eliminate*, one *eliminated*, one more *capture*, and one *ack*). By Corollary 5.4, the message complexity of Algorithm *A_Elect_Leader_C* is then $O(n \log n)$, and because the lengthiest messages (*capture* and *eliminate* messages) are $\lceil \log \lfloor \log n \rfloor \rceil + \lceil \log n \rceil$ bits long, the algorithm's bit complexity is $O(n \log^2 n)$. In order to check that the time complexity of Algorithm *A_Elect_Leader_C* is indeed $O(n)$, it suffices to note that candidates capture nodes independently of one another, in the sense that no candidate depends on another candidate's messages to capture nodes (only to cease being a candidate), and that candidates attempt to capture nodes one at a time.

5.2. Distributed snapshots

The second fundamental technique that we discuss in this chapter is a technique for recording global states during the execution of an asynchronous algorithm. While the concept of a global state, as introduced in Section 3.1, is of fundamental importance by itself, the ability to record a global state over which some of the algorithm's global properties can be analyzed is no less attractive. In the context of this book, areas in which algorithms for global state recording are especially relevant include the treatment of stable properties (discussed in Chapter 6) and the handling of some issues related to timing during a distributed simulation (our subject in Chapter 10).

The bulk of our discussion on global state recording is presented in Section 5.2.1, where we present a distributed algorithm to record a global state and leave the recorded information spread throughout the nodes of G. However, there are special cases, chiefly within the area of distributed simulation, for which the recording of global states with some specific properties is desirable. In these cases, it seems that the use of a leader to perform the global state recording in a centralized fashion is considerably more efficient. We discuss such a centralized approach in Section 5.2.2, aiming at their use in Chapter 10.

Throughout all of Section 5.2, G is taken to be a directed graph, so that the states of edges can be referred to without explicit mention to a particular direction. The extension to the undirected case is immediate, as usual.

5.2.1. An algorithm

In the case of synchronous algorithms, the recording of a global state can be achieved rather simply. At each pulse $s \geq 0$, the states of all nodes and the messages that were sent at pulse $s - 1$ (if $s > 0$), which by assumption must already have arrived at their destinations, constitute a global state. Without further communication, such a global state can be stored in G distributedly, so that a node stores its own state and the state of all edges on which it receives messages.

Clearly, though, nothing like this simple approach can be employed in the asynchronous case, owing to the total absence of global timing. However, with the aid of communication among the nodes in addition to that pertaining to the computation whose global state we wish to record, the task can also be performed for asynchronous algorithms. The algorithm that we discuss next is surprisingly simple given the apparent intricacy of the task, and yields a global state that can be found at the end of the algorithm stored in a distributed fashion throughout G, in much the same way as in the synchronous case we just discussed.

Before we introduce the algorithm for global state recording, it should be noted that, conceptually, we are dealing with two distributed computations. One of them, which we can refer to as the *substrate*, is the computation whose global properties one wishes to study, and then the global state one is seeking to record is a global state of the substrate. It is then to the substrate that the set of events Ξ introduced in Section 3.1 refers. The other distributed computation is an execution of the algorithm for global state recording, which we henceforth call Algorithm *A_Record_Global_State*. Both computations run on G, so each node is responsible for executing its share of the substrate and of Algorithm *A_Record_Global_State*. The two computations are, however, totally independent of each other as far as causality relationships are concerned. Our only assumption about their interaction is that Algorithm *A_Record_Global_State* is capable of "peeking" at the substrate's variables and messages with the purpose of recording a global state. Note that a node participates in both computations in such a way that, when the substrate is being executed by a node, Algorithm *A_Record_Global_State* is suspended, and conversely. This is immaterial from the standpoint of either computation, though. Having been designed to operate in the asynchronous model, the suspension of one to execute the other only adds to the asynchronism already present. Recording a global state during an execution of the substrate is essentially a means of "freezing" that execution in a snapshot (thence this alternative denomination for a global state) to analyze the states of all nodes and edges without actually having to halt the substrate.

This view of the computation at a node as actually comprising the node's participation in two different distributed algorithms is the view that we adopt in this section. What this amounts to when specifying the actions of Algorithm $A\_Record\_Global\_State$ is that there has to exist an action to handle the receipt of messages of the substrate, although in none of the algorithm's actions does one such message get sent. Alternatively, we might have viewed both computations as constituting the execution of a single algorithm, in which case the technique for recording global states would appear truly as a building block. When arguing formally about the recorded global state, however, we would have to be careful to discriminate events associated with the substrate from those associated with the additional communication employed by the recording algorithm, as it is to the former that the recorded global state relates.

The following is an outline of how Algorithm $A\_Record\_Global\_State$ functions. A node is responsible for recording the substrate's local state and the states of all edges directed toward itself. If all nodes carry their recording tasks to their ends, then the resulting overall recording is a system state, as introduced in Section 3.1, because a local state has been recorded for each node and a set of messages for each edge. The algorithm progresses through the exchange between neighbor nodes of a special message called $marker$. A node $n_i \in N_0$ initiates its participation in Algorithm $A\_Record\_Global\_State$ by recording the local state of the substrate, σ_i in the terminology of Section 3.1, and then sending $marker$ on all edges that are directed away from it, without however allowing the substrate to send any messages in the meantime (i.e., after the recording of the local state and before the sending of $marker$). In practice, this can be achieved by "disabling interrupts" so that the node will not switch to execute the other computation while this is undesired. All other nodes behave likewise upon receiving $marker$ for the first time. Every message of the substrate received at n_i from a neighbor n_j after n_i has received the first $marker$ (and consequently recorded a local state) and before n_i receives $marker$ from n_j is added to the set of messages representing Φ_{ji}, which is the state of edge $(n_j \to n_i)$ (cf. Section 3.1 for the appropriate terminology). The state of the edge on which $marker$ was first received is then recorded as the empty set, so the system state recorded by Algorithm $A\_Record\_Global\_State$ can be regarded as containing a forest of empty edges, each of whose trees spanning exactly one node in N_0. The recording is completed at a node when $marker$ has been received on all edges directed toward that node.

It is instructive at this point to notice the very close resemblance of the algorithm we just outlined to Algorithm A_PI, introduced in Section 4.1.1 for the propagation of information on G. While that algorithm was given for an undirected G, Algorithm $A\_Record\_Global\_State$ can be easily recognized as a variation of Algorithm PI to propagate $marker$ messages by flooding when G is a directed graph. Of course, the question of whether every node in G does ever receive a copy of $marker$ in the directed case arises, because there may exist nodes to which no directed path from a node in N_0 exists. One situation in which this can be guaranteed is, for example, the case of a strongly connected G, in which a directed path exists from every node to every other node.

Even before describing and analyzing Algorithm $A\_Record\_Global\_State$ more thoroughly, we are then in position to assess its complexities. Because every edge carries at most one copy of $marker$, the algorithm's message complexity is clearly $O(m)$. The algorithm's time complexity, on the other hand, depends only on how long it takes a $marker$ to reach a node that is not in N_0, and this is clearly $O(n)$ time.

In the description of Algorithm $A\_Record\_Global\_State$ we give next, sub_msg is used to generically denote a message of the substrate. A node n_i maintains a variable to store the substrate's local state at n_i, and for each neighbor $n_j \in I\_Neig_i$ a variable to store the state of edge $(n_j \rightarrow n_i)$. These variables are, respectively, $node\_state_i$ and $edge\_state_i^j$, initialized respectively to **nil** and $\emptyset$. In addition, a variable $recorded_i$ (initially equal to **false**) indicates whether the substrate's local state has already been recorded, and a variable $received_i^j$ for each $n_j \in I\_Neig_i$ (initialized to **false** as well) indicates whether $marker$ has been received from n_j. Clearly, for $n_i \notin N_0$, $recorded_i = $ **true** if and only if $received_i^j = $ **true** for some $n_j \in I\_Neig_i$.

> **Algorithm** $A\_Record\_Global\_State$:

>> ▷ **Variables:**
>> $node_state_i = $ **nil**;
>> $edge\_state_i^j = \emptyset$ for all $n_j \in I\_Neig_i$;
>> $recorded_i = $ **false**;
>> $received_i^j = $ **false** for all $n_j \in I\_Neig_i$.

▷ **Input:**

$msg_i = $ **nil**.

Action if $n_i \in N_0$: $\qquad\qquad\qquad\qquad\qquad\qquad\qquad$ (5.11)

$node\_state_i := \sigma_i;$

$recorded_i := $ **true**;

Send *marker* to all $n_j \in O\_Neig_i$.

▷ **Input:**

$msg_i = marker$ such that $origin_i(msg_i) = (n_j \rightarrow n_i)$.

Action: $\qquad\qquad\qquad\qquad\qquad\qquad\qquad\qquad\qquad\qquad\quad$ (5.12)

$received_i^j := $ **true**;

if not $recorded_i$ **then**

$\qquad$ **begin**

$\qquad\qquad node\_state_i := \sigma_i;$

$\qquad\qquad recorded_i := $ **true**;

$\qquad\qquad$ Send *marker* to all $n_k \in O\_Neig_i$.

$\qquad$ **end**.

▷ **Input:**

$msg_i = sub\_msg$ such that $origin_i(msg_i) = (n_j \rightarrow n_i)$.

Action: $\qquad\qquad\qquad\qquad\qquad\qquad\qquad\qquad\qquad\qquad\quad$ (5.13)

if $recorded_i$ **then**

$\qquad$ **if not** $received_i^j$ **then**

$\qquad\qquad edge\_state_i^j := edge\_state_i^j \cup \{msg_i\}.$

There are two important observations to be made concerning Algorithm *A_Record_Global_State*. The first observation is that the assumed atomicity of actions in Algorithm *A_Template* (cf. Section 2.1) suffices to prevent a node from executing the substrate computation, possibly with the sending of messages, between the recording of the local state and the sending of *marker*'s in (5.11) and (5.12). The second observation concerns (5.13) and the *sub_msg* messages that trigger this action. Because such messages are in fact messages of the substrate, the actions that they trigger do not really belong in a presentation of Algorithm *A_Record_Global_State* based on Algorithm *A_Template*. In fact, we have made no provisions whatsoever to denote an algorithm's peeking at some other algorithm's messages, so that our notation in the description of Algorithm *A_Record_Global_State* is abusive. One of the problems caused by this abuse of notation is that Algorithm *A_Record_Global_State* does not seem to terminate as long as there are *sub_msg*'s in transit on G's edges, while clearly the algorithm is to terminate as soon as every node n_i has received as many *marker*'s as there are edges in In_i (cf. Section 6.2). As long as these issues are clearly understood, however, our slightly licentious use of the notation should not be troublesome. We keep the improper notation for simplicity (here and in other occasions, as in Section 9.3.3), although it appears that adapting Algorithm *A_Template* to properly contemplate such an interaction between two distributed algorithms is a simple matter (cf. Exercise 5).

Theorem 5.5 states two sufficient conditions for the system state that Algorithm *A_Record_Global_State* records to be a global state.

Theorem 5.5. *If G is strongly connected and all of its edges are FIFO, then the system state that Algorithm A_Record_Global_State records is a global state.*

Proof: The fact that G is strongly connected implies that every node n_i receives *marker* exactly once on every edge in In_i, by (5.11) and (5.12).

Recalling that Ξ is the set of events related to the substrate only, let (Ξ_1, Ξ_2) be a partition of Ξ such that $\xi \in \Xi_1$ if and only if ξ occurred before the local state of the node at which it occurred was recorded. In addition, referring back to the notation introduced in Section 3.1, let $\prec_t^+$ be any total order of the events in Ξ consistent with $\prec^+$, and consider two consecutive events $\xi_2 \in \Xi_2$ and $\xi_1 \in \Xi_1$ in $\prec_t^+$.

By the definition of Ξ_1 and of Ξ_2, it is clear that ξ_2 did not happen at the same node as ξ_1 and before the occurrence of ξ_1. Now consider a scenario in which a sequence of events follow ξ_2 at the node at which it happened, and then a message is sent in connection with the last event in this sequence, which in turn eventually causes the sending of another message by its destination node, and then the eventual sending of another message by the destination node of this second message, and so on, and then the arrival of the last message causes a sequence of events to happen at its destination node culminating with the occurrence of ξ_1. By (5.11) and (5.12), and by the definition of Ξ_1 and Ξ_2, the node at which ξ_2 happened must have sent *marker*'s before ξ_2 happened. Likewise, the node at which ξ_1 happened must not have received any *marker* before ξ_1 happened. Clearly, these two requirements are inconsistent with the scenario we just described, as the edges are all FIFO, and the sequence of messages alluded to in the description of the scenario would then have to have been overrun by a *marker*. In summary, $(\xi_2, \xi_1) \notin \prec^+$, so the total order $\prec_t^+$ can be altered by substituting (ξ_1, ξ_2) for (ξ_2, ξ_1) in it, and yet remain consistent with $\prec^+$.

Clearly, it takes no more than $|\Xi_1||\Xi_2|$ such substitutions to obtain a total order in which at most one pair (ξ_1, ξ_2) of consecutive events exists such that $\xi_1 \in \Xi_1$

and $\xi_2 \in \Xi_2$. The events in all other pairs of consecutive events are in this total order both in Ξ_1 or in Ξ_2. By (5.11) through (5.13), and by the definition of Ξ_1 and Ξ_2, this distinguished pair of consecutive events is such that $system\_state(\xi_1, \xi_2)$ is precisely the system state recorded by Algorithm $A\_Record\_Global\_State$, which is then a global state, by our first definition of global states in Section 3.1. ∎

Before we finalize this section, there are a couple of important observations to be made regarding Algorithm $A\_Record\_Global\_State$. The first observation is that, as we mentioned previously, the global state that the algorithm records is stored in a distributed fashion among G's nodes. Often the recorded global state can be used without having to be concentrated on a single node for analysis (cf. Section 6.3.2 for an example), but equally as frequently it must first be concentrated on a leader, which then works on the global state in a centralized manner.

The second observation is that the global state that the algorithm records is in principle any global state, in the sense that no control is provided to make "choices" regarding desirable characteristics of the resulting global state. While this is fine for many applications (as for example the detection of the stable properties we treat in Chapter 6), for others it does matter which global state is used, and then a centralized approach may be advisable. We elaborate on this a little more in Section 5.2.2.

We end the discussion in this section by returning to the issue of knowledge in distributed computations, treated in Section 2.3, in order to illustrate one of the concepts introduced in that section. Specifically, let $\mathcal{P}$ be any sentence related to a global state that has been recorded by Algorithm $A\_Record\_Global\_State$. Because of the distributed fashion in which this global state is stored after it is recorded, $\mathcal{P}$ is clearly implicit knowledge that the members of N have, that is, $I_N\mathcal{P}$.

5.2.2. Some centralized alternatives

In this section, we briefly comment on two centralized alternatives to the recording of global states, drawing mainly on motivations to be found in Chapter 10. As we mentioned in the previous section, these centralized alternatives are a solution when the global state that one seeks to record cannot be just any global state, but instead must be a global state with certain specific characteristics.

The first case that we examine is that of a computation for which it is known that the system state in which every node n_i is in the kth local state in the sequence Σ_i (cf. Section 3.1) for some $k \geq 1$ is a global state. This is the case, for example, of the algorithms we discuss in Section 10.2, where for $k > 1$ a function of the kth such global state has to be compared with the result of applying the same function to the $k - 1$st such global state, regardless of whatever messages may be in transit on the edges. It turns out that computing such a function of a global state is a trivial task if done by a single node, and because the edge states do not matter, the natural choice is for every node n_i to report every new local state to a leader, which then performs the necessary function evaluation and global state comparison whenever a new global state is completed with information received from the other nodes.

The second case is motivated by the needs of Sections 10.3.2 and 10.6, where in the global states to be recorded every edge state must be the empty set. Again, a centralized approach is preferable because it renders the task of checking for empty edges quite simple. The approach is then the following. Whenever a node n_i is in a local state with which it may participate in a global state of interest (or simply periodically), it sends the leader this local state, together with the numbers of messages it has so far received on each edge in In_i and sent on each edge in Out_i. Whenever the information the leader receives from all nodes is such that the number of messages sent on each edge is equal to the number of messages received on that edge, the corresponding system state is surely a global state, because every system state in which all edges are empty is a global state (cf. Exercise 7).

5.3. Network synchronization

This section is dedicated to the third major design technique to be discussed in this chapter, namely network synchronization. As we have anticipated in various occasions, especially in Sections 2.1 and 3.3, a synchronous algorithm can be turned into an asynchronous algorithm at the expense of additional message and time complexities, so that the lack of a global time basis and of bounds on delays for message delivery can be dealt with, and the resulting algorithm can be guaranteed to function as in the synchronous model.

As we remarked in Section 3.3 when presenting Algorithm *S-to-A_Template*, essentially the technique of network synchronization amounts to determining that a node n_i that has been executing the action corresponding to pulse $s \geq 0$ of the synchronous algorithm is ready to proceed to pulse $s + 1$ under the asynchronous model. In Algorithm *S-to-A_Template*, such a decision is embodied in a Boolean function $\text{DONE}_i(s_i)$, where s_i is a variable that indicates the interval n_i is currently involved with.

Our approach in this section is to take G to be an undirected graph, and then consider a generic synchronous algorithm, call it Algorithm *S_Alg*, written in accordance with Algorithm *S_Template* of Section 2.1. The asynchronous algorithm resulting from translating Algorithm *S_Alg* into the asynchronous model will be called Algorithm *A_Alg(Sync)*, where *Sync* indicates the particular technique, or *synchronizer*, employed in the translation. In essence, Algorithm *A_Alg(Sync)* follows Algorithm *S-to-A_Template*.

The essential property that we seek to preserve in translating Algorithm *S_Alg* into Algorithm *A_Alg(Sync)* is that no node n_i proceeds to pulse $s + 1$ before all messages sent to it at pulse s have been delivered and incorporated into $MSG_i(s)$ (the reader should recall from Sections 2.1 and 3.3 that this is the set of messages sent to n_i at pulse s). In order to ensure that this property holds for all nodes and at all pulses, we begin by requiring that all messages of Algorithm *S_Alg* be acknowledged. These messages are denoted by *comp_msg*, and the acknowledgements by *ack*. A node is said to be *safe* with respect to pulse s if and only if it has received an *ack* for every *comp_msg* it sent at pulse s. In order to guarantee that our essential property holds for n_i at pulse s, it then suffices that n_i receive information stating that every one of its neighbors is safe with respect to pulse s. The task of a synchronizer is then to convey this information to all nodes concerning all pulses of the synchronous computation.

A synchronizer is then to be understood as an asynchronous algorithm that is repeated at every pulse of Algorithm *S_Alg* in order to convey to all nodes the safety information we have identified as fundamental. Now let *Messages(Alg)* and *Time(Alg)* denote, respectively, the message complexity and the time complexity of a distributed algorithm *Alg* (synchronous or asynchronous). Then *Messages(Sync)* and *Time(Sync)* stand for the message and time complexities, respectively, introduced by Synchronizer *Sync* per pulse of Algorithm *S_Alg* to yield Algorithm *A_Alg(Sync)*. These two quantities constitute the *synchronization overhead* introduced by Synchronizer *Sync*.

Regardless of how Synchronizer *Sync* operates, we can already draw some conclusions regarding the final complexities of Algorithm *A_Alg(Sync)*. Let us, first of all, recognize that the use of the *ack* messages does not add to the message complexity of Algorithm *S_Alg*, as exactly one *ack* is sent per *comp_msg*. Considering in addition that *Messages(Sync)* is the message complexity introduced by Synchronizer *Sync* per pulse of the execution of Algorithm *S_Alg*, and that there are *Time(S_Alg)* such pulses, we then have

$$Messages\big(A\_Alg(Sync)\big)$$
$$= Messages(S\_Alg) + Time(S\_Alg)Messages(Sync) + Messages_0(Sync),$$

where $Messages_0(Sync)$ is the message complexity, if any, that Synchronizer $Sync$ incurs with initialization procedures.

Similarly, as $Time(Sync)$ is the time complexity introduced by Synchronizer $Sync$ per each of the $Time(S\_Alg)$ pulses of Algorithm S_Alg, we have

$$Time\big(A\_Alg(Sync)\big) = Time(S\_Alg)\,Time(Sync) + Time_0(Sync),$$

where $Time_0(Sync)$ refers to the time, if any, needed by Synchronizer $Sync$ to be initialized.

Depending on how Synchronizer $Sync$ is designed, the resulting complexities $Messages\big(A\_Alg(Sync)\big)$ and $Time\big(A\_Alg(Sync)\big)$ can vary considerably. In Section 5.3.1, we discuss three types of general synchronizers, and in Section 5.3.2 consider some special variations of interest.

5.3.1. General synchronizers

The essential task of a synchronizer is to convey to every node and for every pulse the information that all of the node's neighbors are safe with respect to that pulse. This safety information indicates that the node's neighbors have received an ack for every $comp\_msg$ they sent at that pulse, and therefore the node may proceed to the next pulse.

The first synchronizer we present is known as Synchronizer $Alpha$. The material that we present in Section 5.3.2 comprises variants of this synchronizer. In Synchronizer $Alpha$, the information that all of a node's neighbors are safe with respect to pulse $s \geq 0$ is conveyed directly by each of those neighbors by means of a $safe(s)$ message. A node may then proceed to pulse $s + 1$ when it has received a $safe(s)$ from each of its neighbors. Clearly, we have

$$Messages(Alpha) = O(m)$$

and

$$Time(Alpha) = O(1),$$

as a $safe$ message is sent between each pair of neighbors in each direction, and causes no effect that propagates farther than one edge away. We also have $Messages_0(Alpha) = Time_0(Alpha) = 0$.

Algorithm $A\_Alg(Alpha)$ is described next. In this section, we do not assume that edges are FIFO, and for this reason $comp\_msg$'s and ack's sent in connection with pulse $s \geq 0$ are sent as $comp\_msg(s)$ and $ack(s)$ (cf. Exercise 8). In Algorithm $A\_Alg(Alpha)$, node n_i maintains, in addition to the variables employed by

Algorithm *S-to-A_Template*, the following others. A variable $expected_i(s)$, initially equal to zero, records for all $s \geq 0$ the number of $ack(s)$'s n_i expects. This variable is assumed to be incremented accordingly whenever n_i sends $comp\_msg(s)$'s, although this is part of the "Send one message..." that generically appears in all our templates and then the sending of the messages is not explicitly shown. Node n_i also maintains a variable $safe_i^j(s)$ for each neighbor n_j and all $s \geq 0$, initially set to **false** and used to indicate whether a $safe(s)$ has been received from n_j.

Despite the simplicity of Synchronizer *Alpha*, designing the initial actions of Algorithm *A_Alg(Alpha)* requires that we reason carefully along the following lines. A node in N_0 behaves initially just as it would in the synchronous model. A node that is not in N_0, however, although in Algorithm *S_Alg* it might remain idle for any number of pulses, in Algorithm *A_Alg(Alpha)* it must take actions corresponding to every pulse, because otherwise its neighbors would never receive the *safe* messages that it should send and then not progress in the computation. The way we approach this is by employing an additional message, called *startup*, which is sent by the nodes in N_0 to all of their neighbors when they start computing. This message, upon reaching a node that is not in N_0 for the first time, serves the purpose of "waking" that node up and then gets forwarded by it to all of its neighbors as well. Loosely, this *startup* message can be though of as a "$safe(-1)$" message that is propagated in the manner of Algorithm *A_PI* of Section 4.1.1, and is intended to convey to the nodes that are not in N_0 the information that they should participate in pulse $s = 0$ too, as well as in all other pulses (although for $s > 0$ this can be taken for granted by the functioning of Synchronizer *Alpha*). All nodes, including those in N_0, only proceed to executing pulse $s = 0$ of the synchronous computation upon receiving a *startup* from every neighbor. This is controlled by a variable go_i^j, initially set to **false**, maintained by n_i for every neighbor n_j to indicate whether a *startup* has been received from n_j. An additional variable, $initiated_i$, initially set to **false** as well, indicates whether $n_i \in N_0$.

Algorithm *A_Alg(Alpha)*:

▷ **Variables:**

$s_i = 0$;
$MSG_i(s) = \emptyset$ for all $s \geq 0$;
$initiated_i = \mathbf{false}$;
$go_i^j = \mathbf{false}$ for all $n_j \in Neig_i$;
$expected_i(s) = 0$ for all $s \geq 0$;
$safe_i^j(s) = \mathbf{false}$ for all $n_j \in Neig_i$ and all $s \geq 0$.

▷ **Input:**
    $msg_i = $ **nil.**
  Action if $n_i \in N_0$:   (5.14)
        $initiated_i := $ **true;**
        Send $startup$ to all $n_j \in Neig_i$.

▷ **Input:**
    $msg_i = startup$ such that $origin_i(msg_i) = (n_i, n_j)$.
  Action: (5.15)
        if not $initiated_i$ **then**
              begin
                    $initiated_i := $ **true;**
                    Send $startup$ to all $n_k \in Neig_i$
              end;
        $go_i^j := $ **true;**
        if go_i^j for all $n_j \in Neig_i$ **then**
              begin
                    Do some computation;
                    Send one $comp\_msg(s_i)$ on each edge of a (possibly empty)
                    subset of Inc_i;
                    if $expected_i(s_i) = 0$ **then**
                          Send $safe(s_i)$ to all $n_k \in Neig_i$
              end.

▷ **Input:**
    $msg_i = comp\_msg(s)$ such that $origin_i(msg_i) = (n_i, n_j)$.
  Action: (5.16)
        $MSG_i(s + 1) := MSG_i(s + 1) \cup \{msg_i\}$;
        Send $ack(s)$ to n_j.

▷ **Input:**
    $msg_i = ack(s)$.
  Action: (5.17)
        $expected_i(s) := expected_i(s) - 1$;
        if $expected_i(s) = 0$ **then**
              Send $safe(s)$ to all $n_j \in Neig_i$.

▷ **Input:**

$msg_i = safe(s)$ such that $origin_i(msg_i) = (n_i, n_j)$.

Action: (5.18)

$safe_i^j(s) :=$ **true**;

if $safe_i^k(s_i)$ for all $n_k \in Neig_i$ **then**

> **begin**
>
> > $s_i := s_i + 1$;
> >
> > Do some computation;
> >
> > Send one $comp\_msg(s_i)$ on each edge of a (possibly empty) subset of Inc_i;
> >
> > **if** $expected_i(s_i) = 0$ **then**
> >
> > > Send $safe(s_i)$ to all $n_k \in Neig_i$
>
> **end**.

As we indicated earlier, Algorithm $A\_Alg(Alpha)$ can be viewed as a specialization of Algorithm $S\text{-}to\text{-}A\_Template$ when the synchronization technique is Synchronizer $Alpha$. Indeed, the reader may without any difficulty check that (5.14) and (5.15) essentially do the job of (3.3), although the former involve nodes that are not in N_0 while the latter does not. Similarly, (5.16) through (5.18) offer a detailed view of (3.4) under the rules of Synchronizer $Alpha$. In particular, $\text{DONE}_i(s_i)$ returns a **true** value in (3.4) if and only if $safe_i^j(s_i) = $ **true** for all $n_j \in Neig_i$ in (5.18).

Synchronizer $Alpha$ is only one of the possibilities. For generic synchronous computations like Algorithm S_Alg, there are two other synchronizers of interest. The first one is called Synchronizer $Beta$, and requires for its operation a spanning tree already established on G, so the initial complexities $Messages_0(Beta)$ and $Time_0(Beta)$ are no longer equal to zero, but depend instead on the distributed algorithm used to generate the tree (cf. Section 7.1.2). These complexities must also account for the election of a leader, which, as we mentioned in Section 5.1, may be carried out rather closely to the construction of the spanning tree (cf. Section 7.1.1, and Section 7.1.2 as well).

The function of the leader in Synchronizer $Beta$ is to gather from all other nodes the safety information needed to proceed to further pulses, and then broadcast this information to all of them. The specifics of this procedure are the following. When a node that is not the leader becomes safe with respect to a certain pulse and has received a *safe* message from all but one of its neighbors on the tree, it then sends a *safe* message to the single neighbor from which it did not receive a *safe* (the tree edge connecting to this neighbor leads towards the leader). The leader, upon receiving *safe* messages on all the tree edges that are incident to it, and being itself safe with respect to that pulse, broadcasts a message on the tree indicating that the computation of a new pulse may be undertaken. This message may be a *safe* message as well, and then the rule for a node to proceed to another pulse is to do it after having received a *safe* message on all tree edges incident to it.

Once the leader has been elected and the spanning tree built, the asynchronous algorithm that results from applying Synchronizer *Beta* to Algorithm *S_Alg*, Algorithm *A_Alg(Beta)*, is initiated as follows. The leader broadcasts on the tree that all nodes may begin the computation of pulse $s = 0$.

Clearly, the messages that Synchronizer *Beta* introduces traverse only tree edges, so we have

$$Messages(Beta) = O(n)$$

and

$$Time(Beta) = O(n).$$

For generic computations, Synchronizer *Beta* does better than Synchronizer *Alpha* in terms of message complexity, whereas the reverse holds in terms of time complexity.

The other synchronizer of interest, called Synchronizer *Gamma*, arises from a combination of Synchronizers *Alpha* and *Beta*. In this combination, nodes are conceptually grouped into clusters. Inside clusters, Synchronizer *Gamma* operates as Synchronizer *Alpha*; among clusters, it operates as Synchronizer *Beta*. The size and disposition of clusters are regulated by a parameter k such that $2 \leq k < n$, and in such a way that Synchronizer *Gamma*'s complexities are

$$Messages(Gamma) = O(kn)$$

and

$$Time(Gamma) = O\left(\frac{\log n}{\log k}\right).$$

As k varies, Synchronizer *Gamma* resembles more Synchronizer *Alpha* or Synchronizer *Beta*. Once again the costs of initialization $Messages_0(Gamma)$ and $Time_0(Gamma)$ are nonzero and depend on the mechanisms utilized. Values that can be attained for these measures are $Messages_0(Gamma) = O(kn^2)$ and $Time_0(Gamma) = O(n \log n / \log k)$.

Something instructive for the reader to do, having become acquainted with the synchronizers we discussed in this section, is to return to the various synchronous algorithms we have already seen in the book and assess their complexities when each of the three synchronizers is employed. Some of the conclusions to be drawn from this assessment are the following. First, no synchronizer can beat the complexities of Algorithm *A_Compute_f* when applied to either Algorithm *S_Compute_AND* or Algorithm *S_Locally_Orient*. Secondly, Synchronizer *Alpha* (the only one whose application to a synchronous leader election algorithm is meaningful), when applied to Algorithm *S_Elect_Leader_C*, does not yield improvements over the complexity of Algorithm *A_Elect_Leader_C*.

What these two conclusions indicate is that synchronizers do not necessarily lead to better complexities when compared with asynchronous algorithms that were designed without recourse to synchronization techniques. However, as we remarked at the end of Section 3.4 in the context of establishing a breadth-first numbering on the nodes of a directed graph, historically there have been occasions in which such improvements were obtained. Incidentally, it may also be an instructive exercise for the reader to verify that the complexities claimed in that occasion for the asynchronous solution obtained from the synchronous one are consistent with the message and time complexities of Synchronizer *Gamma* as discussed in this section. (Although in this section G is taken to be undirected, no conflict exists when addressing the computation for breadth-first numbering discussed in Section 3.4. The graph is in that case a directed graph, and it is on such a graph that the synchronous algorithm operates. On the other hand, the synchronizer, and consequently the resulting asynchronous algorithm, operate on the corresponding undirected graph, essentially by being allowed to send synchronization-related messages against the direction of the edges when needed—cf. Exercise 10.)

In Chapter 7, when we discuss algorithms to find maximum flows in networks, synchronizers will come to the fore once again in the book.

5.3.2. Important special cases

Of the synchronous algorithms we have seen so far in the book, another that deserves our attention in the light of a synchronizer is Algorithm *S_Compute_Distances*, introduced in Section 4.3 for the computation of the shortest distances among all pairs of nodes in G. As we claimed in that section, this algorithm yields Algorithm *A_Compute_Distances*, also introduced in Section 4.3, through the utilization of a synchronizer. Interestingly, and contrary to the intuition we built during our study in the previous section, both algorithms have the same message and time complexities. The reason for this is that the synchronizer employed to transform the synchronous algorithm into the asynchronous one is a particular case of Synchronizer *Alpha*, as we discuss next.

Let us first, however, examine the following scenario in the context of Synchronizer *Alpha*. Suppose, for the sake of example, that node n_i has two neighbors, n_j and n_k. Suppose further that n_j has only one neighbor (n_i) and that n_k has many neighbors. Consider the situation in which n_i has just become safe with respect to pulse $s \geq 0$ and then sends $safe(s)$ to n_j and n_k. Node n_i can only proceed to pulse $s + 1$ after receiving similar messages from its two neighbors. Suppose that such a message has been received from n_j but not from n_k (which depends on many more neighbors other than n_i to become safe with respect to pulse s). It is possible at this moment that a $safe(s + 1)$ too is received from n_j before the $safe(s)$ from n_k arrives, at which time n_i will have received two $safe$ messages from n_j without the respective counterparts from n_k, and will therefore be unable to proceed to pulse $s + 1$ immediately. It is simple to see, nevertheless, that n_j will at this time be unable to proceed to pulse $s + 2$, as it now depends on a $safe(s + 1)$ from n_i. If we compute the number of $safe$ messages n_i has received since the beginning of the computation from its two neighbors, we will see that the numbers corresponding to n_j and n_k differ by no more than two. The particular topological situation we described was meant to help the understanding of this issue, but the maximum difference we just stated is true in general.

This relative "boundedness," when coupled with the assumption that all edges are FIFO, allows various simplifications to be carried out on Algorithm $A\_Alg(Alpha)$. For one thing, no message or variable needs to depend explicitly on s any longer, so that the "per-pulse bit complexity" of Synchronizer *Alpha*, which we have not introduced formally but clearly might be unbounded, becomes constant. In addition, under the FIFO assumption ack's are no longer needed, and n_i may send $safe$ messages to all of its neighbors immediately upon completion of its computation for the corresponding pulse. Such $safe$ messages will certainly be delivered after the $comp\_msg$'s sent during that computation, indicating that every such message sent by n_i during the current pulse has already arrived.

We now present a version of Algorithm $A\_Alg(Alpha)$ in which edges are assumed to be FIFO, and, in addition, the following important assumption is made. At each pulse $s \geq 0$, node n_i sends exactly one $comp\_msg$ to each of its neighbors. These two assumptions allow *startup*, *ack*, and *safe* messages to be done away with altogether, and so render the variables go_i^j, $expected_i$, and $safe_i^j$ useless for all neighbors n_j of n_i. Also, the sets $MSG_i(s)$ for $s \geq 0$ are no longer needed; instead, one single set MSG_i for use at all pulses suffices, as we see next.

The behavior of n_i is now considerably simpler, and goes as follows. It starts upon receiving the first $comp\_msg$ (unless it belongs to N_0), and proceeds to the next pulse upon receiving exactly one $comp\_msg$ from each of its neighbors. However, it is still possible to receive two consecutive *comp_msg*'s from one neighbor without having received any *comp_msg* from another neighbor. This issue is essentially the same we discussed above concerning the reception of multiple *safe* messages from a same neighbor, and some control mechanism has to be adopted. What we need is, for each neighbor, a queue with one single position in which *comp_msg*'s received from that neighbor are kept until they can be incorporated into MSG_i. (From our previous discussion, it would seem that two-position queues are needed. However, we can think of MSG_i as containing the queue heads for all of n_i's queues.) We then let $queue_i^j$ denote this queue at n_i for neighbor n_j. The new version we present is called Algorithm *A_Schedule_AS* ("AS" for Alpha Synchronization), in allusion to its use in Section 10.2.

> **Algorithm** *A_Schedule_AS*:

> ▷ **Variables:**
>> $s_i = 0$;
>> $MSG_i = \emptyset$;
>> $initiated_i =$ **false**;
>> $queue_i^j =$ **nil** for all $n_j \in Neig_i$.

> ▷ **Input:**
>> $msg_i =$ **nil**.
>> **Action if** $n_i \in N_0$:   (5.19)
>>> $initiated_i :=$ **true**;
>>> Do some computation;
>>> Send exactly one *comp_msg* on each edge of Inc_i.

▷ **Input:**
$msg_i = comp\_msg$ such that $origin_i(msg_i) = (n_i, n_j)$.

Action: (5.20)

    if not $initiated_i$ **then**

        begin

            $initiated_i := $ **true**;

            Do some computation;

            Send exactly one $comp\_msg$ on each edge of Inc_i

        end;

    if there exists $msg \in MSG_i$ such that $origin_i(msg) = n_j$ **then**

        $queue_i^j := msg_i$

    else

        $MSG_i := MSG_i \cup \{msg_i\}$;

    if $|MSG_i| = |Neig_i|$ **then**

        begin

            $s_i := s_i + 1$;

            Do some computation;

            Send exactly one $comp\_msg$ on each edge of Inc_i;

            $MSG_i := \emptyset$;

            for all $n_k \in Neig_i$ **do**

                $MSG_i := MSG_i \cup \{queue_i^k\}$;

            $queue_i^k := $ **nil** for all $n_k \in Neig_i$

    end.

In Algorithm *A_Schedule_AS*, (5.19) and (5.20) reflect the considerable simplification that the assumptions of this section entail with respect to Algorithm *A_Alg(Alpha)*. In addition to the elimination of many messages and variables with respect to that algorithm, it should also be noted that, unless n_i employs the value of s_i for its computation at any pulse, this variable too may be eliminated.

When comparing this algorithm with the general template given by Algorithm *S-to-A_Template*, one verifies that $\text{DONE}_i(s_i)$ returns **true** in (3.4) if and only if $|MSG_i| = |Neig_i|$ in (5.20), although the dependency on s_i is no longer explicit, as MSG_i is a single set for use at all pulses.

We are now in position to return to the problem of computing shortest distances where we left it in Section 4.3. Clearly, Algorithm *S_Compute_Distances* complies with the assumption of this section that every node sends exactly one message to every one of its neighbors at all pulses. This, combined with the assumption of FIFO edges, allows a corresponding synchronous algorithm to be obtained along the lines of Algorithm *A_Schedule_AS*. Indeed, it should take little effort to realize that Algorithm *A_Compute_Distances* is merely an instance of Algorithm *A_Schedule_AS* (cf. Exercise 11). Because the latter, when viewed as a synchronous algorithm that underwent synchronization, does not contain any synchronization overhead, the complexities of Algorithm *A_Compute_Distances* are indeed the same as those of Algorithm *S_Compute_Distances*.

5.4. Exercises

1. Show that a leader can only be elected if in G all nodes have distinct identifications.

2. Discuss what happens to Algorithm *S_Elect_Leader_C* if the base is no longer 2, but rather c such that $2 \leq c < n - 1$.

3. Consider the $O(n^2)$-message, $O(1)$-time synchronous algorithm that we discussed in Section 5.1 for leader election on a complete graph, and discuss how it can be adapted to the asynchronous case. Show that the message complexity remains the same, but the time complexity becomes $O(n)$. Compare the resulting algorithm with Algorithm *A_Elect_Leader_C*.

4. Derive a leader-election algorithm from multiple executions of Algorithm *A_PI*.

5. Discuss alternatives to Algorithm *A_Template* that allow the treatment of messages belonging to another computation as well. Show how this affects the way Algorithm *A_Record_Global_State* is expressed.

6. Consider a computation in which nodes halt independently of one another, and consider the system state in which all nodes are halted. Is this system state a global state? If it is, is it completely known to the nodes?

7. Show that every system state in which all edges are empty is a global state.

8. Discuss what may happen if the pulse number is omitted from the messages *comp_msg* and *ack* in Algorithm *A_Alg(Alpha)* when edges are not FIFO.

9. In the context of Section 1.5, find the $r(c)$'s for Algorithm *A_Schedule_AS*.

10. Discuss the fundamental alterations synchronizers must undergo when G is a directed graph.

11. Discuss in detail the reasons why Algorithm *A_Compute_Distances* is an instance of Algorithm *A_Schedule_AS*.

12. Explain how to modify Algorithm *A_Compute_Distances* so that useless work is avoided after all distances have been determined (instead of keeping running up to the maximum possible distance of $n - 1$).

5.5. Bibliographic notes

The impossibility of electing leaders in the absence of distinct identifications for all nodes is discussed in Angluin (1980). Our treatment in Section 5.1 is based on Afek and Gafni (1991). Many other authors have investigated the problem of electing a leader under various restrictions on G, including synchronous rings (Overmars and Santoro, 1989; Bodlaender and Tel, 1990) and cases in which G is directed (Afek and Gafni, 1994). Awerbuch (1987) has addressed the problem for generic graphs, and appears to have given the first time-optimal algorithm to solve it—cf. Section 7.4. Additional work on leader election includes the contributions by Peleg (1990), Singh (1992), Tsaan Huang (1993), and Singh and Kurose (1994).

Most of Section 5.2 is based on the seminal work by Chandy and Lamport (1985). Other authors have recently addressed the problem of global state recording in different contexts, as for example Acharya and Badrinath (1992), Alagar and Venkatesan (1994), and Saleh, Ural, and Agarwal (1994). Applications of algorithms for global state recording other than those presented in other chapters can be found in Chaves Filho and Barbosa (1992) and in Choy and Singh (1993), in both cases for scheduling purposes.

A great portion of Section 5.3 is based on the work in which synchronizers were first introduced (Awerbuch, 1985a). Further developments on the theme can be looked up in Awerbuch and Peleg (1990), Shabtay and Segall (1992), Garofalakis, Spirakis, Tampakas, and Rajsbaum (1994), and Rajsbaum and Sidi (1994).

Distributed snapshots and synchronizers are often regarded as essential building blocks for the design of distributed algorithms in general. The reader interested in such a view of the design of distributed algorithms may refer to Gafni (1986), and to additional publications in which techniques with potential to occupy similar positions as building blocks have been introduced (Afek, Awerbuch, and Gafni, 1987; Afek and Ricklin, 1993).

Part 2

Advances and Applications

This second part of the book comprises five additional chapters, each dedicated to a class of problems for which distributed algorithms have been devised. These algorithms constitute advances on the basic algorithms and techniques introduced in the chapters of Part 1, and are in most cases geared toward particular classes of applications.

Chapter 6 contains a study of stable properties from the standpoints of self-stabilization and of stability detection. The investigation of self-stabilizing computations may be ultimately applicable to the recovery from faults, while the detection of stability finds much more immediate applicability, for example in the areas of termination and deadlock detection, both discussed in the chapter.

Chapter 7 expands on material seen previously in Part 1 (Chapters 4 and 5) with the study of two graph problems. The first graph problem is that of finding a minimum spanning tree on a graph, and relates directly to the leader election problem, studied in Chapter 5. The second graph problem is that of finding a maximum flow in a graph with a few special features. This problem, like those seen in Chapter 4, are related to problems in the operation of distributed-memory systems.

Chapter 8 is dedicated to the study of distributed algorithms to ensure mutual exclusion in the access to shared resources, while guaranteeing deadlock- and starvation-freedom as well. This problem is studied from two broad perspectives, which in essence can be reduced to the sharing of one single resource or of multiple resources concomitantly. One of the algorithms studied in this chapter provides the basis for part of the discussion in Chapter 10.

Techniques for the deterministic re-execution of distributed algorithms in an asynchronous setting, and for detecting breakpoints during executions of such algorithms, are studied in Chapter 9. Both problems constitute essential parts of the process of program debugging, and present difficulties far beyond those encountered in a sequential setting. For the detection of breakpoints, we restrict our attention to a few classes of breakpoints only.

Chapter 10 contains material on the distributed simulation of physical systems, which are models of natural systems occurring in various scientific fields. We present approaches for two broad classes of systems, called the time-stepped and event-driven approaches. Within the latter, we expand on the so-called conservative and optimistic methods. The chapter also contains a brief discussion of methods for systems that do not exactly fall into either of the two classes, as well as a short digression on how the various approaches may be unified.

6

Stable Properties

A *stable property* is a global property of G that holds for all global states in the future of a global state for which it holds. This chapter is devoted to the study of stable properties from two essentially distinct perspectives. The first perspective is that of ensuring that a stable property is achieved regardless of the initial global state, and the second perspective is that of detecting that a stable property holds for some global state.

We address stable properties as a desired goal from any initial global state in Section 6.1, where we relate such a type of behavior to the issue of fault-tolerance. Although fault-tolerance is outside the intended scope of this book, our approach in Section 6.1 blends quite well with material to be studied in Chapter 8, and in addition provides us with the opportunity to discuss a class of distributed algorithms exhibiting nontrivial stable behavior for any initial global state.

The second perspective from which we study stable properties is the perspective of stability detection, more specifically the detection of the termination of distributed computations and the detection of deadlocks. This second perspective contrasts with the first one not only because of widely differing objectives (achieving stability, in the former case, as opposed to detecting it, in the latter), but also because termination and deadlocks are far from the sort of stable properties one is seeking to achieve in the former case.

Termination detection is treated in Section 6.2, where we discuss techniques for detecting the termination of distributed computations in general and of distributed computations that that are of the diffusing type. These, as we will see, are characterized by the fact that N_0 is a singleton.

In Section 6.3, we discuss the detection of deadlocks in a distributed computation. Because deadlocks can occur in a variety of situations, and under assumptions that differ widely from one case to another, in Section 6.3 we concentrate on a distributed computation that controls the providing of services by the nodes to one another. Such a computation, as we describe it in that section, is deadlock-prone. The algorithm that we provide to detect the occurrence of deadlocks is very elegantly contrived, and moreover allows techniques that we have seen previously in the book, chiefly in Chapter 4, to be exercised.

Exercises and bibliographic notes appear, respectively, in Sections 6.4 and 6.5.

Before we proceed to the remaining three major sections of this chapter, it may be instructive to once again return to the issue of implicit knowledge introduced in Section 2.3 for another example. Quite simply, if $\mathcal{P}$ is a sentence related to some stable property in some global state, then $\mathcal{P}$ is implicit knowledge that N has in that global state and in all global states in its future, that is, $I_N\mathcal{P}$. So, for example, an algorithm that has terminated or deadlocked is such that N has implicit knowledge of either condition. In these cases, what the detection procedures studied in Sections 6.2 and 6.3 do is to turn such implicit knowledge into knowledge by one or more individual nodes.

6.1. Self-stabilization

If a distributed algorithm over G can be guaranteed to lead G to a global state where a particular stable property holds regardless of the global state at which the computation starts out, then the system comprising G and this distributed algorithm is said to be a *self-stabilizing system*. Every self-stabilizing system is fault-tolerant in the following sense. If the local states of nodes are allowed to change infrequently as the result of a failure, then by definition the system recovers from that failure by reaching a global state at which the desired stable property is once again valid. Just how infrequent such failures have to be for self-stabilization to be still guaranteed is of course an issue, but for our purposes it suffices to recognize that failures have to be infrequent enough for the system to reach stability again once it has been disturbed.

Self-stabilizing systems do not need to be initialized, because by definition the stable property that the distributed algorithm seeks to achieve is certain to be reached from any initial global state. Also, because of the fault-tolerance connotation that inevitably accompanies the subject, once started at some initial global state, the distributed computation is supposed to be infinite, in the sense of never terminating. For this reason, not every stable property is meaningful in the context of self-stabilization, as one is interested in computations that do useful work despite the initial state and occasionally corrupted local states. Stable properties such as global termination and deadlocks are then naturally ruled out.

In order to close in on the subject more objectively, we consider the following example. Suppose that the nodes in G need to utilize certain resources for their computations, but such resources cannot be utilized concurrently by any two nodes. In the context of self-stabilization, the task is to devise a distributed algorithm that, starting at any global state and given the possibility that local states may be occasionally corrupted, guarantees that the system eventually reaches a global state in which (and in whose future) no two nodes access the shared resources concurrently. (The reader may wish to check Section 8.1 for a more thorough treatment of this problem, although in that section self-stabilization is not an issue.) The stable property at hand is then that no two nodes access shared resources concurrently, so long as this can be guaranteed to remain true once it becomes true.

Henceforth in this section, G is an undirected ring with FIFO edges. Referring back to the terminology of Section 2.2, the edges incident to node n_i are called $left_i$ and $right_i$, and the ring is assumed to be locally oriented (employing these edge denominations is only for notational convenience, though, because in this section the issue of anonymity is unimportant). Associated with a node n_i is a variable v_i. The right of a node to access the shared resources depends on the value of its variable and on the values of the variables of its neighbors. The task of a self-stabilizing computation on G is then to assign values to all nodes' variables so that no two nodes have such a right concurrently from a certain global state onward, regardless of the initial global state (i.e., the initial assignment of values to the variables).

Although a justification of this fact falls outside the scope we have intended for this book, for a ring of arbitrary size no self-stabilizing solution exists employing the exact same algorithm for all nodes. For this reason, in the solution that we present next the behavior of n_1 is distinct from that of the other nodes. Our solution is given as Algorithm $A\_Self\_Stabilize$, and is essentially the following. Every node n_i initiates by sending the value of v_i on $right_i$. Upon receiving a value v on edge $left_i$, n_i checks whether $v_i \neq v$. In the affirmative case, n_i accesses the shared resources, and after using them sets v_i to v and sends v_i's new value on $right_i$. An exception to this behavior is the case of n_1, which accesses the shared resources if $v_1 = v$ and then sets v_1 to $v + 1$ before sending the new value on $right_1$.

At node n_i, a Boolean variable $initiated_i$, initially set to **false**, is used to indicate whether $n_i \in N_0$. The simple behavior we just described is all there is to the algorithm, except for the possibility of faults that may corrupt a node's local state (i.e., the value of its variable). Before explaining how the algorithm is augmented to handle such faults, a few assumptions on their nature are in order. First we assume that actions do indeed take no time to be performed (cf. Section 3.2.2), and consequently the occasional faults that may corrupt a node's local state can only occur in the intervals between successive actions at that node. Faults occurring prior to the first action at a node are immaterial (because the algorithm is intended to be insensitive to initial conditions), and then it is reasonable to assume that faults can only occur at n_i if $initiated_i = $ **true** (as in previous occasions when dealing with asynchronous algorithms, $initiated_i$ is set to **true** immediately upon arrival of the first message if $n_i \notin N_0$). Finally, another assumption is that n_i is capable of detecting the occurrence of a fault that may have corrupted its local state. This detection is modeled as the arrival of a *fault* message (of purposefully undetermined origin).

The handling by n_i of a fault that may have corrupted its local state goes as follows. In response to the *fault* message, n_i sets $initiated_i$ to **true** (since by assumption it must have been **true** prior to the occurrence of the fault) and then reproduces the flow of messages involving n_i during initiation. That is, it sends the value of v_i (which may or may not be the same as before the occurrence of the fault) on $right_i$ and a *query* message on $left_i$, the latter meant to prompt its corresponding neighbor to send the value of its variable to n_i.

> **Algorithm** $A\_Self\_Stabilize$:
>
> ▷ **Variables:**
> $initiated_i = $ **false**;
> v_i.
>
> ▷ **Input:**
> $msg_i = $ **nil**.
>   **Action if** $n_i \in N_0$:   (6.1)
> $initiated_i := $ **true**;
>   Send v_i on $right_i$.

▷ **Input:**

$msg_i = fault.$

Action:

$initiated_i := \textbf{true};$

Send v_i on $right_i$;

Send $query$ on $left_i$.

(6.2)

▷ **Input:**

$msg_i = query.$

Action:

Send v_i on $right_i$.

(6.3)

▷ **Input:**

$msg_i = v.$

Action if $n_i = n_1$:

if $v_i = v$ **then**

begin

Access shared resources;

$v_i := v_i + 1;$

Send v_i on $right_i$

end.

(6.4)

▷ **Input:**

$msg_i = v.$

Action if $n_i \in \{n_2, \ldots, n_n\}$:

if $v_i \neq v$ **then**

begin

Access shared resources;

$v_i := v;$

Send v_i on $right_i$

end.

(6.5)

The first fact to notice with respect to Algorithm $A\_Self\_Stabilize$ is that we have not assigned any initial value to v_i for $n_i \in N$, precisely because of the intended insensitivity to the initial global state. Secondly, it should be noticed that (6.1) and the pair consisting of (6.2) and (6.3) are meant to be executed upon initiation, triggered respectively by the spontaneous initiation by n_i if it is in N_0 and by the detection by n_i of a the occurrence of a fault that may have corrupted the value of v_i. As we remarked previously, (6.2) and (6.3) are supported by our assumptions on the nature of such faults, in the sense that the response to a fault may be thought of as a re-initiation of the algorithm as far as n_i is concerned.

The necessary asymmetry that we alluded to earlier is reflected in Algorithm *A_Self_Stabilize* in (6.4) and (6.5), representing respectively the action that n_1 and $n_i \in \{n_2, \dots, n_n\}$ take upon receipt of a variable's value on the ring. It follows easily from these two actions that, if initially all variables have the same value, then by (6.4) v_1 is incremented and by (6.5) its new value is propagated on the FIFO edges around the ring until all variables have this same value. Then v_1 is incremented again, and so on. If, on the other hand, at least two variables have distinct values in any global state, then either the value of v_1 or that of $v_1 + 1$ (if $v_1 = v_n$ in that global state) is propagated on the ring as well, until v_n becomes equal to v_1, and then the process continues repeatedly. So, although in the latter case the shared resources may be concurrently accessed by more than one node during a transient phase of some global states, a global state in which (6.4) and (6.5) cannot be executed concurrently by any two nodes is certain to occur, the same property holding for all global states in its future.

The solution by Algorithm *A_Self_Stabilize* can be turned into a solution by finite-state nodes by doing additions modulo V in (6.4), so that variables are confined to the range $\{0, \dots, V - 1\}$. Any V strictly larger than n will do, so that the range of values for a variable contains at least the set $\{0, \dots, n\}$ (cf. Exercise 1).

6.2. Termination detection

The issue of algorithm termination appeared in this book as early as in Chapter 1, where, in Section 1.4, Algorithm *Task_t* runs until "global termination is known to t." As we discussed in that section, what is meant by this is that task t must execute its disjunction of guarded commands until it is signaled, by means of messages that it receives, that no further messages will ever reach it and it may therefore cease executing the guarded commands and terminate its computation. The notation used in Algorithm *Task_t* was later modified to emphasize the reactive character of the algorithm, so that in the resulting template algorithms (Algorithms *A_Template* and *S_Template*) only the atomic actions corresponding to a task's response to the receipt of messages appear. Such messages, of course, should include those intended to convey to t the information that it may terminate.

Tasks have since been called nodes, and in none of the algorithms we have seen so far (or will see in chapters still ahead in the book) have we included actions to handle the treatment of the termination-related messages we have from Chapter 1 learned to be important. There are essentially two reasons why we have delayed such a treatment until this far into the book. The first reason is that global termination, as we will shortly see, is clearly an instance of stable properties, so that placing its treatment elsewhere in the book might seem a little unnatural. Secondly, and more importantly, the techniques we investigate in this section build naturally on top of what we saw in Chapters 4 and 5, often explicitly, but also sometimes simply in terms of the maturity of reasoning one must have acquired by studying those chapters.

Of course, for some of the algorithms we have seen, the issue of termination is a trivial one. For example, all the synchronous algorithms we have investigated terminate when a certain number of pulses have gone by. Similarly, in the case of all the asynchronous algorithms we have seen so far, a node should have no problem detecting that messages need no longer be expected, mostly because those algorithms are all very well structured and have very great regularity. For example, it is clear that Algorithm A_PI terminates at a node when that node has received inf from all of its neighbors, at which time it can be certain that no further message related to that algorithm will ever reach it again. Similar lines of reasoning apply to all the other asynchronous algorithms we have seen (cf. Exercise 2), as well as to many of the algorithms yet to be seen in the book. For asynchronous algorithms lacking the regularity that allows such simple termination analyses, however, the issue of detecting global termination with the purpose of relieving the various nodes from having to be on the lookout for new messages needs to be addressed from a general perspective. Asynchronous algorithms like these appear, for example, in Section 7.2.3.

The remainder of Section 6.2 is dedicated exclusively to asynchronous algorithms, although for various synchronous computations (e.g., those in Section 7.2.2) the detection of termination is not as straightforward as it has been with some of the other synchronous algorithms we have seen so far. However, the central issue in treating the termination of such algorithms is that, if they do indeed terminate, then it is essentially possible to detect that by counting pulses. Clearly, such a statement has no clear counterpart in the asynchronous case, thence our emphasis henceforth.

What we do in the next two sections is essentially to provide the atomic actions to make up for the treatment of global termination in asynchronous algorithms that do not exhibit enough regularity for its termination to be treated without messages related explicitly to termination. These actions complement those of the asynchronous algorithms proper so that the resulting asynchronous algorithms behave as intended and in addition are also capable of terminating properly. It should be clear to the reader that the techniques we describe henceforth are also applicable to asynchronous algorithms exhibiting high regularity, although of course in such cases they are totally superfluous and the resulting algorithm can in all likelihood be simplified back to the one whose regularity is enough to indicate termination. Section 6.2.1 is dedicated to the case of general computations, in the sense that N_0 may be any subset of N. Section 6.2.2, on the other hand, is specific to the case in which N_0 is a singleton. Before entering specifics in either section, however, we must formalize a little further our concept of global termination.

An asynchronous algorithm is said to have *terminated globally* or reached *global termination* at a certain global state if every node is idle and all edges are empty in that global state. A node is *idle* when it is not executing any of the actions that specify its participation in the algorithm. Obviously, then, global termination is indeed a stable property, owing essentially to the reactive character of all the asynchronous computations we treat in this book. What a node needs to detect in order to be able to terminate its computation at a given local state is that, in every possible global state in which it participates with that local state, the edges on which it receives messages are all empty. Such a detection may be achieved in a variety of ways. In the case of Algorithm *A_PI*, for example, as soon as *inf* has been received from all of a node's neighbors, that node enters a local state with which it can only participate in global states that have empty edges leading to itself, and then it may terminate. When this conclusion cannot be reached in such a straightforward manner, additional computation needs to take place globally over G until a global state in which the algorithm has terminated globally is detected by a leader. The leader is then responsible for spreading this information over G, and every node, upon receiving it, does finally terminate. Without any loss in generality, we assume that such a leader is node n_1.

In both Sections 6.2.1 and 6.2.2, we present the termination detection algorithms as expansions of Algorithm *A_Template*. The resulting algorithms should be regarded as further elaborations over Algorithm *A_Template* to make the termination-related actions explicit. Messages that are not related to the detection of termination are referred to as *comp_msg*'s.

6.2.1. General computations

The distributed computation of interest in this section is initiated by any subset N_0 of N and progresses through the exchange of messages generically referred to as *comp_msg*'s. We take G to be a strongly connected directed graph, so that the case of an undirected G can also be handled in a straightforward manner. Our approach to termination detection in this section is based strongly on Algorithm *A_Record_Global_State*, and then we assume that G's edges are FIFO.

The approach we take goes essentially as follows. Before going idle, a node that "suspects" it may have terminated initiates the recording of a global state. This suspicion is of course highly dependent upon the particular computation at hand, so we let it be indicated by a Boolean variable $suspects_i$ at $n_i \in N$. This variable is set to either **false** or **true** after, in accordance with Algorithm $A\_Template$, n_i has computed and possibly sent out some messages, either spontaneously if $n_i \in N_0$ or upon the receipt of a $comp\_msg$ (the initial value assigned to the variable is then unimportant). A global state in which $suspects_i = $ **true** for all $n_i \in N$ does not imply global termination in that global state (because there may be messages in transit), but we assume that global termination does imply that $suspects_i = $ **true** for all $n_i \in N$.

This recording of a global state proceeds entirely along the lines of Algorithm $A\_Record\_Global\_State$, that is, through the exchange of $marker$ messages, and may as in that case be initiated concurrently by more than one node if for such nodes the $suspects$ variables become **true** concurrently. When the recording of a global state is completed at n_i, it then sends what it recorded to n_1 (the assumed leader), which, upon receiving similar information from every node, checks whether the global state that was recorded indicates global termination. If it does, then a $terminate$ message is broadcast by n_1 to all of G's nodes, which then terminate.

Clearly, this procedure may be wasteful because a node n_i that receives a $marker$ when $suspects_i = $ **false** should not propagate the $marker$'s onward because the resulting global state cannot possibly indicate global termination. Aborting a global state recording is not something we have considered before, and there are a few implications to be considered. In our present context, the two problems that result from prematurely aborting a global state recording are the need to terminate the aborted recording properly and the possibility that n_1 receives incomplete global states which must somehow be dealt with. We tackle both problems simultaneously, as follows. Every $marker$ is sent with a tag, and every node keeps record of the greatest tag it has seen so far in a $marker$. If the tag a node attaches to a $marker$ it sends out when initiating a new global state recording is strictly greater than any tag it has ever seen, then the rule for participating in global state recordings is very simple. A node only participates in a new global state recording if the tag accompanying the corresponding $marker$ is strictly larger than every tag it has known of and in addition its $suspects$ variable is **true**. Any $marker$ received in different circumstances is ignored. The reader should note that this provides the necessary control for terminating aborted global state recordings, and also allows n_1 to discard useless information it has recorded if the information that it receives from nodes on a recorded global state is itself accompanied by the tag that was attached to the *marker*'s during the recording of that global state.

This strategy is adopted by Algorithm *A_Detect_Termination*, given next. In addition to the Boolean variable $suspects_i$, node n_i needs some of the variables employed by Algorithm *A_Record_Global_State* as well. These are $edge\_state_i^j$, initialized to $\emptyset$, for each node $n_j \in I\_Neig_i$, and the Booleans $recorded_i$ and $received_i^j$, all initialized to **false**. The maximum tag n_i has seen in a *marker* is denoted by max_tag_i. Finally, another Boolean variable, $terminated_i$, initially equal to **false**, is used by n_i to indicate whether a *terminate* message has been received from n_1 ($terminated_1$ is used to indicate that global termination has been detected). This variable, in Algorithm *Task_t*, can be used to exit the **repeat** ... **until** loop.

In Algorithm *A_Detect_Termination*, *marker* messages are sent as $marker(t)$ messages, where t is a positive tag. The initial value of max_tag_i is then zero.

Algorithm *A_Detect_Termination*:

▷ **Variables:**

$suspects_i$;
$edge\_state_i^j = \emptyset$ for all $n_j \in I\_Neig_i$;
$recorded_i = $ **false**;
$received_i^j = $ **false** for all $n_j \in I\_Neig_i$;
$max\_tag_i = 0$;
$terminated_i = $ **false**;
Other variables used by n_i, and their initial values, are listed here.

▷ **Input:**

$msg_i = $ **nil**.
Action if $n_i \in N_0$:   (6.6)
Do some computation;
Send one *comp_msg* on each edge of a (possibly empty) subset of
Out_i;
if $suspects_i$ **then**
    begin
        $max\_tag_i := max\_tag_i + 1$;
        $recorded_i := $ **true**;
        Send $marker(max\_tag_i)$ to all $n_j \in O\_Neig_i$
    end.

▷ **Input:**

   $msg_i = comp\_msg$ such that $origin_i(msg_i) = (n_j \to n_i)$.

Action: (6.7)

   Do some computation;

   Send one *comp_msg* on each edge of a (possibly empty) subset of
   Out_i;

   if $recorded_i$ **then**

       if not $received_i^j$ **then**

           $edge\_state_i^j := edge\_state_i^j \cup \{msg_i\}$;

   if $suspects_i$ **then**

       begin

           $edge\_state_i^k := \emptyset$ for all $n_k \in I\_Neig_i$;

           $received_i^k := \textbf{false}$ for all $n_k \in I\_Neig_i$;

           $max\_tag_i := max\_tag_i + 1$;

           $recorded_i := \textbf{true}$;

           Send $marker(max\_tag_i)$ to all $n_j \in O\_Neig_i$

       end.

▷ **Input:**

$msg_i = marker(t)$ such that $origin_i(msg_i) = (n_j \rightarrow n_i)$.

Action: (6.8)

    if $t = max\_tag_i$ **then**

        $received_i^j := \textbf{true}$;

    if $t > max\_tag_i$ **then**

        begin

            $max\_tag_i := t$;

            $edge\_state_i^k := \emptyset$ for all $n_k \in I\_Neig_i$;

            $recorded_i := \textbf{false}$;

            $received_i^k := \textbf{false}$ for all $n_k \in I\_Neig_i$;

            if $suspects_i$ **then**

                begin

                    $received_i^j := \textbf{true}$;

                    $recorded_i := \textbf{true}$;

                    Send $marker(max\_tag_i)$ to all $n_k \in O\_Neig_i$

                end

        end;

    if $received_i^k$ for all $n_k \in I\_Neig_i$ **then**

        Send $edge\_state_i^k$ for all $n_k \in I\_Neig_i$, along with max_tag_i, to

        n_1.

▷ **Input:**

$msg_i = terminate.$

    Action if $n_i \neq n_1$**:**   (6.9)

    $terminated_i := \textbf{true}.$

This algorithm is, in essence, a blend of Algorithm *A_Template* on *comp_msg*'s and Algorithm *A_Record_Global_State*. Specifically, (6.6) is (2.1) enlarged by (5.11) to initiate a global state recording if $suspects_i = \textbf{true}$. Similarly, (6.7) is (2.2) enlarged by (5.11) and (5.13), respectively to initiate a global state recording if $suspects_i = \textbf{true}$ and to record the messages that comprise an edge's state in the global state being recorded. Finally, (6.8) is (5.12), conveniently adapted to abort ongoing global state recordings upon receipt of a *marker* carrying a tag strictly greater than the greatest one the node has seen.

Let us consider the functioning of Algorithm *A_Detect_Termination* more carefully. Node n_i performs computation, possibly with the sending of some *comp_msg*'s, either spontaneously, if it is a member of N_0, or upon receiving a *comp_msg*. In the former case, n_i may also start a global state recording with *marker*'s carrying a tag increased by one with respect to the greatest tag it has seen (cf. (6.6)). In the latter case, n_i may record the *comp_msg* as part of the state of the edge on which it was received, or it may, as in the other case, start the recording of a global state, after re-initializing its variables related to the recording of global states, or it may do both, in which case the recording of *comp_msg* will have been in vain (cf. (6.7)). Notice that these two possibilities account for all the opportunities n_i has to start a global state recording, and in both cases such a start is done with properly initialized variables. Because n_i maintains only one set of variables for global state recording, it may only participate in the recording of one global state at a time, so that upon initiating its participation in a new recording it must quit its participation in whatever recording it may have been participating so far. This is the reason for variable re-initialization in (6.7) if *suspects*$_i$ becomes **true**.

The other occasion in which n_i may have to forsake its current participation in a global state recording is upon receiving a *marker*(t) such that $t > max\_tag_i$. When this happens, n_i re-initializes its variables related to global state recording and, if *suspects*$_i$ = **true**, joins in the new global state recording, as in (6.8). If $t < max\_tag_i$, then the *marker*(t) is ignored (it clearly belongs to a long-forsaken global state recording), whereas if $t = max\_tag_i$, then it may correspond to a recording in which n_i is currently engaged. The receipt of a *marker* in (6.8) may also imply that n_i has finished its participation in the current global state recording, and then what it recorded is sent to the leader for analysis (it only sends the edge states, though, because by (6.6) through (6.8) n_i does not participate in the recording of a global state if its local state is anything other than *suspects*$_i$ = **true**). This information is sent to the leader along with the tag with which it was recorded, and the leader, upon having received information with the same tag from all nodes, decides whether global termination has been reached, in which case a *terminate* message is broadcast to all nodes. We have omitted from the algorithm the actions for n_1 to perform its role as a leader, and we have also omitted any specific mention to how the broadcast of the *terminate* order is performed. Filling in these blanks should pose no difficulty, though, especially after our discussion of information propagation in Section 4.1 (cf. Exercise 3). The response of $n_i \neq n_1$ to the *terminate* message is in (6.9).

The correctness of Algorithm *A_Detect_Termination* is based on Theorem 5.5 on the correctness of Algorithm *A_Record_Global_State* if G is strongly connected with FIFO edges, and on the following observation. Suppose a global state in which global termination holds does exist. As we assumed earlier in this section, at this global state it must hold that *suspects*$_i$ = **true** for all $n_i \in N$, so we may consider the greatest value of max_tag_i over all of N when the corresponding $suspects_i$'s became **true** for the last time. The nodes at which this greatest value occurred must by (6.6) and (6.7) have initiated a global state recording concurrently, and by (6.8) this global state recording must have been propagated by all nodes. Consequently, at least one global state recording is carried out to completion, including the recording of a global state in which global termination holds.

Before leaving this section, a couple of observations are worth making. The first observation concerns obvious possible simplifications to Algorithm *A_Detect_Termination*, especially in what concerns the reports that are sent to n_1. We elaborate no further on the issue, but encourage the reader to further investigate it (cf. Exercise 4). The second observation relates to the treatment of computations for which global termination does not hold at any global state. Computations like these appear in Section 10.2, and because they ordinarily do not terminate by themselves, what we seek is to force their termination by detecting termination-related properties that appear in some global states with special characteristics. As we discussed briefly in Section 5.2.2, in this case a leader can be employed to search for the special global states, and upon finding one of them for which the desired termination-related properties do hold the leader then directs all other nodes to terminate. In Chapter 10, we address these issues with more detail.

6.2.2. Diffusing computations

In this section, we concentrate on detecting the termination of asynchronous algorithms for which N_0 has one single member, assumed to be n_1, the leader. G is in this section taken to be an undirected graph. The approach we described in the previous section is of course applicable to this case as well (and, for that matter, so is the approach of this section applicable to cases in which N_0 is not a singleton—cf. Exercise 5), although in that case n_1 would no longer be required to be a member of N_0.

Distributed computations for which N_0 is a singleton are referred to as *diffusing computations*, because in such computations the causality that the flow of messages induces is "diffused" from one single node. Of course this same intuition is also present in the cases of larger sets of initiators, but the denomination as a diffusing computation is not generally used in those cases because it would seem unnatural to say that the computation is diffused from the members of N_0 when such a set can be arbitrarily large, possibly equal to N.

The algorithm we saw in Section 4.1.1 to propagate information with feedback from n_1 is an example of diffusing computations, and, as we will shortly see, it is an example of particular interest in the context of detecting the termination of diffusing computations in general. In Algorithm *A_PIF*, the role played by n_1 can be thought of as being not only that of the original propagator of *inf*, but also that of the detector of when the propagation has terminated throughout all of G. Although, as we remarked earlier in Section 6.2, in that algorithm every node can decide upon its termination rather easily (without the need for intervention from n_1), the general idea of having a wave of information collapse back to n_1 upon global termination is quite useful for computations whose termination cannot be detected so simply.

One of the main motivations to look for a different solution in the case of diffusing computations, rather than just employ the general technique of the previous section, is the potentially very high complexity of the methodology realized by Algorithm *A_Detect_Termination*. Although, due to its generality, we did not attempt any analysis when presenting that algorithm, clearly its complexity depends on the number of global state recordings it performs, so that the overall complexities may be too high. The specialized solution we study in this section, on the other hand, allows global termination to be detected without affecting the complexities of the computation proper.

The following is an outline of Algorithm *A_Detect_Termination_D* ("D" for Diffusing). Every *comp_msg* is acknowledged with an *ack* message. Node n_i maintains a counter $expected_i$, initially equal to zero, to indicate the number of *ack* messages it expects from its neighbors (we assume that $expected_i$ is automatically increased whenever a *comp_msg* is sent by n_i). As in the case of Algorithm *A_PIF*, n_i also maintains a variable $parent_i$, initialized to **nil**, to indicate the origin of a *comp_msg* received in a special situation to be described shortly. The behavior of n_i is then the following. Whenever n_i receives a *comp_msg* and $expected_i > 0$, an *ack* is immediately sent in response. If, on the other hand, a *comp_msg* is received and $expected_i = 0$, then the *ack* is withheld and sent only when $expected_i$ becomes equal to zero again (if it at all changes with the computation n_i does in response to the arriving *comp_msg*, otherwise the *ack* is sent immediately after that computation). The variable $parent_i$ is in this case set to point to the node that sent the *comp_msg* until the *ack* can be sent. We say that n_i has reached a state of *tentative termination*, or that n_i has *tentatively terminated* when $expected_i$ becomes zero and the pending *ack*, if any, is sent to $parent_i$. This condition may, however, change many times during the computation, for $expected_i$ may again acquire a positive value as a consequence of the reception of a *comp_msg*. Global termination is detected when n_1 has tentatively terminated, which in the case of n_1 may happen only once.

The resulting algorithm is Algorithm *A_Detect_Termination_D*, presented next. As in the previous section, a *terminate* message is employed by n_1 to broadcast the detection of global termination. A Boolean variable $terminated_i$, initially set to **false**, is employed by n_i to signal that n_i may exit the **repeat** ... **until** loop in Algorithm $Task\_t$. This variable is set to **true** by n_i upon detection of global termination, if $n_i = n_1$, or upon receipt of the $terminate$ message, otherwise.

Algorithm $A\_Detect\_Termination\_D$:

▷ **Variables:**
　　　$expected_i = 0$;
　　　$parent_i = $ **nil**;
　　　$terminated_i = $ **false**.

▷ **Input:**
　　　$msg_i = $ **nil**.
　　Action if $n_i \in N_0$:　　　　　　　　　　　　　　　　　　　　(6.10)
　　　　Do some computation;
　　　　Send one $comp\_msg$ on each edge of a (possibly empty) subset of Inc_i.

▷ **Input:**
　　　$msg_i = comp\_msg$ such that $origin_i(msg_i) = (n_i, n_j)$.
　　Action:　　　　　　　　　　　　　　　　　　　　　　　　　　(6.11)
　　　　if $expected_i > 0$ **then**
　　　　　　begin
　　　　　　　　Send ack to n_j;
　　　　　　　　Do some computation;
　　　　　　　　Send one $comp\_msg$ on each edge of a (possibly empty) subset of Inc_i
　　　　　　end
　　　　else
　　　　　　begin
　　　　　　　　Do some computation;
　　　　　　　　Send one $comp\_msg$ on each edge of a (possibly empty) subset of Inc_i;
　　　　　　　　if $expected_i > 0$ **then**
　　　　　　　　　　$parent_i := n_j$
　　　　　　　　else
　　　　　　　　　　Send ack to n_j
　　　　　　end.

> ▷ **Input:**
>
> $msg_i = ack.$
>
> **Action:** (6.12)
>
> $expected_i := expected_i - 1;$
> **if** $expected_i = 0$ **then**
> **if** $parent_i \neq$ **nil then**
> Send ack to $parent_i.$

> ▷ **Input:**
>
> $msg_i = terminate.$
>
> **Action if** $n_i \notin N_0$**:** (6.13)
>
> $terminated_i := $ **true.**

In Algorithm *A_Detect_Termination_D*, (6.10) and (6.11) are, in essence, (2.1) and (2.2), respectively, in Algorithm *A_Template* on *comp_msg*'s, while (6.12) and (6.13) deal with the reception of *ack* and *terminate* messages, respectively (the latter for $n_i \neq n_1$). Together, (6.11) and (6.12) can be seen to be closely related to (4.4) in Algorithm *A_PIF* in that all of them are involved with withholding acknowledgements from a *parent* neighbor until it is appropriate for that acknowledgement to be sent. This similarity with those two algorithms allows Algorithm *A_Detect_Termination_D* to be interpreted as a general template for asynchronous diffusing computations in which n_1, the computation's sole initiator, detects global termination upon being reached by a collapsing wave of acknowledgements. This view of a computation as a propagating wave is the same that we employed in various occasions in Chapter 4, and in the present context allows the following pictorial interpretation. In Algorithm *A_Detect_Termination_D*, a wave is initiated by n_1 in (6.10) and throughout G it propagates back and forth with respect to n_1. It propagates away from n_1 with *comp_msg*'s and backwards in the direction of n_1 with *ack*'s. When the wave hits n_i in its forward propagation, it may bounce back immediately (if $expected_i > 0$ at the beginning of (6.11) or $expected_i = 0$ at the end of (6.11)) or it may continue further on from that node (otherwise). Node n_i may in this case be n_1 itself, in which case the wave is sure to bounce back at once. The wave that propagates backwards in the direction of n_1 does so by means of *ack* messages, and continues to propagate at each node n_i that it encounters so long as $expected_i$ becomes zero with its arrival. What differentiates the wave propagations in this case from those of Algorithm *A_PIF* is that a node that has already seen the *ack* wave go by may be hit by a forward-moving wave again (that is, by a *comp_msg*), so that overall the picture is that of a wave that may oscillate back and forth several times, and in different patterns on the various portions of G, before it finally collapses back onto n_1.

Before proceeding with a more formal analysis of this behavior, we mention that, as in the case of Algorithm $A\_Detect\_Termination$ of the previous section, we have not in Algorithm $A\_Detect\_Termination\_D$ been complete to the point of specifying the termination of n_1 and the propagation of the *terminate* broadcast. The reader should work on providing the missing details (cf. Exercise 6).

The correctness of Algorithm $A\_Detect\_Termination\_D$ is established by the following theorem.

Theorem 6.1. *Every global state in which n_1 has tentatively terminated in Algorithm $A\_Detect\_Termination\_D$ is a global state in which global termination holds.*

Proof: If n_1 has tentatively terminated, then by (6.11) and (6.12) every node must have sent a finite number of *comp_msg*'s. As these *comp_msg*'s and the corresponding *ack*'s were received, the value of $expected_i$ for node n_i, initially equal to zero, became positive and zero again, possibly several times. Whenever a transition occurred in the value of $expected_i$ from zero to a positive value, $parent_i$ was set to point to the node that sent the corresponding *comp_msg*. Consider the system states in which every node n_i is either in a state of positive $expected_i$ following the last transition from zero of its value, if it ever sent a *comp_msg* during the diffusing computation, or in any state, otherwise. Clearly, at least one of these system states is a global state, as for example the one in which every node that ever sent *comp_msg*'s is in its state that immediately precedes the reception of the last *ack* (Figure 6.1). In this global state, only *ack*'s flow on the edges, none of which sent as a consequence of the reception of a last *ack*. Let us consider one of these global states.

In this global state, the variables $parent_i$ for $n_i \neq n_1$ induce a tree that spans all nodes in G corresponding to nodes that sent at least one *comp_msg* during the diffusing computation. (This tree is in fact dynamically changing with the progress of the algorithm, as $parent_i$ may point to several of n_i's neighbors along the way; it is always a tree, nevertheless.) This tree is rooted at n_1, and its leaves correspond to those nodes from which no other node n_i received the *comp_msg* that triggered the last transition from zero to a positive value of $expected_i$. As in the proof of Theorem 4.1, we proceed by induction on the subtrees of this tree. Along the induction, the assertion to be shown is that every global state in which the subtree's root has tentatively terminated is a global state in which every other node in the subtree has also tentatively terminated.

The basis of the induction is given by the subtrees rooted at the leaves, and then the assertion clearly holds, as no leaf n_i is such that $n_i = parent_j$ for some

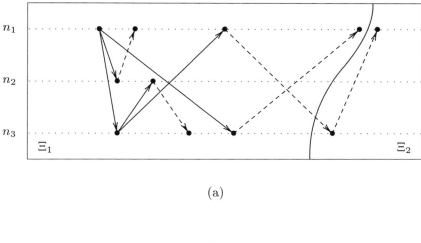

(a)

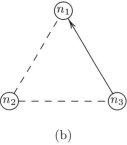

(b)

Figure 6.1. *Edges in the precedence graph fragment shown in part (a) are drawn as either solid lines or dashed lines. Solid lines represent comp_msg's, dashed lines represent ack's, and the remaining edges of the precedence graph are omitted. In this case, system_state(Ξ_1, Ξ_2) is clearly a global state, and is such that every node that ever sent a comp_msg during the diffusing computation (i.e., n_1 and n_3) is in the state that immediately precedes the reception of the last ack. In part (b), the spanning tree formed by the variables parent$_i$ for each node n_i in this global state is shown with directed edges that point from n_i to n_j to indicate that parent$_i = n_j$. In this case, the tree has n_1 for root and its single leaf is n_3.*

node n_j. As the induction hypothesis, assume the assertion for all the subtrees rooted at nodes n_j such that $parent_j$ is n_1. Then n_1 receives $expected_1$ ack's, at which time it has tentatively terminated, and by the induction hypothesis so have all other nodes.   ∎

Let us now return briefly to the question, raised earlier in this section, of the algorithm's complexities. Because exactly one ack is sent for each $comp\_msg$, the message complexity of Algorithm $A\_Detect\_Termination\_D$ is exactly the message complexity that Algorithm $A\_Template$ would have to realize the same computation without having to detect global termination. The same holds with respect to the algorithms' time complexities, because the time that Algorithm $A\_Detect\_Termination\_D$ spends in addition to that already spent by the corresponding instance of Algorithm $A\_Template$ is used solely for the final collapsing of the ack wave onto n_1. This additional time, clearly, does not exceed that of Algorithm $A\_Template$, as this wave that propagates backwards comes from as far as the corresponding forward-propagating wave got.

6.3. Deadlock detection

Deadlocks are a very close acquaintance of anyone who has been involved with any of the many facets of concurrency at any depth. In this book, our concern for deadlock situations has already appeared explicitly in a couple of places, as in Sections 1.3 and 1.5, and less conspicuously it has also appeared in some other situations, as for example in our discussion on the importance of distinct identifications for nodes in the context of leader election (cf. Section 5.1). Also, in chapters to come our concern for deadlocks will be often explicit, as in Chapters 8 and 10.

Informally, a group of nodes is in *deadlock* when every node in the group is suspended for a condition that can only be realized by nodes that belong to the group as well. Clearly, then, deadlocks are indeed stable properties. The classical approaches to the treatment of deadlocks range from its prevention (as for example in Sections 1.3 and 1.5) to its detection after it has occurred. The prevention of deadlocks is based on making sure, by design, that at least one of the conditions necessary for the occurrence of deadlocks can never hold. One of these conditions is the so-called *wait cycle*, which in our context consists of a subset of N whose members are cyclically waiting for one another. Forbidding the occurrence of such cycles constitutes the strategy we described in Section 1.5 to prevent deadlocks related to message buffering (cf. Theorem 1.1).

The detection of deadlocks, on the other hand, is based on the rationale that it may be simpler, or less restrictive in a variety of senses, not to impose conditions leading to the prevention of deadlocks, but rather to let them occur occasionally and then proceed to detecting them when the suspicion exists that they may have indeed occurred. Because deadlocks are stable properties, an approach to detecting their occurrence is to record a global state of the system and then work on this global state to check for the presence of any deadlock. If a deadlock is found in the global state that was recorded, then because of its stability it must have persisted as the system continued to evolve following the recording of the global state. If, on the other hand, no deadlock was found, then naturally the only possible conclusion is that no deadlock existed in any global state in the past of the recorded global state, although it may have occurred in global states in its future.

This section is dedicated to the study of deadlock detection in the case of a very specific distributed computation. Aside from the deadlock issue *per se*, the benefits of this study are manifold. In particular, the approach we describe to deadlock detection yields a distributed algorithm to perform the detection that works on a recorded global state in a completely distributed fashion. This is in contrast with our previous use of recorded global states in this chapter, for example in Section 6.2.1, where the analysis of the recorded global state to detect the desired stable property was performed in a centralized fashion by a leader. By contrast, our approach in this section performs the detection without moving any of the recorded information from the node where it was recorded. Another benefit is that the algorithm we describe constitutes another elegant example of the wave techniques we have seen so far in the book, notably in Chapters 4, 5, and in this very chapter.

We proceed in the following two sections as follows. In Section 6.3.1, the asynchronous computation that may deadlock is introduced. In Section 6.3.2, an algorithm is given to look for deadlocks in a recorded global state of that computation. In both sections, G is taken to be an undirected graph with FIFO edges.

6.3.1. The computation

Every node in G is the provider of a service to some of the other nodes. An edge (n_i, n_j) exists in G if and only if at least one of n_i and n_j may request the service provided by the other node. Node n_i has a Boolean variable $available_i$, initially set to **true**, to indicate whether it is available to provide a service it is requested or not. Because n_i may only respond to one request at a time, every request that it receives when $available_i = $ **false** must wait to be serviced when $available_i$ becomes **true**.

A node requests a service to one of its neighbors by sending it a message *request*. When the request is finally honored, a message *done* is used to indicate that. In the computations that we consider, nodes are allowed to request the same service to more than one neighbor at a time. In addition, if n_i wishes to request a service to x_i of its neighbors, then it is also allowed to do the request to $y_i \geq x_i$ neighbors. Upon receiving x_i *done* messages, it then sends a *quit* message to the $y_i - x_i$ nodes from which it did not receive a *done*. Clearly, $0 < x_i \leq y_i \leq |Inc_i|$ for all $n_i \in N$. For simplicity, we assume that x_i and y_i are constants for each $n_i \in N$.

What accounts for the possibility of deadlocks in this computation is that a node, while servicing the request of one of its neighbors, may itself issue requests for services that it needs some of its neighbors to perform in order to finish its own task. The possibility of deadlocks is then obvious, given that no node accepts a new request if it has a pending request itself. A node that receives a *quit* on a service for which it sent *request*'s sends out *quit*'s itself.

This computation is given more formally next, in the form of Algorithm *A_Provide_Service*. In this algorithm, a variable $requester_i$, initially equal to **nil**, is used by n_i to point to the node to which it is currently providing service. This variable is maintained in such a way that, for $n_i \notin N_0$, $available_i = $ **true** if $requester_i = $ **nil** (but not conversely, so no redundancy really exists between the two variables). In addition, a set $pending_i \subseteq Neig_i$ is used by n_i to keep track of the neighbors to which it sent *request* messages without however having received a *done*. This variable is such that $y_i - x_i \leq |pending_i| \leq y_i$.

Algorithm *A_Provide_Service*:

▷ **Variables:**
      $available_i = $ **true**;
      $requester_i = $ **nil**;
      $pending_i$.

▷ **Input:**
      $msg_i = $ **nil**.
   Action if $n_i \in N_0$:   (6.14)
      Let $Y_i \subseteq Neig_i$ be such that $y_i = |Y_i|$;
      Send *request* to all $n_j \in Y_i$;
      $pending_i := Y_i$.

▷ **Input:**

$msg_i = request$ such that $origin_i(msg_i) = (n_i, n_j)$.

Action when $available_i$:

$\quad$ **if** service from other nodes is needed **then**

$\qquad$ **begin**

$\qquad\qquad$ Let $Y_i \subseteq Neig_i$ be such that $y_i = |Y_i|$;

$\qquad\qquad$ Send $request$ to all $n_k \in Y_i$;

$\qquad\qquad$ $pending_i := Y_i$;

$\qquad\qquad$ $requester_i := n_j$;

$\qquad\qquad$ $available_i := \textbf{false}$

$\qquad$ **end**

$\quad$ **else**

$\qquad$ **begin**

$\qquad\qquad$ Perform requested service;

$\qquad\qquad$ Send $done$ to n_j

$\qquad$ **end.**

(6.15)

▷ **Input:**

$msg_i = done$ such that $origin_i(msg_i) = (n_i, n_j)$.

Action:

$\quad$ $pending_i := pending_i - \{n_j\}$;

$\quad$ **if** $|pending_i| = y_i - x_i$ **then**

$\qquad$ **begin**

$\qquad\qquad$ Send $quit$ to all $n_k \in pending_i$;

$\qquad\qquad$ **if** $requester_i \neq \textbf{nil}$ **then**

$\qquad\qquad\qquad$ **begin**

$\qquad\qquad\qquad\qquad$ Perform requested service;

$\qquad\qquad\qquad\qquad$ Send $done$ to $requester_i$

$\qquad\qquad\qquad$ **end;**

$\qquad\qquad$ $available_i := \textbf{true}$

$\qquad$ **end.**

(6.16)

▷ **Input:**

$msg_i = quit$.

Action:

$\quad$ **if** $pending_i \neq \emptyset$ **then**

$\qquad$ Send $quit$ to all $n_j \in pending_i$;

$\quad$ $available_i := \textbf{true}$.

(6.17)

The reader should have no difficulties to check that (6.14) through (6.17) do indeed realize the computation we outlined earlier on G. Even so, it may be instructive to check the use of $available_i$ as a condition for (6.15) to be carried out (cf. Algorithm $A\_Template$).

6.3.2. An algorithm

The possibility of deadlocks in Algorithm $A\_Provide\_Service$ is very clearly visible in (6.14) and (6.15), because $request$ messages may be sent in such a way that a wait cycle is formed in G. One simple example is the situation in which some of the nodes in N_0 send $request$'s to one another in a cyclic fashion. Another example is the case in which a node triggers a chain of $request$'s that ends up in itself.

When a node n_i has waited "too long" (or longer than would be "typical") for the x_i $done$ messages that it expects to be received, it may start a deadlock-detection procedure to verify whether it is involved in a deadlock. The procedure that we describe in this section is, in much the same way as Algorithm A_PIF, designed to be started by one node only (so N_0 must be a singleton). We assume, without any loss in generality, that such a node is n_1, but it should be clear that in general all the messages related to this detection must bear an indication of which node initiated the process so that multiple concurrent detections started by different nodes do not interfere with one another.

What n_1 does to detect the occurrence of a deadlock is to start the recording of a global state, and then to start a detection procedure on the global state that was recorded. The global state is stored in the same distributed fashion as it was recorded, and the detection procedure is itself an asynchronous algorithm in which various nodes participate. However, the deadlock detection does not operate on the entirety of G. Instead, this procedure runs on some portions of G given in accordance with what is known as a *wait graph*. The node set of the wait graph is a subset of N, and its edges are directed versions of some of the edges in E. In order for a node n_i to be in the wait graph, at least one of the edges incident to it in G must also be in the wait graph.

The conditions for edges of G to be edges of the wait graph vary dynamically as the computation given by Algorithm $A\_Provide\_Service$ evolves. In a particular global state of that computation, an edge (n_i, n_j) is an edge of the wait graph if and only if, in that global state, all of the following three conditions hold.

- n_i has sent n_j a *request*.

- n_j has not sent n_i a *done*.

- n_i has not sent n_j a *quit*.

These three conditions include messages that have been received as well as messages in transit. In particular, in that global state there may be a *request* in transit from n_i to n_j, but no *done* in transit from n_j to n_i and no *quit* in transit from n_i to n_j, so that what the conditions imply is that n_i has requested a service to n_j and is in that global state waiting for the service to be performed. In the wait graph, such an edge is directed from n_i to n_j to indicate precisely that wait. At n_i, and in the context of a particular global state, *out_wait*$_i$ is the subset of *Neig*$_i$ such that $n_j \in$ *out_wait*$_i$ if and only if an edge directed from n_i to n_j exists in the wait graph in that global state. The set *in_wait*$_i$ is defined likewise to include those nodes n_j such that an edge directed from n_j to n_i exists.

It is on the portions of G that intersect the wait graph that the deadlock detection should run, as it is on those portions that the waiting is taking place. This should pose no problem, because the detection runs on a recorded global state and in that global state the wait graph is well defined, as we just discussed. However, the recording of the global state cannot quite run on the wait graph as well, because no such graph has yet been determined (determining it is, in fact, the very purpose of the global state recording). On the other hand, it seems clearly a waste to perform the global state recording all over G, because a great portion of it may not have the slightest chance of participating in the wait graph once the global state is recorded. However, the only other appropriate structure related to G that the global state recording might utilize is that given by the sets *pending*$_i$ for $n_i \in N$ if they are nonempty (cf. Section 6.3.1), but they are not enough to describe the desired graph that would be "between" G and the wait graph to be eventually obtained (cf. Exercise 7).

So what n_1 does is to initiate a global state recording over G as in Algorithm *A_Record_Global_State*, and then to initiate a deadlock detection procedure on the wait graph, which we describe next as Algorithm *A_Detect_Deadlock*. Because all edges are FIFO, n_1 might in principle initiate the deadlock detection immediately after initiating the global state recording. If this were done, then Algorithm *A_Detect_Deadlock* would need a little extra control to ensure that a node would only participate in the latter computation after being through with its participation in the former. In order to avoid this unnecessary complication, we assume that n_1 is somehow notified of the global termination of the global state recording. The reader should consider with care the design of an asynchronous algorithm to record global states and signal its initiator (assumed unique) upon the recording's global termination (cf. Exercise 8).

For each node n_i, the local state to be recorded comprises the variables $available_i$, $requester_i$, and $pending_i$. The edge states to be recorded may in turn contain $request$, $done$, and $quit$ messages. Once the recording is completed at n_i (i.e., n_i's local state has been recorded and so have the states of all edges leading toward n_i), the sets in_wait_i and out_wait_i that describe the wait graph at n_i can be determined as follows. The set in_wait_i must include the node $requester_i$ (if $available_i = $ **false** and n_i is not in the N_0 of Algorithm $A\_Provide\_Service$) and every neighbor n_j such that the recorded state of the edge (n_i, n_j) in the direction from n_j to n_i contains a $request$ but does not contain a $quit$. Similarly, the set out_wait_i must include every neighbor n_j that is in $pending_i$ and such that neither the recorded state of (n_i, n_j) in the direction from n_j to n_i has a $done$ nor the recorded state of (n_i, n_j) in the opposite direction has a $quit$. It is a simple matter to check that these sets are consistent over all edges, that is, $n_j \in out\_wait_i$ if and only if $n_i \in in\_wait_j$, and conversely, for all edges (n_i, n_j).

The following is a general outline of Algorithm $A\_Detect\_Deadlock$. First a wave of $notify$ messages is propagated by n_1 along the edges leading to nodes in the out_wait sets. Because an in_wait set may contain more than one node, this wave may reach a node more than once and should only be sent forward upon receipt of the first $notify$. A node having an empty out_wait set does not propagate the $notify$'s onward, but rather starts the propagation of another wave, this time with $grant$ messages and on edges leading to nodes in the in_wait sets. Such waves simulate the concession of the services upon which nodes wait. A node that receives as many $grant$'s as it needs (this is given by its x constant) propagates the wave onward on its own in_wait set, as in the simulation such a node has already been granted services from as many neighbors as it needs. This wave is propagated as far back as nodes with empty in_wait sets, from which it collapses back with $grant\_done$ messages. A node with an empty in_wait set sends a $grant\_done$ message immediately upon receiving a $grant$. Other nodes withhold the $grant\_done$ that corresponds to the xth $grant$, but do respond with immediate $grant\_done$'s upon receiving all other $grant$'s. At node n_i, the node from which the $grant\_done$ is withheld is pointed to by out_parent_i. The $grant\_done$ to out_parent_i is sent when n_i has received as many $grant\_done$'s as there are nodes in in_wait_i. What remains now is to collapse back onto n_1 the wave that it propagated with $notify$ messages. This is accomplished with $notify\_done$ messages as follows. Node n_i, upon receiving the first $notify$, points to its sender with a variable in_parent_i. Every other notify is replied to immediately with a $notify\_done$ message. Whenever the nodes that initiated the $grant$ waves have received as many $grant\_done$'s as there are nodes in their in_wait sets, they send a $notify\_done$ to their in_parent neighbors. Other nodes do the same upon receiving as many *notify_done*'s as there are nodes in their *out_wait* sets. When n_1 receives all the *notify_done*'s that are due, it then checks the number of *grant*'s it received along the process. Node n_1 is in deadlock if and only if this number is less than x_1.

In this algorithm, nodes behave as if they could grant service concomitantly for all the requests they receive. This is of course untrue by assumption, so that what nodes do during the simulation is to optimistically assume that they can grant service for all of their pending requests, whereas in fact they can only be sure to be able to honor one such request. The consequence of this optimism is that, if n_1 concludes that it is not deadlocked, what this conclusion means is that there exists at each of the nodes in the wait graph an order according to which service should be granted by that node so that n_1 will not deadlock. Of course that order may happen not to be followed and then n_1 may deadlock in future global states.

In Algorithm *A_Detect_Deadlock*, node n_i maintains the following additional variables. The Boolean variable *notified$_i$*, initialized to **false**, is employed to indicate whether n_i has received at least one *notify*. Another variable is a counter, *granted$_i$* (initialized to zero), to keep track of the number of *grant*'s n_i receives during the simulation. Two other counters, *in_dones$_i$* and *out_dones$_i$*, both initially equal to zero, indicate respectively the number of *grant_done* and *notify_done* messages received. The variables *in_parent$_i$* and *out_parent$_i$* are both initialized to **nil**. Node n_1 detects that it is deadlocked if and only if *granted$_1$* $< x_1$ at the end.

Algorithm *A_Detect_Deadlock*:

▷ **Variables:**
    $in_parent_i = $ **nil**;
    $out_parent_i = $ **nil**;
    $notified_i = $ **false**;
    $granted_i = 0$;
    $in\_dones_i = 0$;
    $out\_dones_i = 0$.

▷ **Input:**
    $msg_i = $ **nil**.
    Action if $n_i \in N_0$:
        $notified_i := $ **true**;
        Send *notify* to all $n_j \in out\_wait_i$.

(6.18)

▷ **Input:**

  $msg_i = notify$ such that $origin_i(msg_i) = (n_i, n_j)$.

  Action: (6.19)

    if $notified_i$ **then**

      Send $notify\_done$ to n_j

    else

      begin

        $notified_i :=$ **true**;

        $in\_parent_i := n_j$;

        if $|out\_wait_i| = 0$ **then**

          Send $grant$ to all $n_k \in in\_wait_i$

        else

          Send $notify$ to all $n_k \in out\_wait_i$

      end.

▷ **Input:**

  $msg_i = grant$ such that $origin_i(msg_i) = (n_i, n_j)$.

  Action: (6.20)

    $granted_i := granted_i + 1$;

    if $|in\_wait_i| = 0$ **then**

      Send $grant\_done$ to n_j

    else

      if $granted_i \neq x_i$ **then**

        Send $grant\_done$ to n_j

      else

        begin

          $out\_parent_i := n_j$;

          Send $grant$ to all $n_k \in in\_wait_i$

        end.

▷ **Input:**

  $msg_i = grant\_done$.

  Action: (6.21)

    $in\_dones_i := in\_dones_i + 1$;

    if $in\_dones_i = |in\_wait_i|$ **then**

      if $out\_parent_i \neq$ **nil** **then**

        Send $grant\_done$ to out_parent_i

      else

        Send $notify\_done$ to in_parent_i.

> ▷ **Input:**
> $\quad msg_i = notify\_done.$
> **Action:**
> $\quad out\_dones_i := out\_dones_i + 1;$
> $\quad$ **if** $out\_dones_i = |out\_wait_i|$ **then**
> $\quad\quad$ **if** $in\_parent_i \neq$ **nil then**
> $\quad\quad\quad$ Send $notify\_done$ to $in\_parent_i.$

$$(6.22)$$

Like several other asynchronous algorithms we have seen so far in the book (e.g., Algorithms *A_PIF* and *A_Detect_Termination_D*), this algorithm for deadlock detection by n_1 relies essentially on feedback information to achieve its purposes. Like those other algorithms, it maintains tree structures on the graph so that the feedbacks are sent only when appropriate.

In the case of Algorithm *A_Detect_Deadlock*, the pointers *in_parent* establish a tree that spans all the nodes that can be reached from n_1 in the wait graph. This tree is rooted at n_1 and its leaves are nodes for which the *out_wait* sets are empty. Its creation and eventual collapse are achieved by the pair (6.18) and (6.19), and by (6.22), respectively. In the same vein, for each of these nodes with empty *out_wait* sets, the pointers *out_parent* establish a tree that spans some of the nodes in the wait graph from which that node can be reached. Considered as a set of trees, they constitute a forest rooted at the nodes with empty *out_wait* sets spanning all the nodes in the wait graph from which at least one of the roots can be reached. The leaves of this forest are nodes whose *grant* messages sent during the simulation either never were the xth such message to reach their destinations or reached nodes with empty *in_wait* sets. This forest is created and collapses back onto its roots by means of (6.20) and (6.21), respectively.

It comes naturally from this discussion that the message, complexity of Algorithm *A_Detect_Deadlock* is $O(m)$ while its time complexity is $O(n)$.

6.4. Exercises

1. Show that Algorithm *A_Self_Stabilize* is still correct if the variables are restricted to $0, \ldots, V-1$ for $V > n$.

2. For each of the asynchronous algorithms seen so far in the book (except for the templates), indicate the condition of global termination that allows the loop in Algorithm *Task_t* to be exited.

3. Give the details of node n_1's participation in Algorithm *A_Detect_Termination*, as well as of the participation of all other nodes in the propagation of the *terminate* message.

4. Indicate how in Algorithm *A_Detect_Termination* the sending of reports to node n_1 can be simplified.

5. Discuss how to apply the technique of Section 6.2.2 to the cases in which N_0 does not contain one single element.

6. Repeat Exercise 3 for Algorithm *A_Detect_Termination_D*.

7. Show, in the context of Section 6.3, that the sets *pending* do not suffice to describe a graph that is necessarily "between" a wait graph and G.

8. Design an algorithm for global state recording, which, if initiated by one single node, is capable of informing that node of the global termination of the recording.

6.5. Bibliographic notes

The notion of self-stabilization was introduced by Dijkstra (1974), along with three algorithms on rings for which only considerably later proofs were provided (Dijkstra, 1986). Algorithm *A_Self_Stabilize* of Section 6.1 is based on one of the algorithms of Dijkstra (1974). For a survey of the investigations that this paper has spawned, the reader is referred to Schneider (1993). These investigations are quite broad in scope, ranging from a technique to prove self-stabilizing properties (Kessels, 1988) to applications to problems such as finding a minimum spanning tree (Chen, Yu, and Huang, 1991; Aggarwal and Kutten, 1993), computing on rings as in the original formulation by Dijkstra (1974) (Burns and Pachl, 1989; Flatebo and Datta, 1994), depth-first traversal (Huang and Chen, 1993; Collin and Dolev, 1994), leader election (Dolev and Israeli, 1992), coloring planar graphs (Ghosh and Karaata, 1993), finding maximal matchings (Hsu and Huang, 1992; Tel, 1994a), breadth-first numbering (Huang and Chen, 1992), establishing a local orientation on a ring (Israeli and Jalfon, 1991; 1993), and computing shortest distances (Tsai and Huang, 1994).

The literature on self-stabilization has become quite overwhelming. In addition to the aforementioned works, the reader may also wish to check further developments by a number of authors, including Gouda, Howell, and Rosier (1990), Afek and Kutten (1991), Awerbuch and Varghese (1991), Dolev, Israeli, and Moran (1991), Ghosh (1991), Flatebo and Datta (1992b; 1992c), Hoover and Poole (1992),

Lin and Simon (1992), Sur and Srimani (1992), Dolev (1993), Ghosh (1993), Katz and Perry (1993), Lentfert and Swierstra (1993), Sur and Srimani (1993), Huang, Wuu, and Tsai (1994), and Itkis and Levin (1994).

Section 6.2 is based on Huang (1989) for general computations and on Dijkstra and Scholten (1980) for diffusing computations. For an alternative account on the material in Dijkstra and Scholten (1980), the reader is referred to Bertsekas and Tsitsiklis (1989). Additional publications on termination detection include those by Chandrasekaran and Venkatesan (1990), Kavianpour and Bagherzadeh (1990), Ronn and Saikkonen (1990), Sheth and Dhamdhere (1991), Kumar (1992), Brzezinski, Hélary, and Raynal (1993), and Hélary and Raynal (1994).

Our treatment of deadlock detection in Section 6.3 follows Bracha and Toueg (1984). Sources of additional material are Singhal (1989b), Flatebo and Datta (1992a; 1992b), and Kshemkalyani and Singhal (1994).

7

Graph Algorithms

The problems that we consider in this chapter are graph problems posed on G, similarly to what we did in Sections 4.2 and 4.3, in which we addressed the problems of graph connectivity and shortest distances, respectively. As in those sections, the aim here is to provide distributed algorithms in which all of G's nodes participate in the solution based only on the partial knowledge of G's structure that they have locally. However, our discussion in Section 3.2.2 should be recalled with special care throughout this chapter. Specifically, one alternative to the fully distributed approach we just mentioned is to elect a leader and have that leader obtain information on the entire structure of G. Having done this, the leader is then in position to solve the graph problem locally. As we remarked in that section, it takes $O(nm)$ messages and $O(n)$ time to concentrate all the relevant information in the leader, so that these two measures should be compared to the complexities of the fully distributed solution. But one must never lose sight of the possible impact of the resulting local time complexity (cf. Section 3.2.2) and of the implications of the nonconstant memory demand at the leader, in addition to the complexities associated with electing the leader in the first place.

We consider two graph problems in this chapter. The first problem is that of determining a minimum spanning tree on G. In addition to the role played by spanning trees in some of the problems we have studied so far, particularly in Sections 4.1 and 5.3, establishing a minimum spanning tree on G is, as we remarked in Section 5.1, closely related to electing a leader in G, and then the relevance of the former problem is enlarged by its relation to all the situations in which having a leader is important. When a minimum spanning tree is sought with the purpose of electing a leader, then of course the alternative that we mentioned earlier of employing a leader to solve graph problems becomes meaningless. We deal with the minimum spanning tree problem in Section 7.1.

The other graph problem that we consider in this chapter is that of finding a maximum flow in a directed graph related to G with certain characteristics. We address this problem in Section 7.2, where we present three asynchronous algorithms to solve it. What is interesting in our discussion in that section is that two of the algorithms that we discuss are originally conceived as synchronous algorithms. By employing the synchronization techniques we studied in Section 5.3, we may obtain a variety of corresponding asynchronous algorithms. Some of them are such that the resulting complexities of all the three asynchronous algorithms we consider are the same.

Sections 7.3 and 7.4 contain, respectively, exercises and bibliographic notes.

7.1. Minimum spanning trees

G is in this section an undirected graph with FIFO edges. Our discussion is presented in three sections. Section 7.1.1 presents a statement of the problem, and Section 7.1.2 contains an asynchronous algorithm to solve it. Improvements leading to a reduced time complexity are given in Section 7.1.3.

7.1.1. The problem

As in Section 5.1, nodes in N are assumed to have distinct identifications (id_i for node n_i) totally ordered by $<$. Associated with every edge $(n_i, n_j) \in E$ is a finite weight w_{ij}, known to both n_i and n_j. The *weight* of a spanning tree is the sum of the weights of the $n - 1$ edges that constitute the tree. The *minimum spanning tree problem* asks that a spanning tree of minimum weight, called a *minimum spanning tree*, be found on G. Another related problem, that of finding any spanning tree on G, is clearly reducible to the problem of finding a minimum spanning tree, so that our discussion in this section applies to that problem as well. Although the problem of finding a spanning tree on G (any one) is conceptually what we have needed in other occasions in this book (as in Sections 4.1 and 5.3), the more general problem has greater appeal for at least two reasons. The first reason is that edge weights can in some situations be used to model delays (or other related quantities) for message transmission over the edges, in which case a minimum spanning tree represents a tree of globally minimum transmission delay.

The other reason why considering the more general problem of determining a minimum spanning tree is more appealing is related to the use of such a tree as a first step in the election of a leader. A distributed algorithm to find a minimum spanning tree on G can be built such that, at the end, every node has an indication of which edges incident to it are on the tree and which of these leads to the *core* of the tree, which is a single edge in the tree possessing properties that we describe later. Because only one core edge exists, the two nodes to which it is incident are natural candidates to be the leader. Clearly, under the usual assumption of totally ordered distinct identifications for all nodes, one of the two can be elected leader and the result broadcast over the tree with $O(n)$ message and time complexities. The core edge is only identified at the end of the algorithm, and may in principle be any edge, so the procedure we just described for leader election is only applicable to cases in which all of G's nodes are candidates originally (cf. Section 5.1 for the appropriate terminology). If such is not the case, however, then the tree can still be employed as a basis to choose among the existing candidates according to the procedure we discussed in Section 5.1.

For simplicity, in this section we assume that all edge weights are distinct and totally ordered by $<$. If the particular connotation associated with edge weights poses difficulties with respect to this assumption, then the assumed existence of distinct identifications for all nodes can be used to break ties. Specifically, in such cases the weight of edge (n_i, n_j) can be taken to be the pair

$$\big(w_{ij}, \min\{id_i, id_j\}\big),$$

and then all edge weights are totally ordered by $<$ in the lexicographic sense. Note that such a weight for edge (n_i, n_j) can be computed easily by both n_i and n_j by simply sending their identifications to each other. All over G, this can be regarded as a first step in the computation of the minimum spanning tree. This first step requires $O(m)$ messages and $O(1)$ time, which, as we will see, does not add to the overall complexities of determining the minimum spanning tree.

A *fragment* of a minimum spanning tree is any subtree of the minimum spanning tree. An edge is said to be an *outgoing edge* of a fragment if one of the two nodes to which it is incident is in the fragment while the other is not. The distributed algorithms we study in this section to build a minimum spanning tree on G are based on the following two properties (cf. Exercise 1).

(i) If a fragment of a minimum spanning tree is enlarged by the addition of the fragment's minimum-weight outgoing edge, then the resulting subtree is also a fragment of the minimum spanning tree.

(ii) If all edge weights are distinct, then G has a unique minimum spanning tree.

Properties (i) and (ii) hint at the following basis for an algorithm to find a minimum spanning tree on G. Nodes in N_0 constitute single-node fragments initially. By property (i), these fragments can be enlarged independently of one another by simply absorbing nodes that are connected to the fragments by minimum-weight outgoing edges. Property (ii) ensures that the union of two fragments that grow to the point of sharing a node is also a fragment.

7.1.2. An algorithm

The algorithm we describe in this section employs properties (i) and (ii) along with the following rules for the creation of new fragments. The first rule is that every node in N is initially a single-node fragment. This is achieved by having the nodes in N_0 broadcast a *startup* message by flooding over G (similarly to the case of Algorithm $A\_Alg(Alpha)$ of Section 5.3.1) with a message complexity of $O(m)$ and a time complexity of $O(n)$. Upon receiving a *startup* from every neighbor, a node initiates the algorithm as a single-node fragment. The second rule is that every fragment with at least two nodes has a special edge, called the *core* of the fragment, whose weight is taken to be the identification of the fragment. When the fragment is large enough to encompass all nodes (and then by properties (i) and (ii) it is the minimum spanning tree), its core is the tree's core, alluded to in the previous section.

The third overall rule regulates the process whereby fragments are combined to yield larger fragments. This combination is based on the *level* of each fragment, which is a nonnegative integer determined as follows. The level of a single-node fragment is zero. Now consider a fragment at level $\ell \geq 0$, and let ℓ' be the level of the fragment to which the fragment of level ℓ is connected by its minimum-weight outgoing edge. If $\ell = \ell'$ and the minimum-weight outgoing edges of both fragments are the same edge, then the two fragments are combined into a new fragment, whose level is set to $\ell + 1$ and whose core is the edge joining the former level-ℓ fragments.

If $\ell \neq \ell'$ or the two fragments' minimum-weight outgoing edges are not the same edge, then there are additional five cases to be considered. In two of the cases, $\ell \neq \ell'$ and the two minimum-weight outgoing edges are the same. In these cases, the lower-level fragment is absorbed by the higher-level fragment and the resulting fragment inherits the higher level. In the remaining three cases, the two minimum-weight outgoing edges are not the same, and either $\ell < \ell'$, or $\ell = \ell'$, or $\ell > \ell'$. In the case of $\ell < \ell'$, the absorption of the level-ℓ fragment by the level-ℓ' fragment takes place just as we described earlier. If $\ell \geq \ell'$, then the level-ℓ fragment simply waits until the level of the other fragment has increased from ℓ' enough for the combination to take place via one of the other possibilities.

Before we proceed, we should pause to investigate whether the waiting of fragments upon one another may ever lead to a deadlock. Specifically, the only situation one might be concerned about is that of a wait cycle comprising fragments, all of the same level, and such that the minimum-weight outgoing edge of every fragment leads to the next fragment in the cycle. By property (i), however, no such cycle may exist, as all the minimum-weight outgoing edges would have to be in the minimum spanning tree, which is impossible because they form a cycle.

Another property that may be investigated without any further details on how the algorithm functions is given by the following lemma.

Lemma 7.1. *The level of a fragment never exceeds* $\lfloor \log n \rfloor$.

Proof: For $\ell > 0$, a fragment of level ℓ is only formed when two level-$(\ell - 1)$ fragments are such that their minimum-weight outgoing edges lead from one fragment to the other. An immediate inductive argument shows that a level-ℓ fragment must then contain at least 2^ℓ nodes (this holds for $\ell = 0$ as well), so $n \geq 2^\ell$, thence the lemma.   ■

Let us now provide the details of an algorithm to find a minimum spanning tree on G based on the overall strategy we just outlined. The algorithm is called Algorithm *A_Find_MST* ("MST" for Minimum Spanning Tree), and essentially proceeds repeatedly as follows, until the minimum spanning tree is found. First the minimum-weight outgoing edge of all fragments must be determined, then fragments must be combined with one another, and then (if the combination yielded a new, higher-level fragment) new fragment cores must be determined. During an execution of Algorithm *A_Find_MST*, node n_i maintains a variable $state_i$, which may be one of **find** or **found**. Initially, $state_i = $ **found**, and along the execution $state_i$ switches back and forth between the two possibilities, indicating whether n_i is involved in the process of determining its fragment's minimum-weight outgoing edge ($state_i = $ **find**) or not ($state_i = $ **found**). For each edge $(n_i, n_j) \in E$, n_i also maintains a variable $state_i^j$, which can be one of **on_tree**, **off_tree**, or **basic**, to indicate respectively whether the edge has been found by n_i to be an edge of the minimum spanning tree, not to be an edge of the minimum spanning tree, or still neither. Initially, this variable is set to **basic** for all $n_j \in Neig_i$.

When a minimum-weight outgoing edge has been found for a fragment of level ℓ, a message $connect(\ell)$ is sent over that edge. If such an edge is (n_i, n_j) and n_i belongs to the level-ℓ fragment, than such a message is sent by n_i. There are two possibilities for the response that n_i gets from n_j, whose fragment we take to be at level ℓ'. It may receive another $connect(\ell)$, meaning that $\ell = \ell'$ and (n_i, n_j) is both fragments' minimum-weight outgoing edge, or it may happen that $\ell < \ell'$. In the former case, the two fragments are joined into a level-$(\ell + 1)$ fragment whose core is (n_i, n_j) and whose identification is the weight w_{ij}. Nodes n_i and n_j are referred to as the "coordinators" of the new fragment, and their first task is to broadcast over the fragment the new level and new identification, as well as to direct all nodes in the fragment to begin a new search for a minimum-weight outgoing edge. The message that this broadcast carries is an $initiate(\ell + 1, w_{ij}, \textbf{find})$, where the **find** is the instruction for every node in the fragment to participate in looking for the fragment's minimum-weight outgoing edge.

In the latter case, i.e., $\ell < \ell'$, n_j's fragment absorbs n_i's fragment. In order to do this, n_j sends n_i either a message $initiate(\ell', w, \textbf{find})$ or a message $initiate(\ell', w, \textbf{found})$, where w is the identification of the fragment to which n_j belongs. This message is then broadcast by n_i over its own fragment to inform every node of their new fragment's level and identification. In addition, it prompts nodes to behave differently depending on whether a **find** or a **found** is in the message. If it is a **find**, then the nodes join in the search for the minimum-weight outgoing edge of the fragment they now belong to. If it is a **found**, then the nodes simply acquire information on their new fragment's level and identification. What remains to be explained on this interaction between n_i and n_j is the choice that n_j makes between attaching a **find** or a **found** to the $initiate$ message that it sends. Node n_j attaches a **find** if $state_j = \textbf{find}$; it attaches a **found** if $state_j = \textbf{found}$. Sending a **found** in the $initiate$ message is only correct if it can be argued that the weight of n_j's fragment's minimum-weight outgoing edge is strictly less than w_{ij}, so that no edge outgoing from n_i's fragment could possibly be a candidate (because (n_i, n_j) is that fragment's minimum-weight outgoing edge). We provide this argument in what follows. The remaining cases cause n_i to wait for the level of n_j's fragment to increase from ℓ'.

So far we have seen that the coordinators of a newly formed fragment broadcast $initiate$ messages with a **find** parameter over the edges of the new fragment. This broadcast is meant to inform all the nodes in the fragment that the fragment has a new level and a new identification. It also carries a **find** parameter that directs the nodes to engage in seeking the minimum-weight outgoing edge of the new fragment. A node n_i that is reached by an $initiate$ message with a **find** parameter sets $state_i$

to **find** and participates in locating the fragment's minimum-weight outgoing edge. When n_i's participation in this process is finished, then $state_i$ is reset to **found**. If, on the other hand, the *initiate* message carries a **found** parameter, then its effect upon n_i is simply the fragment level and identification update. The broadcast of an *initiate* message may go beyond the boundaries of the fragment if a node n_i that it has reached receives a *connect* message from another fragment whose level is strictly less than the level being carried by the *initiate* message. The broadcast is then propagated through that fragment as well, representing its absorption by the higher-level fragment. The *initiate* messages that n_i propagates into the lower-level fragment carry either a **find** or a **found** parameter, depending on whether $state_i = $ **find** or $state_i = $ **found**. Let us now discuss in detail the process whereby the minimum-weight outgoing edge of a fragment is found. If the fragment has level zero, and therefore comprises one single node, than that node simply inspects the edges that are incident to it and sends a *connect*(0) message over the edge having minimum weight. In addition, if that node is n_i, then $state_i$ is set to **found**. If the fragment's level is strictly positive, then it must rely on the *initiate* message broadcast by its coordinators to have all the nodes participate in the process.

After receiving an *initiate*$(\ell, w, $**find**$)$ and setting $state_i$ to **find**, node n_i considers all edges (n_i, n_j) for which $state_i^j = $ **basic** in increasing order of weights. On each edge that it considers, n_i sends a *test*(ℓ, w) and waits to receive either a *reject* message or an *accept* message. If ℓ' is the level of the fragment to which n_j belongs and w' that fragment's identification (or at least n_j's view of that level and that identification, which may already have changed), then the *reject* is sent by n_j, after it sets $state_j^i$ to **off_tree**, if $w = w'$ (in this case, n_i and n_j are in the same fragment and the edge between them cannot possibly be on the minimum spanning tree). If $w \neq w'$ and $\ell' \geq \ell$, then n_j sends n_i an *accept*. If $w \neq w'$ and $\ell' < \ell$, then n_j is not in position to send any response immediately and waits to do so until its level has increased to be at least equal to ℓ (at which time it must also re-evaluate the relation between w and w', as the latter may have changed along with ℓ').

An *accept* received from n_j makes n_i stop the search. A *reject* that it receives from n_j causes it to set $state_i^j$ to **off_tree**. When n_i receives an *accept* from a neighbor n_j, the edge (n_i, n_j) becomes its "candidate" for minimum-weight outgoing edge of the fragment. In order to compare the various candidates in the fragment, nodes proceed as follows. When a leaf of the fragment (i.e., n_i such that $state_i^j = $ **on_tree** for exactly one neighbor n_j) has found its own candidate, say of weight w, or when it has exhausted all the possibilities without receiving any *accept*, it then sends a *report*(w) message on the fragment in the direction of the coordinators ($w = \infty$ if n_i does not have a candidate). Every other node does the same after taking w to be the minimum among its own candidate's weight and the weights that it receives in *report* messages over all fragment edges that lead away from the coordinators. Upon sending a *report* message, a node n_i sets $state_i$ to **found**. If it receives a *connect* message from a lower-level fragment, it may then safely respond with an *initiate* message carrying a **found** parameter, because an *accept* must not have been received on that edge (*accept*'s only come from fragments that are not at a lower level), and then that edge could not possibly have been the node's candidate for minimum-weight outgoing edge of the fragment.

When the *report* messages finally reach the coordinators, they exchange report messages themselves (over the fragment's core) and then determine the weight of the fragment's minimum-weight outgoing edge. If this weight is infinity, then the fragment has no outgoing edge and is therefore the minimum spanning tree that was being sought.

If every node keeps track of the edge corresponding to the weight it sent along with its *report* message, then the path through the fragment from the core to the fragment's minimum-weight outgoing edge can be traced easily. At node n_i, we let $best\_edge_i$ denote either n_i's candidate edge, if this edge's weight is what n_i sends along with its *report*, or the edge on which it received the weight that it sends. Another special edge that n_i keeps track of is the edge on the fragment leading to the core. This edge is denoted by to_core_i, and it is on this edge that n_i sends its *report* message. After the coordinators have decided upon the fragment's minimum-weight outgoing edge, one of them sends a *change_core* message along the path given by the $best\_edge$'s. Upon reaching n_i, this message has the effect of changing to_core_i to be equal to $best\_edge_i$. When the *change_core* message reaches the node n_i to which the fragment's minimum-weight outgoing edge is incident, all to_core's in the fragment lead to this node, which is then in position to send its *connect* message over that edge. If such an edge is (n_i, n_j), then n_i sets $state_i^j$ to **on_tree** as it sends the message.

As in various occasions so far in the book, interpreting Algorithm A_Find_MST as propagating waves over G can be very helpful in building some intuitive understanding on how it works. What happens in this case is that a fragment's core propagates a wave of *initiate* messages over **on_tree** edges. This wave collapses back with *report* messages onto the core, and then a new fragment is formed after the *change_core* and *connect* messages have played their roles. The *initiate* waves may occasionally "leak" from the fragment when neighboring fragments are absorbed.

We now turn to the presentation of the algorithm's actions. In addition to the variables that we have already introduced during our preceding discussion, Algorithm A_Find_MST also employs the following variables at node n_i. The Boolean $initiated_i$, initially equal to **false**, is used to indicate whether $n_i \in N_0$. For all $n_j \in Neig_i$, the Boolean go_i^j, equal to **false** initially, indicates whether a $startup$ has been received from n_j. At n_i, the level and identification of the fragment to which it belongs are denoted respectively by $level_i$ (set to zero initially) and $frag_i$. The weight of $best\_edge_i$ is stored in $best\_weight_i$. The counter $expected_i$, initialized to zero, is used by n_i to indicate the number of messages it must receive before being in position to send its $report$ message. An additional group of variables is used to control the wait of higher-level fragments upon lower-level ones. For all $n_j \in Neig_i$, these are the Booleans $got\_connect_i^j$ and $got\_test_i^j$, both initialized to **false**, and also $test\_level_i^j$ and $test\_frag_i^j$. The two Booleans are used, respectively, to indicate that a $connect$ or a $test$ has been received from a higher-level fragment and cannot therefore be replied to at once. When $got_test_i^j = $ **true**, then $test\_level_i^j$ and $test\_frag_i^j$ store respectively the level and the identification that the $test$ message carried.

> **Algorithm** A_Find_MST:

> $\triangleright$ **Variables:**

$initiated_i = $ **false**;
$go_i^j = $ **false** for all $n_j \in Neig_i$;
$state_i = $ **found**;
$state_i^j = $ **basic** for all $n_j \in Neig_i$;
$level_i = 0$;
$frag_i$;
$best\_edge_i$;
$best\_weight_i$;
to_core_i;
$expected_i = 0$;
$got_connect_i^j = $ **false** for all $n_j \in Neig_i$;
$got_test_i^j = $ **false** for all $n_j \in Neig_i$;
$test\_level_i^j$ for all $n_j \in Neig_i$;
$test\_frag_i^j$ for all $n_j \in Neig_i$.

> $\triangleright$ **Input:**

$msg_i = $ **nil**.
Action if $n_i \in N_0$:   (7.1)
$initiated_i := $ **true**;
Send $startup$ to all $n_j \in Neig_i$.

▷ **Input:**
   $msg_i = startup$ such that $origin_i(msg_i) = (n_i, n_j)$.
  Action: (7.2)
      if not $initiated_i$ **then**
          begin
              $initiated_i := $ **true**;
              Send $startup$ to all $n_k \in Neig_i$
          end;
      $go_i^j := $ **true**;
      if go_i^j for all $n_j \in Neig_i$ **then**
          begin
              Let (n_i, n_k) be such that $w_{ik} \leq w_{il}$ for all $n_l \in Neig_i$;
              $state_i^k := $ **on_tree**;
              Send $connect(level_i)$ to n_j
          end.

▷ **Input:**
   $msg_i = connect(\ell)$ such that $origin_i(msg_i) = (n_i, n_j)$.
  Action: (7.3)
      if $\ell < level_i$ **then**
          begin
              $state_i^j := $ **on_tree**;
              Send $initiate(level_i, frag_i, state_i)$ to n_j;
              if $state_i = $ **find then**
                  $expected_i := expected_i + 1$
          end
      else
          if $state_i^j = $ **basic then**
              $got_connect_i^j := $ **true**
          else
              Send $initiate(level_i + 1, w_{ij}, $ **find**$)$ to n_j.

▷ **Input:**

$msg_i = initiate(\ell, w, st)$ such that $origin_i(msg_i) = (n_i, n_j)$.

Action: (7.4)

$level_i := \ell;$

$frag_i := w;$

for all $n_k \in Neig_i$ such that $got\_test_i^k$ **do**

    if $test\_level_i^k \leq level_i$ **then**

        if $test\_frag_i^k \neq frag_i$ **then**

            Send $accept$ to n_k

        else

            begin

                if $state_i^k = $ **basic then**

                    $state_i^k := $ **off_tree**;

                Send $reject$ to n_k

            end;

$state_i := st;$

$to\_core_i := (n_i, n_j);$

$best\_weight_i := \infty;$

for all $n_k \in Neig_i - \{n_j\}$ such that $state_i^k = $ **on_tree do**

    begin

        Send $initiate(level_i, frag_i, state_i)$ to n_k;

        if $state_i = $ **find then**

            $expected_i := expected_i + 1$

    end;

if $state_i = $ **find then**

    if $n_k \in Neig_i$ exists such that $state_i^k = $ **basic then**

        begin

            Let $B \subset Neig_i$ be such that $state_i^k = $ **basic** for all

            $n_k \in B$;

            Let $n_k \in B$ be such that $w_{ik} \leq w_{il}$ for all $n_l \in B$;

            Send $test(level_i, frag_i)$ to n_k

        end

    else

        if $expected_i = 0$ **then**

            begin

                $state_i := $ **found**;

                Send $report(best\_weight_i)$ on to_core_i

            end.

▷ **Input:**

   $msg_i = test(\ell, w)$ such that $origin_i(msg_i) = (n_i, n_j)$.

Action: (7.5)

   if $\ell > level_i$ **then**

      begin

         $got\_test_i^j := \textbf{true}$;

         $test\_level_i^j := \ell$;

         $test\_frag_i^j := w$

      end

   else

      if $w \neq frag_i$ **then**

         Send $accept$ to n_j

      else

         begin

            if $state_i^j = \textbf{basic}$ **then**

               $state_i^j := \textbf{off\_tree}$;

            Send $reject$ to n_j

         end.

▷ **Input:**

   $msg_i = accept$ such that $origin_i(msg_i) = (n_i, n_j)$.

Action: (7.6)

   if $w_{ij} < best\_weight_i$ **then**

      begin

         $best\_weight_i := w_{ij}$;

         $best\_edge_i := (n_i, n_j)$

      end;

   if $expected_i = 0$ **then**

      begin

         $state_i := \textbf{found}$;

         Send $report(best\_weight_i)$ on to_core_i

      end.

$\triangleright$ **Input:**

$msg_i = reject$ such that $origin_i(msg_i) = (n_i, n_j)$.

Action: (7.7)

   if $state_i^j = $ **basic then**

      $state_i^j := $ **off_tree**;

   if $n_k \in Neig_i$ exists such that $state_i^k = $ **basic then**

      begin

         Let $B \subset Neig_i$ be such that $state_i^k = $ **basic** for all $n_k \in B$;

         Let $n_k \in B$ be such that $w_{ik} \leq w_{il}$ for all $n_l \in B$;

         Send $test(level_i, frag_i)$ to n_k

      end

   else

      if $expected_i = 0$ **then**

         begin

            $state_i := $ **found**;

            Send $report(best\_weight_i)$ on to_core_i

         end.

▷ **Input:**
$msg_i = report(w)$ such that $origin_i(msg_i) = (n_i, n_j)$.
Action when $(n_i, n_j) \neq to\_core_i$ **or** $state_i = $ **found:**   (7.8)
    if $(n_i, n_j) \neq to\_core_i$ **then**
        begin
            $expected_i := expected_i - 1;$
            if $w < best\_weight_i$ **then**
                begin
                    $best\_weight_i := w;$
                    $best\_edge_i := (n_i, n_j)$
                end;
            if $expected_i = 0$ **then**
                begin
                    $state_i := $ **found**;
                    Send $report(best\_weight_i)$ on to_core_i
                end
        end
    else
        if $w > best\_weight_i$ **then**
            begin
                Let $n_k \in Neig_i$ be such that $(n_i, n_k) = best\_edge_i;$
                if $state_i^k = $ **on_tree then**
                    Send $change\_core$ on $best\_edge_i$
                else
                    begin
                        Send $connect(level_i)$ on $best\_edge_i;$
                        if $got\_connect_i^k$ **then**
                            Send $initiate(level_i + 1, w_{ik}, $ **find**$)$ on
                            $best\_edge_i;$
                        $state_i^k := $ **on_tree**
                  end
            end.

▷ **Input:**

$msg_i = change\_core$ such that $origin_i(msg_i) = (n_i, n_j)$.

Action: (7.9)

Let $n_k \in Neig_i$ be such that $(n_i, n_k) = best\_edge_i$;

if $state_i^k = $ **on_tree then**

   Send $change\_core$ on $best\_edge_i$

else

   begin

   Send $connect(level_i)$ on $best\_edge_i$;

   if $got\_connect_i^k$ **then**

   Send $initiate(level_i + 1, w_{ik}, $ **find**$)$ on $best\_edge_i$;

   $state_i^k := $ **on_tree**

   end.

Actions (7.1) through (7.9) implement the overall strategy we described in detail earlier to find a minimum spanning tree on G. These actions, the reader must have noticed, account for far more complex a behavior than that of any of the algorithms we have seen (or will see) in other chapters. Although a complete proof of correctness cannot be offered within the scope of this book, we now pause momentarily to offer some more detailed comments on each of the actions, so that the reader may have additional guidance in studying them.

Actions (7.1) and (7.2) are the standard initial actions so that all nodes can begin participating in the algorithm after the initial flood of *startup* messages. A node's initial participation consists of sending a $connect(0)$ message over the minimum-weight edge that is incident to it.

Upon receiving a $connect(\ell)$ message from n_j in (7.3), n_i either immediately absorbs the originating fragment (if $\ell < level_i$), or it recognizes that this *connect* is the response to a *connect* that it sent previously on the same edge, and therefore the two fragments must be merged into another of higher level (if $\ell \geq level_i$ and $state_i^j \neq$ **basic**). If $\ell \geq level_i$ and $state_i^j = $ **basic**, then this must be a *connect* from a higher-level fragment and must not be replied to immediately.

The receipt of an *initiate* message by n_i in (7.4) first causes the node to update its fragment level and identification and then to reply to any of its neighbors that may have sent a *test* message in the past with a level higher than its own. It then forwards the *initiate* message on all the other **on_tree** edges that are incident to it and, if $state_i = $ **find**, begins the search for its minimum-weight outgoing edge by means of *test* messages, if **basic** edges exist that are incident to it (otherwise, it may be in position to send its *report*).

When node n_i receives a $test(\ell, w)$ message from n_j in (7.5) and $\ell > level_i$, then it cannot reply immediately and saves both ℓ and w for later consideration when its own level increases in (7.4). If $\ell \leq level_i$, then either an *accept* gets sent to n_j (if $w \neq frag_i$) or a *reject* gets sent (otherwise).

The receipt of an *accept* by n_i in (7.6) may cause $best\_edge_i$ to be updated (along with $best\_weight_i$), and may in addition signal to n_i that it may send its *report* message. If a *reject* is received in (7.7) and there are additional **basic** edges incident to n_i, then the node continues its probing with *test* messages; if no such edges are left, then n_i checks whether its *report* may be sent.

Upon receiving a $report(w)$ message in (7.8), there are two possibilities for n_i. The first possibility is that the message is received on edge to_core_i, in which case n_i must be a coordinator of the fragment and has to decide on which side of the core the fragment's minimum-weight outgoing edge lies. If that edge is to be found on its own side (i.e., if $w > best\_weight_i$), then either it sends a *change_core* or a *connect* on $best\_edge_i$, the former if $best\_edge_i$ is an **on_tree** edge, the latter otherwise (and then the fragment's minimum-weight outgoing edge is incident to n_i, thence the *connect* that it sends). The second possibility is that of $(n_i, n_j) \neq to\_core_i$, in which case n_i checks whether it is time for its own *report* to be sent.

It is important to notice, in (7.8), that the action is only executed upon receipt of the *report* on (n_i, n_j) when $(n_i, n_j) \neq to\_core_i$ or $state_i = $ **found**. This ensures that a *report* arriving on the core $((n_i, n_j) = to\_core_i)$ is only acted upon when n_i has already identified the least weight on its side of the fragment ($state_i = $ **found**) and may therefore decide on the fragment's minimum-weight outgoing edge. (Associating Boolean conditions to actions can also be an approach to delaying the receipt of a message that cannot be replied to immediately, as in (7.3) and (7.5); however, this can only be done in the presence of edges that are not FIFO— cf. Exercise 2.)

Action (7.9) corresponds to the receipt by n_i of a *change_core* message, which is either forwarded on $best\_edge_i$ or causes a *connect* to be sent on that edge, depending on whether the fragment's minimum-weight outgoing edge is incident to n_i, just as in the case of (7.8). When sending a *connect* in either (7.8) or (7.9), n_i may also have to send an *initiate* after it, if in (7.3) a *connect* was received that could not be replied to immediately.

The algorithm's termination is detected by each coordinator n_i upon receiving a $report(w)$ message on the core when $state_i = $ **found** such that $w = best\_weight_i = \infty$. After the minimum spanning tree has been found on G, at every node the **on_tree** edges indicate which of the edges incident to it are on the tree, while the to_core edge indicates which of the **on_tree** edges leads to the tree's core.

Next we present Algorithm *A_Find_MST*'s complexities.

Theorem 7.2. *Algorithm A_Find_MST has a message complexity of $O(m+n \log n)$ and a time complexity of $O(n \log n)$. In addition, the algorithm's bit complexity is $O\big((m + n \log n)(\log W + \log \log n)\big)$, where $W \geq |w_{ij}|$ for all $(n_i, n_j) \in E$.*

Proof: Let ℓ and w denote respectively a generic fragment level and edge weight. A node can never send more than one *reject* message on the same edge in the same direction. In addition, to each such message there corresponds a *test*(ℓ, w) message, therefore accounting for $O(m)$ messages and, by Lemma 7.1, $O\big(m(\log W + \log \log n)\big)$ bits. At each level, a node can receive at most one *initiate*(ℓ, w, st) and one *accept*, and it can send no more than one *test*(ℓ, w) resulting in an *accept*, one *report*(w), and one *change_core* or *connect*(ℓ), where st is one of **find** or **found** and requires a constant number of bits to be expressed. By Lemma 7.1, we have another $O(n \log n)$ messages and $O\big(n \log n(\log W + \log \log n)\big)$ bits, which, added to what we already have, yields the algorithm's message and bit complexities.

The algorithm's time complexity follows directly from Lemma 7.1 and from the observation that, for each level, the propagation of messages within a fragment takes no more than $O(n)$ time.

It should be noted that the initial complexities for determining edge weights (if not distinct originally, in which case node identifications must be used) and for exchanging the *startup* messages do not add to the complexities we have determined.

■

We finalize the section by returning to some issues raised earlier in the book. The first issue is that of electing a leader once the minimum spanning tree has been found. As we observed earlier in Section 7.1.1, the final coordinators (nodes to which the tree's core is incident) may elect a leader in $O(n)$ time and with $O(n)$ messages. The resulting complexities for the leader election (including those of finding the minimum spanning tree) are then the same as those given by Theorem 7.2. When compared with the $O(nm)$-message, $O(n)$-time procedure for leader election described in Section 5.1, the new approach has a better message complexity, but its time complexity turns out to be somewhat worse.

The second issue is that of the complexities to initialize Synchronizer *Beta* in Section 5.3.1. The reader should recognize quickly that Theorem 7.2, together with the observation we just made on the election of a leader on the tree, provides the values of *Messages*$_0$ and *Time*$_0$ for Synchronizer *Beta*.

7.1.3. Further improvements

Although it can be argued that the $O(m + n \log n)$ message complexity is the best one can hope for when finding a minimum spanning tree on G, reducing the time complexity from the $O(n \log n)$ of Algorithm A_Find_MST has been the subject of investigations, aiming at bringing it down to $O(n)$. We do not in this section aim at conveying the details of how this improved time complexity can be achieved, but rather point at some of the inessential sources of time complexity in Algorithm A_Find_MST and at some possible improvements.

In order to identify the reason for the excessive time complexity of Algorithm A_Find_MST, we must look at the proof of Lemma 7.1, where we argue that, for $\ell \geq 0$, a level-ℓ fragment has at least 2^{ℓ} nodes. Although for $\ell = 0$ this number is exactly 2^{ℓ} (level-0 fragments comprise exactly one node), for $\ell > 0$ a level-ℓ fragment may include a lot more than the minimum 2^{ℓ} nodes. Because the algorithm is such that higher-level fragments wait for lower-level fragments to have their levels increased before they can be merged, a level-$(\ell + 1)$ fragment that happens to be waiting for such an oversized level-ℓ fragment may have to wait for as long as $O(n)$ time before the merge (this is what is argued in the proof of Theorem 7.2 as far as the time complexity is concerned).

So the attempts at improving the algorithm's time complexity concentrate on relating a fragment's size to its level more tightly. One such attempt is, for example, to force level-ℓ fragments (which have at least 2^{ℓ} nodes each) to have strictly less than $2^{\ell+1}$ nodes. With a few modifications to Algorithm A_Find_MST, this strategy can be shown to be able to reduce the number of fragments by an $O(\log n)$ factor within $O(n)$ time. As a consequence, the reduction from the initial n fragments to the final single fragment representing the minimum spanning tree can be achieved in as many $O(n)$-time portions as it takes at a rate of $O(\log n)$ per portion. Employing the usual notation $\log^{*} k$ to denote the number of times log has to be applied to reduce $k > 1$ to a number no greater than one, we see that the number of $O(n)$-time portions that we need is $\log^{*} n$. The time complexity of the resulting algorithm is then $O(n \log^{*} n)$, and its message complexity can be shown to remain the same as that of Algorithm A_Find_MST.

7.2. Maximum flows in networks

In all of Section 7.2, G is an undirected graph with two distinguished nodes, called a *source* (which we assume to be n_1) and a *sink* (which we assume to be n_n). G is an undirected graph, in conformity with our practice in this book that only in such graphs may communication between neighbors flow in both directions. However, the denominations of n_1 and n_n respectively as source and sink are only meaningful when we consider a directed variation of G, denoted by G^d, which is the graph on which the problem that we deal with is posed. The reason for employing the two graphs is that we want to be able to state the problem properly and yet, during the execution of the algorithms that we shall investigate, be able to have messages sent between neighbors in both directions.

The directed graph G^d is obtained from G by associating a direction with each of G's edges. These directions are such that n_1 must not have any edge directed toward itself (thence its denomination as a source) and n_n must not have any edge directed away from itself (thence its denomination as a sink). In addition, n_1 must be the only source in G^d and n_n the only sink, which implies that all the other nodes must in G^d lie on a directed path from n_1 to n_n. As a side remark, the reader should notice that, in Section 6.3.2, we were faced with the same notational issue of being able to refer to G as an undirected graph and at the same time to another directed graph defined as a function of G. A similar situation will occur once again in the book, specifically in Sections 8.3 and 8.4.

The problem that we study in the next three sections is the problem of computing a maximum flow in G^d, which in this context is referred to as a "network," although we refrain from employing this denomination any further in the book, lest there may be confusion with the more pervasive meanings we employ for the term. This problem captures the essence of various problems appearing in the field of computer networks, and that is what justifies our interest in fully distributed approaches to solve it. The study of flows in G^d, both aiming at computing a maximum flow in this graph as well as other quantities, constitutes a research area with issues of its own and a considerable body of knowledge. In particular, arguing for the correctness of many of the pertinent algorithms (and consequently for their complexities) requires a level of detail that does not befit a text on distributed algorithms. Our approach in this section to presenting the algorithms is then far less rigorous than in previous occasions in the book, and this extends to our treatment of the algorithms' complexities. The specialized literature is abundant, though, and the interested reader may deepen the treatment by resorting to it.

We continue our discussion in three further sections. The statement of the problem, as well as a preview of how the algorithms to be studied relate to one another, is given in Section 7.2.1. Sections 7.2.2 and 7.2.3 then follow with the presentation of two synchronous algorithms and one asynchronous algorithm, respectively.

7.2.1. The problem

Let E^d be the set of directed edges in G^d (that is, $G^d = (N, E^d)$). The *capacity* of G^d is a function $c : N \times N \to \mathbf{R}$ such that, for all $n_i, n_j \in N$, $c(n_i, n_j) \geq 0$. In addition, $c(n_i, n_j) = 0$ if $(n_i \to n_j) \notin E^d$. A *flow* in G^d is a function $f : N \times N \to \mathbf{R}$ satisfying the following three properties.

(i) $f(n_i, n_j) \leq c(n_i, n_j)$ for all $n_i, n_j \in N$.

(ii) $f(n_i, n_j) = -f(n_j, n_i)$ for all $n_i, n_j \in N$.

(iii) $\sum_{n_j \in N} f(n_i, n_j) = 0$ for all $n_i \in N - \{n_1, n_n\}$.

For all $n_i, n_j \in N$ such that $(n_i, n_j) \notin E$, the definition of G^d's capacity is such that $c(n_i, n_j) = c(n_j, n_i) = 0$. By property (i), $f(n_i, n_j) \leq 0$ and $f(n_j, n_i) \leq 0$; by property (ii), it must then be that $f(n_i, n_j) = f(n_j, n_i) = 0$. Under the weaker condition that $(n_i \to n_j) \notin E^d$, we still have $c(n_i, n_j) = 0$ by definition, and then by property (i) $f(n_i, n_j) \leq 0$, while by property (ii) $f(n_j, n_i) \geq 0$. So the definitions of capacity and of flow imply that nonzero flow may only exist from node n_i to node n_j if $(n_i, n_j) \in E$. Furthermore, this flow is necessarily nonnegative if $(n_i \to n_j) \in E^d$, or nonpositive if $(n_j \to n_i) \in E^d$.

These observations, together with property (iii), imply that if node n_i is not the source n_1 or the sink n_n, then the flow that "comes into it" must be equal to the flow that "goes out from it," that is,

$$\sum_{n_j \in N} f(n_i, n_j) = \sum_{(n_i \to n_j) \in E^d} f(n_i, n_j) + \sum_{(n_j \to n_i) \in E^d} f(n_i, n_j)$$

$$= \sum_{(n_i \to n_j) \in E^d} f(n_i, n_j) - \sum_{(n_j \to n_i) \in E^d} f(n_j, n_i)$$

$$= 0,$$

so that

$$\sum_{(n_j \to n_i) \in E^d} f(n_j, n_i) = \sum_{(n_i \to n_j) \in E^d} f(n_i, n_j).$$

If $n_i = n_1$, then property (iii) does not hold, because

$$\sum_{(n_1 \to n_j) \in E^d} f(n_1, n_j) \geq 0$$

and

$$\sum_{(n_j \to n_1) \in E^d} f(n_j, n_1) = 0.$$

Analogously, if $n_i = n_n$, then

$$\sum_{(n_j \to n_n) \in E^d} f(n_j, n_n) \geq 0$$

and

$$\sum_{(n_n \to n_j) \in E^d} f(n_n, n_j) = 0.$$

The *value* of a flow f, denoted by F, is given by the summation in either of the two previous inequalities, that is,

$$F = \sum_{(n_1 \to n_j) \in E^d} f(n_1, n_j) = \sum_{(n_j \to n_n) \in E^d} f(n_j, n_n)$$

(cf. Exercise 3). The *maximum-flow problem* asks for a flow f of maximum value.

For $n_i, n_j \in N$, the *residual capacity* of the ordered pair (n_i, n_j) given a flow f is

$$c_f(n_i, n_j) = c(n_i, n_j) - f(n_i, n_j),$$

being therefore equal to zero if $(n_i, n_j) \notin E$. Readily, $c_f(n_i, n_j) \geq 0$ if $(n_i \to n_j) \in E^d$, whereas $c_f(n_i, n_j) = f(n_j, n_i)$ if $(n_j \to n_i) \in E^d$. The *residual network* of G given f is the directed graph $G_f = (N, E_f)$, and is such that $(n_i \to n_j) \in E_f$ if and only if $(n_i, n_j) \in E$ and $c_f(n_i, n_j) > 0$. Clearly, if $(n_i \to n_j) \in E^d$, then both $(n_i \to n_j)$ and $(n_j \to n_i)$ may be members of E_f, so long as $f(n_i, n_j) < c(n_i, n_j)$ and $f(n_j, n_i) > 0$ (these are, respectively, the conditions for each of the memberships in E_f). A directed path from n_1 to n_n in G_f is called an *augmenting path*. The intuitive support for this denomination is that, along such a path, the residual capacity of $(n_i \to n_j) \in E_f$ can be decreased by either increasing $f(n_i, n_j)$ if $(n_i \to n_j) \in E^d$ or decreasing $f(n_j, n_i)$ if $(n_j \to n_i) \in E^d$.

When f does not satisfy property (iii), but rather the weaker property that

$$\sum_{n_j \in N} f(n_i, n_j) \leq 0$$

for all $n_i \in N - \{n_1, n_n\}$, then it is called a *preflow* instead of a flow. In this case, there exists an *excess flow* coming into n_i, denoted by $e_f(n_i)$ and given by

$$e_f(n_i) = - \sum_{n_j \in N} f(n_i, n_j).$$

The next two sections are devoted to the presentation of three distributed algorithms for the maximum-flow problem. Two of these algorithms are synchronous and appear in Section 7.2.2. The other algorithm is asynchronous, and is presented in Section 7.2.3. The first of the synchronous algorithms is based on the concepts of residual networks and augmenting paths, and is called Algorithm *S_Find_Max_Flow*. The other synchronous algorithm and the asynchronous algorithm are both based on the concept of preflows. These two algorithms are considerably simpler than Algorithm *S_Find_Max_Flow*, and for this reason are not presented with all the details as that one is.

Algorithm *S_Find_Max_Flow* and the preflow-based synchronous algorithm can both be shown to have the same message and time complexities, being respectively of $O(n^3)$ and $O(n^2)$. The asynchronous algorithms that result from applying Synchronizer *Gamma* to Algorithm *S_Find_Max_Flow* and to the other synchronous algorithm, following our discussion in Section 5.3.1, both have message complexity and time complexity, for $2 \leq k < n$, respectively of $O(kn^3)$ and $O(n^2 \log n / \log k)$. If Synchronizer *Alpha* is used instead, then the resulting asynchronous algorithms have message complexity of $O(n^2 m)$ and time complexity of $O(n^2)$. Interestingly, these are the complexities that the preflow-based asynchronous algorithm has been shown to have as well.

7.2.2. Two synchronous algorithms

The essence of Algorithm *S_Find_Max_Flow* is the following. It proceeds in iterations, and at each iteration a "layered" residual network (to be explained shortly) is built. A maximal flow is then found on this network and then added to the cumulative flow that is maintained throughout the iterations. A flow in the layered residual network is said to be *maximal* when it is equal to the residual capacity of at least one edge on every n_1-to-n_n path. When a layered residual network with at least one augmenting path can no longer be found, the flow is maximum and the algorithm terminates.

The layered residual network is built at each iteration as follows. Let f be the cumulative flow obtained at the end of the previous iteration (the initial flow, for the first iteration). The source n_1 is included in the first layer and a process similar to the breadth-first numbering discussed in Section 3.4 is started to determine the subsequent layers. For $l > 1$, the lth layer contains every node n_j that is not in any of the previous $l - 1$ layers and such that there exists a node n_i in the $l - 1$st layer such that $c_f(n_i, n_j) > 0$. The synchronous algorithm to build the layered residual network is then very simple. For $l > 1$ and $\sigma \geq 0$ to indicate the pulses within each iteration, the lth layer is determined at pulse $\sigma = l - 2$ as follows. Those nodes

n_i belonging to the $l-1$st layer send a message to their neighbors n_j such that $c_f(n_i, n_j) > 0$. In the next pulse (i.e., $\sigma = l - 1$), n_j replies positively or not at all to n_i, depending on whether it had already been included in a layer at any of the previous pulses.

Once the layered residual network has been constructed based on a flow f, a maximal flow on it is determined by a process that is started at n_1 by assigning to each $(n_1 \rightarrow n_i) \in E_f$ a flow equal to $c_f(n_1, n_i)$, thereby providing n_i with a positive excess flow. This process continues on to the succeeding layers, and along the way the excess flow at the nodes is either pushed to the next layer or returned to the previous one (and then possibly re-routed through other edges). Termination occurs when no node can take any additional flow. The synchronous algorithm to find a maximal flow on the layered residual network works by sending flow between neighbors in the form of messages. Whenever flow is received at n_j from n_i on edge (n_i, n_j) such that $(n_i \rightarrow n_j) \in E_f$, the amount of flow received is pushed onto a stack along with a pointer to its sender, n_i. At each pulse, a node n_j may receive flow from n_i on edge (n_i, n_j) such that $(n_i \rightarrow n_j) \in E_f$ or such that $(n_j \rightarrow n_i) \in E_f$ (this is returned flow). At the beginning of the next pulse, all the flow n_j received is either sent to the succeeding layer, if at all possible, or returned to the previous one, in this case by popping the amount of flow to be returned and its destination off the stack. In case no more flow can be sent to the next layer, n_j informs its neighbors in the preceding layer that it is "blocked," so no further attempts will be made to send flow to it in the remainder of the iteration.

Algorithm *S_Find_Max_Flow* proceeds in iterations $k = 1, \ldots, K$, where K is initially viewed as being equal to infinity and is set to its correct value upon detection by the nodes that the current iteration is the last one. Incidentally, the detection of termination in this case is, like for the other synchronous algorithms we have seen, essentially a matter of counting pulses as they elapse. However, as we mentioned in Section 6.2, in this case such a strategy is supported by the nontrivial arguments (which we do not reproduce here) that lead to the algorithm's time complexity.

For $1 \leq k < K$, the kth iteration comprises two phases, each no more than $2n$ pulses long. The first phase of an iteration is used to find the layered residual network, while the second phase is used to find a maximal flow on that network, so for the Kth iteration only the first phase is needed. The value of K, however, can only be known after a first phase in which n_n could not be reached during the construction of the layered residual network has occurred.

Intuitively, Algorithm *S_Find_Max_Flow* proceeds through the propagation of synchronous waves emanating from n_1. During the first phase of an iteration, such a wave expands from n_1 to construct the layered residual network, with feedback information sent to n_1 when the network is constructed. During the second phase, the wave that n_1 initiates pushes flow onward on the layered residual network, with occasional "ripples" of returned flow in the opposite direction that may in turn be sent onward again.

The following are the messages employed in Algorithm *S_Find_Max_Flow*. A message *layer* is employed to build the layered residual network. It is propagated, starting at n_1, on edges that have positive residual capacity (except the edge, if any, on which it was received) when received for the first time in an iteration. Every *layer* message, if belonging to the first group of such messages to be received in the current iteration, is replied to with an *ack*. This propagation of *layer* messages, as well as *ack*'s, accounts for at most the first n pulses of an iteration. Additional n pulses (at most) are employed for a *success* message to be sent by n_n toward n_1 if it is reached by the *layer* messages. If within $2n$ pulses of the beginning of an iteration n_1 does not receive a *success*, then it may conclude that the *layer* messages did not reach n_n and therefore may set K to the number of the current iteration to terminate the algorithm. The second phase employs *flow*(x) and *block* messages, respectively to ship an amount x of flow and to signal that the sender of the message should not be sent any more flow during the iteration.

Node n_i employs the following variables. A $stack_i$, initialized to **nil**, is employed for n_i to store the flow shipments it receives, and their origins, for later return if the need arises. The excess flow at n_i is stored in the variable $excess_i$, initially equal to zero. A Boolean $reached_i$, initially equal to **false**, indicates whether during the current iteration n_i has already been reached by a *layer* message. As in previous occasions, the node from which n_i receives *layer* for the first time is pointed to by $parent_i$, initially set to **nil** (if a *layer* is received from more than one neighbor at the same pulse, then the choice of which neighbor $parent_i$ is to point to is arbitrary). For all $n_j \in Neig_i$, the following variables are used. The Booleans $in\_previous\_layer_i^j$ and $in\_next\_layer_i^j$, initially set to **false**, are used respectively to indicate, for each iteration, whether n_j is in the previous layer or in the next layer of the layered residual network with respect to n_i. The variables $flow_i^j$ and $residue_i^j$ give, respectively, the value of the current flow and current residual capacity of the ordered pair (n_i, n_j). They are both initialized to zero, unless $(n_i \to n_j) \in E^d$, in which case $residue_i^j$ is initialized to $c(n_i, n_j)$. The Booleans $blocked_i^j$ and $returned_i^j$, both initially equal to **false**, indicate respectively whether more flow can be sent to n_j during the current iteration and whether flow has been returned to n_j during the current iteration. Finally, node n_i employs an auxiliary variable y_i.

The initial values we have given for the variables are employed either at the beginning of the algorithm, and they appear when the variables are first listed, or at the beginning of each iteration. Variables whose initial values are used only once at the beginning of the algorithm are the variables related to flows and capacities (these are the *excess*, *flow*, and *residue* variables). Variables that need to be initialized at the beginning of every iteration are all the others, which are related either to the construction of the layered residual networks (these are the *reached*, *parent*, *in_previous_layer*, and *in_next_layer* variables) or to the control of flow return (these are the *stack*, *blocked*, and *returned* variables). As a final observation on the variables employed by the algorithm, it should be noted that some of them are not used at all by some nodes, but do nonetheless appear listed for the sole sake of simplicity.

The reception of *layer* messages at n_i at a certain pulse in which $reached_i =$ **false** causes $parent_i$ to point to one of the neighbors that sent the *layer*'s. Each such neighbor n_j is sent an *ack* and in addition $in\_previous\_layer_i^j$ is set to **true**. Reception by n_i of an *ack* from n_j causes n_i to set $in\_next\_layer_i^j$ to **true**. Whenever a *flow* message is sent by n_i to n_j or received by n_i from n_j, the variables $excess_i$, $flow_i^j$, and $residue_i^j$ are updated accordingly. When n_i cannot rid itself of its excess flow by sending it forward on the layered residual network, it returns that flow on a "last-in, first-out" basis (supported by $stack_i$) to the nodes that sent it. Nodes in the previous layer that do not get returned flow are sent a *block* message. Both returned flows and *block* messages signal the receiver that no more flow should during the current iteration be sent to n_i.

In Algorithm *S_Find_Max_Flow*, $N_0 = \{n_1\}$ and $1 \leq k < K$. Again for the sake of simplicity (though at the expense of a longer algorithm), we have chosen to provide separate actions for n_1, $n_i \in N - \{n_1, n_n\}$, and n_n.

Algorithm *S_Find_Max_Flow*:

▷ **Variables:**

$reached_i$;

$parent_i$;

$in\_previous\_layer_i^j$ for all $n_j \in Neig_i$;

$in\_next\_layer_i^j$ for all $n_j \in Neig_i$;

$stack_i$;

$excess_i = 0$;

$flow_i^j = 0$ for all $n_j \in Neig_i$;

$residue_i^j = c(n_i, n_j)$ for all $(n_i \to n_j) \in E^d$;

$residue_i^j = 0$ for all $(n_j \to n_i) \in E^d$;

$blocked_i^j$ for all $n_j \in Neig_i$;

$returned_i^j$ for all $n_j \in Neig_i$;

y_i.

▷ **Input:**

$s = 4n(k-1)$ or $s = 4n(K-1)$, $MSG_i(s) = \emptyset$.

Action if $n_i = n_1$ (if $n_i \in N_0$, for $k = 1$):   (7.10)

$in_next_layer_i^j := $ **false** for all $n_j \in Neig_i$;

$blocked_i^j := $ **false** for all $n_j \in Neig_i$;

$K := k$;

Send *layer* to all $n_j \in Neig_i$ such that $residue_i^j > 0$.

▷ **Input:**

$s = 4n(k-1)$ or $s = 4n(K-1)$, $MSG_i(s) = \emptyset$.

Action if $n_i \neq n_1$ and $n_i \neq n_n$:   (7.11)

$reached_i := $ **true**;

$parent_i := $ **nil**;

$in_previous_layer_i^j := $ **false** for all $n_j \in Neig_i$;

$in_next_layer_i^j := $ **false** for all $n_j \in Neig_i$;

$stack_i := $ **nil**;

$blocked_i^j := $ **false** for all $n_j \in Neig_i$;

$returned_i^j := $ **false** for all $n_j \in Neig_i$;

$K := k$.

▷ **Input:**

  $s = 4n(k - 1)$ or $s = 4n(K - 1)$, $MSG_i(s) = \emptyset$.

Action if $n_i = n_n$:   (7.12)

  $reached_i := $ **true**;

  $parent_i := $ **nil**;

  $K := k$.

▷ **Input:**

  $4n(k - 1) + 1 \leq s \leq 4nk - 2n - 1$ or $4n(K - 1) + 1 \leq s \leq 4nK - 2n - 1$, $MSG_i(s)$ such that $origin_i(msg) = (n_i, n_j)$ for $msg \in MSG_i(s)$.

Action if $n_i = n_1$:   (7.13)

  for all $ack \in MSG_i(s)$ **do**

    $in_next_layer_i^j := $ **true**;

  if there exists $success \in MSG_i(s)$ **then**

    $K := \infty$.

▷ **Input:**

$4n(k-1) + 1 \leq s \leq 4nk - 2n - 1$ or $4n(K-1) + 1 \leq s \leq 4nK - 2n - 1$, $MSG_i(s)$ such that $origin_i(msg) = (n_i, n_j)$ for $msg \in MSG_i(s)$.

Action if $n_i \neq n_1$ and $n_i \neq n_n$:   (7.14)

    if not $reached_i$ **then**

        if there exists $layer \in MSG_i(s)$ **then**

            begin

                $reached_i := $ **true**;

                for all $layer \in MSG_i(s)$ **do**

                    begin

                        if $parent_i = $ **nil then**

                            $parent_i := n_j$;

                            $in_previous_layer_i^j := $ **true**;

                            Send ack to n_j

                    end;

                  Send $layer$ to all $n_k \in Neig_i$ such that $n_k \neq n_j$ and $residue_i^k > 0$

            end;

        for all $ack \in MSG_i(s)$ **do**

            $in_next_layer_i^j := $ **true**;

        for $success \in MSG_i(s)$ **do**

            begin

                $K := \infty$;

                Send $success$ to $parent_i$

        end.

▷ **Input:**

$4n(k-1)+1 \leq s \leq 4nk - 2n - 1$ or $4n(K-1) + 1 \leq s \leq 4nK - 2n - 1$, $MSG_i(s)$ such that $origin_i(msg) = (n_i, n_j)$ for $msg \in MSG_i(s)$.

Action if $n_i = n_n$:   (7.15)

    if not $reached_i$ **then**

        begin

            if there exists $layer \in MSG_i(s)$ **then**

                begin

                    $reached_i := $ **true**;

                    for all $layer \in MSG_i(s)$ **do**

                        begin

                            if $parent_i = $ **nil then**

                                $parent_i := n_j$;

                            Send ack to n_j

                        end

                end

        end

    else

        if $K = k$ **then**

            begin

                $K := \infty$;

                Send $success$ to $parent_i$

            end.

▷ **Input:**

$s = 4nk - 2n$, $MSG_i(0) = \emptyset$.

Action if $n_i = n_1$:   (7.16)

    for all $n_j \in Neig_i$ such that $in\_next\_layer_i^j$ **do**

        begin

            $y_i := residue_i^j$;

            $flow_i^j := flow_i^j + y_i$;

            $residue_i^j := 0$;

            Send $flow(y_i)$ to n_j

        end.

▷ **Input:**

$4nk - 2n + 1 \le s \le 4nk - 1$, $MSG_i(s)$ such that $origin_i(msg) = (n_i, n_j)$ for $msg \in MSG_i(s)$.

Action if $n_i = n_1$:   (7.17)

    for all $flow(x) \in MSG_i(s)$ **do**

        begin

            $flow_i^j := flow_i^j - x;$

            $residue_i^j := residue_i^j + x$

        end.

▷ **Input:**

$4nk - 2n + 1 \leq s \leq 4nk - 1$, $MSG_i(s)$ such that $origin_i(msg) = (n_i, n_j)$ for $msg \in MSG_i(s)$.

Action if $n_i \neq n_1$ and $n_i \neq n_n$:   (7.18)

    for all $flow(x) \in MSG_i(s)$ **do**

        begin $excess_i := excess_i + x$;

          $flow_i^j := flow_i^j - x$;

          $residue_i^j := residue_i^j + x$;

          if $in\_previous\_layer_i^j$ **then**

             Push (n_j, x) onto $stack_i$;

          if $in\_next\_layer_i^j$ **then**

             $blocked_i^j :=$ **true**

        end;

    for all $block \in MSG_i(s)$ **do**

      $blocked_i^j :=$ **true**;

    while (there exists $n_k \in Neig_i$ such that $in\_next\_layer_i^k$ **and not** $blocked_i^k$) **and** $excess_i > 0$ **do**

        begin $y_i := \min\{excess_i, residue_i^k\}$;

          $excess_i := excess_i - y_i$;

          $flow_i^k := flow_i^k + y_i$;

          $residue_i^k := residue_i^k - y_i$;

          Send $flow(y_i)$ to n_k

        end;

    while $excess_i > 0$ **do**

        begin Pop (n_k, x) off $stack_i$;

          $y_i := \min\{excess_i, x\}$;

          $excess_i := excess_i - y_i$;

          $flow_i^k := flow_i^k + y_i$;

          $residue_i^k := residue_i^k - y_i$;

          $returned_i^k :=$ **true**;

          Send $flow(y_i)$ to n_k

        end;

    if there exists $n_k \in Neig_i$ such that $returned_i^k$ **then**

      for all $n_k \in Neig_i$ such that $in\_previous\_layer_i^k$ **and not** $returned_i^k$ **do**

        begin $returned_i^k :=$ **true**;

          Send $block$ to n_k

        end.

> ▷ **Input:**
> $4nk - 2n + 1 \leq s \leq 4nk - 1$, $MSG_i(s)$ such that $origin_i(msg) = (n_i, n_j)$ for $msg \in MSG_i(s)$.
>   **Action if $n_i = n_n$:**   (7.19)
>   **for** all $flow(x) \in MSG_i(s)$ **do**
>   **begin**
> $flow_i^j := flow_i^j - x;$
> $residue_i^j := residue_i^j + x$
>   **end**.

In Algorithm *S_Find_Max_Flow*, (7.10) through (7.19) realize the K-iteration, two-phase-per-iteration method that we described. Actions (7.10) through (7.15) handle the first phases of the K iterations, while actions (7.16) through (7.19) handle the second phases of the $K - 1$ first iterations. Actions (7.10) through (7.12) last for exactly one pulse per iteration each, and are intended respectively for n_1, $n_i \in N - \{n_1, n_n\}$, and n_n to initialize their variables for the new iteration and for n_1 to send out the initial *layer* messages. Actions (7.13) through (7.15) are executed for $2n - 1$ pulses each in every iteration, and specify the participation of the nodes in the remainder of the first phase. What these actions contain are the responses, respectively by n_1, $n_i \in N - \{n_1, n_n\}$, and n_n, to the receipt of *layer*, *ack*, and *success* messages. Note, however, that n_1 never receives a *layer* and n_n never receives an *ack* or *success*. It is through (7.15) that a *success* message first gets sent in each iteration.

In (7.16), which is executed for exactly one pulse in each iteration, n_1 sends out the initial *flow* messages of the iteration. The handling of such messages, and of *block* messages, is achieved through (7.17) through (7.19) for nodes n_1, $n_i \in N - \{n_1, n_n\}$, and n_n, respectively (n_n never receives any *block* message, though). Each of these actions lasts for $2n - 1$ pulses, and is tuned to the peculiarities of the corresponding node or nodes. Specifically, (7.17) and (7.19), for execution respectively by n_1 and n_n, do not include the sending of any messages at all. Also, in (7.17) n_1 does not act upon the receipt of *block* messages. Note that no action is explicitly given for nodes $n_i \neq n_1$ at pulse $s = 4nk - 2n$, as this is the first pulse in the second phase of iteration k and is as such meant for n_1 only.

When a new iteration is initiated in (7.10) through (7.12) and the pertinent variables get initialized, nodes also set K to the number k of the current iteration, in preparation for the possibility that this may be the last one. When n_n sends a *success* message in (7.15), or upon receipt of such a message by n_1 or $n_i \in N - \{n_1, n_n\}$, respectively in (7.13) and (7.14), K is reset to infinity, thereby indicating that the current iteration will include a second phase, and then is not the last one. When the algorithm terminates, the *flow* variables contain a maximum flow in G^d.

The other synchronous algorithm that we study in this section is considerably simpler than Algorithm *S_Find_Max_Flow*. For this reason, we only describe it superficially, and leave to the reader the task of expressing it more formally in the style of notation we have been employing (cf. Exercise 4). This algorithm works with the notion of preflows, and continually tries to push excess flow along the edges of the residual network that the nodes estimate to be on the shortest paths to n_1 or n_n. The algorithm starts with a preflow f such that $f(n_1, n_j) = c(n_1, n_j)$ for all $(n_1 \to n_j) \in E^d$ and $f(n_i, n_j) = 0$ for all $(n_i \to n_j) \in E^d$ with $n_i \neq n_1$.

Every node n_i maintains an estimate d_i of its shortest distance to either n_1 or n_n in the residual network. Any initial values for these estimates will do, as long as $d_1 = n$, $d_n = 0$, and $d_i \leq d_j + 1$ for all $(n_i \to n_j) \in E^d$. In the first pulse of the algorithm, these estimates are exchanged between neighbors; at node n_i, the estimate of neighbor n_j is stored in d_i^j. At all times during the execution of the algorithm, these estimates are such that either d_i is a lower bound on the distance from n_i to n_n, if $d_i < n$, or $d_i - n$ is a lower bound on the distance from n_i to n_1, if $d_i \geq n$.

At each pulse of the algorithm, the active nodes attempt to get rid of their excess flows by pushing flow in the direction of n_1 or n_n. Letting f be the preflow at the end of the previous pulse (the initial preflow, in the first pulse), a node n_i is said to be *active* if $n_i \in N - \{n_1, n_n\}$ and $e_f(n_i) > 0$. An active node n_i, at the current pulse, first sends an amount of flow equal to

$$\min\{e_f(n_i), c_f(n_i, n_j)\}$$

to a neighbor n_j such that $d_i = d_i^j + 1$ and $c_f(n_i, n_j) > 0$, and updates f (as well as $e_f(n_i)$ and $c_f(n_i, n_j)$) accordingly. This is repeated until either $e_f(n_i) = 0$ or $c_f(n_i, n_j) = 0$ for all n_j such that $d_i = d_i^j + 1$. If after this $e_f(n_i) > 0$, then d_i is updated to the minimum, over all neighbors n_j of n_i such that $c_f(n_i, n_j) > 0$, of $d_i^j + 1$, and this value, if different from the previous one, is sent to n_i's neighbors. The next pulse is initiated by adding to $e_f(n_i)$ all the flow received during the pulse. The algorithm terminates when no nodes are any longer active, although a termination criterion that, as in previous occasions, only considers the number of pulses elapsed is also possible.

7.2.3. An asynchronous algorithm

In this section, we discuss briefly the asynchronous version of the preflow-based synchronous algorithm that we introduced in the previous section. As with its synchronous counterpart, we leave all the details for the reader to pursue as an exercise (cf. Exercise 5).

The essential difficulty in the asynchronous case is that the condition that $d_i = d_i^j + 1$, necessary for n_i to send flow to n_j (cf. Section 7.2.2 on the preflow-based synchronous algorithm), cannot be trivially ensured, as the values of d_j and of d_i^j may differ substantially. The solution adopted when proposing the corresponding asynchronous algorithm has been that every flow sent from n_i to n_j must carry the value of d_i, and be explicitly accepted or rejected by n_j before additional flow may be sent.

When n_j receives flow from n_i and verifies that in fact $d_i = d_j + 1$, then the flow is accepted and this is reported back to n_i. If, on the other hand, $d_i \neq d_j + 1$, then the flow is rejected and this is reported back to n_i along with the value of d_j. Upon receiving this rejection message, n_i updates $e_f(n_i)$, $c_f(n_i, n_j)$, d_i^j, and possibly d_i. Whenever d_i changes, its new value is reported to all of n_i's neighbors.

7.3. Exercises

1. Prove properties (i) and (ii) of Section 7.1.1 on minimum spanning trees.

2. Discuss how to modify Algorithm *A_Find_MST* for the case in which edges are not FIFO. In particular, show that the situations in which a *connect* or *test* message cannot be replied to immediately can be handled with the aid of conditions for actions to be executed, instead of auxiliary variables.

3. In the context of Section 7.2.1, show that the definitions of the value of f as the total flow "going out from" n_1 or "coming into" n_n are indeed equivalent to each other.

4. Express the second synchronous algorithm of Section 7.2.2 according to Algorithm *S_Template*.

5. Express the asynchronous algorithm of Section 7.2.3 according to Algorithm *A_Template*.

7.4. Bibliographic notes

Our treatment in Section 7.1 of the problem of finding a minimum spanning tree follows the original paper of Gallager, Humblet, and Spira (1983) closely, except for the material in Section 7.1.3, which is based on Gafni (1985) and Chin and Ting (1990). For an algorithm with time complexity even lower than the one mentioned in Section 7.1.3, the reader is referred to Awerbuch (1987). Another publication of interest is Janssen and Zwiers (1992).

For material on maximum flows in networks to complement our treatment in Section 7.2.1, the reader can count on books dedicated exclusively to the subject (Ford and Fulkerson, 1962; Ahuja, Magnanti, and Orlin, 1993), chapters in more general books (Lawler, 1976; Even, 1979; Papadimitriou and Steiglitz, 1982; Cormen, Leiserson, and Rivest, 1990), and surveys (Ahuja, Magnanti, and Orlin, 1989; Goldberg, Tardos, and Tarjan, 1990).

Algorithm *S_Find_Max_Flow* of Section 7.2.2 is from Awerbuch (1985b), and the concepts of augmenting paths and of layered residual networks that it employs are originally from Ford and Fulkerson (1962) and Dinic (1970), respectively. The algorithm in Awerbuch (1985b) is an adaptation of the algorithm given by Shiloach and Vishkin (1982) for a shared-memory model (Karp and Ramachandran, 1990). The other synchronous algorithm of Section 7.2.2 and the asynchronous algorithm of Section 7.2.3 can be found in detail in Goldberg and Tarjan (1988). The concept of preflows on which they are based is originally from Karzanov (1974).

Parallel implementations of the algorithms of Goldberg and Tarjan (1988) have been discussed by Anderson and Setubal (1992) and by Portella and Barbosa (1992). In the latter publication, the authors describe an experimental evaluation of all the three algorithms discussed in Section 7.2. This evaluation employs random graphs (Bollobás, 1985) in the style suggested in DIMACS (1990).

8

Resource Sharing

When the nodes in G share resources with one another that must not be accessed by more than one node at the same time, distributed algorithms must be devised to ensure the *mutual exclusion* in the access to those resources, that is, ensure that nodes exclude one another in time to access the shared resources. This problem is not entirely new to us, having been treated in Section 6.1 in the context of self-stabilization on a ring, and in Section 6.3 in the context of detecting deadlocks in a distributed computation in which nodes provide service to one another, but never to more than one node at a time.

In this chapter, G is an undirected graph, and our treatment spans two main problems. The first problem is to ensure mutual exclusion when all the nodes share one single resource, or a group of resources that always have to be accessed as a single one. In this case, G may be as dense as a complete graph, reflecting the need, in some algorithms, for a node to communicate with all others to secure exclusive resource access. Mentions in the literature to the "mutual exclusion problem" normally refer to this first problem, which we address in Section 8.1.

The second problem that we treat in this chapter is that of ensuring mutual exclusion when each node may require access to a different set of resources. When a node accesses the same set of resources whenever it accesses any resource, the problem is a generalized form of the paradigmatic dining philosophers problem. When the set of resources that a node accesses may vary from one time to the next, then the problem has become known as the drinking philosophers problem. We dedicate Sections 8.3 and 8.4 respectively to each of these problems, after a common introduction in Section 8.2.

Two important notions that pervade all of our resource sharing studies in this chapter are those of a deadlock, which already we are acquainted with, and of *starvation*. Acceptable algorithms for resource sharing must ensure that neither conditions are ever present, unless it can be argued, in the particular situation at hand, that resorting to deadlock detection is preferable, as we discussed in Section 6.3. In the context of ensuring mutual exclusion in the access to shared resources by the group N of nodes, deadlock exists when none of the nodes ever succeeds in obtaining access to the resources. If there always exists at least one node that does succeed, but at least one other node does not succeed indefinitely, then the situation is one of starvation.

Exercises and bibliographic notes are given, respectively, in Sections 8.5 and 8.6.

8.1. Algorithms for mutual exclusion

In this section, as in other occasions in the book, we assume that nodes have distinct identifications totally ordered by $<$. For node n_i, such an identification is id_i. Nodes share a resource, or a group of resources, that must be accessed with the guarantee of mutual exclusion. If it is a group of resources that the nodes share, then we assume that all the resources in the group are always accessed together, as if they constituted one single resource, so that for all purposes it is legitimate to assume that the nodes share one single resource.

For the first algorithm that we study, G is a complete graph, because the algorithm is based on the strategy that a node, in order to access the shared resource, must obtain permission to do so from all the other $n - 1$ nodes. This first algorithm is called *A_Mutually_Exclude_C* (the suffix "C" here indicates, as in Section 5.1, that a complete graph is involved), and is based on the following simple approach. In order to request permission to access the shared resource, node n_i sends a *request*(seq, id_i) message to all the other nodes in G. The parameters that this message carries are, respectively, a "sequence number" (akin to the tag attached to *marker*'s in Algorithm *A_Detect_Termination* of Section 6.2.1) and n_i's identification. The sequence number is an integer, and is obtained by adding one to the largest such number n_i has received or sent in a *request* message (or to zero, if no *request* has ever been received or sent by it). Node n_i proceeds to access the resource upon receiving one *reply* message from each of the other nodes.

Upon receiving a $request(seq, id_j)$, node n_i replies immediately to n_j with a *reply* message if it is not waiting for *reply*'s itself. If it is waiting for *reply*'s, then it is also competing for exclusive access to the shared resource, and the parameters that it sent out with its *request* messages, namely a sequence number seq' and id_i, must be compared to those received with the message from n_j to determine which node takes priority. Lower sequence numbers indicate earlier *request* messages (in the sense of the partial order $\prec^+$ of Section 3.1), so that n_j takes priority (i.e., is sent a *reply* by n_i) if

$$(seq, id_j) < (seq', id_i),$$

where the comparison is done lexicographically. Otherwise, n_i delays the sending of a *reply* to n_j until after it has accessed the shared resource.

In Algorithm *A_Mutually_Exclude_C*, the following are the variables employed by node n_i. Two integers, seq_i and $highest\_seq_i$ (the latter initialized to zero), are used respectively to indicate the sequence number n_i sent with the last group of *request* messages it sent (if any) and the highest sequence number to have been sent or received by n_i in a *request* message. Another integer, $expected_i$ (set to zero initially), indicates the number of *reply* messages n_i must receive before accessing the shared resource. For all $n_j \in Neig_i$, a Boolean $owes\_reply_i^j$ (initially set to **false**) is used to indicate whether n_i has postponed the sending of a *reply* to n_j.

Algorithm *A_Mutually_Exclude_C*:

▷ **Variables:**

seq_i;
$highest\_seq_i = 0$;
$expected_i = 0$;
$owes\_reply_i^j =$ **false** for all $n_j \in Neig_i$.

▷ **Input:**

$msg_i =$ **nil**.

Action when $expected_i = 0$ **and access to the shared resource is needed:**

(8.1)

$seq_i := highest\_seq_i + 1$;
$highest\_seq_i := seq_i$;
$expected_i := n - 1$;
Send $request(seq_i, id_i)$ to all $n_j \in Neig_i$.

▷ **Input:**
$msg_i = request(seq, id)$ such that $origin_i(msg_i) = (n_i, n_j)$.
Action: (8.2)
$highest\_seq_i := \max\{highest\_seq_i, seq\}$;
if $expected_i = 0$ **or** $(seq, id) < (seq_i, id_i)$ **then**
        Send *reply* to n_j
else
        $owes\_reply_i^j := \textbf{true}$.

▷ **Input:**
$msg_i = reply$.
Action: (8.3)
$expected_i := expected_i - 1$;
if $expected_i = 0$ **then**
    begin
            Access shared resource;
            for all $n_j \in Neig_i$ such that $owes\_reply_i^j$ **do**
                begin
                        $owes\_reply_i^j := \textbf{false}$;
                        Send *reply* to n_j
                end
    end
end.

In Algorithm *A_Mutually_Exclude_C*, actions (8.1) through (8.3) indicate n_i's participation respectively as a spontaneous initiator, upon receipt of a *request*, and upon receipt of a *reply*. Action (8.1), in particular, is executed whenever there is need for n_i to access the shared resource and in addition $expected_i = 0$ (indicating that n_i is not already engaged in seeking access to that resource). As in Algorithm *A_FIFO* of Section 2.1, a node may initiate its participation in the algorithm spontaneously more than once, in that case by deciding to migrate a task to run elsewhere, in this case by deciding that access to the shared resource is needed. What this amounts to is that N_0 must be regarded as a maximal set of nodes that send out *request*'s concurrently. Each such set initiates a new execution of the algorithm, and executions operate on variables that persist, in the sense of not being re-initialized, from one execution to another.

Theorem 8.1 establishes important properties of this algorithm.

Theorem 8.1. *Algorithm A_Mutually_Exclude_C ensures mutual exclusion in the access to the shared resource, and is in addition deadlock- and starvation-free.*

Proof: Two nodes can only access the shared resource concurrently if they receive the $n-1$st *reply* message concurrently. This follows from (8.3) and, in particular, indicates that each of the two nodes must have received a *reply* from the other as well. But by (8.2) and (8.3), and because node identifications are all distinct from one another, this can only have happened if at least one of the two was not requesting access to the resource, which is in contradiction with the possibility that they access the resource concurrently.

By (8.2), node n_i only refrains from sending n_j a *reply* if $expected_i > 0$ and $(seq, id) \not< (seq_i, id_i)$, where seq and id are the parameters of n_j's *request* message. In this case, n_j is forced to wait for n_i's *reply*. Because node identifications are totally ordered by $<$, a wait cycle cannot be formed among the nodes, and then no deadlock can ever occur (cf. Section 6.3).

Now consider the number of resource accesses that may take place after node n_i has sent *request*'s and before it has received *reply*'s (because mutual exclusion is ensured, resource accesses are totally ordered, so that the "before" and "after" are meaningful with respect to this order). By (8.1) and (8.2), the sequence number a node sends along with a *request* message is strictly greater than those it has received in *request*'s itself, so that by (8.2) every node sending out *request*'s after receiving n_i's *request* will only access the shared resource after n_i has done so. The number of resource accesses we are considering is then finite, and as a consequence no starvation ever occurs. ∎

Let us now examine the complexities of Algorithm *A_Mutually_Exclude_C*. Clearly, each access to the shared resource involves $n-1$ *request* messages and $n-1$ *reply*'s. The algorithm's message complexity per access to the shared resource is then $O(n)$. The time complexity per access to the shared resource refers to the chain of messages that may occur starting with a *request* sent by a node and the last *reply* that it receives. The longest such chain occurs when a global state exists in which $n-1$ nodes in a row have withheld *reply*'s from the next node in the sequence (by Theorem 8.1, the number of nodes involved in this wait cannot be greater than $n-1$, because otherwise there would be deadlock). If n_i and n_j are, respectively, the first and last nodes in this wait chain (that is, n_i is the only node not to have been withheld a *reply* from), and if the *request* from n_j arrives at n_i before n_i accesses the shared resource, then the *reply*'s that n_i sends out when it finally does access the resource start a causal chain of *reply*'s through the other nodes to n_j. The time complexity of the algorithm per access to the shared resource is then $O(n)$ as well.

The algorithm's bit complexity is in principle unbounded, because, although a node's identification can be as usual assumed to be expressible in $\lceil \log n \rceil$ bits, the other parameter that *request* messages carry, the sequence number, does not in the algorithm have any bound. However, it can be argued relatively easily that no two sequence numbers that a node has to compare in (8.2) are ever farther apart from each other than $n - 1$, and then it is possible to implement them as $O(\log n)$-bit numbers (cf. Exercise 1). The algorithm's bit complexity is then $O(n \log n)$.

Unlike Algorithm *A_Mutually_Exclude_C*, the next algorithm that we consider in this section does not require every node to receive explicit permission from every other node before accessing the shared resource. What makes this possible is the following interesting observation. For $n_i \in N$, let $S_i \subseteq N$ denote the set of nodes from which n_i must receive explicit permission before accessing the shared resource (in the previous algorithm, $S_i = N - \{n_i\}$ for all $n_i \in N$). In order for S_i not to have to include every node in $N - \{n_i\}$ and yet mutual exclusion to be ensured in the access to the shared resource when the nodes in S_i grant permission for n_i to proceed, for every two nodes n_i and n_j we must have $S_i \cap S_j \neq \emptyset$. If the S sets can be built such that this property holds, then every pair of conflicting requests to access the shared resource will reach at least one node, which will then be able to arbitrate between the two requests and ensure mutual exclusion.

Once the sets $S_1, \ldots, S_n$ have been determined, the following is how a node n_i proceeds in order to access the shared resource. For simplicity when describing the algorithm, we assume that $n_i \notin S_i$, so that the number of *request*'s that n_i sends is $|S_i|$. First n_i sends a *request* message to every node in S_i, and then waits to receive one *granted* message corresponding to each of the *request* messages it sent. It may then access the shared resource, and after doing so sends a *release* message to each of the nodes in S_i. A node that has sent a *granted* and receives another *request* before receiving the corresponding *release*'s must somehow postpone its permission corresponding to the new *request*.

Although the *granted* messages may be thought of as corresponding to the *reply* messages of the previous algorithm, the need to explicitly indicate that the resource is no longer in use through the *release* messages reflects some of the important differences between the two approaches. The essential reason why *release* messages are now needed is that a *request* does not reach every node, and thence the double meaning that a *reply* message had of both granting permission and signaling the end of an access to the shared resource can no longer be exploited with the *granted* messages. In fact, another consequence of the selective broadcast of *request*'s, in addition to the need of explicit *release*'s, is that deadlocks can no longer be taken as prevented even if the *request*'s carry the same information that they did in the previous case. Because different nodes obtain their permissions from different sets of nodes, it is rather simple to imagine situations in which wait cycles appear.

The following is then the overall strategy to handle conflicts and the waits that result from them, and yet ensure that deadlocks are not possible. A *request* message is, as in the previous algorithm, sent by n_i as $request(seq_i, id_i)$, where seq_i is strictly greater than every other sequence number n_i has ever sent or received in such a message. Node n_i maintains a Boolean variable, called $locked_i$ and initialized to **false**, to indicate whether it has sent a *granted* message to some node without having received any other message from that node. When n_i receives a $request(seq, id)$ and $locked_i = $ **false**, a *granted* is immediately sent to its originator. If $locked_i = $ **true**, then n_i marks the origin of the *request* message for later consideration. Upon delaying the response to a node in this way, n_i must ensure that no deadlock will arise, and to this end proceeds as follows. If the newly received *request* takes precedence (in the sense of a lexicographically smaller pair (seq, id)) over the *request* to which n_i has replied with a *granted* as well as all the others that n_i has not yet replied to, then a *probe* message is sent to the same node to which the *granted* was sent. Otherwise, a *delayed* message is sent in response to the new *request*, which is then kept waiting. A node that receives a *probe* responds to it right away with a *relinquish* if it has already received a *delayed*, or when it does receive a *delayed* if it still has not. Node n_i does not send another *probe* until a *relinquish* or a *release* has arrived for the one it has sent. A node only sends a *relinquish* in response to a *probe* if a *granted* was not received from each of the nodes that sent it a *delayed*.

Algorithm *A_Mutually_Exclude*, presented next, is based on this approach. In contrast with the previous approach, G is no longer a complete graph, but rather has its set of edges given in accordance with the sets $S_1, \ldots, S_n$ in such a way that $(n_i, n_j) \in E$ if and only if $n_j \in S_i$ or $n_i \in S_j$. Also, we assume that all edges are FIFO, and then a *granted* never overruns a *delayed* or a *probe* a *granted*.

In addition to the variables seq_i, $highest\_seq_i$, and $expected_i$, used here as in the previous algorithm, and the already introduced variable $locked_i$, Algorithm *A_Mutually_Exclude* employs the following additional variables. A *request* in response to which a *granted* has been sent has its origin and *seq* and *id* parameters recorded by n_i in the variables $granted\_node_i$, $granted\_seq_i$, and $granted\_id_i$, respectively. Node n_i maintains a queue, called $queue_i$ and initialized to **nil**, to store these same attributes for all *request*'s that cannot be immediately replied to. This queue is maintained in lexicographically increasing order of (seq, id). Finally, the Booleans has_probed_i, and $got\_probe_i^j$ and $got\_delayed_i^j$ for all $n_j \in S_i$, all initialized to **false**, are employed to indicate respectively whether n_i has sent a *probe* for which a *relinquish* or a *release* was not received in response, whether n_i has received a *probe* from n_j, and whether a *delayed* was received from n_j without a succeeding *granted*.

Algorithm *A_Mutually_Exclude*:

▷ **Variables:**

seq_i;
$highest\_seq_i = 0$;
$expected_i = 0$;
$locked_i = $ **false**;
$granted\_node_i$;
$granted\_seq_i$;
$granted\_id_i$;
$queue_i = $ **nil**;
$has_probed_i = $ **false**;
$got_probe_i^j = $ **false** for all $n_j \in S_i$;
$got_delayed_i^j = $ **false** for all $n_j \in S_i$.

▷ **Input:**

$msg_i = $ **nil**.

Action when $expected_i = 0$ **and access to the shared resource is needed:** (8.4)

$seq_i := highest\_seq_i + 1$;
$highest\_seq_i := seq_i$;
$expected_i := |S_i|$;
Send *request*(seq_i, id_i) to all $n_j \in S_i$.

▷ **Input:**
  $msg_i = request(seq, id)$ such that $origin_i(msg_i) = (n_i, n_j)$.
 Action: (8.5)
  $highest\_seq_i := \max\{highest\_seq_i, seq\};$
  if not $locked_i$ **then**
    begin
      $locked_i := \textbf{true};$
      $granted\_node_i := n_j;$
      $granted\_seq_i := seq;$
      $granted\_id_i := id;$
      Send $granted$ to n_j
    end
  else
    begin
      Add (n_j, seq, id) to $queue_i;$
      if $(seq, id) < (granted\_seq_i, granted\_id_i)$ **and** (n_j, seq, id) is
      first in $queue_i$ **then**
        begin
          if not has_probed_i **then**
            begin
              $has\_probed_i := \textbf{true};$
              Send $probe$ to $granted\_node_i$
            end
        end
      else
        Send $delayed$ to n_j
    end.

▷ **Input:**

$msg_i = granted$ such that $origin_i(msg_i) = (n_i, n_j)$.

(8.6)

Action:

$expected_i := expected_i - 1$;

if $got\_delayed_i^j$ **then**

$got_delayed_i^j := $ **false**;

if $expected_i = 0$ **then**

begin

Access shared resource;

for all $n_k \in S_i$ such that $got\_probe_i^k$ **do**

$got_probe_i^k := $ **false**;

Send $release$ to all $n_k \in S_i$

end.

▷ **Input:**

$msg_i = release$.

(8.7)

Action:

if has_probed_i **then**

$has_probed_i := $ **false**;

if $queue_i = $ **nil then**

$locked_i := $ **false**

else

begin

Let $(granted\_node_i, granted\_seq_i, granted\_id_i)$ be first in $queue_i$;

Remove $(granted\_node_i, granted\_seq_i, granted\_id_i)$ from $queue_i$;

Send $granted$ to $granted\_node_i$

end.

▷ **Input:**

$msg_i = probe$ such that $origin_i(msg_i) = (n_i, n_j)$.

Action: (8.8)

if there exists $n_k \in S_i$ such that $got\_delayed_i^k$ **then**

begin

$expected_i := expected_i + 1$;

Send $relinquish$ to n_j

end

else

$got_probe_i^j := $ **true**.

▷ **Input:**

$msg_i = delayed$ such that $origin_i(msg_i) = (n_i, n_j)$.

Action: (8.9)

$got_delayed_i^j := $ **true**;

for all $n_k \in S_i$ such that $got\_probe_i^k$ **do**

begin

$expected_i := expected_i + 1$;

Send $relinquish$ to n_k

end.

▷ **Input:**

$msg_i = relinquish$.

Action: (8.10)

$has_probed_i := $ **false**;

Add $(granted\_node_i, granted\_seq_i, granted\_id_i)$ to $queue_i$;

Let $(granted\_node_i, granted\_seq_i, granted\_id_i)$ be first in $queue_i$;

Remove $(granted\_node_i, granted\_seq_i, granted\_id_i)$ from $queue_i$;

Send $granted$ to $granted\_node_i$.

Actions (8.4) through (8.10) realize the algorithm we described informally earlier. In this algorithm, the set N_0 is to be interpreted as in the case of Algorithm $A\_Mutually\_Exclude\_C$. Some of the algorithm's properties are established by the following theorem.

Theorem 8.2. *Algorithm $A\_Mutually\_Exclude$ ensures mutual exclusion in the access to the shared resource, and is in addition deadlock- and starvation-free.*

Proof: By (8.4) and (8.6), any two nodes n_i and n_j can only access the shared resource concurrently if they receive, respectively, the $|S_i|$th and $|S_j|$th *granted* messages concurrently. However, by definition S_i and S_j have at least one node in common, say n_k, which by (8.5), (8.7), and (8.10) only sends *granted* messages when $locked_k = \textbf{false}$ upon receipt of a *request* or when a *release* or a *relinquish* is received. In addition, $locked_k$ is only **false** initially or upon receipt by n_k of a *release*, so that either n_k receives a *release* or a *relinquish* from n_i before sending a *granted* to n_j, or conversely. In either case, a contradiction exists with the possibility of concurrent access to the shared resource by n_i and n_j.

Because different nodes send *request*'s to different subsets of N, a wait cycle (cf. Section 6.3) may indeed be formed, but only momentarily though, because (8.5) ensures that a *request*(seq, id) arriving at n_i prompts the sending by n_i of a *probe* if (seq, id) is lexicographically minimum among ($granted\_seq_i$, $granted\_id_i$) and all the pairs in $queue_i$. All node identifications are totally ordered by $<$, and for this reason at least one *probe* must succeed in breaking the wait cycle through the sending of a *relinquish* by (8.8) or (8.9). Deadlocks are then not possible.

Ensuring mutual exclusion has the effect that all accesses to the shared resource are totally ordered. With respect to this total order, it is then legitimate to consider the number of accesses that may take place after an access by node n_i and before the next access by the same node. Considering that in all nodes queues are kept in increasing lexicographic order of sequence numbers and node identifications, and that nodes issue *request*'s with strictly increasing sequence numbers, the number of accesses we are considering is then clearly finite, and therefore starvation never occurs.   ∎

Analyzing Algorithm *A_Mutually_Exclude* for its complexity measures requires that we consider the sets $S_1, \ldots, S_n$ more closely, because, by the algorithm's actions, the message complexity per access to the shared resource by node n_i is intimately dependent upon the number of nodes in S_i. Before proceeding any further with this discussion, though, we make two additional assumptions concerning these sets. The first assumption is that $|S_1| = \cdots = |S_n|$, and the second assumption is that every node is contained in the same number of sets. The first assumption seeks to guarantee that every node requests an equal number of permissions in order to access the shared resource, while the second assumption aims at distributing evenly the "responsibility" for granting permission to access the shared resource. Combined, the two assumptions are to be regarded as an attempt at "fairness," however this may be defined.

If we let K denote the size of each of the n sets and D the number of sets of which each node is a member, then we have

$$n = \frac{|S_1| + \cdots + |S_n|}{D}$$
$$= \frac{nK}{D},$$

which yields $D = K$.

One of the possibilities for the sets $S_1, \ldots, S_n$ is of course $S_i = N$ for all $n_i \in N$. It is a trivial matter, in this case, to simplify Algorithm *A_Mutually_Exclude* until Algorithm *A_Mutually_Exclude_C* is obtained, as G is clearly a complete graph. Our interest, however, is in obtaining the smallest sets whose pairwise intersections are nonempty, because this is what will improve the algorithm's message complexity from that of Algorithm *A_Mutually_Exclude_C*.

Now consider the set S_i, for some node n_i. This set has K members, each of which belonging to other $D - 1$ sets, so the number of distinct sets involving the members of S_i is at most $K(D - 1) + 1$. Because we need n such sets (S_1 through S_n), and considering that $D = K$ and that the largest number of sets leads to the smallest sets, we then have

$$n = K(K - 1) + 1,$$

which immediately yields $K \geq \sqrt{n}$. If n is the square of some integer, then we adopt

$$|S_1| = \cdots = |S_n| = \sqrt{n}.$$

Otherwise, a little imbalance cannot be avoided as some sets must necessarily have more nodes than the others, although no more than the square root of the least perfect square greater than n. It should be clear that this square root is still $O(\sqrt{n})$.

Under the two assumptions that led to the determination of the $\sqrt{n}$ lower bound for K, the message complexity of Algorithm *A_Mutually_Exclude* can be seen to be of $O(\sqrt{n})$ per access to the shared resource. This is so because, in the worst case, there will be $\sqrt{n}$ *request* messages, each one causing a *probe* message, this one being replied to by a *relinquish* message, in turn generating a *granted* message and eventually a *release* message. Notice that the argument we employed earlier on the possibility of bounding sequence numbers in the case of Algorithm *A_Mutually_Exclude_C* is no longer applicable, so that the bit complexity is in this case unbounded (cf. Exercise 2).

As in the case of the previous algorithm, the time complexity of Algorithm *A_Mutually_Exclude* per access to the shared resource refers to the chain of messages that may occur starting with a *request* sent by a node and the *release*'s that it sends. One possibility for this chain occurs in the following situation. Node n_j sends n_i

a *request*, which is queued and only replied to with a *granted* after n_i has sent a *granted* and received a *release* for each of the requests ahead of n_j's in $queue_i$. Because of our assumption that n_i is in the S sets of exactly D other nodes, this scenario would account for an $O(D)$ delay. However, such a chain is not the longest that may occur, as we see next. Suppose that n_i and n_k are two nodes in S_j, and in addition that a wait chain exists starting at n_k and ending at n_i. In this wait chain, n_k is waiting for a *release* from the next node in the chain, which is waiting for a *granted* from the next node, which in turn is waiting for a *release*, and so on, all the way to the node that precedes n_i in the chain, which is waiting for a *granted* from n_i. By Theorem 8.2, the algorithm is deadlock-free, so that this chain cannot involve more than $n - 1$ nodes. If the *granted* that n_i sends to the node that is waiting on it on the chain is sent after n_i receives the *request* from n_j, we see that a chain of messages of length $O(n)$ exists between a *request* sent by n_j and its sending of *release*'s. This is then the algorithm's time complexity, therefore the same as in the previous case.

As one last remark in this section, we encourage the reader to pursue the exercise of modifying Algorithm *A_Mutually_Exclude* for the case in which node n_i is allowed to belong to S_i (cf. Exercise 3).

8.2. Sharing multiple resources

Henceforth in this chapter, we no longer assume that only one single resource (or a group of resources that have to be accessed as a single entity) is shared by the nodes, but instead consider the more general case in which nodes may require access to resources in groups of varied composition. One immediate consequence of this relaxed view is that it is now possible for more than one node to be accessing shared resources concurrently, so long as no resource belongs to the group of resources accessed by any node.

Let R be a set of resources, and let $R = |\text{R}|$. The members of R are the resources $\rho_1, \ldots, \rho_R$, and for $1 \le r \le R$ with each resource $\rho_r \in \text{R}$ a set of nodes $S_r \subseteq N$ is associated. Nodes in S_r are the only ones that may have access to resource ρ_r. In the algorithms that we investigate in Sections 8.3 and 8.4, nodes coordinate the shared access to resources by communicating with the other nodes that may have access to those resources, and then the definitions we just introduced are instrumental in establishing the structure of G for those algorithms.

The graph G to be used in Sections 8.3 and 8.4 has its edge set defined as follows. For $n_i, n_j \in N$ such that $n_i \ne n_j$, $(n_i, n_j) \in E$ if and only if there exists $\rho_r \in \text{R}$ such that $n_i \in S_r$ and $n_j \in S_r$. In other words, nodes n_i and n_j

are neighbors if and only if there exists a resource that both may access. In G, every resource in R is then represented by a clique (i.e., a completely connected subgraph) involving the nodes that may have access to that particular resource (but not conversely, though, as there may be cliques in G that do not correspond to any resource). For $\rho_r \in$ R, such a clique spans the nodes in S_r. As a side remark, the reader may note that a more natural representation would in this case be the hypergraph $\mathcal{H} = (N, \{S_1, \ldots, S_R\})$, having the same set of nodes as G and one hyperedge for each of the sets S_1 through S_R. However, the use of such a representation would be unnatural in our context of message-passing computations, which in the point-to-point case calls for a graph representation (cf. Section 1.1).

In Sections 8.3 and 8.4, we study algorithms to coordinate the sharing of resources in two different cases. The first case is treated in Section 8.3, and corresponds to the situation in which nodes always access the resources they may access as a group including all such resources (if all nodes may access all resources, then this is equivalent to the case of Section 8.1). The second case is treated in Section 8.4, and corresponds to the situation in which nodes access the resources that they may access in groups of any admissible size. Both cases are similar, in that a node only has to communicate with its neighbors when seeking mutual exclusion. There are also differences, however, the most important one being that, in the latter case, neighbors may access resources concurrently if they request disjoint sets of resources.

8.3. The dining philosophers problem

The resource-sharing problem that we treat in this section is a generalization of the following paradigmatic problem, called the *dining philosophers problem*. Five philosophers sit at a round table, and five forks are placed on the table so that there is one fork between the plates of every two adjacent philosophers. A philosopher requires both forks that are adjacent to him in order to eat, and then it is impossible for neighbor philosophers to eat concurrently. The life of a philosopher is a cycle of thinking and eating for alternating finite periods of time. A solution to the problem consists of an algorithm that ensures mutual exclusion (a fork may only be used by one philosopher at a time), prevents deadlocks (at least one hungry philosopher must be eating), and prevents starvation (every philosopher must get to eat within a finite time of becoming hungry; incidentally, it is from the context of this problem that the term "starvation" in resource sharing comes).

In terms of our modeling of the previous section, in the dining philosophers problem N is the set of philosophers with $n = 5$, R is the set of forks with $R = 5$, and every one of S_1 through S_5 includes two philosophers that sit next to each other at the table (conversely, each philosopher is a member of exactly two such sets, specifically those that correspond to the forks that are adjacent to him). The graph G is then a five-node ring in which an edge corresponds to a fork.

In the generalized form of this problem, G is any connected undirected graph with one philosopher per node and one fork per edge. In order to eat, a philosopher must acquire all the forks that are adjacent to him. It is very important for the reader to note that the dining philosophers problem in this generalized form is entirely equivalent to the resource sharing problem, described in the previous section, in which a node always accesses the same set of resources. Although there is in principle no correspondence between the forks that are adjacent to a philosopher and those resources, a fork can be used to represent all the resources that two neighboring nodes share. Acquiring every adjacent fork is then equivalent to securing mutual exclusion in the access to all the resources a node needs. It is then to this generalized form of the dining philosophers problem that we dedicate the remainder of Section 8.3. Our discussion proceeds in two parts. In the first part, presented in Section 8.3.1, we give an algorithm to solve this generalized formulation of the problem. The second part, in Section 8.3.2, is dedicated to the extreme situation in which the thinking period of philosophers is negligibly small. Under this situation of perennial hunger, interesting issues appear related to the concurrency that can be achieved in the sharing of forks by the philosophers.

8.3.1. An algorithm

The solution to the generalized dining philosophers problem that we discuss in this section is given as Algorithm A_Dine. In this algorithm, node n_i employs a Boolean variable, called $hungry_i$ and initialized to **false**, to indicate the need to access the resources that it shares with its neighbors. Whenever this variable becomes **true**, n_i employs request messages to ask its neighbors to send it the forks it still does not have. Upon acquiring the forks corresponding to all the edges incident to it, n_i accesses the shared resources and, perhaps contrary to our intuitive expectation, it does not send the forks to the corresponding neighbors, but rather keeps them to be sent when they are requested. However, if forks are indiscriminately distributed among the nodes at the beginning, deadlocks may, as it takes little effort to realize, occur. In addition, in the absence of some sort of priority among the nodes, the simple sending of forks upon receiving request's may easily lead to starvation.

The priority scheme that we adopt employs what we call a "turn" object per edge of G, much like forks. In addition, the turn associated with an edge can only be possessed by one of the nodes to which the edge is incident at a time, much like forks as well. What distinguishes turns from forks is that a node does not need to acquire turns for all the edges incident to it in order to access the shared resources, and also that turns get sent over the edges to a node's neighbors as soon as the node is through with accessing the shared resources. The essential goal of an edge's turn is to indicate which of its end nodes has the priority to hold that edge's fork when there is conflict. However, in the absence of conflict, that fork may be held by either node, even against the current location of the turn. Sending a turn over to the corresponding neighbor is a guarantee that the priority to hold that edge's fork alternates between the two nodes. In Algorithm A_Dine, a $fork$ message is used to send a fork, while a $turn$ message is used to send a turn. For all $n_j \in Neig_i$, node n_i maintains two Boolean variables to indicate whether n_i holds the fork and the turn that it shares with n_j. These are, respectively, $holds\_fork_i^j$ and $holds\_turn_i^j$, and should be initialized so that consistency is maintained over the edge (n_i, n_j) (that is, exactly one of n_i and n_j must hold the fork and exactly one of them, not necessarily the same, must hold the turn). We do not provide these initial values when presenting the algorithm, but return to the issue later with a more detailed discussion.

When n_j sends n_i a $request$ and this message finds $hungry_i = $ **true** and $holds_turn_i^j = $ **true** upon arrival, n_i does not send the corresponding fork over to n_j, but rather postpones the sending of this fork to after it has accessed the shared resource. If, on the other hand, the $request$ message finds $hungry_i = $ **true** and $holds_turn_i^j = $ **false** upon arrival, then the fork is sent at once to n_j, but n_j must know that the fork is to be returned when it has completed its access to the shared resource. In order not to have to send two messages in each case (a $turn$ and a $fork$ in the former case, a $fork$ and a $request$ in the latter), every $fork$ message is sent with a parameter, either as $fork(\mathbf{nil})$, if all that needs to be achieved is the sending of a fork, or as $fork(turn)$, to indicate that a turn is also being sent, or yet as $fork(request)$, when a request for the fork is implied. For all $n_j \in Neig_i$, node n_i employs the additional Boolean variable $owes\_fork_i^j$, initially set to **false**, to remind it to send n_j a $fork$ when it finishes accessing the shared resources.

We assume that G's edges are FIFO, so that a $request$ never overruns a $fork$ or a $turn$, thereby ensuring that the arrival of a $request$ at n_i from n_j only occurs when $holds_fork_i^j = $ **true**.

Algorithm A_Dine:

▷ **Variables:**
$hungry_i =$ **false**;
$holds\_fork_i^j$ for all $n_j \in Neig_i$;
$holds\_turn_i^j$ for all $n_j \in Neig_i$;
$owes\_fork_i^j =$ **false** for all $n_j \in Neig_i$.

▷ **Input:**
$msg_i =$ **nil**.
Action when not $hungry_i$ **and access to shared resources is needed:**   (8.11)
$hungry_i :=$ **true**;
Send $request$ to all $n_j \in Neig_i$ such that $holds\_fork_i^j =$ **false**.

▷ **Input:**
$msg_i = request$ such that $origin_i(msg_i) = (n_i, n_j)$.
Action: (8.12)
if not $hungry_i$ **or not** $holds\_turn_i^j$ **then**
$\quad$ **begin**
$\qquad holds\_fork_i^j :=$ **false**;
$\qquad$ **if not** $hungry_i$ **then**
$\qquad\quad$ Send $fork(\textbf{nil})$ to n_j
$\qquad$ **else**
$\qquad\quad$ Send $fork(request)$ to n_j
$\quad$ **end**
else
$\quad owes\_fork_i^j :=$ **true**.

▷ **Input:**

$\quad msg_i = fork(t)$ such that $origin_i(msg_i) = (n_i, n_j)$.

Action: (8.13)

$\quad holds\_fork_i^j :=$ **true**;

$\quad$**if** $t = turn$ **then**

$\quad\quad holds\_turn_i^j :=$ **true**;

$\quad$**if** $t = request$ **then**

$\quad\quad owes\_fork_i^j :=$ **true**;

$\quad$**if** $holds\_fork_i^k$ for all $n_k \in Neig_i$ **then**

$\quad\quad$**begin**

$\quad\quad\quad$Access shared resources;

$\quad\quad\quad hungry_i :=$ **false**;

$\quad\quad\quad$**for** all $n_k \in Neig_i$ **do**

$\quad\quad\quad\quad$**if** $holds\_turn_i^k$ **then**

$\quad\quad\quad\quad\quad$**begin**

$\quad\quad\quad\quad\quad\quad holds\_turn_i^k :=$ **false**;

$\quad\quad\quad\quad\quad\quad$**if** $owes\_fork_i^k$ **then**

$\quad\quad\quad\quad\quad\quad\quad$**begin**

$\quad\quad\quad\quad\quad\quad\quad\quad owes\_fork_i^k :=$ **false**;

$\quad\quad\quad\quad\quad\quad\quad\quad holds\_fork_i^k :=$ **false**;

$\quad\quad\quad\quad\quad\quad\quad\quad$Send $fork(turn)$ to n_k

$\quad\quad\quad\quad\quad\quad\quad$**end**

$\quad\quad\quad\quad\quad$**else**

$\quad\quad\quad\quad\quad\quad$Send $turn$ to n_k

$\quad\quad\quad\quad\quad$**end**

$\quad\quad$**end.**

▷ **Input:**

$\quad msg_i = turn$ such that $origin_i(msg_i) = (n_i, n_j)$.

Action: (8.14)

$\quad holds\_turn_i^j :=$ **true.**

In Algorithm A_Dine, as in previous occasions in this chapter, the set N_0 comprises nodes for which the need to access the shared resources arises concurrently. Multiple executions of the algorithm coexist, and no variables are re-initialized for executions other than the very first. In this algorithm, actions (8.11) through (8.14) realize, respectively, the sending of *request*'s for forks when the need arises for a node to access the shared resources, and the handling of *request*, *fork*, and *turn* messages.

In order to discuss the algorithm's main properties, we must at last be more specific about the initial values to be assigned to the *holds_fork* and *holds_turn* variables. Whereas any consistent assignment of values to the *holds_fork* variables will do, the algorithm's properties are quite sensitive to the values that are assigned to the *holds_turn* variables, and simple consistency across edges will not do in general.

Before continuing with this discussion on initial values, let us pause and introduce the concept of an *orientation* of the undirected graph G. As in Sections 6.3 and 7.2, such an orientation is a means of regarding G as a directed graph, without however sacrificing the ability for messages to traverse G's edges in both directions. In the present case, as in Section 6.3, G's orientation will change dynamically, thereby increasing the importance of assigning directions to edges in a manner that is not too inflexible as assuming that G is directed in the first place. An orientation of G is a function

$$\omega : E \to N$$

such that, for $(n_i, n_j) \in E$, $\omega\big((n_i, n_j)\big)$ is either n_i or n_j, indicating respectively that, according to ω, (n_i, n_j) is directed from n_j to n_i or from n_i to n_j. An orientation is said to be *acyclic* if it does not induce any directed cycle in G.

The following is then how the assignment of turns to neighbors is performed, and consequently the consistent assignment of values to the *holds_turn* variables. Say that the edge (n_i, n_j) is directed from n_i to n_j if the turn that corresponds to it is given to n_j. The initial assignment that we adopt is then such that the resulting orientation is acyclic. The essential importance of such an initial acyclic orientation is that, as the orientation changes by the sending of turns when a node is done with accessing the shared resources in (8.13), that node becomes a source in the new orientation, that is, a node with all incident edges directed away from it. The resulting orientation is then acyclic as well, because the only changes in an orientation correspond to nodes that become sources, and then directed cycles that might have been formed would have to go through those nodes, which is impossible.

We now turn to a more formal statement of the algorithm's properties.

Theorem 8.3. *Algorithm A_Dine ensures mutual exclusion in the access to the shared resources, and is in addition deadlock- and starvation-free.*

Proof: By (8.13), a node only accesses the shared resources if it holds the forks corresponding to all the edges incident to it. By (8.12) and (8.13), only one of every two neighbors may hold the fork that they share in any global state, and then no two neighbors can access the shared resources concurrently. Because by construction of G nodes that are not neighbors never share any resources, mutual exclusion is guaranteed.

G's orientation is always acyclic, and then G always has at least one sink. Sinks are nodes that hold the turns corresponding to all the edges incident to them, and then by (8.11) and (8.12) must acquire all the forks that they do not hold within a finite time of having responded to the need to access the shared resources. No deadlock is then possible.

A node that is not a sink but does execute (8.11) in order to access the shared resources is also guaranteed to acquire all the necessary forks within a finite time, and then no starvation ever occurs either. What supports this conclusion is that either such a node acquires all the forks because its neighbors that hold turns do not need to access the shared resources (by (8.12) and (8.13)), or because it eventually acquires all the turns (by (8.13) and (8.14)) and then the forks as a consequence of the acyclicity of G's orientations.   ■

The number of messages that need to be exchanged per access to the shared resources can be computed as follows. First a node may send as many *request* messages as it has neighbors, that is $|Neig_i|$ in the case of node n_i. The worst that can happen is that n_i does not hold any turns and the *request*'s that it sends find nodes that do not need to access the shared resources and then send n_i forks. Because n_i does not hold any turns, it may happen that these forks may have to be returned as *fork(request)* messages if n_i receives at least one *request* from its neighbors before receiving the last fork. By (8.13), n_i will then eventually receive all these forks back, then access the shared resources, and then send turns out. If we let

$$\Delta = \max_{n_i \in N} \{|Neig_i|\},$$

then clearly the algorithm's message complexity per access to the shared resources is $O(\Delta)$. Message lengths are constant, and then the algorithm's bit complexity is also of $O(\Delta)$.

The time complexity of Algorithm *A_Dine* per access to the shared resources is related to the longest chain of messages beginning with the sending of *request*'s by a node and ending with the reception by that node of the last *fork* message that it expects. Such a chain happens for a node that is a source in the current acyclic orientation when all nodes require access to shared resources. In this case, the directed distance from that node to the sinks may be as large as $n - 1$, and then the time complexity that we seek is $O(n)$. One situation in which this worst case may happen is that of a ring with a single sink.

All of Algorithm A_Dine's properties rely strongly on the assumption of an initial acyclic orientation for G. Determining this initial acyclic orientation constitutes an interesting problem by itself, and appears to require randomized techniques to be solved unless nodes can be assumed to have distinct identifications totally ordered by $<$, as in Section 8.1 and other occasions in the book. If such is the case, then the initial acyclic orientation that we need can be determined with $O(m)$ messages and $O(1)$ time as follows. Every node sends its identification to its neighbors. For each edge (n_i, n_j), the turn stays initially with n_i if $id_i < id_j$; it stays with n_j if $id_j < id_i$. When compared with the algorithms of Section 8.1, the approach of assigning priorities based on a dynamically evolving acyclic orientation of G can be regarded as trading the nonconstant message length in those cases by an initial overhead to establish the initial acyclic orientation.

8.3.2. Operation under heavy loads

A heavy-load situation is characterized by the fact that nodes require access to shared resources continually. Clearly, under such circumstances Algorithm A_Dine may be simplified to a great extent. Specifically, a node may send forks to all of its neighbors immediately upon finishing accessing the shared resources. As a consequence, $request$ and $turn$ messages are no longer needed, provided it is the placement of forks, instead of turns, that gives G's orientation. The only variables that are needed at n_i are then $holds\_fork_i^j$ for all $n_j \in Neig_i$. The simplified algorithm is presented next as Algorithm A_Dine_H ("H" for Heavy), with N_0 being the set of nodes that are sinks (i.e., hold all forks corresponding to incident edges) initially.

    Algorithm A_Dine_H**:**

      ▷ **Variables:**
        $holds\_fork_i^j$ for all $n_j \in Neig_i$.

      ▷ **Input:**
        $msg_i = $ **nil**.
      Action if $n_i \in N_0$**:**   (8.15)
        Access shared resources;
        $holds_fork_i^j := $ **false** for all $n_j \in Neig_i$;
        Send $fork$ to all $n_j \in Neig_i$.

▷ **Input:**

$msg_i = fork$ such that $origin_i(msg_i) = (n_i, n_j)$.

Action: (8.16)

$holds\_fork_i^j :=$ **true**;

if $holds\_fork_i^k$ for all $n_k \in Neig_i$ **then**

    begin

        Access shared resources;

        $holds\_fork_i^k :=$ **false** for all $n_k \in Neig_i$;

        Send $fork$ to all $n_k \in Neig_i$.

    end.

Actions (8.15) and (8.16) are both related to (8.13) of Algorithm *A_Dine*. It should then come with no difficulty that Theorem 8.3 is equally applicable to Algorithm *A_Dine_H* as well. In the remainder of this section, we turn to the synchronous model of computation for a more detailed analysis of Algorithm *A_Dine_H*. Our choice of a synchronous model for this analysis is motivated by the simplicity that ensues from that model, although corresponding results for the asynchronous model also exist and can be found in the literature.

The synchronous counterpart of Algorithm *A_Dine_H* starts off with an initial acyclic orientation at pulse $s = 0$ and generates a sequence of acyclic orientations for pulses $s > 0$. For $s \geq 0$, at pulse s all sinks concurrently access shared resources and then send forks to neighbors. The evolution of acyclic orientations in synchronous time is such that a new acyclic orientation is generated by reversing the orientation of all edges incident to sinks, which then become sources in the new orientation. This mechanism is referred to as the *edge-reversal mechanism*, having applications beyond the context of resource sharing. For example, together with Algorithm *A_Schedule_AS* of Section 5.3.2, an algorithm based on the edge-reversal mechanism is of key importance as a technique for time-stepped simulation (cf. Section 10.2). Both in this section and in Section 10.2, the edge-reversal mechanism is employed to schedule nodes for operation so that neighbors do not operate concurrently. In this section, the "operation" is to access resources that nodes share with neighbors, while in Section 10.2 the term has a different meaning. Because of its role as a scheduler, it is also common to find the edge-reversal mechanism referred to as *scheduling by edge reversal*.

Let $\omega_1, \omega_2, \ldots$ denote the sequence of acyclic orientations created by the edge-reversal mechanism, and $Sinks_1, Sinks_2, \ldots$ denote the corresponding sets of sinks. For $k \geq 1$, ω_k is the orientation at pulse $s = k - 1$. For $n_i \in N$ and $k \geq 1$, let $m_i(k)$ be the number of times n_i appears in $Sinks_1, \ldots, Sinks_k$.

Theorem 8.4. *Consider two nodes n_i and n_j, and let $r \geq 1$ be the number of edges on a shortest undirected path between them in G. Then $\left| m_i(k) - m_j(k) \right| \leq r$ for all $k \geq 1$.*

Proof: We use induction on the number of edges on a shortest undirected path between n_i and n_j. The case of one edge constitutes the basis of the induction, and then the assertion of the theorem holds trivially, as in this case n_i and n_j are neighbors in G, and must therefore appear in alternating sets in $Sinks_1, Sinks_2, \ldots$. As the induction hypothesis, assume the assertion of the theorem holds whenever a shortest undirected path between n_i and n_j has a number of edges no greater than $r - 1$. When n_i and n_j are separated by a shortest undirected path with r edges, consider any node n_ℓ (other than n_i and n_j) on this path and let d be the number of edges between n_i and n_ℓ on the path. By the induction hypothesis,

$$\left| m_i(k) - m_\ell(k) \right| \leq d$$

and

$$\left| m_\ell(k) - m_j(k) \right| \leq r - d,$$

yielding

$$\left| m_i(k) - m_j(k) \right| \leq r,$$

thence the theorem.   ∎

Theorem 8.4 is in fact more than a mere starvation-freedom statement, as not only does it imply that all nodes become sinks within a bounded number of pulses, but it also establishes a bound on the relative frequency with which nodes become sinks. This theorem is then a stronger version of Theorem 8.3 as far as starvation is concerned.

The number of distinct acyclic orientations of G is of course finite, so the sequence $\omega_1, \omega_2, \ldots$ must at some pulse embark in a periodic repetition of orientations, which we call a *period of orientations*, or simply a *period* (Figure 8.1). Orientations in a period are said to be *periodic orientations*. The next corollary establishes an important property of periods.

Corollary 8.5. *The number of times that a node becomes a sink in a period is the same for all nodes.*

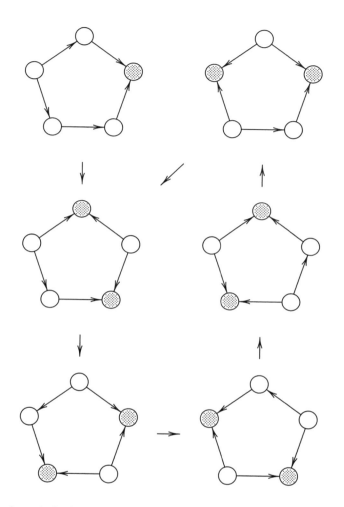

Figure 8.1. *A period of five orientations results from the edge-reversal mechanism started at the orientation shown in the upper left corner of the figure, which is outside the period. In this period, every node becomes a sink twice.*

Proof: Suppose, to the contrary, that two nodes n_i and n_j exist that become sinks different numbers of times in a period. Suppose, in addition, that a shortest undirected path between n_i and n_j in G has r edges. Letting p be the number of orientations in the period and $k = (r+1)p$ yields

$$\left| m_i(k) - m_j(k) \right| \geq r + 1,$$

which contradicts Theorem 8.4.   ∎

Clearly, the period is unequivocally determined given ω_1. We let $m(\omega_1)$ denote the number of times that nodes become sinks in this period, and $p(\omega_1)$ denote the number of orientations in the same period.

One issue of great interest is the "amount of concurrency" that scheduling by edge reversal is capable to yield from an initial acyclic orientation ω_1. The importance of this issue comes from the very nature of the resource-sharing computations we have been considering in all of Section 8.3, and from the intuitive realization that the choice of ω_1 greatly influences the number of nodes that become sinks concurrently.

The measure that we adopt for the concurrency attainable from ω_1, denoted by $Conc(\omega_1)$, is the average, over a large number of pulses and over n, of the number of times each node becomes a sink in those pulses. More formally,

$$Conc(\omega_1) = \lim_{k \to \infty} \frac{1}{kn} \sum_{n_i \in N} m_i(k).$$

Clearly, we get more concurrency as more nodes become sinks earlier.

Theorem 8.6. $Conc(\omega_1) = m(\omega_1)/p(\omega_1)$.

Proof: For some $\ell \geq 1$, let ω_ℓ be the first periodic orientation in $\omega_1, \omega_2, \dots$. For $k \geq \ell$, the first k orientations of $\omega_1, \omega_2, \dots$ include $\lfloor (k - \ell + 1)/p(\omega_1) \rfloor$ repetitions of the period, so

$$k = \left\lfloor \frac{k - \ell + 1}{p(\omega_1)} \right\rfloor p(\omega_1) + u$$

and

$$\sum_{n_i \in N} m_i(k) = n \left\lfloor \frac{k - \ell + 1}{p(\omega_1)} \right\rfloor m(\omega_1) + v,$$

where $\ell - 1 \leq u \leq \ell + p(\omega_1) - 2$ and $u \leq v \leq nu$. The theorem then follows easily in the limit as $k \to \infty$.   ∎

It follows immediately from Theorem 8.6 that

$$\frac{1}{n} \leq Conc(\omega_1) \leq \frac{1}{2}.$$

This is so because it takes at most n pulses for a node to become a sink (the longest directed distance to a sink is $n - 1$), so

$$m(\omega_1) \geq \frac{p(\omega_1)}{n},$$

and because the most frequently that a node can become a sink is in every other pulse, so

$$m(\omega_1) \leq \frac{p(\omega_1)}{2}.$$

If G is a tree, then it can be argued relatively simply that $Conc(\omega_1) = 1/2$, regardless of the initial orientation ω_1. If G is not a tree, then, interestingly, $Conc(\omega_1)$ can also be expressed in purely graph-theoretic terms, without recourse to the dynamics of the edge-reversal mechanism. For such, let κ denote an undirected cycle in G (with $|\kappa|$ nodes). Let also $n^+(\kappa, \omega_1)$ and $n^-(\kappa, \omega_1)$ denote the number of edges in κ oriented by ω_1 clockwise and counter-clockwise, respectively. Define

$$\rho(\kappa, \omega_1) = \frac{1}{|\kappa|} \min\{n^+(\kappa, \omega_1), n^-(\kappa, \omega_1)\},$$

and let K denote the set of all of G's undirected cycles.

Theorem 8.7. *If G is not a tree, then $Conc(\omega_1) = \min_{\kappa \in K} \rho(\kappa, \omega_1)$.*

Proof: The proof is quite involved, and escapes the intended scope of this book. The interested reader is referred to the pertaining literature. ∎

There are in the literature additional results concerning scheduling by edge reversal that we do not explicitly reproduce here. Some are positive, as the one that states that this mechanism is optimal (provides most concurrency) among all schemes that prevent neighbors from operating concurrently and require neighbors to operate alternately. Other results are negative, as for example the computational intractability (*NP*-hardness) of finding the initial acyclic orientation ω_1 that optimizes $Conc(\omega_1)$.

8.4. The drinking philosophers problem

If nodes may access different subsets of resources whenever they require access to shared resources, then the possibility that neighbors in G access shared resources concurrently exists, provided the sets of resources they access have an empty intersection. In such cases, the technique of employing one single fork per edge to secure exclusive access to the resources that two neighbors share is no longer sufficient. Instead, associated with every edge there has to be one object for each resource that the corresponding neighbors share. Such objects are bottles from which the philosophers drink, and the problem of ensuring mutual exclusion, deadlock-freedom, and starvation-freedom in the drinking of the philosophers is referred to as the *drinking philosophers problem*.

At node n_i, the set of bottles shared over edge (n_i, n_j) is denoted by B_i^j (which, clearly, is the same as B_j^i). For all $n_j \in Neig_i$, and for all $b_k \in B_i^j$, node n_i employs the Boolean variable *needs_bottle*$_i^{jk}$, initially set to **false**, to indicate whether $b_k \in B_i^j$ is needed. The need to access shared resources is indicated at n_i by the Boolean variable *thirsty*$_i$, initialized to **false**. In order to access the shared resources that it requires, n_i must acquire all the bottles corresponding to those resources, i.e., $b_k \in B_i^j$ such that *needs_bottle*$_i^{jk}$ = **true** for all $n_j \in Neig_i$.

Except for this need to acquire multiple objects corresponding to a same edge, the solution that we describe for the drinking philosophers problem is quite similar to that of the dining philosophers problem. In particular, the same priority scheme based on the turn objects that we employed in Algorithm *A_Dine* is also used in the new solution. In contrast with the multiplicity of bottles for each edge, the turns continue to exist in the number of one per edge, as in the dining philosophers case. What this amounts to is that turns are sent out on all edges when a node finishes accessing a group of shared resources, even in those edges whose bottles were not needed.

This solution to the drinking philosophers problem is given next as Algorithm *A_Drink*. Additional variables employed by node n_i are, for all $n_j \in Neig_i$, the Boolean *holds_turn*$_i^j$ (employed as in the dining philosophers case), and for all $b_k \in B_i^j$ the Booleans *holds_bottle*$_i^{jk}$ and *owes_bottle*$_i^{jk}$ (this one initially set to **false**), employed respectively to indicate whether n_i holds b_k and whether n_i has postponed the sending of b_k to n_j until it is through with accessing the shared resources. As in the dining philosophers case, the *holds_turn* and *holds_bottle* variables must be initialized to consistency across edges. In addition, the *holds_turn* variables must be initialized as to induce an acyclic orientation on G. Auxiliary set variables X_i and Y_i, both initially empty, are used by n_i.

The messages employed by Algorithm *A_Drink* are completely analogous to those of Algorithm *A_Dine*, but with some slight modifications. A message *request*(X) is sent by n_i to n_j to request a set of bottles $X \subseteq B_i^j$. A set X of bottles is sent via the message *bottle*(X), which similarly to the *fork* message of the dining philosophers case may carry an additional **nil**, *turn*, or *request*(Y) parameter. Finally, a *turn* message is used to send a turn over an edge.

Algorithm *A_Drink*:

▷ **Variables:**

$thirsty_i = \textbf{false}$;

$holds\_bottle_i^{jk}$ for all $n_j \in Neig_i$ and all $b_k \in B_i^j$;

$holds\_turn_i^j$ for all $n_j \in Neig_i$;

$owes\_bottle_i^{jk} = \textbf{false}$ for all $n_j \in Neig_i$ and all $b_k \in B_i^j$;

$needs\_bottle_i^{jk} = \textbf{false}$ for all $n_j \in Neig_i$ and all $b_k \in B_i^j$;

$X_i = \emptyset$;

$Y_i = \emptyset$.

▷ **Input:**

$msg_i = \textbf{nil}$.

Action when not $thirsty_i$ **and access to shared resources is needed:**   (8.17)

$thirsty_i := \textbf{true}$;

$needs\_bottle_i^{jk} := \textbf{true}$ for all $n_j \in Neig_i$ and all $b_k \in B_i^j$ such that access to the resource for which b_k stands is needed;

for all $n_j \in Neig_i$ such that there exists $b_k \in B_i^j$ with $needs\_bottle_i^{jk} = \textbf{true}$ and $holds\_bottle_i^{jk} = \textbf{false}$ **do**

> **begin**
>
> > Let X_i be the subset of B_i^j such that $b_k \in X_i$ if and only if $needs\_bottle_i^{jk} = \textbf{true}$ and $holds\_bottle_i^{jk} = \textbf{false}$;
> >
> > Send *request*(X_i) to n_j;
> >
> > $X_i := \emptyset$
>
> **end**.

▷ **Input:**
$msg_i = request(X)$ such that $origin_i(msg_i) = (n_i, n_j)$.
Action: (8.18)
   for all $b_k \in X$ **do**
     if not $thirsty_i$ **or not** $holds\_turn_i^j$ **or not** $needs\_bottle_i^{jk}$ **then**
       begin
         $holds_bottle_i^{jk} := $ **false**;
         $X_i := X_i \cup \{b_k\}$;
         if $thirsty_i$ **and** $needs\_bottle_i^{jk}$ **then**
           $Y_i := Y_i \cup \{b_k\}$
       end
     else
       $owes_bottle_i^{jk} := $ **true**;
   if $X_i \neq \emptyset$ **then**
     begin
       if $Y_i = \emptyset$ **then**
         Send $bottle(X_i, \mathbf{nil})$ to n_j
       else
         begin
           Send $bottle\big(X_i, request(Y_i)\big)$ to n_j;
           $Y_i := \emptyset$
         end;
       $X_i := \emptyset$
     end.

▷ **Input:**

    $msg_i = bottle(X, t)$ such that $origin_i(msg_i) = (n_i, n_j)$.

Action: (8.19)

    $holds_bottle_i^{jk} := $ **true** for all $b_k \in X$;

    if $t = turn$ **then**

        $holds_turn_i^j := $ **true**;

    if $t = request(Y)$ **then**

        $owes_bottle_i^{jk} := $ **true** for all $b_k \in Y$;

    if $holds\_bottle_i^{k\ell}$ for all $n_k \in Neig_i$ and all $b_\ell \in B_i^k$ **then**

        begin

            Access shared resources;

            $thirsty_i := $ **false**;

            for all $n_k \in Neig_i$ **do**

                if $holds\_turn_i^k$ **then**

                    begin

                        $holds_turn_i^k := $ **false**;

                        for all $b_\ell \in B_i^k$ **do**

                            if $owes\_bottle_i^{k\ell}$ **then**

                                begin

                                      $owes_bottle_i^k := $ **false**;

                                      $holds_bottle_i^{k\ell} := $ **false**;

                                      $X_i := X_i \cup \{b_\ell\}$

                              end;

                      if $X_i \neq \emptyset$ **then**

                        begin

                            Send $bottle(X_i, turn)$ to n_k;

                            $X_i := \emptyset$

                      end

                    else

                      Send $turn$ to n_k

                end

        end.

▷ **Input:**

    $msg_i = turn$ such that $origin_i(msg_i) = (n_i, n_j)$.

Action: (8.20)

    $holds_turn_i^j := $ **true**.

Actions (8.17) through (8.20) are entirely analogous to actions (8.11) through (8.14), respectively, of Algorithm A_Dine. Because the same priority scheme is used in both algorithms, Theorem 8.3 is, in essence, applicable to Algorithm A_Drink as well. With the exception of the bit complexity, the two algorithms also share the same complexity measures. The bit complexity of Algorithm A_Drink is different because $request$ and $bottle$ messages carry references to a set of bottles (possibly two sets of bottles, in the case of $bottle$ messages) with a nonconstant number of bottles. Because two neighbors share as many bottles as they share resources, and because they share at most R resources (cf. Section 8.2), the algorithm's bit complexity is $O(\Delta R \log R)$, provided every resource can be identified with $\lceil \log R \rceil$ bits.

8.5. Exercises

1. In Algorithm $A\_Mutually\_Exclude\_C$, show that the sequence numbers can be implemented with $O(\log n)$ bits.

2. Show, for Algorithm $A\_Mutually\_Exclude$, that it may be necessary to compare two sequence numbers differing from each other by an arbitrarily large amount.

3. Modify Algorithm $A\_Mutually\_Exclude$ for the case in which node n_i may belong to S_i.

4. In the context of Section 1.5, find the $r(c)$'s for Algorithm A_Dine_H.

8.6. Bibliographic notes

In order to sort through the plethora of approaches and algorithms for mutual exclusion, the reader can resort to the book by Raynal (1986), or the more current taxonomic studies by Raynal (1991) and Singhal (1993). Our treatment in Section 8.1 is derived from Ricart and Agrawala (1981) and from Maekawa (1985), where Algorithms $A\_Mutually\_Exclude\_C$ and $A\_Mutually\_Exclude$ first appeared, respectively. Further developments on these algorithms, as well as new approaches, can be found in numerous sources, including Carvalho and Roucairol (1983), Agrawal and Abbadi (1989), Raymond (1989), Singhal (1989a), Ramarao and Brahmadathan (1990), Neilsen and Mizuno (1991), Singhal (1991), Bouabdallah and Konig (1992), Satyanarayanan and Muthukrishnan (1992), Woo and Newman-Wolfe (1992), Chang and Yuan (1994), Chen and Tang (1994), Hélary, Mostefaoui, and Raynal (1994), and Madhuram and Kumar (1994).

The formulation of Section 8.2 can be found in Barbosa (1986) and in Barbosa and Gafni (1987; 1989b).

The dining philosophers problem appeared originally in Dijkstra (1968), and received attention in a distributed setting, either as posed originally or as variations thereof, in Chang (1980), Lynch (1980), Lynch (1981), and Rabin and Lehmann (1981). Algorithm *A_Dine* of Section 8.3.1 is based on Chandy and Misra (1984), but the idea of transforming sinks into sources to maintain the acyclicity of a graph's orientation appeared previously (Gafni and Bertsekas, 1981) in the context of routing in computer networks. The analysis that appears in Section 8.3.2 for the heavy-load case is from Barbosa (1986) and Barbosa and Gafni (1987; 1989b), where the omitted proof of Theorem 8.7 also appears, as well as other results related to optimality and intractability (in the sense of *NP*-hardness, as in Karp (1972) and Garey and Johnson (1979)). Most of the concurrency notions involved with scheduling by edge reversal are closely related to the concept of a multicoloring of a graph's nodes. Such a concept can be looked up in Stahl (1976), for example. Other sources of information on scheduling by edge reversal are Bertsekas and Tsitsiklis (1989), Malka, Moran, and Zaks (1993), Calabrese and França (1994), and França (1994). The latter addresses the randomized determination of *G*'s initial acyclic orientation.

Section 8.4 is based on Chandy and Misra (1984).

9

Program Debugging

Debugging is the part of the program development process whereby conceptual and programming errors are detected and corrected. The debugging of a sequential program is achieved mainly through the use of rather simple techniques that involve the ability to re-execute a program and to halt its execution at certain points of interest (the so-called breakpoints). Asynchronous algorithms like the ones we have been treating in this book lack both the determinism that makes the re-execution of sequential programs simple, and the unique total order of events that facilitates the detection of states where a halt is desired. Clearly, then, the debugging of programs based on such algorithms is altogether a different matter.

Notwithstanding this difference in levels of difficulty, approaches to the debugging of programs based on asynchronous algorithms have concentrated on the same two major techniques on which the debugging of sequential programs is based, namely deterministic re-execution and breakpoint detection. It is then to these two major topics that we dedicate this chapter, beginning in Section 9.1 with some preliminary concepts, and then progressing through Sections 9.2 and 9.3, respectively on techniques for program re-execution and breakpoint detection. Throughout the chapter, G is an undirected graph.

The detection of breakpoints can be an especially intricate endeavor, depending on the characteristics of the breakpoint one is seeking to detect. For this reason, in Section 9.3 we limit ourselves to very special classes of breakpoints, chiefly those that are either unconditional or depend on predicates that can be expressed as logical disjunctions or conjunctions of local predicates. In this context, we provide techniques that fall into two classes, specifically those that are based on a re-execution (in the style of Section 9.2), and those that are not so.

Sections 9.4 and 9.5 contain, respectively, exercises and bibliographic notes.

9.1. Preliminaries

The debugging of a sequential program is a cyclic process supported by two basic techniques, those of program re-execution and of breakpoint detection. We assume henceforth that the programs that we treat in this chapter, sequential and distributed alike, never act on probabilistic decisions, and then a sequential program is guaranteed to go through the same sequence of states whenever it is re-executed from the same initial conditions. In the asynchronous distributed case, however, there are sources of nondeterminism other than those related to probabilistic decisions, specifically those related to the model's unsynchronized local clocks and unpredictable delays for message delivery among neighbors. As a consequence, the simple re-execution from the same initial conditions is not enough to ensure that all nodes will repeat the same behavior as in the previous execution.

This issue of nondeterminacy is also what distinguishes the sequential and asynchronous distributed cases when it comes to the detection of breakpoints during an execution. In the sequential case, all operations on variables are totally ordered, and then checking for the occurrence of particular states where predefined predicates hold poses no conceptual difficulties. In the asynchronous distributed case, on the other hand, no such unique total order exists, and the detection of global states with the characteristics required by a predefined predicate becomes a much harder problem.

The key to approaching the two problems is the treatment of timing issues under the asynchronous model that we pursued in Section 3.1. Specifically, in order to reproduce an execution of an asynchronous algorithm, it suffices to ensure that the re-execution follows the exact same partial order of events that was generated by the original execution. Detecting breakpoints correctly is also very much dependent upon the concepts introduced in that section, because, as we already mentioned, what is required is the detection of global states at which the required predicates hold. However, what is needed is not just an algorithm like Algorithm *A_Record_Global_State* of Section 5.2.1, which offers no control as to which global state it records, but rather algorithms that are guaranteed not to miss a global state with the desired characteristics if one exists.

Before we proceed to the remaining sections of the chapter, let us pause briefly for a few terminological comments. Although in these first two sections we have attempted to comply with the standard practice of reserving the terms "algorithm" and "program" for different entities (a program is normally a realization of an algorithm, involving a particular programming language and often assumptions on the system's architecture), henceforth we shall drop the distinction and refer to the debugging of an algorithm as encompassing the debugging of programs as well (even though what is normally true is the converse). We do this to simplify the terminology only, and no further presumptions are implied.

9.2. Techniques for program re-execution

As we remarked in the previous section, the aim when attempting to re-execute an asynchronous algorithm is to re-generate the same set of events, and hence the same partial order among them, as in the original execution. What is needed to achieve this goal is twofold. First of all, the set N_0 of spontaneous initiators must be the same as in the original execution. Secondly, from the perspective of individual nodes, messages must be received in the same order as in the original execution. Note that this involves more than the order of message reception on a particular edge, as in reality what is required is the preservation of the order of message reception across all edges incident to a node. If edges are FIFO, then it suffices that a node, during the re-execution, consider the edges to receive messages in the same order as they happened to be considered in the original execution. Put differently, if node n_i has as neighbors nodes $n_{j_1}, \ldots, n_{j_k}$ for $k = |Neig_i|$, and in the original execution the first message was received at n_i from $n_a \in \{n_{j_1}, \ldots, n_{j_k}\}$, the second message from $n_b \in \{n_{j_1}, \ldots, n_{j_k}\}$, and so on, then during the re-execution the same order must be respected. The solution that we describe next is given for this case of FIFO edges, although an extension to the case in which edges are not FIFO can also be devised (cf. Exercise 1).

Preserving this order of appearance of a node's neighbors (equivalently, of a node's incident edges) in the sequence of messages the node receives during the re-execution of an algorithm can be achieved through the following two-phase process. During the original execution, every node records a sequence of pointers to neighbors; this recording is the process's first phase. The second phase occurs during the re-execution, in which the sequences recorded during the first phase are employed to force nodes to receive messages from neighbors in the order implied by the recorded sequence. The combined sequences recorded by all nodes during the first phase constitute a *trace* of the original execution. This trace, along with the composition of the N_0 set associated with the original execution, clearly suffice for the algorithm to be deterministically re-executed.

Before we proceed to describe more precisely the mechanism whereby the trace is employed during the re-execution, it must be mentioned that the recording of the trace may cause the original execution to be different from what it would be if no recording were being done. This is the so-called *probe effect* of the trace-recording process, and is of little consequence from a purely theoretical point of view, because under the assumptions of the asynchronous model any execution is as good as any other. However, in a practical setting where certain executions would be favored by certain prevailing timing conditions, the probe effect can be misleading, in the sense of causing the trace of an "atypical" execution to be recorded. In such circumstances, probe effects are important and the recording of traces (i.e., the "probe") should be designed to keep them to a minimum.

During the trace recording, node n_i employs the Boolean variable $initiator_i$, initialized to **false**, to indicate whether n_i turns out to be a member of N_0. In addition, a queue of pointers to neighbors is employed by n_i to record the origins of all the messages it receives during the execution. This queue is called $queue_i$ and is initialized to **nil**. At all times, $first\_in\_queue_i$ is assumed to be the first element in $queue_i$, being equal to nil if $queue_i =$ **nil**. During the re-execution phase, the Boolean $initiator_i$ is used to make up an N_0 set that is equal to the one of the original execution. Similarly, $queue_i$ is employed to control the reception of messages by node n_i. This is achieved by conditioning actions on the reception of a message msg_i to be executed only when

$$origin_i(msg_i) = (n_i, first\_in\_queue_i),$$

provided $queue_i$ is updated by the removal of its first element whenever a message is received. The mechanism whereby this takes place is through the use of the Boolean conditions allowed in our general template, Algorithm *A_Template* of Section 2.1.

Next we present two asynchronous algorithms, one for each of the phases involved in the deterministic re-execution of asynchronous algorithms. These algorithms are called Algorithm *A_Record_Trace* and Algorithm *A_Replay*, respectively for the first phase and the second phase. These two algorithms are derived directly from Algorithm *A_Template*, and are therefore intended for generic asynchronous computations that fit that template.

Algorithm *A_Record_Trace*:

  ▷ **Variables:**

      $initiator_i = $ **false**;

      $queue_i = $ **nil**;

      $first_in_queue_i = $ **nil**;

      Other variables used by n_i, and their initial values, are listed here.

  ▷ **Input:**

      $msg_i = $ **nil**.

    Action if $n_i \in N_0$:   (9.1)

      $initiator_i := $ **true**;

      Do some computation;

      Send one message on each edge of a (possibly empty) subset of Inc_i.

  ▷ **Input:**

      msg_i such that $origin_i(msg_i) = (n_i, n_j)$.

    Action: (9.2)

      Append n_j to $queue_i$;

      Do some computation;

      Send one message on each edge of a (possibly empty) subset of Inc_i.

In Algorithm *A_Record_Trace*, the variable $initiator_i$ is set to **true** in (9.1) to signal to the re-execution phase what the members of N_0 must be. Similarly, the portion of the trace that corresponds to message receptions at n_i is recorded in $queue_i$ in (9.2). In Algorithm *A_Replay*, presented next, the members of N_0 are exactly those nodes n_i for which $initiator_i = $ **true** at the end of the execution of Algorithm *A_Record_Trace*. In this sense, N_0 is no longer a set of spontaneous initiators, but rather the set of nodes that are forced to initiate the computation so the original execution of the algorithm can be faithfully reproduced.

Algorithm *A_Replay*:

  ▷ **Variables:**

      $queue_i$;

      $first\_in\_queue_i$;

      Other variables used by n_i, and their initial values, are listed here.

▷ **Input:**
$\quad$ $msg_i = $ **nil.**
$\quad$ **Action if** $n_i \in N_0$: $\hspace{6cm}$ (9.3)
$\qquad$ Do some computation;
$\qquad$ Send one message on each edge of a (possibly empty) subset of Inc_i.

▷ **Input:**
$\quad$ msg_i such that $origin_i(msg_i) = (n_i, n_j)$.
$\quad$ **Action when** $n_j = first\_in\_queue_i$: $\hspace{4cm}$ (9.4)
$\qquad$ Remove $first\_in\_queue_i$ from $queue_i$;
$\qquad$ Do some computation;
$\qquad$ Send one message on each edge of a (possibly empty) subset of Inc_i.

Action (9.3) is executed by the nodes that initiate the re-execution according to the trace recorded by Algorithm A_Record_Trace. Action (9.4), which is only executed by n_i on a message arriving on edge (n_i, n_j) when $n_j = first\_in\_queue_i$, ensures that message receptions are acted upon by n_i in the same order as they were in the execution of Algorithm A_Record_Trace.

As a final remark in this section, note that the message, time, and bit complexities of both Algorithm A_Record_Trace and Algorithm A_Replay are the same. This is only expected, in view of the correctness of Algorithm A_Replay in reproducing the execution of Algorithm A_Record_Trace, if we consider that neither the recording process nor the deterministic re-execution employ any messages in addition to those already present in the original computation.

9.3. Breakpoint detection

This section is devoted to the second major problem we discuss in this chapter in connection with the debugging of asynchronous algorithms, namely that of detecting breakpoints. Our discussion proceeds in Sections 9.3.1 through 9.3.3 as follows. Section 9.3.1 contains fundamental definitions and concepts, especially those related to the types of breakpoints to be treated in the sequel. The remaining two sections are devoted each to a different aspect of the problem. Section 9.3.2 contains a trace-based approach, and Section 9.3.3 an approach that does not depend on a trace of a previous execution.

The bulk of Section 9.3 is contained in Section 9.3.3, where we introduce a collection of distributed algorithms for the detection of some types of breakpoints. Although Section 9.3.2 also contains interesting insights into the problem, it is on Section 9.3.3 that the reader should concentrate.

9.3.1. Fundamentals

A breakpoint in the execution of an asynchronous algorithm is a global state at which one wishes the computation to halt so that nodes' variables can be examined. All the breakpoints we study in the forthcoming sections refer to local states of the nodes only, so that for our purposes in this chapter messages in transit on edges are an unimportant part of a global state. Whenever the need arises for a global state to be represented, we shall then do so by considering nodes' local states only. For node n_i, we let $lt_i \geq 0$ be n_i's local time. For simplicity when describing our algorithms, we assume that lt_i is in fact an event counter at n_i, that is, $lt_i = 0$ initially and is increased by one either upon the spontaneous sending of messages by n_i if $n_i \in N_0$ or upon the reception of a message by n_i. Clearly, a node n_i's local state is unequivocally determined given lt_i.

Because messages in transit play no role in the global states of our interest, and considering the relationship we just described between a node's local state and local time, a node's view of a global state can be represented by an n-component array of local times. In such an array, and for $1 \leq i \leq n$, the ith component contains some value of lt_i. If we revisit our initial study of global states in Section 3.1, then clearly an n-component array φ of natural numbers is a global state if and only if no $n_i \in N$ exists that ever receives a message earlier than (or at) $\varphi[i]$ that was sent by some $n_j \in Neig_i$ later than $\varphi[j]$. The definition of an earliest global state with respect to some property that we alluded to in Section 3.1 can in this simplified view of a global state be given as follows. A global state φ is the *earliest* global state for which a certain property holds if and only if no other global state φ' for which the property also holds is such that $\varphi'[i] \leq \varphi[i]$ for all $n_i \in N$. Depending on the particular property one is considering, it is conceivable, as we will see later in Section 9.3.3, that more than one earliest global state exists. In this case, all the earliest global states are *incomparable* to one another, in the sense that the past of none of them is in the past of another (or, equivalently, if we resort to the terminology of Section 3.1, none of them comes earlier than any other).

There is a great variety of problems that may be considered when studying breakpoints of asynchronous algorithms, so right at this introductory section it must remain very clear which the problems that we consider are. The first important distinction is related to the so-called "weak" and "strong" senses in which breakpoints can be treated. The weak sense refers to breakpoints as global states of one single execution of the algorithm, while the strong sense is about breakpoints in all possible executions of the algorithm. Although attempts are described in the literature that focus on strong-sense problems, it is to be intuitively expected that such attempts invariably result in computationally intractable problems for general computations, given the prohibitively large number of possible executions of an asynchronous algorithm. It is then to problems in the weak sense that we dedicate our study. One important consequence of restricting ourselves to such problems is that, if a particular execution of an asynchronous algorithm fails to contain a global state with certain desired properties, one cannot infer that no execution exists in which such a global state would appear.

Although in many situations the ultimate goal of considering breakpoints in asynchronous algorithms is to halt the execution at the corresponding global state, with one single exception it is not to this halting problem that we dedicate most of our efforts in the forthcoming sections within Section 9.3, but rather to the problem of only detecting the occurrence of the breakpoints. The exception is the material that we present in Section 9.3.2, where the halting problem is considered. In all other situations, that is, those discussed in Section 9.3.3, if halting is desired after the detection, then special techniques of the so-called "checkpointing and rollback recovery" type must be employed so that the execution can be "returned" to the global state where the breakpoint was detected. We pursue the issue no further in this book, but in Section 10.4 the reader can find closely related techniques, only in a totally different context.

A breakpoint can be unconditional or conditional. An *unconditional breakpoint* is specified by providing a *local unconditional breakpoint* for each $n_i \in N$, denoted by lub_i. The local unconditional breakpoint of n_i is either a nonnegative integer specifying the value of lt_i with which n_i is to participate in the breakpoint, or such that $lub_i = \infty$ if n_i does not participate in the breakpoint. This flexibility of allowing nodes not to participate in breakpoints is fundamental from a practical perspective, because it allows global properties of interest to be monitored on subsets of nodes instead of on N as a whole. The goal of detecting an unconditional breakpoint is to find a global state φ such that $\varphi[i] = lub_i$ for all $n_i \in N$ such that $lub_i < \infty$. If no such global state exists, then the detection algorithm must be able to report this as an error.

A *conditional breakpoint* is specified by providing for each $n_i \in N$ a *local predicate*, that is, a Boolean function that depends on n_i's variables. The local predicate of n_i is denoted by lp_i, and can be a constant (either **true** or **false**) if n_i does not participate in the breakpoint. The conditional breakpoints that we consider are either disjunctive or conjunctive. A *disjunctive breakpoint* is a global state at which the *disjunctive predicate* given by the logical disjunction of all participating nodes' local predicates is **true**. In other words, a global state is a disjunctive breakpoint if and only if at least one of the participating nodes has a **true** local predicate in that global state. A *conjunctive breakpoint* is defined likewise, being a global state at which the *conjunctive predicate* given by the logical conjunction of all participating nodes' local predicates is **true**. Put differently, a global state is a conjunctive breakpoint if and only if all participating nodes have a **true** local predicate in that global state.

The goal of detecting a disjunctive breakpoint is that of finding a global state φ such that $lp_i = \textbf{true}$ at local time $\varphi[i]$ for at least one node n_i that participates in the breakpoint. In the same vein, the goal of detecting a conjunctive breakpoint is to find a global state φ such that $lp_i = \textbf{true}$ at time $\varphi[i]$ for all nodes n_i that participate in the breakpoint. If node n_i does not participate in a breakpoint, then it suffices to set lp_i to **false** in the disjunctive case, or to **true** in the conjunctive case, for the goal of the corresponding detections to be re-stated more simply as follows. Detecting a disjunctive breakpoint is to find a global state φ such that $lp_i = \textbf{true}$ at time $\varphi[i]$ for at least one $n_i \in N$; in the conjunctive case, it is to find a global state φ such that $lp_i = \textbf{true}$ at time $\varphi[i]$ for all $n_i \in N$.

The following is how Sections 9.3.2 and 9.3.3 are organized. In Section 9.3.2, a trace-based algorithm is presented to halt an execution at the earliest conjunctive breakpoint. Section 9.3.3, which is where most of our study is concentrated, contains distributed algorithms for the detection of earliest disjunctive breakpoints, earliest unconditional breakpoints, and earliest conjunctive breakpoints. In the case of unconditional breakpoints, requiring the earliest such breakpoint to be detected is only meaningful if there is at least one node that does not participate in the breakpoint. As we have seen earlier in this section, nodes like this have the *lub* variables set to infinity, and may then be required to appear in the detected breakpoint with as early a local state as possible.

Most of the algorithms that we study employ messages other than the messages of the computation proper, and for this reason a distinction must be made between such messages and those additional messages that the algorithms employ. Messages of the computation proper are then referred to as *comp_msg*'s.

9.3.2. A trace-based technique

In this section, we discuss a trace-based technique to halt the execution of an asynchronous algorithm at the earliest conjunctive breakpoint that occurs. It is trace-based because, as in Section 9.2, it is based on two phases, the first one being the recording of a trace and the second one a re-execution with special attention to the detection of the earliest conjunctive breakpoint. The trace recording is achieved precisely as in Algorithm *A_Record_Trace* of Section 9.2, where the variables $queue_i$ and $first\_in\_queue_i$, respectively a queue of node references and a pointer to its first element, are employed by node n_i to record the neighborhood-wide order according to which it receives *comp_msg*'s. The difference in this case is that not only a deterministic re-execution is sought, but a re-execution that does not progress beyond the earliest conjunctive breakpoint. As in Section 9.2, G's edges are assumed to be FIFO. Also, for the sake of simplicity when writing the algorithm, we assume that a node's local predicate can only become **true** after the node has computed and sent messages out (unless the node does not participate in the breakpoint, in which case its local predicate is perpetually **true**).

The approach that we adopt has the following essential ingredients. During the re-execution phase, node n_i may be *active* or *inactive*. It is active initially and becomes inactive when lp_i becomes **true**. A node only receives *comp_msg*'s (and therefore only computes and sends *comp_msg*'s out) if it is active, so that becoming inactive when its local predicate becomes **true** is a means of cooperating for the execution to halt at the earliest conjunctive breakpoint. The problem with such a naïve way of cooperating is that, by becoming inactive and therefore not sending any *comp_msg*'s out, a node may be precluding other nodes from reaching local states in which their local predicates can become **true** as well, which is an absolute must if the execution is to halt at a conjunctive breakpoint.

One way to go around this difficulty is the following. For $n_j \in Neig_i$, node n_i maintains two counters, $last\_received_i^j$ and $last\_sent_i^j$, both initially set to zero, to indicate respectively the number of *comp_msg*'s received from n_j and the number of *comp_msg*'s sent to n_j. Whenever n_i is finished with computing and sending *comp_msg*'s out, either initially or in response to the reception of a *comp_msg*, and has remained active, it sends a *request*($last\_received_i^j + 1$) message to n_j such that $n_j = first\_in\_queue_i$. This message is intended to activate n_j if it is inactive, so that it can send n_i the *comp_msg* that it needs to proceed according to the trace. When the *request* message reaches n_j with an x parameter, then it must be that $x - 1 \leq last\_sent_j^i$ (if n_i is requesting the xth *comp_msg*, then it must have received exactly $x - 1$ *comp_msg*'s prior to sending the request and n_j must have sent at least as many *comp_msg*'s prior to receiving the request). If $x - 1 = last\_sent_j^i$, then n_j does indeed owe n_i a *comp_msg*. If it is not active, it then becomes active and sends a *request* itself, and only becomes inactive when its local predicate becomes **true** after having sent that *comp_msg* to n_i. Because *request*'s may accumulate before a node's computation is such that the corresponding *comp_msg*'s get sent, node n_i employs the variable $owed_i^j$, initially equal to zero, to indicate the number of *comp_msg*'s that need to be sent to $n_j \in Neig_i$ before it may become inactive.

The problem that still persists with this approach is that, because edges are FIFO (as they must be for correct re-execution) and a node only receives

$comp\_msg$'s when it is active and the origin of the $comp\_msg$ coincides with the node's $first\_in\_queue$ variable, it may happen that a $request$ never reaches its destination. The final fix is then to allow a node to receive all $comp\_msg$'s that reach it, and then to queue them up internally (along with their origins) on edge-specific queues if the node happens to be inactive or the $comp\_msg$ that arrived is not the one that was expected for re-execution. Upon receipt of a $request$ from n_j, an inactive node n_i works on the messages in those queues until the re-execution can no longer progress or $owed_i^j = 0$ and $lp_i = \textbf{true}$. If $owed_i^j > 0$ or $lp_i = \textbf{false}$ when n_i exits this loop, then n_i becomes active and sends out a $request$. The reader should reflect on the reasons why this procedure ensures that the re-execution halts (i.e., all nodes become inactive) at the earliest conjunctive breakpoint (cf. Exercise 2).

Algorithm $A\_Replay\_\&\_Halt\_CB$ ("CB" for Conjunctive Breakpoint), given next, realizes the procedure we just described. In addition to the variables we already introduced, node n_i also employs the Boolean $active_i$, initialized to $\textbf{not}\ lp_i$, to indicate whether it is active. Also, for each $n_j \in Neig_i$, the queue where $comp\_msg$'s from n_j may have to be queued is $msg\_queue_i^j$, initially set to $\textbf{nil}$, whose first element is assumed to be the pair $(first\_origin\_in\_msg\_queue_i^j, first\_msg\_in\_msg\_queue_i^j)$, initially equal to $(\textbf{nil}, \textbf{nil})$, at all times. In this algorithm, as in Algorithm A_Replay, the set N_0 is given as determined by Algorithm A_Record_Trace.

Algorithm $A\_Replay\_\&\_Halt\_CB$:

▷ **Variables:**

   $queue_i$;
   $first\_in\_queue_i$;
   $last\_received_i^j = 0$ for all $n_j \in Neig_i$;
   $last\_sent_i^j = 0$ for all $n_j \in Neig_i$;
   $owed_i^j = 0$ for all $n_j \in Neig_i$;
   $active_i = \textbf{not}\ lp_i$;
   $msg\_queue_i = \textbf{nil}$ for all $n_j \in Neig_i$;
   $first\_origin\_in\_msg\_queue_i = \textbf{nil}$ for all $n_j \in Neig_i$;
   $first\_msg\_in\_msg\_queue_i = \textbf{nil}$ for all $n_j \in Neig_i$;
   Other variables used by n_i, and their initial values, are listed here.

▷ **Input:**

$msg_i = \textbf{nil}$.

Action if $n_i \in N_0$:   (9.5)

Do some computation;

Send one *comp_msg* on each edge of a (possibly empty) subset of Inc_i and update the *last_sent*$_i^j$'s accordingly;

if lp_i **then**

$active_i := \textbf{false}$.

▷ **Input:**

$msg_i = comp\_msg$ such that $origin_i(msg_i) = (n_i, n_j)$.

Action: (9.6)

if $active_i$ **and** $n_j = first\_in\_queue_i$ **then**

begin

$last\_received_i^j := last\_received_i^j + 1$;

Remove $first\_in\_queue_i$ from $queue_i$;

Do some computation;

Send one *comp_msg* on each edge of a (possibly empty) subset of Inc_i and update the *last_sent*$_i^k$'s and the *owed*$_i^k$'s accordingly;

if $owed_i^k = 0$ for all $n_k \in Neig_i$ **then**

if lp_i **then**

$active_i := \textbf{false}$;

if $active_i$ **then**

begin

Let $n_k = first\_in\_queue_i$;

Send $request(last\_received_i^k + 1)$ to n_k

end

end

else

Append (n_j, msg_i) to $msg\_queue_i^j$.

▷ **Input:**

  $msg_i = request(x)$ such that $origin_i(msg_i) = (n_i, n_j)$.

Action: (9.7)

  if not $active_i$ **and** $x - 1 = last\_sent_i^j$ **then**

    begin

      $owed_i^j := owed_i^j + 1;$

      while ($owed_i^j > 0$ **or not** lp_i) **and** there exists $n_k \in Neig_i$

      such that $first\_in\_queue_i = first\_origin\_in\_msg\_queue_i^k$ **do**

        begin

          $last\_received_i^k := last\_received_i^k + 1;$

          Remove $first\_in\_queue_i$ from $queue_i$;

          Remove the pair

          ($first\_origin\_in\_msg\_queue_i^k, first\_msg\_in\_msg\_queue_i^k$)

          from $msg\_queue_i^k$;

          Do some computation;

          Send one $comp\_msg$ on each edge of a (possibly

          empty) subset of Inc_i and update the $last\_sent_i^\ell$'s

          and the $owed_i^\ell$'s accordingly

        end;

      if $owed_i^j > 0$ **or not** lp_i **then**

        begin

          $active_i := \textbf{true};$

          Let $n_k = first\_in\_queue_i$;

          Send $request(last\_received_i^k + 1)$ to n_k

        end

  end.

There is some correspondence between the actions in this algorithm and those in Algorithm A_Replay for simple re-execution, but they differ greatly, too. Specifically, actions (9.3) and (9.5) are related to each other, although (9.5) also undertakes the incrementing of $last\_sent_i^j$ when a $comp\_msg$ is sent to neighbor n_j and checks lp_i to see if n_i must become inactive. Likewise, actions (9.4) and (9.6) are also related to each other. The differences are in the internal queueing of $comp\_msg$'s and in that (9.6) increments $last\_received_i^j$ to account for the receipt of the triggering msg_i on (n_i, n_j), increments $last\_sent_i^k$ (decrements $owed_i^k$, if positive) upon sending a $comp\_msg$ to neighbor n_k, and in addition checks lp_i to possibly set $active_i$ to **false** (if $active_i$ remains **true**, then (9.6) includes the sending of a $request$ as well). Action (9.7) deals with the reception of a $request$ from n_j. This $request$, if indeed corresponding to a *comp_msg* that was not sent, and if n_i is inactive, causes $owed_i^j$ to be incremented and n_i to compute on its internal queues of messages. If $owed_i^j$ remains positive or $lp_i = \textbf{false}$ after this, then n_i becomes active and sends a *request*.

As in the case of Algorithm *A_Replay*, the message and time complexities of Algorithm *A_Replay_&_Halt_CB* are the same as those of Algorithm *A_Record_Trace*. This is so because the additional *request* messages only increase the total number of messages exchanged and the longest causal chain of messages by a constant factor. However, the new algorithm's bit complexity may be higher, because *request* messages carry integers that depend on how many *comp_msg*'s were received by the sending node during the trace-recording phase.

We finalize the section with a couple of observations leading to issues that the reader may find worth pursuing further. The first observation is that devising a procedure similar to Algorithm *A_Replay_&_Halt_CB* to halt at the earliest disjunctive breakpoint during a re-execution is a very different matter. The reader is encouraged to pursue a proof that no such procedure exists, be it trace-based or otherwise (cf. Exercise 3).

As the second observation, notice that Algorithm *A_Replay_&_Halt_CB* does not entirely conform to the standards set by Algorithm *A_Template*, in the sense that in both (9.6) and (9.7) a *request* may follow a *comp_msg* to the same node, whereas Algorithm *A_Template* only allows one message to be sent to a node per action. An instructive exercise is to rewrite Algorithm *A_Replay_&_Halt_CB* so that this constraint is respected (cf. Exercise 4).

9.3.3. A trace-independent approach

In this section we introduce three asynchronous algorithms for the detection of breakpoints. One of the algorithms detects earliest disjunctive breakpoints, another detects earliest unconditional breakpoints, and the last one detects earliest conjunctive breakpoints whose corresponding conjunctive predicates are stable (in the sense of Chapter 6). As we remarked earlier in Section 9.3.1, not always is the requirement that an unconditional breakpoint be the earliest such breakpoint meaningful—in fact, it only makes sense when at least one node does not participate in the unconditional breakpoint. If such is not the case, then what the algorithm that we discuss achieves is the detection of the requested unconditional breakpoint. Another pertinent observation regarding the algorithms of this section is the assumed stability of the conjunctive predicate used to detect the conjunctive breakpoints. This assumption simplifies matters tremendously, and it is in the wake of this simplicity that we adopt it. However, there do exist techniques to detect conjunctive breakpoints in the absence of stability (as in Section 9.3.2), and at least a couple of recent algorithms that do not employ traces can be found in the literature.

In contrast with the detection procedure discussed in the previous section, which was based on a trace of a previous execution, the overall approach in this section does not depend on any trace, but rather attempts to detect the required breakpoint as the computation progresses. As in the case of the global state recording discussed in Section 5.2.1, what we must handle is then the interaction of two computations on G. One of the computations is the computation proper, the one that progresses by the exchange of the already introduced $comp\_msg$ messages. The other computation is the computation for breakpoint detection, which, as in Section 5.2.1, must be endowed with certain privileges with respect to the former computation, because it must be able to inspect nodes' states in that computation as well as the flow of $comp\_msg$'s. In the case of Algorithm $A\_Record\_Global\_State$, we were able to get away without being more specific about the way the two computations interacted, but in the present case we must face the need to provide some of the details, especially because the computation for breakpoint detection will have to be able to attach additional fields, in the form of parameters, to the $comp\_msg$'s that flow among nodes.

Let us then fill in some of the details on how the two computations interact. We begin by assuming that the message complexity of the computation proper is $O(c(n, m))$, or more succinctly $O(c)$. Likewise, we assume that every node's local clock can only represent local times up to a value T (i.e., $lt_i \leq T$ for all $n_i \in N$), which can be arbitrarily large but needs nevertheless be such that we can refer to it when assessing our algorithms' complexities.

The following is how we henceforth assume the computation proper and the detection algorithms to interact. At $n_i \in N$, the actions of both computations exclude one another in time, as usual. For clarity, we view node n_i as comprising two processes that can send messages to each other. One of the processes is referred to as p_i, while the other is referred to as q_i. For all $n_i \in N$, process q_i is responsible for the detection algorithm, while process p_i is responsible for the computation proper. Process q_i may send messages to every other process q_j such that $n_j \in Neig_i$ and to p_i, while process p_i may only send messages to q_i. In this way, q_i is capable of intercepting every $comp\_msg$ that p_i sends or receives, for the purpose of detecting breakpoints. In doing so, q_i may add fields to, or strip fields off, the $comp\_msg$'s that it intercepts. Of course, every $comp\_msg$ sent by p_i must somehow contain an indication of which p_j it is destined to, so that q_i can forward it appropriately to q_j. Process q_i responds to messages it receives either on edges $(n_i, n_j) \in E$ or "internally" from p_i. When specifying the algorithms for breakpoint detection, we provide actions for process q_i only, and then mentions to the set N_0 never appear, as clearly actions performed by nodes in this set are actions of the computation proper.

Perhaps the most important assumption on how processes p_i and q_i interact is that the atomicity of p_i's actions may be violated, in the following sense. Process q_i is activated (and then p_i is suspended, while lt_i remains constant) when lt_i becomes equal to lub_i (in the case of unconditional breakpoints) or when the local predicate lp_i becomes **true** (in the case of conditional breakpoints), or yet upon the sending by p_i of a $comp\_msg$ or the arrival of a message from q_j such that $n_j \in Neig_i$. What this amounts to is that q_i has some sort of "preemptive priority" over p_i.

When evaluating our algorithms' complexities, this dual character of a node's behavior may at first seem confusing, so that it is advisable to spell out the criteria to be used right away. All the complexity measures to be given in this section are measures related to the breakpoint detection computation only, and then may involve messages sent especially for detection purposes as well as $comp\_msg$'s to which additional fields were attached (although in the latter case only the message and bit complexities are affected, not the global time complexity, which is already accounted for by the computation proper). Such measures are then aimed at capturing the "overhead" of breakpoint detection only.

Our algorithms for breakpoint detection are based on the following general approach. For $1 \leq i \leq n$, process q_i maintains an array gs_i of length n representing its view of the global state to be detected. This array is initialized with zeroes (representing the earliest global state of the computation) and is updated when information is received concerning the other nodes' local unconditional breakpoints or local predicates. Such information is conveyed from node to node either by means of special $broadcast$ messages or as additional fields attached to the $comp\_msg$'s that constitute the communication traffic of the computation proper. This information, when sent by q_i, comprises the array gs_i, and may, depending on the type of breakpoint to be detected, comprise additional data as well. In each of the cases we consider, this information is exchanged among nodes in such a way as to allow at least one node, say $n_k \in N$, to detect locally that the breakpoint has occurred at the global state recorded in the current gs_k maintained by q_k, which is in all cases the earliest global state at which the breakpoint can be said to have occurred.

Let us now examine Algorithm A_Detect_DB ("DB" for Disjunctive Breakpoint) for the detection of disjunctive breakpoints. Such a breakpoint is a global state at which for at least one of the participating nodes the local predicate holds. Clearly, the earliest global state at which a disjunctive predicate holds does not

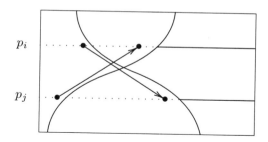

Figure 9.1. *In this figure, the solid segment in a process's horizontal line indicates the time interval during which the corresponding local predicate is* **true**. *The two cuts shown clearly correspond to global states, in fact earliest global states in which the disjunctive predicate holds.*

have to be unique (Figure 9.1), as we mentioned in Section 9.3.1, so it is conceivable that more than one node detects the occurrence of the breakpoint, however at different global states.

Because of the inherent ease with which disjunctive predicates can be detected in a distributed fashion, Algorithm *A_Detect_DB* is quite straightforward. It does not employ any *broadcast* messages, and attaches the array $gs_i(lt_i)$, in addition to a "status bit" (to be discussed shortly), to the *comp_msg*'s sent by process q_i on behalf of p_i. This array is identical to gs_i in all components except the ith, which is given by lt_i. Our earlier assumptions imply that the value of lt_i is in this case the local time at p_i when it sent the message that q_i intercepted, and then corresponds to p_i's local state immediately succeeding the sending of the message. The *comp_msg*'s sent by q_i are then sent as *comp_msg*("status bit", $gs_i(lt_i)$). Likewise, when q_i receives a message *comp_msg*("status bit", gs) from q_j such that $n_j \in Neig_i$, it is *comp_msg* that gets forwarded to p_i.

Attaching the modified gs_i to *comp_msg*'s is a procedure with important properties in the context of this section, not only for the algorithm we are beginning to present, but also for other algorithms presented in the sequel. We then pause briefly to introduce the following two supporting lemmas.

Lemma 9.1. *For all $n_i \in N$, if gs_i is a global state such that $gs_i[i] < lt_i$ and no message is received at p_i at time t such that $gs_i[i] < t \leq lt_i$, then $gs_i(lt_i)$ is also a global state.*

Proof: If $gs_i(lt_i)$ is not a global state, then there must exist $n_k, n_\ell \in N$ such that a *comp_msg* was sent by p_k strictly later than $gs_i(lt_i)[k]$ and received at p_ℓ earlier than (or at) $gs_i(lt_i)[\ell]$. By the definition of $gs_i(lt_i)$, and by hypothesis, it follows that the message must have been sent later than $gs_i[k]$ and arrived at p_ℓ earlier than (or at) $gs_i[\ell]$, and then gs_i must not be a global state, which is a contradiction. ■

Lemma 9.2. *If φ and φ' are global states, then the component-wise maximum of the two is also a global state.*

Proof: Let φ'' be the component-wise maximum of φ and φ', and suppose that it is not a global state. Then there must exist $n_k, n_\ell \in N$ such that a message was sent by p_k strictly later than $\varphi''[k]$ and received at p_ℓ earlier than (or at) $\varphi''[\ell]$. Because $\varphi''[k] \geq \varphi[k]$ and $\varphi''[k] \geq \varphi'[k]$, then φ must not be a global state if $\varphi''[\ell] = \varphi[\ell]$. Likewise, if $\varphi''[\ell] = \varphi'[\ell]$, then φ' must not be a global state. Either case yields a contradiction. ■

The essence of Algorithm *A_Detect_DB* is the following for $n_i \in N$. Variable lp_i is initialized with **false** at process p_i, and is assumed never to become **true** if n_i does not participate in the breakpoint. Whenever q_i detects that lp_i has become **true**, it sets $gs_i[i]$ to lt_i and declares the disjunctive breakpoint detected at the global state gs_i. Because every *comp_msg* it received from q_j such that $n_j \in Neig_i$ prior to lt_i carried a copy of q_j's view of the global state with jth component updated to the time the message was sent, gs_i must indeed be a global state by Lemmas 9.1 and 9.2. In order to ensure that it is also an earliest global state with respect to the disjunctive predicate, the simple procedure we just described must only be allowed to be performed if no other node has already detected a global state that renders the one q_i would detect not an earliest one. This is where the "status bit" comes in. This bit will indicate, upon arriving along with a *comp_msg*, whether any other such global state has already been detected.

Algorithm *A_Detect_DB* is presented next. Two additional variables employed by the algorithm are the Booleans *found$_i$* and *found_elsewhere$_i$*, both initially set to **false**, which indicate respectively whether q_i has detected the disjunctive breakpoint and whether such a breakpoint has already been detected elsewhere so that the one detected by q_i would necessarily not be an earliest one.

Algorithm A_Detect_DB:

▷ **Variables:**

$gs_i[k] = 0$ for all $n_k \in N$;
$found_i = $ **false**;
$found_elsewhere_i = $ **false**.

▷ **Input:**

$msg_i = $ **nil**.
Action when lp_i **becomes true:** (9.8)
if not $(found_i$ **or** $found\_elsewhere_i)$ **then**
begin
$gs_i[i] := lt_i$;
$found_i := $ **true**
end.

▷ **Input:**

$msg_i = comp\_msg$ from p_i to p_j.
Action: (9.9)
Send $comp\_msg\big(found_i$ **or** $found\_elsewhere_i, gs_i(lt_i)\big)$ to q_j.

▷ **Input:**

$msg_i = comp\_msg(b, gs)$.
Action: (9.10)
$found\_elsewhere_i := b$ **or** $found\_elsewhere_i$;
if not $(found_i$ **or** $found\_elsewhere_i)$ **then**
for $k := 1$ **to** n **do**
if $gs_i[k] < gs[k]$ **then**
$gs_i[k] := gs[k]$;
Send $comp\_msg$ to p_i.

The next theorem establishes the correctness of Algorithm A_Detect_DB. This theorem, like the others to follow in this section, state the equivalence of several conditions. The proof strategy in all theorems is then to show that the first condition implies the second, which implies the third, and so on, and finally that the last condition implies the first.

Theorem 9.3. *There exist $n_i \in N$ and $t \geq 0$ such that the following three conditions are equivalent to one another for Algorithm A_Detect_DB.*

(i) *There exists a global state φ such that $lp_k = $ **true** at time $\varphi[k]$ for at least one $n_k \in N$.*

(ii) $found_i$ becomes **true** at time $lt_i = t$.

(iii) At time $lt_i = t$, gs_i is the earliest global state at which $lp_k = $ **true** for at least one $n_k \in N$.

Proof:

(i) $\Rightarrow$ (ii):

At least one of the nodes n_k for which lp_k ever becomes **true** must by actions (9.9) and (9.10) have reached this state for the first time when $found_elsewhere_k = $ **false**. The assertion then follows immediately by action (9.8), with n_i being this particular node and t being the local time at which lp_i becomes **true** for the first time.

(ii) $\Rightarrow$ (iii):

By hypothesis and by action (9.8), $found\_elsewhere_i$ can only have become **true** after time t. By Lemmas 9.1 and 9.2, the gs_i produced by action (9.8), the $gs_i(lt_i)$ used in action (9.9), and the gs_i yielded by action (9.10) must all be global states. As a consequence of this, by action (9.8) gs_i is at time t a global state at which $lp_i = $ **true**. If gs_i were not an earliest global state at which $lp_k = $ **true** for at least one $n_k \in N$, then either $found\_elsewhere_i$ would by actions (9.9) and (9.10) have become **true** prior to t, and then $found_i$ would be **false** at t, which is a contradiction, or lp_k would for some $n_k \in N$ be **true** right from the start, which is ruled out by our assumption on the initial values of these variables.

(iii) $\Rightarrow$ (i):

This is immediate.   ■

Each of the $O(c)$ $comp\_msg$'s carries an n-component array, each of whose components is an integer no larger than T, so the bit complexity of Algorithm A_Detect_DB is $O(cn \log T)$. Because only $comp\_msg$'s are employed, the algorithm's message and global time complexity are of $O(1)$. Each message reception requires $O(n)$ comparisons, which is then the algorithm's local time complexity.

Detecting the other types of breakpoints we consider in this section is a considerably more intricate task in comparison with the detection of disjunctive breakpoints. These other cases comprise unconditional breakpoints and conjunctive breakpoints on stable conjunctive predicates, all of which require some sort of additional "global" information to be monitored. It is the propagation of this global information that makes use of the *broadcast* messages we introduced earlier.

In general, in addition to gs_i process q_i also maintains another array of Booleans with its local view of the global condition to be monitored and detected.

When disseminated by q_i, this array is always accompanied by gs_i as well, so that whenever q_i detects locally that the global condition has occurred (by examination of its array), it also associates the contents of gs_i with the global state at which the condition occurred.

Messages of the *broadcast* type are sent by q_i whenever n_i is one of the nodes participating in the global condition to be detected and either its local unconditional breakpoint is reached (in the case of unconditional breakpoint detection) or its local predicate becomes **true** (in the case of the detection of conjunctive breakpoints). The broadcast we employ follows closely Algorithm *A_PI* of Section 4.1.1, but during the propagation of information an arriving gs from some process q_j is used by q_i to update gs_i. In addition, gs and the other array accompanying it are used to update the local view at q_i of the global condition being monitored.

What further differentiates the broadcast that we employ in this section from Algorithm *A_PI* is that we adopt a "forward-when-true" rule for the propagation of information. This rule states that a process participates in the broadcast (i.e., forwards the information it receives) only when its local condition (local unconditional breakpoint reached or local predicate become **true**) holds. Clearly, if no *comp_msg*'s were ever sent, then this broadcast would suffice for the detection of the desired type of breakpoint. In such a case, whichever process produced an array with **true** values for all the participating processes would declare the breakpoint detected at the global state given by the global-state array obtained along with it.

Algorithm *A_Broadcast_When_True* does this detection in the absence of *comp_msg*'s, so long as the global condition under monitoring is stable. In this algorithm, process p_i maintains a Boolean variable lc_i to indicate whether the local condition with which n_i participates (if at all) in the global condition to be detected is true. It is initialized with **false** if n_i does indeed participate in the global condition, or with **true** otherwise. Stability then means that no $n_k \in N$ exists such that lc_k is reset to **false** once it becomes **true**. The array associated with q_i's view of the global condition is denoted by gc_i. For $1 \leq k \leq n$, $gc_i[k]$ is initialized with the same value assigned initially to lc_k. Only *broadcast* messages are employed in this algorithm (as the computation proper does not employ any), and are sent as *broadcast*(gc_i, gs_i) when q_i is the sender. As in the case of Algorithm *A_Detect_DB* discussed earlier, a Boolean variable *found*$_i$, set to **false** initially, is employed to indicate whether q_i has detected the occurrence of the global condition. In addition, another Boolean variable, *changed*$_i$, is used by q_i to ensure that a *broadcast* message is never sent to a node if not different than the last message sent to that node.

Algorithm $A\_Broadcast\_When\_True$:

▷ **Variables:**

$gs_i[k] = 0$ for all $n_k \in N$;
$gc_i[k]$ for all $n_k \in N$;
$found_i = $ **false**;
$changed_i$.

▷ **Input:**

$msg_i = $ **nil**.

Action when lc_i **becomes true:**   (9.11)

$gc_i[i] := lc_i$;
$gs_i[i] := lt_i$;
if $gc_i[1] \wedge \cdots \wedge gc_i[n]$ **then**
$\qquad found_i := $ **true**
else
$\qquad$ Send $broadcast(gc_i, gs_i)$ to all q_j such that $n_j \in Neig_i$.

▷ **Input:**

$msg_i = (gc, gs)$.

Action: (9.12)

if not $found_i$ **then**
$\quad$ **begin**
$\qquad changed_i := $ **false**;
$\qquad$ **for** $k := 1$ **to** n **do**
$\qquad\quad$ **if** $gs_i[k] < gs[k]$ **then**
$\qquad\qquad$ **begin**
$\qquad\qquad\quad gs_i[k] := gs[k]$;
$\qquad\qquad\quad gc_i[k] := gc[k]$;
$\qquad\qquad\quad changed_i := $ **true**
$\qquad\qquad$ **end**;
$\qquad$ **if** lc_i **and** $changed_i$ **then**
$\qquad\quad$ **if** $gc_i[1] \wedge \cdots \wedge gc_i[n]$ **then**
$\qquad\qquad found_i := $ **true**
$\qquad\quad$ **else**
$\qquad\qquad$ Send $broadcast(gc_i, gs_i)$ to all q_j such that $n_j \in$
$\qquad\qquad Neig_i$
$\quad$ **end.**

Properties of Algorithm $A\_Broadcast\_When\_True$ are given in the following theorem.

Theorem 9.4. *There exist $n_i \in N$ and $t \geq 0$ such that the following three conditions are equivalent to one another for Algorithm $A\_Broadcast\_When\_True$.*

(i) *There exists a global state φ such that $lc_k = \textbf{true}$ at time $\varphi[k]$ for all $n_k \in N$.*

(ii) *$found_i$ becomes $\textbf{true}$ at time $lt_i = t$.*

(iii) *At time $lt_i = t$, gs_i is the earliest global state at which $lc_k = \textbf{true}$ for all $n_k \in N$.*

Proof:

(i) $\Rightarrow$ (ii):

If exactly one node participates in the global condition, then by action (9.11) $found_i$ becomes **true**, with $n_i \in N$ being this node and t the time at which lc_i becomes **true**. No messages are ever sent in this case. If at least two nodes participate, then at least one of them, say $n_k \in N$, is such that q_k does by action (9.11) send a *broadcast* message to n_k's neighbors when lc_k becomes **true**, which by action (9.12) pass the updated information on, so long as the update introduced changes and their local conditions hold as well. Because this broadcast carries lc_k, it must introduce changes when reaching every node for the first time and is therefore propagated. This happens to the local condition of every participating node, and then at least one process, say q_i, upon having been reached by their broadcasts, and having $lc_i = \textbf{true}$, sets $found_i = \textbf{true}$. The value of t here is either the time at which the last broadcast to reach q_i does reach it by action (9.12) or the time at which lc_i becomes **true** by action (9.11).

(ii) $\Rightarrow$ (iii):

By Lemmas 9.1 and 9.2, the gs_i produced in actions (9.11) and (9.12) are global states. Consequently, and by actions (9.11) and (9.12) as well, at time t gs_i is a global state at which $lc_k = \textbf{true}$ for all $n_k \in N$. That gs_i is the earliest such global state is immediate, because of the absence of $comp\_msg$'s, which implies that $gs_i[k]$ is either zero or the time at which lc_k becomes **true**.

(iii) $\Rightarrow$ (i):

This is immediate.   ∎

Let us now assess Algorithm *A_Broadcast_When_True*'s complexities. The worst case is that in which all nodes start the algorithm concurrently, and furthermore the broadcast started by a node traverses all edges. The algorithm's message complexity is then $O(nm)$. Because two n-component arrays are sent along with each message, one comprising single-bit components, the other integers bounded by T, the bit complexity becomes $O(n^2 m \log T)$. No causal chain of messages comprises more than $O(n)$ messages, because this is what it takes for a broadcast to reach all nodes, so this is the algorithm's global time complexity. The local time complexity is like that of Algorithm *A_Detect_DB*, therefore of $O(n)$.

Algorithms *A_Detect_DB* and *A_Broadcast_When_True* detect breakpoints in two extreme situations, respectively when the breakpoint is a disjunctive breakpoint and when the breakpoint is a conjunctive breakpoint but the computation proper does not ever send any message (it is simple to note that the case of unconditional breakpoints in the absence of *comp_msg*'s is in fact a case of conjunctive breakpoints). In the former case only are *comp_msg*'s employed, whereas in the latter case only *broadcast* messages are needed. Other situations between these two extremes are examined in the sequel, and then the messages received by process q_i are either like *comp_msg(gc, gs)* or like *broadcast(gc, gs)*.

Now we introduce *A_Detect_UB* ("UB" for Unconditional Breakpoint), a distributed algorithm to detect the occurrence in a distributed computation of an unconditional breakpoint. As we discussed previously, this unconditional breakpoint is specified, for each node actually participating in the breakpoint, as a local time denoted by lub_i for $n_i \in N$. For nodes n_i that do not participate in the breakpoint, we have chosen to adopt $lub_i = \infty$, so that lt_i can never equal lub_i.

Algorithm *A_Detect_UB* must operate somewhere between the two extreme situations assumed by Algorithms *A_Detect_DB* and *A_Broadcast_When_True*, and then can be regarded as a mixture of those. Put differently, the detection of unconditional breakpoints does require the detection of a global condition (which is ruled out by Algorithm *A_Detect_DB*) and must be applicable to the case when messages of the computation proper exist (which are disallowed by Algorithm *A_Broadcast_When_True*).

The variables employed by Algorithm *A_Detect_UB* are essentially the ones introduced earlier for the other two algorithms, except that for process p_i the Boolean variable lc_i is now replaced with the occurrence of the equality $lt_i = lub_i$, and furthermore the array ub_i, used to indicate q_i's view of the occurrence of the local unconditional breakpoints at all nodes, is now used in lieu of the array gc_i. For $n_k \in N$, $ub_i[k]$ may be either **true**, **false**, or **undefined**. It is **true** or **false** if n_k participates in the unconditional breakpoint and is viewed at n_i as having already reached its local unconditional breakpoint or not, respectively, and is **undefined** if n_k is not one of the nodes participating in the unconditional breakpoint. Initially, $ub_i[k]$ is set to **false** for every participating n_k and to **undefined** if n_k does not participate.

Algorithm A_Detect_UB proceeds as follows. Whenever q_i detects that $lt_i = lub_i$, it updates $ub_i[i]$ and $gs_i[i]$ accordingly and starts a broadcast to disseminate the updated ub_i and gs_i. This broadcast proceeds like the one in Algorithm $A\_Broadcast\_When\_True$, i.e., it is never forwarded by a node whose local unconditional breakpoint has not yet been reached (unless the node does not participate in the unconditional breakpoint), and in addition no duplicate information is ever forwarded by any node. Every $comp\_msg$ is sent with ub_i and $gs_i(lt_i)$ attached to them, in the way of Algorithm A_Detect_DB, so that the global state that is eventually detected is indeed a global state. This detection, if achieved by q_i, corresponds to the verification that $ub_i[k] \neq$ **false** for all $n_k \in N$, that is, every node has either reached its local unconditional breakpoint or is not participating in the unconditional breakpoint.

One of the difficulties in designing Algorithm A_Detect_UB is that it must be able to detect situations in which the requested set of local unconditional breakpoints does not constitute a global state (Figure 9.2). In such situations, an error must be reported and the computation proper must be allowed to progress normally. The detection of such a situation can be achieved along the following lines. Suppose q_i receives a $comp\_msg(ub, gs)$ from some process q_j. If $ub[j] =$ **true** and $ub[i] =$ **false** at this moment, then clearly an error has occurred in the determination of the unconditional breakpoint, as p_i will never reach its local unconditional breakpoint in such a way that is consistent with the local unconditional breakpoint of p_j from the point of view of a global state.

The possibility of having nodes for which no local unconditional breakpoint is specified complicates the treatment of these erroneous conditions a little bit. If a causal chain of $comp\_msg$'s beginning at q_ℓ such that $ub_\ell[\ell] =$ **true** and going through a number of processes q_k for which $ub_k[k] =$ **undefined** eventually leads to q_i such that $ub_i[i] =$ **false**, then an error must be detected just as in the case discussed earlier. The way we approach this is by artificially setting $ub_k[k]$ to **true** for all the q_k's. A Boolean variable in_error_i, initially set to **false**, is employed by q_i to indicate whether an erroneous condition has been detected.

Nodes that do not participate in the unconditional breakpoint also complicate the detection of earliest global states. If such nodes did not exist, or if we did not require the earliest global state to be detected when they did exist, then what we have outlined so far would suffice for Algorithm A_Detect_UB to work as needed.

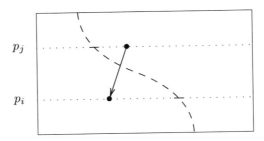

Figure 9.2. *The tiny solid segment in a process's horizontal line indicates the local time to which the corresponding local unconditional breakpoint has been set. Clearly, the settings in this figure are erroneous, as the cut (shown as a dashed line) that goes through them does not correspond to a global state.*

However, the existence of causal chains of *comp_msg*'s similar to the one we just described but beginning at q_ℓ such that $ub_\ell[\ell] =$ **undefined** may lead to distinct earliest global states, depending on whether it leads to q_i such that $ub_i[i] =$ **false** or $ub_i[i] =$ **true** (Figure 9.3). Only in the former case should q_i take into account what it receives attached to the *comp_msg* in updating gs_i, but the senders of the preceding messages in the causal chain have no way of knowing this beforehand. The strategy we adopt to tackle this is the following. In addition to maintaining gs_i as a local view of the global state to be detected, q_i also maintains an alternative view, denoted by alt_gs_i, which is initialized like gs_i but only updated or attached to outgoing *comp_msg*'s (the latter in place of gs_i) if $ub_i[i] =$ **undefined**. Arriving *comp_msg*'s at q_i affect gs_i if $ub_i[i] =$ **false** or alt_gs_i if $ub_i[i] =$ **undefined**. So for q_i such that $ub_i[i] =$ **undefined**, $gs_i[k] \leq alt\_gs_i[k]$ for all $n_k \in N$, and therefore gs_i may constitute an earlier global state than alt_gs_i.

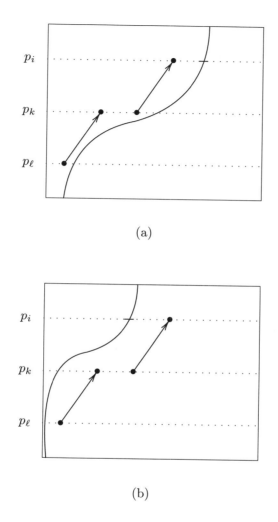

(a)

(b)

Figure 9.3. *Following the same conventions as in Figure 9.2, here a situation is depicted in which only one node participates in the unconditional breakpoint (node n_i). Depending on how the corresponding local unconditional breakpoint is placed with respect to the reception of the message by p_i, the other processes appear in the resulting earliest global state differently, as shown in parts (a) and (b).*

Algorithm *A_Detect_UB*:

▷ **Variables:**
   $gs_i[k] = 0$ for all $n_k \in N$;
   $ub_i[k]$ for all $n_k \in N$;
   $found_i =$ **false**;
   $changed_i$;
   $in\_error_i =$ **false**;
   $alt\_gs_i[k] = 0$ for all $n_k \in N$.

▷ **Input:**
   $msg_i =$ **nil**.

   Action when detecting that $lt_i = lub_i$:   (9.13)
        if not in_error_i **then**
             begin
                  $ub_i[i] :=$ **true**;
                  $gs_i[i] := lt_i$;
                  if $ub_i[k] \neq$ **false** for all $k = 1, \ldots, n$ **then**
                       $found_i :=$ **true**
                  else
                       Send $broadcast(ub_i, gs_i)$ to all q_j such that $n_j \in Neig_i$
             end.

▷ **Input:**

$msg_i = broadcast(ub, gs)$.

   Action: (9.14)

      if not $(in\_error_i$ **or** $found_i)$ **then**

         begin

            $changed_i :=$ **false**;

            for $k := 1$ **to** n **do**

               if $gs_i[k] < gs[k]$ **then**

                  begin

                     $gs_i[k] := gs[k]$;

                     $ub_i[k] := ub[k]$;

                     $changed_i :=$ **true**

                  end;

            if $ub_i[i] =$ **undefined then**

               for $k := 1$ **to** n **do**

                  if $alt\_gs_i[k] < gs[k]$ **then**

                     $alt\_gs_i[k] := gs[k]$;

            if $lub_i \neq$ **false and** $changed_i$ **then**

               if $ub_i[k] \neq$ **false for all** $k = 1, \ldots, n$ **then**

                  $found_i :=$ **true**

            else

               Send $broadcast(ub_i, gs_i)$ to all q_j such that $n_j \in$ $Neig_i$

     end.

▷ **Input:**

$msg_i = comp\_msg$ from p_i to p_j.

   Action: (9.15)

      if $ub_i[i] =$ **undefined then**

         Send $comp\_msg(ub_i, alt\_gs_i(lt_i))$ to q_j

      else

         Send $comp\_msg(ub_i, gs_i(lt_i))$ to q_j.

▷ **Input:**
  $msg_i = comp\_msg(ub, gs)$ such that $origin_i(msg_i) = (n_i, n_j)$.
  Action: (9.16)
    if not $(in\_error_i$ **or** $found_i)$ **then**
        begin
            if $ub[j] =$ **true and** $ub_i[i] =$ **false then**
                $in\_error_i :=$ **true**;
            if $ub[j] =$ **true and** $ub_i[i] =$ **undefined then**
                $ub_i[i] :=$ **true**;
            if $ub[j] =$ **undefined and** $ub_i[i] =$ **false then**
                for $k := 1$ **to** n **do**
                    if $gs_i[k] < gs[k]$ **then**
                        begin
                            $gs_i[k] := gs[k]$;
                            $ub_i[k] := ub[k]$
                        end;
            if $ub[j] =$ **undefined and** $ub_i[i] =$ **undefined then**
                for $k := 1$ **to** n **do**
                    if $alt\_gs_i[k] < gs[k]$ **then**
                        $alt\_gs_i[k] := gs[k]$
        end;
    Send $comp\_msg$ to p_i.

Next we give properties of Algorithm A_Detect_UB related to its correctness.

Theorem 9.5. *There exist* $n_i \in N$ *and* $t \geq 0$ *such that the following four conditions are equivalent to one another for Algorithm* A_Detect_UB.

(i) *There exists a global state* φ *such that* $\varphi[k] = lub_k$ *for every* $n_k \in N$ *such that* $lub_k < \infty$.

(ii) in_error_k *never becomes* **true** *for any* $n_k \in N$.

(iii) $found_i$ *becomes* **true** *at time* $lt_i = t$.

(iv) *At time* $lt_i = t$, gs_i *is the earliest global state at which* $gs_i[k] = lub_k$ *for every* $n_k \in N$ *such that* $lub_k < \infty$.

Proof:

(i) $\Rightarrow$ (ii):

Suppose that there does exist $n_k \in N$ such that in_error_k becomes **true**. By action (9.16), this must happen upon receipt, when $ub_k[k] =$ **false**, of a $comp\_msg$ contained in a causal chain of $comp\_msg$'s started at, say, process q_ℓ, sent when $ub_\ell[\ell] =$ **true**. No array φ such that $\varphi[k] = lub_k$ and $\varphi[\ell] = lub_\ell$ can then be a global state, and because both $lub_k < \infty$ and $lub_\ell < \infty$, we have a contradiction.

(ii) $\Rightarrow$ (iii):

If in_error_k never becomes **true** for any $n_k \in N$, then actions (9.13) and (9.14) are, so far as *broadcast* messages are concerned, identical to actions (9.11) and (9.12), respectively, of Algorithm $A\_Broadcast\_When\_True$. This part of the proof is then analogous to the (i) $\Rightarrow$ (ii) part in the proof of Theorem 9.4.

(iii) $\Rightarrow$ (iv):

By Lemmas 9.1 and 9.2, the gs_i produced by action (9.13), the $gs_i(lt_i)$ and $alt\_gs_i(lt_i)$ used in action (9.15), and the gs_i and alt_gs_i produced by actions (9.14) and (9.16) are all global states. This implies, by actions (9.13) and (9.14) and at time t, that gs_i is a global state at which $ub_i[k] \neq$ **false** for all $n_k \in N$, or, equivalently, a global state such that $gs_i[k] = lub_k$ for every $n_k \in N$ such that $lub_k < \infty$. In order to show that gs_i is the earliest global state with these characteristics, consider any other n-component array of local times, call it φ, such that $\varphi[k] = gs_i[k]$ for all $n_k \in N$ such that $lub_k < \infty$, and $\varphi[k] < gs_i[k]$ for at least one $n_k \in N$ such that $lub_k = \infty$. For this particular n_k, in order for $gs_i[k]$ to have been assigned the value greater than $\varphi[k]$, a causal chain of $comp\_msg$'s must have existed from q_k (leaving at time $gs_i[k]$) to some $q_\ell \in N$, where by action (9.16) it must have arrived at q_ℓ when $ub_\ell[\ell] =$ **false** (otherwise gs_ℓ would not have been updated, and so neither would gs_i through the broadcast). In addition, because in_error_ℓ must have remained **false**, every process involved in this chain (except for q_ℓ but including q_k) must have had an **undefined** in its local record of its local unconditional breakpoint (for q_k, $ub_k[k] =$ **undefined**). But because $ub_\ell[\ell]$ was found to be **false**, φ cannot possibly be a global state such that $\varphi_k = lub_k$ for all $n_k \in N$ such that $lub_k < \infty$.

(iv) $\Rightarrow$ (i):

This is immediate.						∎

The message complexity of Algorithm A_Detect_UB is the same as that of Algorithm $A\_Broadcast\_When\_True$, that is, $O(nm)$. The algorithm's bit complexity is the sum of those of Algorithm A_Detect_DB and Algorithm $A\_Broadcast\_When\_True$, therefore equal to $O\big((c + nm)n\log T\big)$. The global and local time complexities of Algorithm A_Detect_UB are the same as Algorithm $A\_Broadcast\_When\_True$'s, that is, $O(n)$.

We now finally come to Algorithm $A\_Detect\_CB\_Stable$ for the detection of conjunctive breakpoints on stable conjunctive predicates. Such predicates are specified for each participating node $n_i \in N$ as the local predicate lp_i endowed with the property that it remains **true** once it becomes **true**. Unconditional breakpoints are also breakpoints on stable conjunctive predicates, but much more rigid than the ones we consider now, as in that case the detected global state is required to match the local unconditional breakpoints specified for the participating nodes exactly. In contrast, the ones we are now beginning to consider only ask that the local predicates of the participating nodes be **true** in the detected global state, although in some nodes they may have become **true** earlier than the local times given by the global state. Not surprisingly, then, the algorithm that we introduce next can be regarded as a slight simplification of Algorithm A_Detect_UB, as error conditions no longer need to be addressed.

Algorithm $A\_Detect\_CB\_Stable$ is in many senses related to Algorithm A_Detect_UB, and as such can also be viewed as a conceptual mixture of the principles employed in Algorithms A_Detect_DB and $A\_Broadcast\_When\_True$. With respect to the latter, the local condition for $n_i \in N$, lc_i, is now expressed by the very local predicate lp_i we have been considering throughout, and q_i's view of the global condition, gc_i, is now the array cp_i. For all $n_k \in N$, $cp_i[k]$ is initialized like lp_k, that is, to **false** if n_k is participating in the breakpoint, and to **true** otherwise. All the other variables employed by Algorithm $A\_Detect\_CB\_Stable$ have the same meaning they had when used in previous contexts.

The simplification of Algorithm A_Detect_UB to yield $A\_Detect\_CB\_Stable$ does not go any further than the elimination of error detection, as an alternative local view at q_i of the global state to be detected, alt_gs_i, is still needed to aid in the detection of the earliest global state of interest. Similarly to the case of unconditional breakpoints, a causal chain of $comp\_msg$'s beginning at q_ℓ such that $cp_\ell[\ell] = $ **true**, going through a number of q_k's, each with $cp_k[k] = $ **true** as well, and finally reaching q_i with $cp_i[i] = $ **false** requires q_i to take into account what it receives attached to the $comp\_msg$ in updating gs_i. On the other hand, if no such q_i is ever reached, then the detected global state has a chance to be an earlier one (Figure 9.4). Maintaining alt_gs_i has the function of allowing this earlier global state to be saved in gs_i, to be used in case no causal chain of the sort we just described ever occurs. The array alt_gs_i is initialized like gs_i and is attached to $comp\_msg$'s with its ith

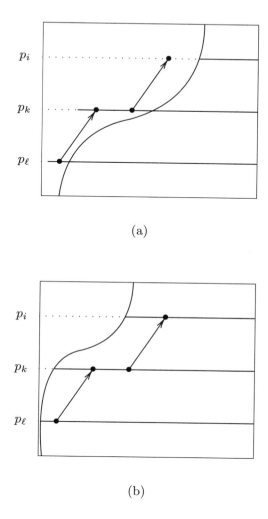

(a)

(b)

Figure 9.4. *The conventions employed in this figure are the same as those of Figure 9.1, and the situation depicted is quite akin to that of Figure 9.3. Specifically, the earliest global state at which the conjunctive predicate holds depends on when n_i's local predicate becomes* **true** *with respect to the reception of the message by p_i, as shown in parts (a) and (b).*

component modified to lt_i. A $comp\_msg$ arriving at q_i affects alt_gs_i and may eventually affect gs_i, which happens if $cp_i[i] = $ **false** upon arrival of the $comp\_msg$, by simply updating gs_i to alt_gs_i when lp_i becomes **true**. Only in this situation, or upon the receipt of $broadcast$ messages, does gs_i get updated, but then so does alt_gs_i, so $gs_i[k] \leq alt\_gs_i[k]$ for every $n_k \in N$.

> **Algorithm** $A\_Detect\_CB\_Stable$:

> ▷ **Variables:**
>> $gs_i[k] = 0$ for all $n_k \in N$;
>> $cp_i[k]$ for all $n_k \in N$;
>> $found_i = $ **false**;
>> $changed_i$;
>> $alt\_gs_i[k] = 0$ for all $n_k \in N$.

> ▷ **Input:**
>> $msg_i = $ **nil**.
>> **Action when** lp_i **becomes true:**   (9.17)
>>> $cp_i[i] := lp_i$;
>>> $alt\_gs_i[i] := lt_i$;
>>> **for** $k := 1$ **to** n **do**
>>>> $gs_i[k] := alt\_gs_i[k]$;
>>> **if** $cp_i[1] \wedge \cdots \wedge cp_i[n]$ **then**
>>>> $found_i := $ **true**
>>> **else**
>>>> Send $broadcast(cp_i, gs_i)$ to all q_j such that $n_j \in Neig_i$.

▷ **Input:**

$\quad\quad msg_i = broadcast(cp, gs)$.

$\quad$ **Action:** $\hfill$ (9.18)

$\quad\quad$ **if not** $found_i$ **then**

$\quad\quad\quad$ **begin**

$\quad\quad\quad\quad changed_i :=$ **false**;

$\quad\quad\quad\quad$ **for** $k := 1$ **to** n **do**

$\quad\quad\quad\quad\quad$ **if** $gs_i[k] < gs[k]$ **then**

$\quad\quad\quad\quad\quad\quad$ **begin**

$\quad\quad\quad\quad\quad\quad\quad gs_i[k] := gs[k]$;

$\quad\quad\quad\quad\quad\quad\quad cp_i[k] := cp[k]$;

$\quad\quad\quad\quad\quad\quad\quad changed_i :=$ **true**

$\quad\quad\quad\quad\quad\quad$ **end**;

$\quad\quad\quad\quad$ **for** $k := 1$ **to** n **do**

$\quad\quad\quad\quad\quad$ **if** $alt\_gs_i[k] < gs[k]$ **then**

$\quad\quad\quad\quad\quad\quad alt\_gs_i[k] := gs[k]$;

$\quad\quad\quad\quad$ **if** $cp_i[i]$ **and** $changed_i$ **then**

$\quad\quad\quad\quad\quad$ **if** $cp_i[1] \wedge \cdots \wedge cp_i[n]$ **then**

$\quad\quad\quad\quad\quad\quad found_i :=$ **true**

$\quad\quad\quad\quad$ **else**

$\quad\quad\quad\quad\quad$ Send $broadcast(cp_i, gs_i)$ to all q_j such that $n_j \in$

$\quad\quad\quad\quad\quad Neig_i$

$\quad\quad$ **end.**

▷ **Input:**

$\quad\quad msg_i = comp\_msg$ from p_i to p_j.

$\quad$ **Action:** $\hfill$ (9.19)

$\quad\quad$ Send $comp\_msg\big(cp_i, alt\_gs_i(lt_i)\big)$ to q_j.

▷ **Input:**
$$msg_i = comp\_msg(cp, gs).$$

(9.20)

   Action:
   if not $found_i$ **then**
      for $k := 1$ **to** n **do**
         if $alt\_gs_i[k] < gs[k]$ **then**
            begin
               $cp_i[k] := cp[k];$
               $alt\_gs_i[k] := gs[k]$
            end;
   Send $comp\_msg$ to p_i.

Correctness properties of Algorithm $A\_Detect\_CB\_Stable$ are established in the following theorem.

Theorem 9.6. *There exist $n_i \in N$ and $t \geq 0$ such that the following three conditions are equivalent to one another for Algorithm $A\_Detect\_CB\_Stable$.*

   (i) *There exists a global state φ such that $lp_k =$ **true** at time $\varphi[k]$ for all $n_k \in N$.*

   (ii) *$found_i$ becomes **true** at time $lt_i = t$.*

   (iii) *At time $lt_i = t$, gs_i is the earliest global state at which $lp_k =$ **true** for all $n_k \in N$.*

Proof:

(i) $\Rightarrow$ (ii):

Actions (9.17) and (9.18) are, from the standpoint of *broadcast* messages alone, identical to actions (9.11) and (9.12), respectively, of Algorithm $A\_Broadcast\_When\_True$. This part of the proof then goes along the same lines as the (i) $\Rightarrow$ (ii) part in the proof of Theorem 9.4, so long as no *comp_msg* overruns any *broadcast* message on any edge. When this happens, however, the propagation of the *broadcast* message may by action (9.18) be interrupted after traversing the edge, specifically upon arriving, say at process q_k, and by action (9.18) finding $cp_k[k] =$ **true** without causing changes to gs_k or to cp_k. This is so because the gs_j carried by the *broadcast* message is no greater than gs_k in any component, which in turn was updated by action (9.17) when lp_k became **true** with the alt_gs_k produced by action (9.20) upon receipt of the *comp_msg*. The broadcast that by action (9.17)

q_k then initiates when lp_k becomes **true** allows the proof to proceed like that of the (i) $\Rightarrow$ (ii) part in the proof of Theorem 9.4 as well.

(ii) $\Rightarrow$ (iii):

By Lemmas 9.1 and 9.2, the gs_i and alt_gs_i produced by actions (9.17) and (9.18), the $alt\_gs_i(lt_i)$ used in action (9.19), and the alt_gs_i produced by action (9.20) must all be global states. A consequence of this is that, by actions (9.17) and (9.18), gs_i is at time t a global state at which $cp_i[k] = $ **true** for all $n_k \in N$. To show that gs_i is the earliest such global state requires that we consider any other n-component array of local times, call it φ, such that $lp_k = $ **true** at time $\varphi[k]$ for all $n_k \in N$ and such that $\varphi[k] < gs_i[k]$ for at least one $n_k \in N$. For this particular n_k, $gs_i[k]$ can only have been assigned the value greater than $\varphi[k]$ if a causal chain of $comp\_msg$'s existed from q_k (leaving at time $gs_i[k]$) to some $q_\ell \in N$, which by action (9.17) must have arrived at q_ℓ when $cp_\ell[\ell] = $ **false** (otherwise gs_ℓ would not have been updated, and so neither would gs_i by means of the broadcast). But because $cp_\ell[\ell]$ was found to be **false**, φ cannot possibly be a global state such that $lp_k = $ **true** at time $\varphi[k]$ for all $n_k \in N$.

(iii) $\Rightarrow$ (i):

This is immediate.   ∎

All the complexities of Algorithm *A_Detect_CB_Stable* are the same as the corresponding complexities of Algorithm *A_Detect_UB*.

In finalizing this section, we suggest that the reader investigate simplifications to the algorithms of this section (except Algorithm *A_Broadcast_When_True*) if they are not required to detect earliest global states, but instead any global state in which the desired properties hold (cf. Exercise 5).

9.4. Exercises

1. Devise a solution for the problem discussed in Section 9.2 if the edges are not FIFO.

2. Prove that Algorithm *A_Replay_&_Halt_CP* halts at the earliest conjunctive breakpoint.

3. Prove that there does not exist an algorithm for halting at an earliest disjunctive breakpoint, unless it is acceptable to progress further than that global state and then return by means of a rollback.

4. Rewrite Algorithm *A_Replay_&_Halt_CP* so that no node sends more than one message to the same neighbor per action.

5. Show how to simplify the algorithms of Section 9.3.3 (except Algorithm *A_Broadcast_When_True*) given that earliest global states do not have to be detected.

9.5. Bibliographic notes

If the reader wishes to check for generalities on the debugging of asynchronous algorithms other than those discussed in Section 9.1, some references are the survey by McDowell and Helmbold (1989), and the publications by Garcia-Molina, Germano, and Kohler (1984), Joyce, Lomow, Slind, and Unger (1987), Haban and Weigel (1988), Miller and Choi (1988b), Hélary (1989), Choi, Miller, and Netzer (1991), Becher and McDowell (1992), Yang and Marsland (1992), Garg and Tomlinson (1993), Hurfin, Plouzeau, and Raynal (1993), and Fromentin and Raynal (1994).

The material in Section 9.2 is inspired in the work by LeBlanc and Mellor-Crummey (1987). Additional sources on the same problem include Netzer and Xu (1993).

The sources for reference within the topic of breakpoint detection and related issues are quite abundant. The material discussed in Section 9.3.1, for example, can be enlarged by checking Cooper and Marzullo (1991) for a strong-sense approach, while the sources for additional insights into the use of arrays of local times as global states are Mattern (1989) and Fidge (1991). Publications of interest on checkpointing and rollback recovery include Kim, You, and Abouelnaga (1986), Koo and Toueg (1987), Bhargava and Lian (1988), Goldberg, Gopal, Lowry, and Strom (1991), Ramanathan and Shin (1993), and Xu and Netzer (1993).

The source of the material discussed in Section 9.3.2 is Manabe and Imase (1992), where the concern for detecting earliest global states seems to have first appeared. Section 9.3.3 is closely based on Drummond and Barbosa (1994), where an algorithm to detect earliest conjunctive breakpoints on predicates that do not need to be stable is also presented. References for material closely related to that of Section 9.3.3 are Miller and Choi (1988a) and Garg and Waldecker (1994). Other publications on the detection of breakpoints include the one by Spezialetti (1991), which is based on an earlier formulation that appears to be prone to missing many possible global states (Spezialetti and Kearns, 1989).

10

Simulation

In this chapter, a *physical system* is to be understood as a collection of physical entities, called *physical processes*, whose states we wish to determine for all times in a certain range, beginning at certain initial conditions. Physical processes interact with one another, and it is as a result of this interaction that their states change. Our interest is in the study of distributed algorithms for the determination by simulation of all physical processes' states in the appropriate time range. We divide our presentation according to the nature of the state changes a physical process may undergo, after detailing the physical-system model and related notions in Section 10.1.

If the state of a physical process may change as a consequence of the processes' continual interaction with one another (often at all time units), then the essential drive of the simulation is time itself, and the simulation is referred to as being time-stepped. Algorithms for this type of simulation are presented in Section 10.2 for two general classes of physical systems. If, on the other hand, only at some special instants do the physical processes interact by means of the so-called events that may cause the state of a physical process to change, then it is the events that drive the simulation, which is then said to be event-driven.

Algorithms for the event-driven simulation of physical systems are discussed in Sections 10.3 and 10.4 from two different perspectives on how to guarantee that the causality that exists among such events is preserved. These sections present, respectively, typical approaches of the so-called conservative and optimistic types.

Sections 10.5 and 10.6 contain brief descriptions of extensions on some of the material discussed in the earlier sections. In the case of Section 10.5, the extension is on methods for simulating systems whose timing nature is not so well defined as those treated earlier, and therefore require simulation methods that provide a hybrid approach between the time-stepped and the event-driven. In Section 10.6, we digress on a general framework encompassing all sorts of physical systems and simulation strategies discussed along the chapter.

Exercises and bibliographic notes appear, respectively, in Sections 10.7 and 10.8.

The complexities of all the algorithms to be discussed in this chapter are highly dependent upon the particular physical system being simulated. For this reason, and unlike our practice so far in the book, in this chapter we do not touch the issue of algorithm complexity at all.

As in earlier occasions (cf. Section 9.3.2), it does occasionally happen during this chapter that a node sends more than one message to the same node in the same action. While this is not in full conformity with Algorithm $A\_Template$, fixing it if necessary should be a simple matter.

10.1. Physical and logical processes

The physical system is represented by either the undirected graph $\mathcal{G} = (\mathcal{N}, \mathcal{E})$ or the directed graph $\mathcal{G} = (\mathcal{N}, \mathcal{D})$, where $\mathcal{N}$ is the set of physical processes. $\mathcal{G}$ is an undirected graph if and only if, for all $\nu_i, \nu_j \in \mathcal{N}$ such that $\nu_i \neq \nu_j$ and ν_i affects the state evolution of ν_j, it is also the case that ν_j affects the state evolution of ν_i. In this case, (ν_i, ν_j) is an edge in $\mathcal{E}$. Otherwise, the representation as a directed graph is chosen, and $(\nu_i \rightarrow \nu_j) \in \mathcal{D}$ if and only if ν_i affects the state evolution of ν_j.

The *state* of a physical process ν_i at time $t \geq 0$ is in this chapter denoted by $x_i(t)$. The goal of a simulation by computer of the physical system is to determine $x_i(t)$ for all $\nu_i \in \mathcal{N}$ and all time t such that $0 \leq t \leq T$. The value of T may be known *a priori* or it may have to be determined as the simulation progresses (for example, in cases in which the system is to be simulated until some sort of convergence is detected).

Physical systems are models of natural systems of interest in various scientific disciplines, so the particular natural system at hand, or the simplifications made when constructing the model, ultimately dictates the nature of the time t that governs the evolution of the physical system. Often t is continuous time (as in all cases in which differential equations are employed to build the model), but equally as often (for example, in the case of cellular automata and some other automaton networks) it is discrete. In either case, however, the simulation by computer of the physical system must be restricted to determining the states of physical processes at discrete instants (determined by the achievable precision within the particular computer system in use), and then it is legitimate to assume, for all purposes in this chapter, that t is a nonnegative integer between 0 and T (also assumed to be an integer).

The simulation of the physical system $\mathcal{G}$ is achieved by a *logical system*, which contains a *logical process* for each of $\mathcal{G}$'s physical processes. Logical processes attempt to mimic the interaction that occurs among physical processes in the physical system, and for all times in the appropriate range output the states of the corresponding physical processes. The approach of a logical process to the simulation of the corresponding physical process depends largely on how physical processes interact. In this respect, a subdivision into two broad classes is normally employed.

If physical processes interact continually in such a way that the instants at which the state of a physical process may change can be determined beforehand, then the main drive of the logical system is time itself, and the simulation that the logical system carries out is called *time-stepped*. If, on the other hand, state changes in the physical processes are restricted to special instants in which they interact, and such instants can only be known as the simulation progresses, then the simulation is referred to as being *event-driven*, in allusion to the denomination as an *event* commonly employed to designate the interactions among physical processes. As the reader will have the opportunity to verify later in this section, such events do bear resemblance to the events employed in Section 3.1 to model distributed computations, but they are not the same at all.

The essence of a time-stepped simulation is quite simple. Basically, at each of the foreseeable instants at which a physical process ν_i's local state may change, the corresponding logical process does the update based on the current state of ν_i and on the states of the other physical processes that exert influence on the state of ν_i (these are either all the physical processes connected to ν_i in $\mathcal{G}$, if $\mathcal{G}$ is undirected, or physical processes ν_j such that $(\nu_j \to \nu_i) \in \mathcal{D}$, otherwise). Time-stepped simulations are treated in Section 10.2.

The essentials of an event-driven simulation are also simple, but are best described if we resort to a sequential version of it first. A sequential event-driven simulation employs a queue of events. In this queue, events are kept in nondecreasing order of the time at which they must happen. The task of a sequential simulator is to iterate on this queue until the queue is empty or no event in it is scheduled to happen at a time no greater than T. At each iteration, the simulator removes the first event from the queue, updates the state of the corresponding physical process, and possibly inserts in the queue new events to happen farther in time at some of the other physical processes. Initially, the queue contains the only events that happen spontaneously, which we assume to happen at time zero. The key ingredient in guaranteeing the correct simulation of the physical system is that events are processed in nondecreasing order of time.

In the distributed case, one possibility is for each logical process to maintain a similar queue for the events that are scheduled to happen at the physical process to which it corresponds. Initially, only a logical process at whose physical process an event happens spontaneously at time zero has a nonempty queue. The set of such physical processes is $\mathcal{N}_0 \subseteq \mathcal{N}$. This queue is maintained in increasing order of time (the reason for increasing in place of nondecreasing is that no two events are allowed to happen at the same physical process at the same time—we return to this issue shortly). The task of a logical process is, similarly to the sequential simulator, to remove the first event from the queue, then to update the state of its physical process, and then possibly to send new events to be inserted in the queues of other logical processes. The problem is, of course, that this simple iterative treatment of a logical process's event queue does not suffice to ensure that, globally, events are processed in nondecreasing order of time. In particular, it is easily conceivable that a logical process receives, for inclusion in its queue, an event scheduled for a time that has already passed in the local simulation.

Classically, the approaches to solving this problem are twofold. Either one makes every effort to ensure that events are indeed globally processed in nondecreasing order of time, or one lets the simulation progress without this constraint and then makes provisions for correcting possible errors when they occur. These two approaches are called, respectively, *conservative* (discussed in Section 10.3) and *optimistic* (our subject in Section 10.4), for reasons that come to mind at once.

Before we leave this section, let us discuss in a little more detail the way logical processes interact with one another in both the time-stepped and the event-driven cases. We let $n = |\mathcal{N}|$, and for $1 \leq i \leq n$ let node n_i be the logical process responsible for simulating the behavior of the physical process ν_i. G is then a graph whose edge set (undirected or directed) has to contain edges at least in one-to-one correspondence to those of $\mathcal{G}$, but G can also be assumed to be a complete undirected graph if the structure of $\mathcal{G}$ is not known. Some of the methods that we discuss require G and $\mathcal{G}$ to be isomorphic, and as a consequence are only applicable to cases in which the structure of $\mathcal{G}$ is known. Other methods do not pose such a requirement, and then it is best to go for generality and assume that the structure of $\mathcal{G}$ is not known, in which case G is taken to be a complete undirected graph.

In a time-stepped simulation by G, the messages that nodes exchange are simply the initial or updated states of the corresponding physical processes. In event-driven simulations, a message sent by node n_i to node n_j stands for an event that the physical process ν_i causes to happen at the physical process ν_j. Such a message is denoted simply by $event(t)$, where t is the time at which the event is to happen in the physical process ν_j. Depending on the particular application at hand, this message will of course have to contain more information for n_j to be able to simulate the event that it stands for in ν_j. However, in a general framework like ours such details are of little importance, and so we keep the notation conveniently minimal.

Unless we explicitly state otherwise, the distributed simulation that the logical system (that is, G) carries out resorts, for termination, to techniques of the sort we discussed in Section 6.2. This is termination in the usual sense, that is, the sense in which all nodes are idle and all edges are empty.

It is very important for the reader to note that the t in the $event(t)$ message has nothing to do whatsoever with the local time at node n_j, in the sense introduced in Section 3.1. This t, sometimes also referred to as *virtual time*, is the time at the physical process ν_j at which the event is to happen during the simulation by n_j, and is as such part of the model of the natural system that the physical system represents. In spite of such a fundamental difference between the two notions of time, the times at which events are to happen at the various physical processes are also related to each other by restrictive properties, in a way similar to the relation $\prec$ on the set of events in a distributed computation.

One fundamental property says that, if an event is generated at time t by physical process ν_i to happen at time t' at physical process ν_j, then $t < t'$. This property expresses the unavoidable delay that accompanies the transmission of information between the two physical processes at any finite speed. Another fundamental property, also originating from inherent limitations of physical processes, is that, if t and t' are times at which two events happen at a certain physical process, then either $t < t'$ or $t' < t$. In the remainder of the chapter, we refer to these two properties as *causality properties*.

The task of an event-driven simulator, be it sequential or otherwise, is to ensure that, from the perspective of every single physical process, no event is processed unless all events that precede it in that physical process have themselves already been processed. As we remarked earlier, a sequential simulator can guarantee this trivially. A distributed simulator, by contrast, has a whole suite of techniques

to choose from with that goal. So an intuitively appealing interpretation for the
differences in the concepts of Section 3.1 to those of this chapter is that, while the
relation $\prec$ emerges from the occurrence of events in that case, in the present case
the aforementioned causality properties have to be forced upon the logical system.

In all further sections in this chapter, we let τ_i be a variable of node n_i to
contain the time at physical process ν_i. This variable is a nonnegative integer,
being initialized to zero. Also, n_i employs a variable $state_i$, initialized to $x_i(0)$, to
contain the state of physical process ν_i. Unless otherwise noted, we assume that,
when updating $state_i$, node n_i also outputs (to the "user") the pair $(\tau_i, state_i)$.

10.2. Time-stepped simulation

Our treatment of time-stepped simulation in this section unfolds along two main
lines, each motivated by a particular class of physical systems. Physical systems
in the first class are said to be *fully concurrent*, while physical systems in the
second class are referred to as being *partially concurrent*. We assume that $\mathcal{G}$ is an
undirected graph, that its structure is known, and that G and $\mathcal{G}$ are isomorphic
graphs.

In a fully concurrent physical system, $x_i(0)$ is provided for every physical process ν_i, and for $t > 0$ $x_i(t)$ is a function of $x_i(t-1)$ and of $x_j(t-1)$ for every physical
process ν_j such that $(\nu_i, \nu_j) \in \mathcal{E}$. In a partially concurrent physical system, $x_i(0)$
is also provided for every physical process ν_i, but the so-called "neighborhood constraints" restrict the values of t at which the state of a physical process may be
updated. Specifically, two physical processes ν_i and ν_j can have their states updated for the same t if and only if $(\nu_i, \nu_j) \notin \mathcal{E}$, that is, x_i and x_j do not depend
on each other to be updated. The set of physical processes that can have states
updated for the same t must then constitute an independent set in $\mathcal{G}$. Because
of these neighborhood constraints, partially concurrent physical systems also come
with the requirement that every node is to be updated infinitely often, which, in
our present context, means the following. If t_1 and t_2 are nonnegative integers such
that $t_2 - t_1 \geq n - 1$, then every physical process ν_i must be such that x_i is updated
for at least one time t such that $t_1 \leq t \leq t_2$.

Examples of fully concurrent physical systems are cellular automata, various
neural networks, and other systems whose behavior is described by differential
equations. Notorious partially concurrent physical systems include binary Hopfield
neural networks, Markov random fields in general (including Boltzmann machines),
and Bayesian networks. Based on what happens in the cases of these examples,
the time-stepped simulations that we consider in this section terminate when they

converge according to some application-dependent criterion. The value of T is then unknown beforehand, and then termination in the sense of idle nodes and empty edges in the logical system never really occurs. This is the situation we referred to in Section 6.2 in which it is convenient to employ a leader-based approach to termination detection. Specifically, every node, upon updating the state of its physical process, sends a report to the leader with the new state. The leader, in possession of such reports, is capable of putting together global states (cf. Section 5.2.2), and on these global states detecting whatever convergence is required for termination. Upon detection, the leader instructs the other nodes to terminate, possibly after some additional exchange of messages for gracefulness at the termination. We pursue this termination issue no more in this section, but do nonetheless advise the reader to consider the problem as an exercise (cf. Exercise 1).

Interestingly, already along the book we have seen solutions to the time-stepped simulation of both types of physical system. Specifically, the simulation of fully concurrent physical systems requires a synchronous algorithm that employs pulse $s = 0$ for initial states to be exchanged among neighbors and for $s > 0$ updates the states of all physical processes for time $t = s$. Because every state of every physical process has to be sent to all of the corresponding logical process's neighbors, such a simulation is a synchronous algorithm with the property that, at every pulse, exactly one message is sent to every neighbor. Couple this property with the assumption of FIFO edges in G, and we see that Algorithm $A\_Schedule\_AS$ of Section 5.3.2 can be employed directly for the time-stepped simulation of fully concurrent physical systems (the case of nonFIFO edges is left for the reader's appreciation—cf. Exercise 2).

Before being more specific about the algorithm we have seen that can also be applied to the time-stepped simulation of partially concurrent physical systems, we provide Algorithm $A\_Simulate\_FC$ ("FC" for Fully Concurrent) for the time-stepped simulation of fully concurrent physical systems based on Algorithm $A\_Schedule\_AS$. The two algorithms are entirely analogous to each other, so essentially we are simply re-writing the previous algorithm to employ appropriate notation. The variables s_i, MSG_i, and $queue_i^j$ for $n_j \in Neig_i$, employed in Algorithm $A\_Schedule\_AS$, are now replaced respectively with τ_i (already introduced), a set of variables $state_i^j$ for $n_j \in Neig_i$, and $next\_state_i^j$. For $n_j \in Neig_i$, $state_i^j$ and $next\_state_i^j$, both initialized to **nil**, contain if different from **nil** the last two states received from n_j ($state_i^j$ is the least recent, therefore to be used first).

Algorithm *A_Simulate_FC*:

▷ **Variables:**

$\tau_i = 0$;
$state_i = x_i(0)$;
$state_i^j = \textbf{nil}$ for all $n_j \in Neig_i$;
$next\_state_i^j = \textbf{nil}$ for all $n_j \in Neig_i$;
$initiated_i = \textbf{false}$.

▷ **Input:**

$msg_i = \textbf{nil}$.

Action if $n_i \in N_0$:   (10.1)

$initiated_i := \textbf{true}$;
Send $state_i$ to all $n_j \in Neig_i$.

▷ **Input:**

$msg_i = x$ such that $origin_i(msg_i) = (n_i, n_j)$.

Action: (10.2)

    if not *initiated_i* **then**
        begin
            $initiated_i := \textbf{true}$;
            Send $state_i$ to all $n_k \in Neig_i$
        end;
    if $state_i^j \neq \textbf{nil}$ **then**
        $next\_state_i^j := x$
    else
        $state_i^j := x$;
    if $state_i^k \neq \textbf{nil}$ for all $n_k \in Neig_i$ **then**
        begin
            $\tau_i := \tau_i + 1$;
            Update $state_i$;
            Send $state_i$ to all $n_k \in Neig_i$;
            for all $n_k \in Neig_i$ **do**
                begin
                    $state_i^k := next\_state_i^k$;
                    $next\_state_i^k := \textbf{nil}$
                end
    end.

Actions (10.1) and (10.2) originate, respectively, from actions (5.19) and (5.20). In this algorithm, the set N_0 is the set of nodes that initiate the simulation concurrently.

Let us now return to our earlier remark that an algorithm has been seen earlier in this book for the time-stepped simulation of partially concurrent physical systems as well. By definition of a partially concurrent physical system, we see that its time-stepped simulation by the corresponding logical system has to obey the constraints that no two neighbors ever update the states of their physical processes concurrently, and that every node update the state of its physical process infinitely often (in the sense explained earlier). Well, aside from the initial exchange of states, this is exactly the type of computation that is carried out by Algorithm A_Dine_H of Section 8.3.2.

That algorithm, as we recall, implements scheduling by edge reversal, and is an asynchronous algorithm that functions as follows. Assume that G is initially oriented by an acyclic orientation (cf. Section 8.3.1). Sinks in this orientation must not be neighbors of one another, and may then update the states of their physical processes concurrently. Upon doing such an update, a node sends the new state to all of its neighbors, thereby implicitly reversing the orientation of all edges incident to it and becoming a source. As we remarked in Section 8.3.1, the resulting acyclic orientations are thus guaranteed to be always acyclic, so sinks always exist and the simulation can always progress. In addition, Theorem 8.4 guarantees the form of infinitely often updates we are seeking.

The simulation algorithm based on Algorithm A_Dine_H is given next as Algorithm $A\_Simulate\_PC$ ("PC" for Partially Concurrent). Unlike the fully concurrent case, now the transformation is a bit more subtle, because initial states need to be spread selectively, that is, node n_i needs the initial state of neighbor n_j's physical process only if n_i is "downstream" from n_j with respect to the initial orientation (i.e., the initial orientation of edge (n_i, n_j) is from n_j to n_i). If such is not the case, then the state of that process to be used when n_i computes for the first time will be the one received from n_j upon reversal of the edge (n_i, n_j), so no initial state is really needed. We encourage the reader to write Algorithm $A\_Schedule\_PC$ in this fashion (cf. Exercise 3), but for simplicity we provide a version in which all nodes send initial states to every neighbor, though at times uselessly.

The additional variables employed by node n_i in Algorithm $A\_Simulate\_PC$ are, for all $n_j \in Neig_i$, $state_i^j$ (initialized to **nil**) and the Boolean $upstream_i^j$. The variable $upstream_i^j$ (which is equivalent to $holds\_fork_i^j$ in Algorithm A_Dine_H) indicates the current orientation of edge (n_i, n_j), and has to be initialized in accordance with the initial acyclic orientation (to **true** if the edge is directed from n_j to n_i, to false otherwise). The variable $state_i^j$, if different from **nil** and if $upstream_i^j = $ **true**, contains the state of n_j's physical process to be used by n_i when it next updates the state of its own physical process.

Algorithm *A_Simulate_PC*:

▷ **Variables:**
$\tau_i = 0$;
$state_i = x_i(0)$;
$state_i^j = $ **nil** for all $n_j \in Neig_i$;
$upstream_i^j$ for all $n_j \in Neig_i$.

▷ **Input:**
$msg_i = $ **nil**.
Action if $n_i \in N_0$:   (10.3)
Send $state_i$ to all $n_j \in Neig_i$.

▷ **Input:**
$msg_i = x$ such that $origin_i(msg_i) = (n_i, n_j)$.
Action: (10.4)
if $state_i^k = $ **nil** for all $n_k \in Neig_i$ **then**
Send $state_i$ to all $n_k \in Neig_i$;
if $state_i^j \neq $ **nil then**
$upstream_i^j := $ **true**;
$state_i^j := x$;
if $(state_i^k \neq $ **nil and** $upstream_i^k)$ for all $n_k \in Neig_i$ **then**
begin
Update τ_i;
Update $state_i$;
$upstream_i^k := $ **false** for all $n_k \in Neig_i$;
Send $state_i$ to all $n_k \in Neig_i$
end.

In Algorithm *A_Simulate_PC*, actions (10.3) and (10.4) relate closely to actions (8.15) and (8.16) of Algorithm *A_Dine_H*. The differences are accounted for by the need for initial states to be exchanged. Specifically, the set N_0 of spontaneous initiators no longer corresponds to the initial set of sinks, but rather to the set of nodes that initiate the propagation of initial states spontaneously. In addition, upon receiving a state x from node n_j, node n_i must decide whether this is the first message it receives (that is, whether $state_i^k = $ **nil** for all $n_k \in Neig_i$), in which case it must send its physical process's initial state out. Node n_i must also be able to distinguish states that it receives from n_j that should be interpreted as edge reversals (when $state_i^j \neq \mathbf{nil}$) from those that are initial values and do not imply edge reversal (when $state_i^j = \mathbf{nil}$). Finally, testing whether n_i has become a sink requires not only that $upstream_i^k$ be checked for all $n_k \in Neig_i$, but $state_i^k$ as well (because if n_i is an initial sink, it may only update $state_i$ after receiving initial states from all of its neighbors).

As a final observation, we note that the way to update τ_i in (10.4) was left purposefully vague. It should be clear that simply adding one as in (10.2) does not suffice, because it is necessary to account for all the time units in which $state_i$ was not updated because n_i was not a sink. We leave it to the reader to remove this vagueness (cf. Exercise 4).

10.3. Conservative event-driven simulation

In this section, we elaborate on conservative approaches to distributed event-driven simulation. As we remarked in Section 10.1, conservative methods seek to guarantee that events are processed in increasing order of time at all nodes, so that, globally, events are processed in nondecreasing order of time.

Our treatment of conservative methods is presented in the two sections that follow. The method that we present in Section 10.3.1 requires isomorphism between G and $\mathcal{G}$, and in addition that the edges of G be FIFO. Such a method is then only applicable to cases in which the structure of $\mathcal{G}$ is known. In Section 10.3.2, by contrast, a conservative method is discussed that does not require such an isomorphism, and consequently is applicable to cases in which the structure of $\mathcal{G}$ is not known. In these cases, G is taken to be a complete undirected graph, but the method still requires FIFO edges in G.

In addition to the causality properties that we discussed in Section 10.1, in the case of conservative methods another property is needed on the physical system. If a sequence of $k \geq 1$ events is generated at times $t_1 < t_2 < \cdots < t_k$ by a physical process ν_i to happen respectively at times $t_1', t_2', \ldots, t_k'$ at physical process ν_j, then we require that $t_1' < t_2' < \cdots < t_k'$ as well. This is a *monotonicity property*. Note that, although conservative methods seek to faithfully mimic the functioning of a sequential simulator, in the sequential case monotonicity is not an issue (i.e., it does not need to happen) so long as the causality properties hold. Requiring monotonicity in the conservative distributed case may be thought of as requiring that $\mathcal{G}$'s edges, like those of G, be FIFO.

10.3.1. A first algorithm

For greater generality, in this section we take $\mathcal{G}$ (and consequently G) to be a directed graph. In addition, if $\mathcal{G}$ is not strongly connected, then we assume that all of it sources are in $\mathcal{N}_0$.

The monotonicity property of the physical system and the assumption that G's edges are FIFO guarantee that, if a node processes $event(t)$ messages that it receives in increasing order of t, then the sequence of $event(t)$ messages that it sends to another node n_i is received in increasing order of t as well. In order to guarantee that n_i too processes the $event(t)$ messages that it receives in increasing order of t, by the causality properties all n_i has to do is to merge the incoming streams of $event(t)$ messages so that the resulting single stream is sorted in increasing order of t. It then suffices for n_i to process $event$ messages as they are queued in this resulting stream.

The approach that suggests itself for the participation of node n_i in the simulation is then the following. For each $n_j \in I\_Neig_i$, node n_i does not really maintain a queue of incoming messages, but rather a variable $next\_time_i^j$, initialized to zero, to contain the t parameter in the next $event(t)$ message to be processed in the stream from n_j (if no such next message has been received, then $next\_time_i^j$ is either the t in the last $event(t)$ message received from n_j or the initial zero). All n_i has to do is then to select for processing the $event$ message from $n_k \in I\_Neig_i$ such that

$$next\_time_i^k < next\_time_i^j$$

for all $n_j \in I\_Neig_i$ such that $n_j \neq n_k$. After processing this $event$ message, n_i waits to receive another $event$ message from n_k so that a new minimum can be found.

The problem with this initial approach is of course that such a message may never be received, and then the simulation may deadlock. In fact, this same problem exists from the very beginning of the simulation, because no node n_i may process any $event$ message before receiving one message from each neighbor in I_Neig_i. As in general situations in which deadlocks may happen, here too we have a choice as to either prevent its occurrence or detect it after it occurs (cf. Section 6.3). We chose the prevention strategy, but approaches based on deadlock detection have also been proposed.

The deadlock-prevention fix that we add to the simulation strategy we just described is based on additional $null(t)$ messages that the nodes exchange. Such messages are sent by n_i to every neighbor in O_Neig_i to which it does not send an $event$ upon computing the aforementioned minimum and simulating the behavior of ν_i up to that minimum. If the message that corresponds to this minimum time is itself a *null* message, then a *null* is sent to all of n_i's neighbors in O_Neig_i. Although *null* messages may account for an excessive increase in the algorithm's message complexity, they can also be used to advance the simulation more rapidly if so the physical system's peculiarities permit, and to enable nodes to terminate their computations locally.

Before proceeding to the presentation of the algorithm, let us be more specific about these alternative uses for a *null* message. When an $event(t)$ or a $null(t)$ is processed by node n_i, a $null(t+1)$ message is sent to every node $n_j \in O\_Neig_i$ to which an *event* message is not sent. This $null(t+1)$ message has the purpose of informing n_j that it will never be sent by n_i any $event(t')$ message such that $t' \le t+1$.

If the physical process being simulated is such that n_i can predict that no $event(t')$ message will ever be sent to n_j such that $t' \le t^+$ for $t^+ > t+1$, then a $null(t^+)$ message is sent instead. This message may be quite beneficial to the processing at n_j, in the sense that it may allow n_j to make more progress before it has to wait for additional messages from n_i. The difference $t^+ - t - 1$ is known as n_i's *lookahead at time t with respect to node n_j*. In the algorithm to be presented, and for all $n_j \in O\_Neig_i$, n_i maintains a variable $lookahead_i^j$, which we assume is properly initialized and maintained based on the physical system's characteristics.

Similarly, when the $event(t)$ message that n_i must send is such that $t > T$, then a $null(T)$ is sent instead, thereby signaling the destination node that n_i is never going to send it another message. This is also what nodes that correspond to sources in $\mathcal{G}$ must do after participating in the algorithm for time zero.

The classical example of a physical system exhibiting the possibility of lookahead determination is that of a network of queues (although it is easy to argue that in general simulating such a system by a distributed algorithm is not a good idea— reliable results for such a physical system require multiple simulations on random initial conditions, and then it is best to employ multiple sequential simulations). In such a system, each physical process is a queue with a server that provides service to each customer in the queue according to a certain distribution of service times. If for a queue it holds that no service time is ever less than, say, z time units, then the lookahead of the corresponding logical process is at all times equal to z with respect to all of its neighbors to which it may send *event* messages.

In order to contain the number of *null* messages when they are also used for lookahead and termination purposes, node n_i keeps track, for all $n_j \in O\_Neig_i$, of the value of t in the last $null(t)$ message sent to n_j. Variable $last\_time_i^j$, initially set to zero, is employed for this purpose.

The algorithm that realizes this conservative simulation strategy is Algorithm $A\_Simulate\_C$ ("C" for Conservative), presented next. In addition to the already introduced variables, it also employs the following. For $n_j \in I\_Neig_i$, the Boolean $needs\_event_i^j$, initialized to **true**, indicates whether n_i must receive a message from n_j before continuing. Also, the Boolean $null\_message_i^j$ indicates, if $needs_event_i^j = $ **false**, whether the message corresponding to $next\_time_i^j$ was a $null$ message. Finally, the auxiliary set X_i and variable t_i are also employed.

> **Algorithm** $A\_Simulate\_C$:

> ▷ **Variables:**
> > $\tau_i = 0$;
> > $state_i = x_i(0)$;
> > $next\_time_i^j = 0$ for all $n_j \in I\_Neig_i$;
> > $lookahead_i^j$ for all $n_j \in O\_Neig_i$;
> > $last\_time_i^j = 0$ for all $n_j \in O\_Neig_i$;
> > $needs_event_i^j = $ **true** for all $n_j \in I\_Neig_i$;
> > $null\_message_i^j$ for all $n_j \in I\_Neig_i$;
> > X_i;
> > t_i.

> ▷ **Input:**
> > $msg_i = $ **nil**.
> > **Action if** $n_i \in N_0$:   (10.5)
> > > Let $X_i \subseteq O\_Neig_i$ be the set of nodes to which $event$'s are to be sent;
> > > **for** $n_j \in X_i$ **do**
> > > > **begin**
> > > > > Let $t_i > \tau_i$ be the time of the $event$ to be sent to n_j;
> > > > > **if** $t_i \leq T$ **then**
> > > > > > Send $event(t_i)$ to n_j;
> > > > > **if** $t_i > T$ **or** $I\_Neig_i = \emptyset$ **then**
> > > > > > Send $null(T)$ to n_j
> > > > **end**;
> > > **for** $n_j \notin X_i$ **do**
> > > > **begin**
> > > > > $last\_time_i^j := \min\{\tau_i + 1 + lookahead_i^j, T\}$;
> > > > > Send $null(last\_time_i^j)$ to n_j
> > > > **end**.

▷ **Input:**

$msg_i = event(t)$ such that $origin_i(msg_i) = (n_j \rightarrow n_i)$.

Action when $needs\_event_i^j$:   (10.6)

$needs\_event_i^j := \textbf{false}$;

$null\_message_i^j := \textbf{false}$;

$next\_time_i^j := t$;

if not $needs\_event_i^k$ for all $n_k \in I\_Neig_i$ **then**

    begin

        Let $n_k \in I\_Neig_i$ be such that $next\_time_i^k \leq next\_time_i^\ell$ for all $n_\ell \in I\_Neig_i$;

        $\tau_i := next\_time_i^k$;

        if $null\_message_i^k$ **then** $X_i := \emptyset$

        else

            begin

                Update $state_i$;

                Let $X_i \subseteq O\_Neig_i$ be the set of nodes to which $event$'s are to be sent

            end;

        for $n_\ell \in X_i$ **do**

            begin

                Let $t_i > \tau_i$ be the time of the $event$ to be sent to n_ℓ;

                if $t_i \leq T$ **then**

                    Send $event(t_i)$ to n_ℓ

                else

                    Send $null(T)$ to n_ℓ

            end;

        for $n_\ell \notin X_i$ **do**

            begin

                if $last\_time_i^\ell < \min\{\tau_i + 1 + lookahead_i^\ell, T\}$ **then**

                    begin

                          $last\_time_i^\ell$

                                $:= \min\{\tau_i + 1 + lookahead_i^\ell, T\}$;

                        Send $null(last\_time_i^\ell)$ to n_ℓ

                  end

            end;

        $needs\_event_i^k := \textbf{true}$

    end.

▷ **Input:**
    $msg_i = null(t)$ such that $origin_i(msg_i) = (n_j \rightarrow n_i)$.

Action when $needs\_event_i^j$:   (10.7)

    $needs_event_i^j := $ **false**;
    $null_message_i^j := $ **true**;
    $next\_time_i^j := t$;
    if not $needs\_event_i^k$ for all $n_k \in I\_Neig_i$ **then**
        begin
            Let $n_k \in I\_Neig_i$ be such that $next\_time_i^k \leq next\_time_i^\ell$ for
            all $n_\ell \in I\_Neig_i$;
            $\tau_i := next\_time_i^k$;
            if $null\_message_i^k$ **then** $X_i := \emptyset$
            else
                begin
                    Update $state_i$;
                    Let $X_i \subseteq O\_Neig_i$ be the set of nodes to which
                    $event$'s are to be sent
                end;
            for $n_\ell \in X_i$ **do**
                begin
                    Let $t_i > \tau_i$ be the time of the $event$ to be sent to
                    n_ℓ;
                    if $t_i \leq T$ **then**
                        Send $event(t_i)$ to n_ℓ
                    else
                        Send $null(T)$ to n_ℓ
            end;
            for $n_\ell \notin X_i$ **do**
                begin
                    if $last\_time_i^\ell < \min\{\tau_i + 1 + lookahead_i^\ell, T\}$ **then**
                    begin
                        $last\_time_i^\ell$
                                $:= \min\{\tau_i + 1 + lookahead_i^\ell, T\}$;
                      Send $null(last\_time_i^\ell)$ to n_ℓ
                  end
            end;
            $needs_event_i^k := $ **true**
    end.

In Algorithm $A\_Simulate\_C$, the set N_0 is the set of all nodes that initiate the simulation spontaneously. These nodes include those whose physical processes are in $\mathcal{N}_0$, but are not restricted to them (if $n_i \in N_0$ but $\nu_i \notin \mathcal{N}_0$, then in (10.5) only *null* messages are sent).

Action (10.5) in the algorithm is executed by the nodes in N_0, while actions (10.6) and (10.7) are executed upon receipt by n_i of an *event* message or a *null* message, respectively. Actions (10.6) and (10.7) are identical to each other, except for the setting of variable $null\_message_i^j$, n_j being the message's origin. It is important to note that, in the algorithm, the causality and monotonicity properties are only implicitly ensured, depending essentially of the portions of the simulation that relate to the nature of the physical system under consideration. Another important observation is that, although in (10.6) and (10.7) the determination of n_k would be unique in the absence of *null* messages (by the causality properties), when such messages are employed it may happen that the minimum $next\_time_i^\ell$ occurs for more than one node in I_Neig_i. However, at most one such node participates in the minimum with an *event* message instead of a *null* message, and it is to such a neighbor that n_k must be preferably set if it exists (the reader should try to be convinced that, if this is the case, then the *null* messages for which the minimum time also holds will not generate the sending of any messages when they are processed).

We now turn to establishing the algorithm's correctness.

Theorem 10.1. *Algorithm $A\_Simulate\_C$ correctly simulates the physical system for all $t \in \{0, \ldots, T\}$.*

Proof: Every node corresponding to a physical process in $\mathcal{N}_0$ is in the set N_0 of spontaneous initiators. In addition, by (10.5) through (10.7) a node never sends any $event(t)$ or $null(t)$ message for which $t > T$. Because the causality and monotonicity properties are guaranteed to hold and all of G's edges are FIFO, what we need to show is that the simulation always progresses so long as there exists at least one node n_i for which $\tau_i < T$.

Suppose, to the contrary, that a deadlock happens. It must then be, following our discussion in Section 6.3, that a wait cycle exists in G. In this cycle, every node n_i is precluded from picking an *event* or *null* message to process because there exists $n_j \in I\_Neig_i$ such that $needs\_event_i^j = \mathbf{true}$. Because N_0 is nonempty, at least one such wait cycle has to exist including at least one node n_i such that either $n_i \in N_0$ or $\tau_i > 0$. The message that this n_i needs from the corresponding n_j in order to continue must carry a parameter t such that $t > \tau_j$ when it is sent (by the causality properties), which means that there exists n_k in the cycle waiting for a message from n_i with parameter t such that $t > \tau_i$. But either by (10.5) (if $n_i \in N_0$) or by (10.6) and (10.7) (if $\tau_i > 0$), such a message must have been sent, respectively spontaneously or when n_i last updated τ_i. It is then impossible for any such wait cycle to exist, thence any deadlock as well.   ■

10.3.2. Conditional events

The need for the structure of $\mathcal{G}$ to be known and the potentially excessive traffic of *null* messages in Algorithm *A_Simulate_C* have led to the search for other conservative methods. As we mentioned earlier, some of the other methods that have been proposed are based on the use of deadlock detection, instead of prevention, although in them the need to know the structure of $\mathcal{G}$ still persists. In this section, we do not assume that the structure of $\mathcal{G}$ is known, and then take G to be a complete undirected graph. G's edges are still assumed to be FIFO edges.

The approach that we discuss in this section is based on the following observation. In a sequential simulation, every event in the single queue of events is a *conditional event*, in the sense that it must only be scheduled to happen when it reaches the head of the queue, at which time it becomes a *definite event*. In Algorithm *A_Simulate_C*, definite events were determined by restraining the input of messages to a node. In other words, only upon having received exactly one message from each neighbor did a node choose from those messages one to be processed. If the chosen message was an *event* message, then *event* messages corresponding to definite events were output.

The method to turn conditional events into definite events is in this section different. The messages exchanged among nodes are still *event* and *null* messages, but the latter no longer have a deadlock-prevention connotation, but rather are only used to convey lookahead and termination information. Node n_i no longer restrains the receipt of messages, but rather assumes that every incoming *event* message corresponds to a definite event and because every edge is FIFO they may therefore be acted upon immediately. In order for this assumption to be valid globally, n_i makes sure that only *event* messages that correspond to definite events are output. To this end, n_i computes on every *event* or *null* message it receives, and as a result produces as many *event* and *null* messages as it can. The *null* messages it produces, having solely a lookahead- or termination-related meaning, are immediately output when they are generated. Messages of the *event* type, however, are stored in a set $events_i$ until the events to which they correspond can become definite, at which time the messages are sent out. At all times, a variable $next_i$ indicates the least time t associated with the $event(t)$'s in $events_i$.

Determining which of the *event* messages are to be sent out as definite events (and when this is to happen) is the crux of the approach, and is achieved as follows. For all $n_k \in N$, node n_i maintains a collection of variables $next_i^k$ to contain local views of $next_k$. For each such n_k, node n_i also maintains the variables $sent_i^k$ and $received_i^k$ to indicate the number of messages (of either type) it ever sent to n_k or received from n_k, respectively. Similarly, for all ordered pairs of nodes (n_k, n_ℓ), a collection of variables $sent_i^{k\ell}$ and $received_i^{k\ell}$ is also maintained to indicate n_i's views of the number of messages sent by n_k to n_ℓ and received by n_k from n_ℓ, respectively.

In order to describe the computation that takes place on these variables, we need to resort to the terminology of Section 5.2.1, where we described an algorithm for global state recording on a substrate computation. In the present case, we regard as a substrate computation the computation that the nodes perform that is related to the simulation proper. That is, n_i's participation in the substrate is to compute on *event* and *null* messages it receives, thereby updating all the variables involved, including the variables $events_i$, $next_i$, the $sent_i^k$'s, and the $received_i^k$'s. On top of this substrate computation, a global state recording is performed periodically. The goal of these recordings is to seek global states in which all edges are empty, and then Algorithm *A_Record_Global_State* of Section 5.2.1 offers no help. Instead, we recall our observation in Section 5.2.2 on the possibility of recording such global states by a leader, except that no leader will in this case be employed, but rather the recording will be done by all nodes acting as "leaders."

The following is then how the substrate and the global state recording interact. The local state to be recorded at node n_i comprises the variables $next_i$, the $sent_i^k$'s, and the $received_i^k$'s. These variables must be recorded (respectively in available $next_i^i$'s, $sent_i^{ik}$'s, and $received_i^{ik}$'s) from time to time, specifically a finite time after one of them changes. In addition, a finite time after the recording they must be broadcast to all other nodes. Node n_i, now in its role as the aforementioned "leader," collects such broadcasts in available $next_i^k$'s, $sent_i^{k\ell}$'s, and $received_i^{k\ell}$'s, and looks for system states in which $sent_i^{k\ell} = received_i^{k\ell}$ for all ordered pairs (n_k, n_ℓ). In these system states, all edges are empty, so they must constitute global states, as we observed in Section 5.2.2. If such a global state is detected at which $next_i^i \leq next_i^k$ for all $n_k \in N$, then n_i is sure never to add another $event(t)$ such that $t \leq next_i^i$ to $events_i$. Consequently, every $event(t) \in events_i$ such that $t = next_i^i$ is seen to correspond to a definite event, and may be sent to its destination, while $states_i$ and $next_i$ are updated accordingly.

We do not provide any further details on this algorithm, but rather leave providing such details for the reader to undertake as an exercise (cf. Exercise 5).

As a final remark, we note that, in addition to the overall scheme for turning conditional events into definite events we just described, node n_i may at any time detect, based on specifics of the application at hand, that certain conditional events are in fact definite and may be sent out without waiting for any global information. This is valid for sequential simulations as well (an event that is not at the head of the queue may, depending on the application, be processed), although it makes little sense in that case.

10.4. Optimistic event-driven simulation

Optimistic methods of distributed simulation are based on the premise that it may be more efficient to let causality errors occur and then fix them than to rely on lookaheads and other application-specific properties in the search for efficiency. Physical systems for which this premise has proven valid include systems of colliding particles and evolving populations. In this section, then, there is no place for such things as lookaheads and *null* messages. Similarly, the structure of $\mathcal{G}$ is not assumed to be known, so that G, whose edges no longer have to be FIFO, is taken to be a complete undirected graph.

The mechanism that we describe in this section for optimistic distributed simulation is known as the *time warp mechanism*, perhaps in allusion to the possibility that, at node n_i, τ_i may move back and forth as the need arises for errors to be corrected. The essence of this mechanism is the following. Whenever n_i receives an $event(t)$ message such that $t > \tau_i$, it sets τ_i to t, computes on the message it received, and possibly sends out $event(t)$'s for some $t > \tau_i$. Because no precautions are taken to ensure that such events are definite (in the terminology of Section 10.3.2), it may well happen that a $event(t)$ reaches n_i with $t \leq \tau_i$, thereby indicating that whatever state updates were done or $event$ messages were sent in the interval $\{t, \ldots, \tau_i\}$ were erroneous and must therefore be corrected. This arriving $event(t)$ message is often referred to as a "straggler."

The approach of the time warp mechanism to correcting such errors when they are detected is to return the simulation globally to a correct global state, and then to proceed from there. In order to be able to perform such "rollbacks," every node must store some of its past history, so that earlier states can be restored when necessary. At node n_i, this history has two queue components, called $state\_queue_i$ and $output\_queue_i$. An element of $state\_queue_i$ is the pair (t, x), indicating the state x of the physical process ν_i at time t. This queue is initialized to **nil**, and receives a new pair whenever $state_i$ is updated. An element of $output\_queue_i$ is the triple (t, t', n_k), indicating that n_i sent n_k an $event(t')$ message when τ_i was equal to t. This queue is initialized to **nil**, and receives a new triple whenever n_i sends an *event* message. Both queues are kept in increasing order of t (nondecreasing for *output_queue$_i$*, for there may be multiple *event*'s sent for fixed τ_i).

When a straggler arrives with a t parameter, τ_i is set to t and *state$_i$* is set to x in the (t', x) pair in *state_queue$_i$*. Here t' is the greatest integer less than t for which a pair exists in *state_queue$_i$*. This queue is then shortened to contain pairs with time components no greater than t'. Before resuming normal processing, however, n_i has to annul the effect of every *event* it sent when $\tau_i = t$ or later. This is achieved by sending an *anti-event*(t') message to the n_k in every triple (t^+, t', n_k) in *output_queue$_i$* such that $t^+ \geq t$, and then shortening the queue by the removal of those triples. It only remains for us to discuss how to handle the reception of such *anti-event*'s.

Because G's edges are not assumed to be FIFO, an *anti-event*(t) arriving at node n_i may be following the *event*(t) to which it corresponds or it may be ahead of the *event*(t). In the former case, the *anti-event* is also a straggler upon arrival, and should be trated as we discussed previously. In the latter case, n_i needs a mechanism to remember the arrival of the *anti-event*(t), so that, when the *event*(t) arrives, it is not acted upon. In order to implement this mechanism, node n_i maintains yet another queue, called *input_queue$_i$* and initialized to **nil**, where the pair (t, n_k) corresponding to an *anti-event*(t) from n_k that does not arrive as a straggler is stored in increasing order of t. An arriving *event*(t) from node n_k that finds the pair (t, n_k) in *input_queue$_i$* is rendered ineffective, while the queue is shortened by the removal of that pair. (Note that, by the causality properties, only the t's would have to be stored in *input_queue$_i$*; however, *anti-message*'s occur in erroneous situations, thence the additional precaution of storing the messages' origins as well.)

This strategy is realized by Algorithm *A_Simulate_TW* ("TW" for Time Warp), given next. In addition to the variables already described, the algorithm also employs the auxiliary variable t_i. Contrasting with our initial approach in Section 10.1, no queue of *event* messages to be processed is really needed. Instead, node n_i in Algorithm *A_Simulate_TW* acts upon such messages as they are received.

Algorithm $A\_Simulate\_TW$:

▷ **Variables:**

$\tau_i = 0$;
$state_i = x_i(0)$;
$state\_queue_i = \textbf{nil}$;
$output\_queue_i = \textbf{nil}$;
$input\_queue_i = \textbf{nil}$;
t_i.

▷ **Input:**

$msg_i = \textbf{nil}$.

Action if $n_i \in N_0$:   (10.8)

Append $(\tau_i, state_i)$ to $state\_queue_i$;
for $n_j \in Neig_i$ **do**
    if there exists event to be sent to n_j **then**
        begin
            Let $t_i > \tau_i$ be the time of the event to be sent to n_j;
            if $t_i \leq T$ **then**
                Send $event(t_i)$ to n_j
        end.

▷ **Input:**

$msg_i = event(t)$ such that $origin_i(msg_i) = (n_i, n_j)$.

Action: (10.9)

if there exists (t, n_j) in $input\_queue_i$ **then**

Remove (t, n_j) from $input\_queue_i$

else

begin

if $t \leq \tau_i$ **then**

begin

Let t' be the greatest integer such that $t' < t$ and there exists (t', x) in $state\_queue_i$;

$state_i := x$;

Remove all (t^+, x') such that $t^+ \geq t$ from $state\_queue_i$;

for all (t^+, t', n_k) in $output\_queue_i$ such that $t^+ \geq t$ **do**

begin

Remove (t^+, t', n_k) from $output\_queue_i$;

Send $anti\text{-}event(t')$ to n_k

end

end;

$\tau_i := t$;

Update $state_i$;

Append $(\tau_i, state_i)$ to $state\_queue_i$;

for $n_k \in Neig_i$ **do**

if there exists event to be sent to n_k **then**

begin

Let $t_i > \tau_i$ be the time of the event to be sent to n_k;

if $t_i \leq T$ **then**

begin

Append (τ_i, t_i, n_k) to $output\_queue_i$;

Send $event(t_i)$ to n_k

end

end

end.

▷ **Input:**
   $msg_i = anti\text{-}event(t)$ such that $origin_i(msg_i) = (n_i, n_j)$.
 Action: (10.10)
   if $t \leq \tau_i$ **then**
       begin
           Let t' be the greatest integer such that $t' < t$ and there
           exists (t', x) in $state\_queue_i$;
           $state_i := x$;
           Remove all (t^+, x') such that $t^+ \geq t$ from $state\_queue_i$;
           for all (t^+, t', n_k) in $output\_queue_i$ such that $t^+ \geq t$ **do**
               begin
                   Remove (t^+, t', n_k) from $output\_queue_i$;
                   Send $anti\text{-}event(t')$ to n_k
               end;
           $\tau_i := t$
       end
   else
       Add (t, n_j) to $input\_queue_i$.

The set N_0 in Algorithm $A\_Simulate\_TW$ comprises the nodes whose physical processes are in $\mathcal{N}_0$. Action (10.8) corresponds to the processing on events at physical processes in $\mathcal{N}_0$, while actions (10.9) and (10.10) correspond, respectively, to the receipt at n_i of an $event(t)$ message and an $anti\text{-}event(t)$ message. Both actions include n_i's participation in a rollback if the message is a straggler. In the case of an $event$ message, this participation in the rollback is followed by the processing of the event. If the message is not a straggler, then the corresponding event is processed in (10.9) or a new element is added to $input\_queue_i$ in (10.10).

The reader will have noticed that the sending of $event$'s in (10.8) and in (10.9) differ from each other in that (10.8) does not include any additions to $output\_queue_i$. As a result, $output\_queue_i$ does not contain any pair $(0, t', n_k)$. What this amounts to is that provisions are not made for a possible rollback of the simulation in which n_i must return to $\tau_i = 0$.

The reason why such provisions are indeed unnecessary, and in fact why numerous other properties of Algorithm $A\_Simulate\_TW$ and variations thereof hold, relies on the following definition. At any global state, consider the minimum of the following quantities: τ_i for all $n_i \in N$, and for every message in transit sent by node n_i the value of τ_i at the moment the message was sent. This minimum is called the *global virtual time* at that global state, known mainly by the acronym GVT (for Global Virtual Time).

Theorem 10.2. *In Algorithm A_Simulate_TW, τ_i is never set to a value $t \leq GVT$.*

Proof: The value of τ_i is only changed to t upon receipt of an *event(t)* in (10.9) or an *anti-event(t)* in (10.10). By the physical system's causality properties, any such message, when sent by $n_k \in N$, must have been sent when $\tau_k < t$. The theorem then follows from the observation that $GVT \leq \tau_k$ (and consequently $GVT < t$) at any global state in which the said message is in transit. ∎

At the initial global state of the simulation, $GVT = 0$. The reason why *output_queue$_i$* does not contain any elements with a zero time component for any node n_i is then immediate from Theorem 10.2. This theorem, in addition, implies the following.

Corollary 10.3. *Algorithm A_Simulate_TW correctly simulates the physical system for all $t \in \{0, \ldots, T\}$.*

Proof: This is an immediate consequence of the fact that every node whose physical process is in $\mathcal{N}_0$ is in N_0, the fact that in (10.8) and in (10.9) *event(t)*'s are never sent with $t > T$, and the physical system's causality properties, if only we consider that, by Theorem 10.2, progress in the simulation is always guaranteed. ∎

In addition to being instrumental in establishing the correctness of Algorithm *A_Simulate_TW*, the GVT concept is also useful in other situations, including memory management at the various nodes. Specifically, the only pairs that need to be maintained in *state_queue$_i$* at any node n_i are those with time component $t' \geq t$, where t is the greatest integer such that $t \leq GVT$ for which a pair exists in *state_queue$_i$*. Similarly, *output_queue$_i$* need not contain any (t, t', n_k) for $t \leq GVT$. These are immediate consequences of Theorem 10.2.

When employed for such memory management purposes, the value of GVT needs from time to time to be accessible locally to the nodes. Regardless of which technique is employed for this to happen (either a global state recording algorithm in the fashion of Section 5.2.1 or some of the other techniques present in the literature requiring fewer messages), *event* and *anti-event* messages can no longer be sent as we have introduced them, but instead must include another time parameter to store the value of the τ variables at the time they are sent. So these messages must then be sent by n_i as *event(τ_i, t)* and *anti-event(τ_i, t)*, respectively.

Let us make one final observation before leaving this section. As we remarked in Section 10.1, the updating by node n_i of *state$_i$* is implicitly taken as also implying that the pair $(\tau_i, state_i)$ is output. It should be clear to the reader that guaranteeing this in Algorithm *A_Simulate_TW* requires a little more elaboration. Specifically, such a pair can only be output if $\tau_i \leq GVT$, thereby providing another justification for the need to acquire estimates of GVT locally from time to time.

10.5. Hybrid timing and defeasible time-stepping

There are physical systems in which the states of the physical processes change in a way that does not entirely fall into any of the two categories we introduced in Section 10.1. For such systems, the methods we have seen so far in the book are inadequate, and other alternatives have to be devised. In this section, we briefly describe an example of such physical systems and outline a simulation strategy that can be regarded as a hybrid between some of the approaches we have studied. The physical system we describe arises from problems in nuclear physics, and it appears that some phenomena associated with the dynamics of stellar cores can be modeled likewise.

The physical system consists of p interacting particles in three-dimensional space. At time $t \geq 0$, the particles' positions are $\mathbf{z}_1(t), \ldots, \mathbf{z}_p(t)$ and their momenta are $\mathbf{p}_1(t), \ldots, \mathbf{p}_p(t)$. All particles have mass m, and their behavior can be modeled by integral-differential equations whose solution cannot be obtained analytically or even numerically within reasonable bounds on the required computational resources. The approach to solving them is then to employ a heuristic that assumes simpler modeling equations and uses randomness to guarantee accuracy. We describe such a heuristic next.

For $1 \leq k \leq p$, the behavior of the kth particle is assumed to follow the equations

$$\frac{d\mathbf{z}_k(t)}{dt} = \frac{\mathbf{p}_k(t)}{m};$$
$$\frac{d\mathbf{p}_k(t)}{dt} = -\nabla U\Big(\rho\big(\mathbf{z}_k(t)\big)\Big),$$

where U is a potential and $\rho\big(\mathbf{z}_k(t)\big)$ is the average particle density in the vicinity of point $\mathbf{z}_k(t)$ at time t. The average here is the average over a large number, call it N, of random initial conditions, so what is required is the solution of Np pairs of differential equations like the ones we showed. These equations are very tightly coupled with one another, so what we have is not the typical situation in which N independent solutions are required, in which case distributed methods can hardly be recommended within the context of obtaining each of the individual solutions. Instead, our problem is to solve for the positions and momenta of Np interacting particles, based on equations that require knowledge, at all times, of the average particle density, over N, near the particles' positions.

Because analytical methods to solve this system of equations are not known either, the sequential approach is to employ simulation. For a conveniently chosen Δt, the simulation starts at initial positions and momenta for all Np particles and computes these quantities for the discrete times $\Delta t, 2\Delta t, \ldots, T$. It is, in this sense, a time-stepped simulation. If t is any of these discrete times, then the solutions at t are computed from the solutions at $t - \Delta t$ and from the average densities corresponding to the interval $[t - \Delta t, t)$. The problem, naturally, is the computation of such densities, because they depend on how the particles interact with one another during that interval. What is done in the sequential method is to perform an event-driven simulation for each of the intervals, with provisions for events not to be generated for occurrence at times t' such that $t' \geq t$.

This hybrid sequential method has an obvious distributed counterpart, which is the following. The time-stepped portion can be achieved by a synchronous algorithm. By means of any of the synchronizers seen in Section 5.3, this synchronous algorithm can be turned into an asynchronous one. The processing for each pulse is an event-driven simulation that must terminate before nodes are allowed to progress to further pulses. This event-driven simulation can employ any of the approaches we discussed in Sections 10.3 and 10.4, for example.

An alternative that is not so tightly synchronized is to employ essentially the same guidelines we just described, with the slight modification that an optimistic method be used within each pulse, and that pulses, like events in the optimistic simulation, be defeasible, in the sense of being prone to annulment by way of rollbacks. Let us be a little more specific on a method, called *defeasible time-stepping*, that proceeds along these lines.

We present the method's essentials for the case of the physical system introduced at the beginning of this section. A physical process is a region in the portion of three-dimensional space to which the particles are confined, so the overall structure of $\mathcal{G}$ is quite well known. Within each time interval, the events that characterize the interaction among the physical processes are the arrival of particles from neighboring regions in space, so $\mathcal{G}$ is an undirected graph. Defeasible time-stepping operates on a graph G that is isomorphic to $\mathcal{G}$, for this particular problem.

In order to carry out the event-driven simulation corresponding to each time interval, a logical process requires the particle densities at points within its own physical process and at points in adjacent physical processes that are in the vicinity of the boundary between the two. What this implies is that logical processes must,

at the end of each time interval, send information on the appropriate densities to
all of their neighbors in G. Clearly, then, the synchronization method that is best
suited is the particularization of Synchronizer *Alpha* that we saw in Section 5.3.2
(i.e., Algorithm *A_Schedule_AS*), provided edges are FIFO, as we do assume for
the sake of simplicity. So the time-stepped portion of the simulation is in principle
performed in much the same lines as those of Section 10.2.

A logical process starts participating in the event-driven simulation that corresponds to a time interval as soon as it receives the necessary densities from all of
its neighbors corresponding to the previous time interval. This event-driven simulation is performed optimistically, say by means of techniques similar to the one
introduced in Section 10.4. When a logical process judges that it may have finished
participating in the simulation for the current time interval, it sends densities out
to its neighbors. If it then receives a straggler to be processed in that same time
interval (or in an earlier one), it must correct the effects of the premature signal
for its neighbors to proceed to the next time interval. Overall, events and messages
carrying densities are processed optimistically, and may then have to be revised
upon the occurrence of errors. The techniques employed to this end are pretty
similar to those of Section 10.4. We provide no further details here, but encourage
the reader to seek additional information in the pertinent literature.

10.6. A general framework

In this section, we provide a brief description of a framework that may help visualize
how all the different approaches to the simulation of physical systems relate to
one another. The overall goal of such a unified understanding has some obvious
aesthetic connotations, but more importantly is to provide an intuitive basis for
the development of new methods for physical systems with new characteristics.

In this unifying framework, the physical system is viewed as a two-dimensional
grid, with one dimension (say the "horizontal") used to represent the physical
processes and the other (the "vertical") used to represent time. Each point in this
grid corresponds to a physical process and a time instant. The goal of a simulation
method is to fill out the grid by assigning to each point the state of the corresponding
physical process at the corresponding time.

In broad terms, a logical process may correspond to any set of points in the
grid. The task of the logical process is to fill out the points in that set. Our approach
throughout this chapter has been to restrict such sets to being vertical stripes, but
there is in principle no reason why logical processes may not have different shapes.

Sequential simulation methods can be viewed as employing one single logical process corresponding to the entire grid. The distributed methods we have studied all restrict each vertical stripe to correspond to exactly one physical process. Sequential methods normally fill out the grid in increasing order of time, and essentially this is what their distributed time-stepped and conservative event-driven counterparts do as well. Optimistic event-driven methods also have the overall goal of doing that, but they do it in a rather unsynchronized manner, and occasionally points that have been filled out may have to be erased for later reconsideration.

Although all the methods we have studied adopt such a vertical-stripe approach to filling out the grid, the use of other subdivisions in the distributed case accounts for interesting possibilities. For example, any arrangement other than the one based on vertical stripes requires more than one logical process to simulate the same physical process, however for different time intervals. Whether physical systems exist for which such an arrangement of logical processes is capable of performing efficiently remains largely to be seen.

10.7. Exercises

1. Provide the termination details for the two cases discussed in Section 10.2. Assume, in both cases, that an additional node, n_0, exists whose function is to detect termination. Provide a solution for each of the following two cases. First, all nodes update the states of their physical processes the same number of times. Second, nodes perform updates until some global convergence criterion is met.

2. Provide an algorithm for the time-stepped simulation of fully concurrent systems when edges are not FIFO.

3. Provide a version of Algorithm *A_Schedule_PC* in which the initial propagation of states is selective, depending on the initial orientation.

4. Complete action (10.4) by specifying how to update τ_i.

5. Write the algorithm described in Section 10.3.2.

6. Discuss an alternative to the use of *anti-event*'s if G's edges are FIFO.

10.8. Bibliographic notes

There are many sources of reference to complement the introductory material presented in Section 10.1. A general introduction to the role played by high-performance computation in the analysis of physical systems is given by Fox and

Otto (1986). Readers wanting to concentrate on the simulation of physical systems based on continuous-time may need to acquire a deeper understanding of the mathematics involved (Wylie, 1975; Luenberger, 1979), while those whose interest lies mainly on the study of discrete-time physical systems may wish to check some of the paradigmatic problems in the area, as the firing squad problem (Jiang, 1989) and the chip firing problem (Spencer, 1986). Overviews of various aspects of distributed event-driven simulation can be found in many places, including Misra (1986), Fujimoto (1990a), Fujimoto (1993), and Nicol and Fujimoto (1994). A discussion on the relation between distributed simulation and the notions of knowledge of Section 2.3 has been given by Loucks and Preiss (1990). Alonso, Frutos, and Palacio (1994) provide a comparative study of conservative and optimistic methods, while Lin (1993) discusses the termination of event-driven simulations. Pohlmann (1991) discusses an approach that departs from our taxonomy.

Section 10.2 is entirely based on Barbosa and Lima (1990) and on Barbosa (1991; 1993), where the time-stepped simulation of numerous physical systems is considered. These include cellular automata (von Neumann, 1966; Wolfram, 1986), analog Hopfield neural networks (Hopfield, 1984), neural networks to solve linear systems and linear programming problems (de Carvalho and Barbosa, 1992), binary Hopfield neural networks (Hopfield, 1982), systems under simulated annealing (Kirkpatrick, Gelatt, and Vecchi, 1983; Gafni and Barbosa, 1986; Barbosa and Gafni, 1989a; Barbosa and Boeres, 1990), Markov random fields (Geman and Geman, 1984), Boltzmann machines (Hinton, Sejnowski, and Ackley, 1984), and Bayesian networks (Pearl, 1988; Eizirik, Barbosa, and Mendes, 1993).

The pioneering work on conservative methods for distributed simulation (and hence for distributed simulation in general) was done independently by Bryant (1977) and by Chandy and Misra (1979). It is on the work of Chandy and Misra (1979) that Section 10.3.1 is based. Section 10.3.2 is based on the later work by Chandy and Sherman (1989b). In the context of conservative methods, various authors have addressed the question of reducing the number of *null* messages, as for example De Vries (1990) and Preiss, Loucks, MacIntyre, and Field (1990). Similarly, the effects of the absence of lookaheads (Lin, Lazowska, and Baer, 1990) and of their presence (Preiss and Loucks, 1990) have also been studied. Other studies on conservative methods have been conducted by Chandy and Misra (1981)—where a deadlock-detection strategy is employed in place of prevention, Mehl (1990), Yu, Ghosh, and DeBenedictis (1990), Lin, Lazowska, and Hwang (1992), Nicol (1992), Ayani and Rajaei (1994), Blanchard, Lake, and Turner (1994), Teo and Tay (1994), and Wood and Turner (1994).

Fujimoto (1990b) presents a survey of optimistic methods for distributed simulation, and Preiss, MacIntyre, and Loucks (1992) elaborate on the relation between "optimism" and memory availability in optimistic methods. Section 10.4 on the time warp mechanism is based on Jefferson (1985). For studies on the management of memory during optimistic simulations, the reader is referred to Lin (1994), for a treatment related to optimistic methods in general, and to Lin and Preiss (1991) and Das and Fujimoto (1994), for a treatment within the context of the time warp mechanism. Methods for the periodic computation of GVT have been proposed by many authors, including, more recently, Mattern (1993), Srinivasan and Reynolds (1993), and D'Souza, Fan, and Wilsey (1994). Strategies for limiting a method's optimism have also been investigated, and can be looked up, for example, in the works by Sokol, Briscoe, and Wieland (1988), Sokol, Stucky, and Hwang (1989), Sokol and Stucky (1990), and Sokol, Weissman, and Mutchler (1991). Additional relevant publications on optimistic methods include Prakash and Subramanian (1992) and Nicol (1993).

Section 10.5 is based on Wedemann, Barbosa, and Donangelo (1995). Details on the physical system described in that section can be found in Aichelin and Bertsch (1985), Bertsch and Gupta (1988), and Bauer, Bertsch, and Schulz (1992).

Material related to our discussion in Section 10.6 is available from Chandy and Sherman (1989a), Bagrodia, Chandy, and Liao (1991), and Jha and Bagrodia (1994).

Bibliography

Acharya, A., and B. R. Badrinath (1992). Recording distributed snapshots based on causal order of message delivery. *Information Processing Letters* **44**, 317–321.

Afek, Y., B. Awerbuch, and E. Gafni (1987). Applying static network protocols to dynamic networks. In *Proc. of the Annual Symposium on Foundations of Computer Science*, 358–370.

Afek, Y., and E. Gafni (1991). Time and message bounds for election in synchronous and asynchronous complete networks. *SIAM J. on Computing* **20**, 376–394.

Afek, Y., and E. Gafni (1994). Distributed algorithms for unidirectional networks. *SIAM J. on Computing* **23**, 1152–1178.

Afek, Y., and S. Kutten (1991). Memory-efficient self stabilizing protocols for general networks. In *Proc. of the (1990) International Workshop on Distributed Algorithms*, 15–28.

Afek, Y., and M. Ricklin (1993). Sparser: a paradigm for running distributed algorithms. *J. of Algorithms* **14**, 316–328.

Agarwal, A., R. Bianchini, D. Chaiken, K. Johnson, D. Kranz, J. Kubiatowicz, B.-H. Lim, K. Mackenzie, and D. Yeung (1995). The MIT Alewife machine: architecture and performance. In *Proc. of the Annual International Symposium on Computer Architecture*, 2–13.

Aggarwal, S., and S. Kutten (1993). Time optimal self-stabilizing spanning tree algorithms. In *Proc. of the Conference on Foundations of Software Technology and Theoretical Computer Science*, 400–410.

Agrawal, D., and A. E. Abbadi (1989). An efficient solution to the distributed mutual exclusion problem. In *Proc. of the Annual ACM Symposium on Principles of Distributed Computing*, 193–200.

Ahuja, R. K., T. L. Magnanti, and J. B. Orlin (1989). Network flows. In G. L. Nemhauser, A. H. G. Rinnooy Kan, and M. J. Todd (Eds.), *Handbooks in Operations Research and Management Science, Vol. 1: Optimization*, 211–369. North-Holland, Amsterdam, The Netherlands.

Ahuja, R. K., T. L. Magnanti, and J. B. Orlin (1993). *Network flows: Theory, Algorithms, and Applications*. Prentice-Hall, Englewood Cliffs, NJ.

Aichelin, J., and G. Bertsch (1985). Numerical simulation of medium energy heavy ion reactions. *Physical Review C* **31**, 1730–1738.

Akl, S. G. (1989). *The Design and Analysis of Parallel Algorithms*. Prentice-Hall, Englewood Cliffs, NJ.

Alagar, S., and S. Venkatesan (1994). An optimal algorithm for distributed snapshots with causal message ordering. *Information Processing Letters* **50**, 311–316.

Ali, H. H., and H. El-Rewini (1993). Task allocation in distributed systems: a split graph model. *J. of Combinatorial Mathematics and Combinatorial Computing* **14**, 15–32.

Ali, H. H., and H. El-Rewini (1994). On the intractability of task allocation in distributed systems. *Parallel Processing Letters* **4**, 149–157.

Almasi, G. S., and A. Gottlieb (1989). *Highly Parallel Computing*. Benjamin/Cummings, Redwood City, CA.

Alonso, J. M., A. A. Frutos, and R. B. Palacio (1994). Conservative and optimistic distributed simulation in massively parallel computers: a comparative study. In *Proc. of the International Conference on Massively Parallel Computing Systems*, 528–532.

Anderson, R. J., and J. C. Setubal (1992). On the parallel implementation of Goldberg's maximum flow algorithm. In *Proc. of the Annual ACM Symposium on Parallel Algorithms and Architectures*, 168–177.

Andrews, G. R. (1991). *Concurrent Programming: Principles and Practice*. Benjamin/Cummings, Menlo Park, CA.

Andrews, G. R., and F. B. Schneider (1983). Concepts and notations for concurrent programming. *ACM Computing Surveys* **15**, 3–43.

Angluin, D. (1980). Local and global properties in networks of processors. In *Proc. of the Annual ACM Symposium on Theory of Computing*, 82–93.

Arjomandi, E., M. J. Fischer, and N. A. Lynch (1983). Efficiency of synchronous versus asynchronous distributed systems. *J. of the ACM* **30**, 449–456.

Arlauskas, S. (1988). iPSC/2 system: a second generation hypercube. In *Proc. of the Conference on Hypercube Concurrent Computers and Applications, Vol. 1*, 38–42.

Attiya, H., and M. Snir (1985). Computing on an anonymous ring. In *Proc. of the Annual ACM Symposium on Principles of Distributed Computing*, 196–203.

Attiya, H., and M. Snir (1991). Better computing on the anonymous ring. *J. of Algorithms* **12**, 204–238.

Attiya, H., M. Snir, and M. K. Warmuth (1988). Computing on an anonymous ring. *J. of the ACM* **35**, 845–875.

Awerbuch, B. (1985a). Complexity of network synchronization. *J. of the ACM* **32**, 804–823.

Awerbuch, B. (1985b). Reducing complexities of the distributed max-flow and breadth-first-search algorithms by means of network synchronization. *Networks* **15**, 425–437.

Awerbuch, B. (1987). Optimal distributed algorithms for minimum weight spanning tree, counting, leader election, and related problems: detailed summary. In *Proc. of the Annual ACM Symposium on Theory of Computing*, 230–240.

Awerbuch, B. (1989). Distributed shortest paths algorithms. In *Proc. of the Annual ACM Symposium on Theory of Computing*, 490–500.

Awerbuch, B., S. Kutten, and D. Peleg (1994). On buffer-economical store-and-forward deadlock prevention. *IEEE Trans. on Communications* **42**, 2934–2937.

Awerbuch, B., and D. Peleg (1990). Network synchronization with polylogarithmic overhead. In *Proc. of the Annual Symposium on Foundations of Computer Science*, 514–522.

Awerbuch, B., and G. Varghese (1991). Distributed program checking: a paradigm for building self-stabilizing distributed protocols. In *Proc. of the Annual Symposium on Foundations of Computer Science*, 258–267.

Ayani, R., and H. Rajaei (1994). Parallel simulation based on conservative time windows: a performance study. *Concurrency: Practice and Experience* **6**, 119–142.

Bae, J. J., and T. Suda (1991). Survey of traffic control schemes and protocols in ATM networks. *Proc. of the IEEE* **79**, 170–189.

Bagheri, B., A. Ilin, and L. Ridgeway Scott (1994). A comparison of distributed and shared memory scalable architectures. 1. KSR shared memory. In *Proc. of the Scalable High-Performance Computing Conference*, 9–16.

Bagrodia, R., K. M. Chandy, and W. T. Liao (1991). A unifying framework for distributed simulation. *ACM Trans. on Modeling and Computer Simulation* **1**, 348–385.

Barbosa, V. C. (1986). Concurrency in systems with neighborhood constraints. Ph.D. dissertation, Computer Science Department, University of California, Los Angeles, CA.

Barbosa, V. C. (1990a). Strategies for the prevention of communication deadlocks in distributed parallel programs. *IEEE Trans. on Software Engineering* **16**, 1311–1316.

Barbosa, V. C. (1990b). Blocking versus nonblocking interprocess communication: a note on the effect on concurrency. *Information Processing Letters* **36**, 171–175.

Barbosa, V. C. (1991). On the time-driven parallel simulation of two classes of complex systems. Technical report ES-248/91, COPPE/UFRJ, Rio de Janeiro, Brazil.

Barbosa, V. C. (1993). *Massively Parallel Models of Computation: Distributed Parallel Processing in Artificial Intelligence and Optimization*. Ellis Horwood, Chichester, UK.

Barbosa, V. C., and M. C. S. Boeres (1990). An Occam-based evaluation of a parallel version of simulated annealing. In *Proc. of Euromicro-90*, 85–92.

Barbosa, V. C., L. M. de A. Drummond, and A. L. H. Hellmuth (1991a). From distributed algorithms to Occam programs by successive refinements. Technical report ES-237/91, COPPE/UFRJ, Rio de Janeiro, Brazil.

Barbosa, V. C., L. M. de A. Drummond, and A. L. H. Hellmuth (1991b). An integrated software environment for large-scale Occam programming. In *Proc. of Euromicro-91*, 393–400.

Barbosa, V. C., L. M. de A. Drummond, and A. L. H. Hellmuth (1994). From distributed algorithms to Occam programs by successive refinements. *The J. of Systems and Software* **26**, 257–272.

Barbosa, V. C., and F. M. G. França (1988). Specification of a communication virtual processor for parallel processing systems. In *Proc. of Euromicro-88*, 511–518.

Barbosa, V. C., and E. Gafni (1987). Concurrency in heavily loaded neighborhood-constrained systems. In *Proc. of the International Conference on Distributed Computing Systems*, 448–455.

Barbosa, V. C., and E. Gafni (1989a). A distributed implementation of simulated annealing. *J. of Parallel and Distributed Computing* **6**, 411–434.

Barbosa, V. C., and E. Gafni (1989b). Concurrency in heavily loaded neighborhood-constrained systems. *ACM Trans. on Programming Languages and Systems* **11**, 562–584.

Barbosa, V. C., and H. K. Huang (1988). Static task allocation in heterogeneous distributed systems. Technical report ES-149/88, COPPE/UFRJ, Rio de Janeiro, Brazil.

Barbosa, V. C., and P. M. V. Lima (1990). On the distributed parallel simulation of Hopfield's neural networks. *Software—Practice and Experience* **20**, 967–983.

Barbosa, V. C., and S. C. S. Porto (1995). An algorithm for FIFO message delivery among migrating tasks. *Information Processing Letters* **53**, 261–267.

Bar-Noy, A., and D. Dolev (1993). A partial equivalence between shared-memory and message-passing in an asynchronous fail-stop distributed environment. *Mathematical Systems Theory* **26**, 21–39.

Bauer, W., G. F. Bertsch, and H. Schulz (1992). Bubble and ring formation in nuclear fragmentation. Technical report MSUCL-840, National Superconducting Cyclotron Laboratory, Michigan State University.

Becher, J. D., and C. E. McDowell (1992). Debugging the MP-2001. In *Proc. of New Frontiers, A Workshop on Future Directions of Massively Parallel Processing*, 48–57.

Bell, G. (1992). Ultracomputers: a teraflop before its time. *Comm. of the ACM* **35**(8), 26–47.

Ben-Ari, M. (1982). *Principles of Concurrent Programming*. Prentice-Hall, Englewood Cliffs, NJ.

Berge, C. (1976). *Graphs and Hypergraphs*. North-Holland, Amsterdam, The Netherlands.

Bernard, G., D. Steve, and M. Simatic (1993). A survey of load sharing in networks of workstations. *Distributed Systems Engineering* **1**, 75–86.

Bertsch, G. F., and S. D. Gupta (1988). A guide to microscopic models for intermediate energy heavy ion collisions. *Physics Reports* **160**, 190–233.

Bertsekas, D. P., and R. G. Gallager (1987). *Data Networks*. Prentice-Hall, Englewood Cliffs, NJ.

Bertsekas, D. P., and J. N. Tsitsiklis (1989). *Parallel and Distributed Computation: Numerical Methods*. Prentice-Hall, Englewood Cliffs, NJ.

Bertsekas, D. P., and J. N. Tsitsiklis (1991). Some aspects of parallel and distributed iterative algorithms—a survey. *Automatica* **27**, 3–21.

Bhargava, B., and S. R. Lian (1988). Independent checkpointing and concurrent rollback for recovery: An optimistic approach. In *Proc. of the IEEE Symposium on Reliable Distributed System*, 3–12.

Blanchard, T. D., T. W. Lake, and S. J. Turner (1994). Cooperative acceleration: robust conservative distributed discrete event simulation. In *Proc. of the Workshop on Parallel and Distributed Simulation*, 58–64.

Blumofe, R. D., and D. S. Park (1994). Scheduling large-scale parallel computations on networks of workstations. In *Proc. of the IEEE International Symposium on High Performance Distributed Computing*, 96–105.

Bodlaender, H. L., S. Moran, and M. K. Warmuth (1994). The distributed bit complexity of the ring: from the anonymous to the non-anonymous case. *Information and Computation* **108**, 34–50.

Bodlaender, H. L., and G. Tel (1990). Bit-optimal election in synchronous rings. *Information Processing Letters* **36**, 53–56.

Bollobás, B. (1985). *Random Graphs*. Academic Press, London, UK.

Bondy, J. A., and U. S. R. Murty (1976). *Graph Theory with Applications*. North-Holland, New York, NY.

Bouabdallah, A., and J.-C. Konig (1992). An improvement of Maekawa's mutual exclusion algorithm to make it fault-tolerant. *Parallel Processing Letters* **2**, 283–290.

Bracha, G., and S. Toueg (1984). A distributed algorithm for generalized deadlock detection. In *Proc. of the Annual ACM Symposium on Principles of Distributed Computing*, 285–301.

Bryant, R. E. (1977). Simulation of packet communication architecture computer systems. Technical report MIT/LCS/TR 88, Laboratory for Computer Science, MIT, Cambridge, MA.

Brzezinski, J., J.-M. Hélary, and M. Raynal (1993). Termination detection in a very general distributed computing model. In *Proc. of the International Conference on Distributed Computing Systems*, 374–381.

Burns, A. (1988). *Programming in Occam2*. Addison-Wesley, Wokingham, England.

Burns, J. E., and J. Pachl (1989). Uniform self-stabilizing rings. *ACM Trans. on Programming Languages and Systems* **11**, 330–344.

Calabrese, A., and F. M. G. França (1994). A randomised distributed primer for the updating control of ANNs. In *Proc. of the International Conference on Artificial Neural Networks*, 585–588.

Carvalho, O., and G. Roucairol (1983). On mutual exclusion in computer networks. *Comm. of the ACM* **26**, 146–147.

Chandrasekaran, S., and S. Venkatesan (1990). A message-optimal algorithm for distributed termination detection. *J. of Parallel and Distributed Computing* **8**, 245–252.

Chandy, K. M., and L. Lamport (1985). Distributed snapshots: determining global states of distributed systems. *ACM Trans. on Computer Systems* **3**, 63–75.

Chandy, K. M., and J. Misra (1979). Distributed simulation: a case study in design and verification of distributed programs. *IEEE Trans. on Software Engineering* **5**, 440–452.

Chandy, K. M., and J. Misra (1981). Asynchronous distributed simulation via a sequence of parallel computations. *Comm. of the ACM* **24**, 198–206.

Chandy, K. M., and J. Misra (1984). The drinking philosophers problem. *ACM Trans. on Programming Languages and Systems* **6**, 632–646.

Chandy, K. M., and J. Misra (1988). *Parallel Program Design: A Foundation.* Addison-Wesley, Reading, MA.

Chandy, K. M., and R. Sherman (1989a). Space-time and simulation. In *Distributed Simulation, Proc. of the SCS Multiconference*, 53–57.

Chandy, K. M., and R. Sherman (1989b). The conditional event approach to distributed simulation. In *Distributed Simulation, Proc. of the SCS Multiconference*, 93–99.

Chang, E. (1980). *n* philosophers: an exercise in distributed control. *Computer Networks* **4**, 71–76.

Chang, H.-K., and S.-M. Yuan (1994). Message complexity of the tree quorum algorithm for distributed mutual exclusion. In *Proc. of the International Conference on Distributed Computing Systems*, 76–80.

Chaves Filho, E. M., and V. C. Barbosa (1992). Time sharing in hypercube multiprocessors. In *Proc. of the IEEE Symposium on Parallel and Distributed Processing*, 354–359.

Chen, H., and J. Tang (1994). An efficient method for mutual exclusion in truly distributed systems. In *Proc. of the International Conference on Distributed Computing Systems*, 97–104.

Chen, N.-S., H.-P. Yu, and S.-T. Huang (1991). A self-stabilizing algorithm for constructing spanning trees. *Information Processing Letters* **39**, 147–151.

Chin, F., and H. F. Ting (1990). Improving the time complexity of message-optimal distributed algorithms for minimum-weight spanning trees. *SIAM J. on Computing* **19**, 612–626.

Choi, J., B. P. Miller, and R. H. B. Netzer (1991). Techniques for debugging parallel programs with flowback analysis. *ACM Trans. on Programming Languages and Systems* **13**, 491–530.

Chou, C.-T., and E. Gafni (1988). Understanding and verifying distributed algorithms using stratified decomposition. In *Proc. of the Annual ACM Symposium on Principles of Distributed Computing*, 44–65.

Choy, M., and A. K. Singh (1993). Distributed job scheduling using snapshots. In *Proc. of the International Workshop on Distributed Algorithms*, 145–159.

Collin, Z., and S. Dolev (1994). Self-stabilizing depth-first search. *Information Processing Letters* **49**, 297–301.

Cooper, R., and K. Marzullo (1991). Consistent detection of global predicates. In *Proc. of the ACM Workshop on Parallel and Distributed Debugging*, 167–174.

Cormen, T. H., C. E. Leiserson, and R. L. Rivest (1990). *Introduction to Algorithms*. The MIT Press, Cambridge, MA.

D'Souza, L. M., X. Fan, and P. A. Wilsey (1994). pGVT: an algorithm for accurate GVT estimation. In *Proc. of the Workshop on Parallel and Distributed Simulation*, 102–109.

Dally, W. J. (1990). Network and processor architecture for message-driven computers. In R. Suaya and G. Birtwistle (Eds.), *VLSI and Parallel Computation*, 140–222. Morgan Kaufmann, San Mateo, CA.

Dally, W. J., L. Chao, A. Chien, S. Hassoun, W. Horwat, J. Kaplan, P. Song, B. Totty, and S. Wills (1987). Architecture of a message-driven processor. In *Proc. of the Annual International Symposium on Computer Architecture*, 189–196.

Dally, W. J., and C. L. Seitz (1987). Deadlock-free message routing in multiprocessor interconnection networks. *IEEE Trans. on Computers* **36**, 547–553.

Das, S. R., and R. M. Fujimoto (1994). An adaptive memory management protocol for Time Warp parallel simulation. In *Proc. of the ACM SIGMETRICS Conference on Measurement and Modeling of Computer Systems*, 201–210.

de Carvalho, L. A. V., and V. C. Barbosa (1992). Fast linear system solution by neural networks. *Operations Research Letters* **11**, 141–145.

De Vries, R. C. (1990). Reducing null messages in Misra's distributed discrete event simulation method. *IEEE Trans. on Software Engineering* **16**, 82–91.

Dijkstra, E. W. (1968). Cooperating sequential processes. In F. Genuys (Ed.), *Programming Languages*, 43–112. Academic Press, New York, NY.

Dijkstra, E. W. (1974). Self-stabilizing systems in spite of distributed control. *Comm. of the ACM* **17**, 643–644.

Dijkstra, E. W. (1975). Guarded commands, nondeterminacy and formal derivation of programs. *Comm. of the ACM* **18**, 453–457.

Dijkstra, E. W. (1986). A belated proof of self-stabilization. *Distributed Computing* **1**, 5–6.

Dijkstra, E. W., and C. S. Scholten (1980). Termination detection for diffusing computations. *Information Processing Letters* **11**, 1–4.

DIMACS (Center for Discrete Mathematics and Theoretical Computer Science) (1990). The first DIMACS international algorithm implementation challenge: general information; problem definitions and specifications; the core experiments. DIMACS, Rutgers University, Piscataway, NJ.

Dinic, E. A. (1970). Algorithm for solution of a problem of maximum flow in networks with power estimation. *Soviet Math. Doklady* **11**, 1277–1280.

Dolev, S. (1993). Optimal time self stabilization in dynamic systems. In *Proc. of the International Workshop on Distributed Algorithms*, 160–173.

Dolev, S., and A. Israeli (1992). Uniform dynamic self-stabilizing leader election. In *Proc. of the (1991) International Workshop on Distributed Algorithms*, 167–180.

Dolev, S., A. Israeli, and S. Moran (1991). Resource bounds for self-stabilizing message driven protocols. In *Proc. of the Annual ACM Symposium on Principles of Distributed Computing*, 281–293.

Drummond, L. M. de A. (1990). Design and implementation of a communication virtual processor. M.Sc. thesis, Programa de Engenharia de Sistemas e Computação, COPPE/UFRJ, Rio de Janeiro, Brazil. In Portuguese.

Drummond, L. M. de A., and V. C. Barbosa (1994). Distributed breakpoint detection in message-passing programs. Technical report ES-306/94, COPPE/UFRJ, Rio de Janeiro, Brazil.

Dwork, C., and Y. Moses (1990). Knowledge and common knowledge in a Byzantine environment: crash failures. *Information and Computation* **88**, 156–186.

Edmonds, J. (1965). Maximum matching and a polyhedron with 0, 1-vertices. *J. of Research of the National Bureau of Standards* **69B**, 125–130.

Eizirik, L. M. R., V. C. Barbosa, and S. B. T. Mendes (1993). A Bayesian-network approach to lexical disambiguation. *Cognitive Science* **17**, 257–283.

Eskicioğlu, M. R., and L.-F. Cabrera (1991). Process migration: an annotated bibliography. Technical Report RJ 7935 (72918), IBM Research Division, San Jose, CA.

Even, S. (1979). *Graph Algorithms*. Computer Science Press, Potomac, MD.

Fagin, R., J. Y. Halpern, and M. Y. Vardi (1992). What can machines know? On the properties of knowledge in distributed systems. *J. of the ACM* **39**, 328–376.

Fagin, R., and M. Y. Vardi (1986). Knowledge and implicit knowledge in a distributed environment: preliminary report. In *Proc. of the Conference on Theoretical Aspects of Reasoning about Knowledge*, 187–206.

Feldman, Y., and E. Shapiro (1992). Spatial machines: a more realistic approach to parallel computation. *Comm. of the ACM* **35**(10), 60–73.

Fernandes, E. S. T., C. L. de Amorim, V. C. Barbosa, F. M. G. França, and A. F. de Souza (1989). MPH: a hybrid parallel machine. *Microprocessing and Microprogramming* **25**, 229–232.

Fidge, C. (1991). Logical time in distributed computing systems. *Computer* **24**(8), 28–33.

Fiorini, S., and R. J. Wilson (1977). *Edge-Colourings of Graphs*. Pitman, London, England.

Fischer, M. J., and N. Immerman (1986). Foundations of knowledge for distributed systems. In *Proc. of the Conference on Theoretical Aspects of Reasoning about Knowledge*, 171–185.

Flatebo, M., and A. K. Datta (1992a). Distributed deadlock detection algorithms. *Parallel Processing Letters* **2**, 21–30.

Flatebo, M., and A. K. Datta (1992b). Self-stabilizing deadlock detection algorithms. In *Proc. of the ACM Computer Science Conference*, 117–122.

Flatebo, M., and A. K. Datta (1992c). Simulation of self-stabilizing algorithms in distributed systems. In *Proc. of the Annual Simulation Symposium*, 32–41.

Flatebo, M., and A. K. Datta (1994). Two-state self-stabilizing algorithms for token rings. *IEEE Trans. on Software Engineering* **20**, 500–504.

Ford, Jr., L. R., and D. R. Fulkerson (1962). *Flows in Networks*. Princeton University Press, Princeton, NJ.

Fox, G. C., and W. Furmanski (1988). Load balancing loosely synchronous problems with a neural network. In *Proc. of the Conference on Hypercube Concurrent Computers and Applications, Vol. 1*, 241–278.

Fox, G. C., M. A. Johnson, G. A. Lyzenga, S. W. Otto, J. K. Salmon, and D. W. Walker (1988). *Solving Problems on Concurrent Processors, Vol. 1*. Prentice-Hall, Englewood Cliffs, NJ.

Fox, G. C., A. Kolawa, and R. Williams (1987). The implementation of a dynamic load balancer. In M. T. Heath (Ed.), *Hypercube Multiprocessors 1987*, 114–121. SIAM, Philadelphia, PA.

Fox, G. C., and S. W. Otto (1986). Concurrent computation and the theory of complex systems. In M. T. Heath (Ed.), *Hypercube Multiprocessors 1986*, 244–268. SIAM, Philadelphia, PA.

Fox, G. C., R. D. Williams, and P. C. Messina (1994). *Parallel Computing Works!* Morgan Kaufmann, San Mateo, CA.

França, F. M. G. (1994). Neural networks as neighbourhood-constrained systems. Ph.D. thesis, Department of Electrical and Electronic Engineering, Imperial College of Science, Technology, and Medicine, London, UK.

Freitas, L. de P. Sá, and V. C. Barbosa (1991). Experiments in parallel heuristic search. In *Proc. of the International Conference on Parallel Processing*, III-62–65.

Fromentin, E., and M. Raynal (1994). Inevitable global states: a concept to detect unstable properties of distributed computations in an observer independent way. In *Proc. of the IEEE Symposium on Parallel and Distributed Processing*, 242–248.

Fujimoto, R. M. (1990a). Parallel discrete event simulation. *Comm. of the ACM* **33**(10), 30–53.

Fujimoto, R. M. (1990b). Optimistic approaches to parallel discrete event simulation. *Trans. of the Society for Computer Simulation* **7**, 153–191.

Fujimoto, R. M. (1993). Parallel and distributed discrete event simulation: algorithms and applications. In *Proc. of the Winter Simulation Conference*, 106–114.

Fulkerson, D. R. (1972). Anti-blocking polyhedra. *J. of Combinatorial Theory, Series B* **12**, 50–71.

Gafni, E. (1985). Improvements in the time complexity of two message-optimal election algorithms. In *Proc. of the Annual ACM Symposium on Principles of Distributed Computing*, 175–185.

Gafni, E. (1986). Perspectives on distributed network protocols: a case for building blocks. In *Proc. of Milcom-86*.

Gafni, E., and V. C. Barbosa (1986). Optimal snapshots and the maximum flow in precedence graphs. In *Proc. of the Allerton Conference on Communication, Control, and Computing*, 1089–1097.

Gafni, E. M., and D. P. Bertsekas (1981). Distributed algorithms for generating loop-free routes in networks with frequently changing topology. *IEEE Trans. on Communications* **29**, 11–18.

Gallager, R. G., P. A. Humblet, and P. M. Spira (1983). A distributed algorithm for minimum weight spanning trees. *ACM Trans. on Programming Languages and Systems* **5**, 66–77.

Garcia-Molina, H., F. Germano, and W. Kohler (1984). Debugging a distributed computing system. *IEEE Trans. on Software Engineering* **10**, 210–219.

Garey, M. R., and D. S. Johnson (1979). *Computers and Intractability: A Guide to the Theory of NP-Completeness*. Freeman, New York, NY.

Garg, V. K., and A. I. Tomlinson (1993). Detecting relational global predicates in distributed systems. In *Proc. of the ACM/ONR Workshop on Parallel and Distributed Debugging*, 21–31.

Garg, V. K., and B. Waldecker (1994). Detection of weak and unstable predicates in distributed programs. *IEEE Trans. on Parallel and Distributed Systems* **5**, 299–307.

Garofalakis, J., P. Spirakis, B. Tampakas, and S. Rajsbaum (1994). Tentative and definite distributed computations: an optimistic approach to network synchronization. *Theoretical Computer Science* **128**, 63–74.

Gaughan, P. T., and S. Yalamanchili (1993). Adaptive routing protocols for hypercube interconnection networks. *Computer* **26**(5), 12–23.

Gehringer, E. F., D. P. Siewiorek, and Z. Segall (1987). *Parallel Processing: The Cm* Experience*. Digital Press, Bedford, MA.

Geman, S., and D. Geman (1984). Stochastic relaxation, Gibbs distributions, and the Bayesian restoration of images. *IEEE Trans. on Pattern Analysis and Machine Intelligence* **6**, 721–741.

Gentleman, W. M. (1981). Message passing between sequential processes: the reply primitive and the administrator concept. *Software—Practice and Experience* **11**, 435–466.

Gerla, M., and L. Kleinrock (1982). Flow control protocols. In P. E. Green, Jr. (Ed.), *Computer Network Architectures and Protocols*, 361–412. Plenum Press, New York, NY.

Ghosh, S. (1991). Binary self-stabilization in distributed systems. *Information Processing Letters* **40**, 153–159.

Ghosh, S. (1993). An alternative solution to a problem on self-stabilization. *ACM Trans. on Programming Languages and Systems* **15**, 735–742.

Ghosh, S., and M. H. Karaata (1993). A self-stabilizing algorithm for coloring planar graphs. *Distributed Computing* **7**, 55–59.

Gibbons, A., and W. Rytter (1988). *Efficient Parallel Algorithms*. Cambridge University Press, Cambridge, England.

Goldberg, A. P., A. Gopal, A. Lowry, and R. Strom (1991). Restoring consistent global states of distributed computations. In *Proc. of the ACM/ONR Workshop on Parallel and Distributed Debugging*, 144–154.

Goldberg, A. V., E. Tardos, and R. E. Tarjan (1990). Network flow algorithms. In B. Korte, L. Lovász, H. J. Prömel, and A. Schrijver (Eds.), *Algorithms and Combinatorics, Vol. 9*, 101–164. Springer-Verlag, Berlin, Germany.

Goldberg, A. V., and R. E. Tarjan (1988). A new approach to the maximum-flow problem. *J. of the ACM* **35**, 921–940.

Gouda, M. G., R. R. Howell, and L. E. Rosier (1990). The instability of self-stabilization. *Acta Informatica* **27**, 697–724.

Grunwald, D. C., and D. A. Reed (1988). Networks for parallel processors: measurements and prognostications. In *Proc. of the Conference on Hypercube Concurrent Computers and Applications, Vol. 1*, 600–608.

Günther, K. D. (1981). Prevention of deadlocks in packet-switched data transport systems. *IEEE Trans. on Communications* **29**, 512–524.

Haban, D., and W. Weigel (1988). Global events and global breakpoints in distributed systems. In *Proc. of the International Conference on System Sciences*, II-166–175.

Haldar, S. (1994). An all pairs shortest paths distributed algorithm using $2n^2$ messages. In *Proc. of the (1993) International Workshop on Graph-Theoretic Concepts in Computer Science*, 350–363.

Halpern, J. Y. (1986). Reasoning about knowledge: an overview. In *Proc. of the Conference on Theoretical Aspects of Reasoning about Knowledge*, 1–17.

Halpern, J. Y., and R. Fagin (1989). Modelling knowledge and action in distributed systems. *Distributed Computing* **3**, 159–177.

Halpern, J. Y., and Y. Moses (1990). Knowledge and common knowledge in a distributed environment. *J. of the ACM* **37**, 549–587.

Halpern, J. Y., and Y. Moses (1992). A guide to completeness and complexity for modal logics of knowledge and belief. *Artificial Intelligence* **54**, 319–379.

Harary, F. (1969). *Graph Theory*. Addison-Wesley, Reading, MA.

Heinlein, J., K. Gharachorloo, S. A. Dresser, and A. Gupta (1994). Integration of message passing and shared memory in the Stanford FLASH multiprocessor. In *Proc. of the International Conference on Architectural Support for Programming Languages and Operating Systems*, 38–50.

Heinrich, M., J. Kuskin, D. Ofelt, J. Heinlein, J. P. Singh, R. Simoni, K. Gharachorloo, J. Baxter, D. Nakahira, M. Horowitz, A. Gupta, M. Rosenblum, and J. Hennessy (1994). The performance impact of flexibility in the Stanford FLASH multiprocessor. In *Proc. of the International Conference on Architectural Support for Programming Languages and Operating Systems*, 274–285.

Hélary, J.-M. (1989). Observing global states of asynchronous distributed applications. In *Proc. of the International Workshop on Distributed Algorithms*, 124–135.

Hélary, J.-M., A. Mostefaoui, and M. Raynal (1994). A general scheme for token- and tree-based distributed mutual exclusion algorithms. *IEEE Trans. on Parallel and Distributed Systems* **5**, 1185–1196.

Hélary, J.-M., and M. Raynal (1994). Towards the construction of distributed detection programs, with an application to distributed termination. *Distributed*

Computing **7**, 137–147.

Hellmuth, A. L. H. (1991). Tools for the development of distributed parallel programs. M.Sc. thesis, Programa de Engenharia de Sistemas e Computação, COPPE/UFRJ, Rio de Janeiro, Brazil. In Portuguese.

Hillis, W. D. (1985). *The Connection Machine*. The MIT Press, Cambridge, MA.

Hinton, G. E., T. J. Sejnowski, and D. H. Ackley (1984). Boltzmann machines: constraint satisfaction networks that learn. Technical report CMU-CS-84-119, Computer Science Department, Carnegie-Mellon University, Pittsburgh, PA.

Hoare, C. A. R. (1978). Communicating sequential processes. *Comm. of the ACM* **21**, 666–677.

Hoare, C. A. R. (1984). *Communicating Sequential Processes*. Prentice-Hall, London, England.

Hoover, D., and J. Poole (1992). A distributed self-stabilizing solution to the dining philosophers problem. *Information Processing Letters* **41**, 209–213.

Hopfield, J. J. (1982). Neural networks and physical systems with emergent collective computational abilities. *Proc. of the National Academy of Sciences USA* **79**, 2554–2558.

Hopfield, J. J. (1984). Neurons with graded response have collective computational properties like those of two-state neurons. *Proc. of the National Academy of Sciences USA* **81**, 3088–3092.

Hsu, S.-C., and S.-T. Huang (1992). A self-stabilizing algorithm for maximal matching. *Information Processing Letters* **43**, 77–81.

Huang, S.-T. (1989). Termination detection by using distributed snapshots. *Information Processing Letters* **32**, 113–119.

Huang, S.-T., and N.-S. Chen (1992). A self-stabilizing algorithm for constructing breadth-first trees. *Information Processing Letters* **41**, 109–117.

Huang, S.-T., and N.-S. Chen (1993). Self-stabilizing depth-first token circulation on networks. *Distributed Computing* **7**, 61–66.

Huang, S.-T., L.-C. Wuu, and M.-S. Tsai (1994). Distributed execution model for self-stabilizing systems. In *Proc. of the International Conference on Distributed Computing Systems*, 432–439.

Hurfin, M., N. Plouzeau, and M. Raynal (1993). Detecting atomic sequences of predicates in distributed computations. In *Proc. of the ACM/ONR Workshop on Parallel and Distributed Debugging*, 32–40.

Israeli, A., and M. Jalfon (1991). Self-stabilizing ring orientation. In *Proc. of the (1990) International Workshop on Distributed Algorithms*, 1–14.

Israeli, A., and M. Jalfon (1993). Uniform self-stabilizing ring orientation. *Information and Computation* **104**, 175–196.

Itkis, G., and L. Levin (1994). Fast and lean self-stabilizing asynchronous protocols. In *Proc. of the Annual Symposium on Foundations of Computer Science*, 226–239.

JáJá, J. (1992). *An Introduction to Parallel Algorithms*. Addison-Wesley, Reading, MA.

Janssen, W., and J. Zwiers (1992). From sequential layers to distributed processes. Deriving a distributed minimum weight spanning tree algorithm. In *Proc. of the Annual ACM Symposium on Principles of Distributed Computing*, 215–227.

Jefferson, D. R. (1985). Virtual time. *ACM Trans. on Programming Languages and Systems* **7**, 404–425.

Jha, V., and R. L. Bagrodia (1994). A unified framework for conservative and optimistic distributed simulation. In *Proc. of the Workshop on Parallel and Distributed Simulation*, 12–19.

Jiang, T. (1989). The synchronization of nonuniform networks of finite automata. In *Proc. of the Annual Symposium on Foundations of Computer Science*, 376–381.

Joyce, J., G. Lomow, K. Slind, and B. W. Unger (1987). Monitoring distributed systems. *ACM Trans. on Computer Systems* **5**, 121–150.

Karp, R. M. (1972). Reducibility among combinatorial problems. In R. E. Miller and J. W. Thatcher (Eds.), *Complexity of Computer Computations*, 85–103. Plenum Press, New York, NY.

Karp, R. M., and V. Ramachandran (1990). Parallel algorithms for shared-memory machines. In J. van Leeuwen (Ed.), *Handbook of Theoretical Computer Science, Vol. A*, 869–941. The MIT Press, Cambridge, MA.

Karzanov, A. V. (1974). Determining the maximal flow in a network by the method of preflows. *Soviet Math. Doklady* **15**, 434–437.

Katz, S., and K. J. Perry (1993). Self-stabilizing extensions for message-passing systems. *Distributed Computing* **7**, 17–26.

Kavianpour, A., and N. Bagherzadeh (1990). A three coloring algorithm for distributed termination detection of nonFIFO distributed systems. In *Proc. of the Annual Parallel Processing Symposium*, II-708–718.

Kermani, P., and L. Kleinrock (1979). Virtual cut-through: a new computer communication switching technique. *Computer Networks* **3**, 267–286.

Kessels, J. L. W. (1988). An exercise in proving self-stabilization with a variant function. *Information Processing Letters* **29**, 39–42.

Kim, K. H., J. H. You, and A. Abouelnaga (1986). A scheme for coordinated execution of independently designed recoverable distributed processes. In *Proc. of the IEEE Fault-Tolerant Computing Symposium*, 130–135.

Kirkpatrick, S., C. D. Gelatt, and M. P. Vecchi (1983). Optimization by simulated annealing. *Science* **220**, 671–680.

Koo, R., and S. Toueg (1987). Checkpointing and rollback-recovery for distributed systems. *IEEE Trans. on Software engineering* **13**, 23–31.

Kranakis, E., D. Krizanc, and J. van den Berg (1994). Computing Boolean functions on anonymous networks. *Information and Computation* **114**, 214–236.

Kranz, D., K. Johnson, A. Agarwal, J. Kubiatowicz, and B.-H. Lim (1993). Integrating message-passing and shared-memory: early experience. In *Proc. of the ACM SIGPLAN Symposium on Principles and Practice of Parallel Programming*, 54–63.

Krumme, D. W., K. N. Venkataraman, and G. Cybenko (1986). Hypercube embedding is *NP*-complete. In M. T. Heath (Ed.), *Hypercube Multiprocessors 1986*, 148–157. SIAM, Philadelphia, PA.

Kshemkalyani, A. D., and M. Singhal (1994). On characterization and correctness of distributed deadlock detection. *J. of Parallel and Distributed Computing* **22**, 44–59.

Kumar, D. (1992). Development of a class of distributed termination detection algorithms. *IEEE Trans. on Knowledge and Data Engineering* **4**, 145–155.

Kuskin, J., D. Ofelt, M. Heinrich, J. Heinlein, R. Simoni, K. Gharachorloo, J. Chapin, D. Nakahira, J. Baxter, M. Horowitz, A. Gupta, M. Rosenblum, and J. Hennessy (1994). The FLASH multiprocessor. In *Proc. of the Annual International Symposium on Computer Architecture*, 302–313.

Lakshman, T. V., and V. K. Wei (1994). Distributed computing on regular networks with anonymous nodes. *IEEE Trans. on Computers* **43**, 211–218.

Lamport, L. (1978). Time, clocks, and the ordering of events in a distributed system. *Comm. of the ACM* **21**, 558–565.

Lamport, L., and N. A. Lynch (1990). Distributed computing: models and methods. In J. van Leeuwen (Ed.), *Handbook of Theoretical Computer Science, Vol. B*, 1156–1199. The MIT Press, Cambridge, MA.

Lamport, L., R. Shostak, and M. Pease (1982). The Byzantine generals problem. *ACM Trans. on Programming Languages and Systems* **4**, 382–401.

Lawler, E. L. (1976). *Combinatorial Optimization: Networks and Matroids*. Holt, Rinehart, and Winston, New York, NY.

LeBlanc, T., and J. M. Mellor-Crummey (1987). Debugging parallel programs with instant replay. *IEEE Trans. on Computers* **36**, 471–482.

Lehmann, D. (1984). Knowledge, common knowledge and related puzzles. In *Proc. of the Annual ACM Symposium on Principles of Distributed Computing*, 62–67.

Leighton, F. T. (1992). *Introduction to Parallel Algorithms and Architectures: Arrays, Trees, Hypercubes*. Morgan Kaufmann, San Mateo, CA.

Lentfert, P. J. A., and S. D. Swierstra (1993). Towards the formal design of self-stabilizing distributed algorithms. In *Proc. of the Annual Symposium on Theoretical Aspects of Computer Science*, 440–451.

Lin, C., and J. Simon (1992). Observing self-stabilization. In *Proc. of the Annual ACM Symposium on Principles of Distributed Computing*, 113–123.

Lin, Y.-B. (1993). On terminating a distributed discrete event simulation. *J. of Parallel and Distributed Computing* **19**, 364–371.

Lin, Y.-B. (1994). Memory management algorithms for optimistic parallel simulation. *Information Sciences* **77**, 119–140.

Lin, Y.-B., E. D. Lazowska, and J.-L. Baer (1990). Conservative parallel simulation for systems with no lookahead prediction. In *Distributed Simulation, Proc. of the SCS Multiconference*, 144–149.

Lin, Y.-B., E. D. Lazowska, and S.-Y. Hwang (1992). Some properties of conservative parallel discrete event simulation. *J. of Information Science and Engineering* **8**, 61–77.

Lin, Y.-B., and B. R. Preiss (1991). Optimal memory management for time warp parallel simulation. *ACM Trans. on Modeling and Computer Simulation* **1**, 283–307.

Loucks, W. M., and B. R. Preiss (1990). The role of knowledge in distributed simulation. In *Distributed Simulation, Proc. of the SCS Multiconference*, 9–16.

Luenberger, D. G. (1979). *Introduction to Dynamic Systems*. Wiley, New York, NY.

Lynch, N. A. (1980). Fast allocation of nearby resources in a distributed system. In *Proc. of the Annual ACM Symposium on Theory of Computing*, 70–81.

Lynch, N. A. (1981). Upper bounds for static resource allocation in a distributed system. *J. of Computer and System Sciences* **23**, 254–278.

Lynch, N. A., and K. J. Goldman (1989). Distributed algorithms: lecture notes for 6.852, fall 1988. Research seminar series MIT/LCS/RSS 5, Laboratory for Computer Science, MIT, Cambridge, MA.

Lynch, N. A., M. Merritt, W. Weihl, and A. Fekete (1994). *Atomic Transactions*. Morgan Kaufmann, San Mateo, CA.

Lynch, N. A., and M. R. Tuttle (1987). Hierarchical correctness proofs for distributed algorithms. In *Proc. of the Annual ACM Symposium on Principles of Distributed Computing*, 137–151.

Ma, P. R., E. Y. S. Lee, and M. Tsuchiya (1982). A task allocation model for distributed computing systems. *IEEE Trans. on Computers* **31**, 41–47.

Madhuram, S., and A. Kumar (1994). A hybrid approach for mutual exclusion in distributed computing systems. In *Proc. of the IEEE Symposium on Parallel and Distributed Processing*, 18–25.

Maekawa, M. (1985). A $\sqrt{N}$ algorithm for mutual exclusion in decentralized systems. *ACM Trans. on Computer Systems* **3**, 145–159.

Maekawa, M., A. E. Oldehoeft, and R. R. Oldehoeft (1987). *Operating Systems: Advanced Concepts.* Benjamin/Cummings, Menlo Park, CA.

Malka, Y., S. Moran, and S. Zaks (1993). A lower bound on the period length of a distributed scheduler. *Algorithmica* **10**, 383–398.

Malka, Y., and S. Rajsbaum (1992). Analysis of distributed algorithms based on recurrence relations (preliminary version). In *Proc. of the (1991) International Workshop on Distributed Algorithms*, 242–253.

Manabe, Y., and M. Imase (1992). Global conditions in debugging distributed programs. *J. of Parallel and Distributed Computing* **15**, 62–69.

Manna, Z., and A. Pnueli (1992). *The Temporal Logic of Reactive and Concurrent Systems: Specification.* Springer-Verlag, New York, NY.

Martonosi, M., and A. Gupta (1989). Tradeoffs in message passing and shared memory implementations of a standard cell router. In *Proc. of the International Conference on Parallel Processing*, III-88–96.

Mattern, F. (1989). Virtual time and global states of distributed systems. In *Proc. of the International Workshop on Parallel and Distributed Algorithms*, 215–226.

Mattern, F. (1993). Efficient algorithms for distributed snapshots and global virtual time approximation. *J. of Parallel and Distributed Computing* **18**, 423–434.

McDowell, C., and D. Helmbold (1989). Debugging concurrent programs. *ACM Computing Surveys* **21**, 593–622.

Mehl, H. (1990). Speed-up of conservative distributed discrete event simulation methods by speculative computing. In *Advances in Parallel and Distributed Simulation, Proc. of the (1991) SCS Multiconference*, 163–166.

Miller, B., and J. Choi (1988a). Breakpoints and halting in distributed programs. In *Proc. of the International Conference on Distributed Computing Systems*, 316–323.

Miller, B., and J. Choi (1988b). A mechanism for efficient debugging of parallel programs. In *Proc. of the ACM SIGPLAN Conference on Programming Language Design and Implementation*, 135–144.

Misra, J. (1986). Distributed discrete-event simulation. *ACM Computing Surveys* **18**, 39–65.

Moran, S., and M. K. Warmuth (1993). Gap theorems for distributed computation. *SIAM J. on Computing* **22**, 379–394.

Neiger, G., and S. Toueg (1993). Simulating synchronized clocks and common knowledge in distributed systems. *J. of the ACM* **40**, 334–367.

Neilsen, M. L., and M. Mizuno (1991). A DAG-based algorithm for distributed mutual exclusion. In *Proc. of the International Conference on Distributed Computing Systems*, 354–360.

Netzer, R. H. B., and J. Xu (1993). Adaptive message logging for incremental program replay. *IEEE Parallel & Distributed Technology* **1**(4), 32–39.

Ni, L. M., and P. K. McKinley (1993). A survey of wormhole routing techniques in direct networks. *Computer* **26**(2), 62–76.

Nicol, D. (1992). Conservative parallel simulation of priority class queuing networks. *IEEE Trans. on Parallel and Distributed Systems* **3**, 294–303.

Nicol, D. M. (1993). Global synchronization for optimistic parallel discrete event simulation. In *Proc. of the Workshop on Parallel and Distributed Simulation*, 27–34.

Nicol, D., and R. Fujimoto (1994). Parallel simulation today. *Annals of Operations Research* **53**, 249–285.

Nicol, D. M., and P. F. Reynolds, Jr. (1990). Optimal dynamic remapping of data parallel computations. *IEEE Trans. on Computers* **39**, 206–219.

Nilsson, N. J. (1980). *Principles of Artificial Intelligence*. Tioga, Palo Alto, CA.

Ogier, R. G., V. Rutenburg, and N. Shacham (1993). Distributed algorithms for computing shortest pairs of disjoint paths. *IEEE Trans. on Information Theory* **39**, 443–455.

Ousterhout, J. K., A. R. Cherenson, F. Douglis, M. N. Nelson, and B. B. Welch (1988). The Sprite network operating system. *Computer* **21**(2), 23–36.

Overmars, M., and N. Santoro (1989). Time vs. bits: an improved algorithm for leader election in synchronous rings. In *Proc. of the Annual Symposium on Theoretical Aspects of Computer Science*, 282–293.

Papadimitriou, C. H., and K. Steiglitz (1982). *Combinatorial Optimization*. Prentice-Hall, Englewood Cliffs, NJ.

Pase, D. M., and A. R. Larrabee (1988). Intel iPSC concurrent computer. In R. G. Babb II (Ed.), *Programming Parallel Processors*, 105–124. Addison-Wesley, Reading, MA.

Pearl, J. (1984). *Heuristics: Intelligent Search Strategies for Computer Problem Solving*. Addison-Wesley, Reading, MA.

Pearl, J. (1988). *Probabilistic Reasoning in Intelligent Systems: Networks of Plausible Inference*. Morgan Kaufmann, San Mateo, CA.

Peleg, D. (1990). Time-optimal leader election in general networks. *J. of Parallel and Distributed Computing* **8**, 96–99.

Perrott, R. H. (1987). *Parallel Programming*. Addison-Wesley, Wokingham, England.

Pnueli, A. (1981). The temporal semantics of concurrent programs. *Theoretical Computer Science* **13**, 45–60.

Pohlmann, W. (1991). A fixed point approach to parallel discrete event simulation. *Acta Informatica* **28**, 611–629.

Portella, C. F., and V. C. Barbosa (1992). Parallel maximum-flow algorithms on a transputer hypercube. Technical report ES-251/92, COPPE/UFRJ, Rio de Janeiro, Brazil.

Prakash, A., and R. Subramanian (1992). An efficient optimistic distributed simulation scheme based on conditional knowledge. In *Proc. of the Workshop on Parallel and Distributed Simulation*, 85–94.

Preiss, B. R., and W. M. Loucks (1990). The impact of lookahead on the performance of conservative distributed simulation. In *Modelling and Simulation, Proc. of the European Simulation Multiconference*, 204–209.

Preiss, B. R., W. M. Loucks, I. D. MacIntyre, and J. A. Field (1990). Null message cancellation in conservative distributed simulation. In *Advances in Parallel and Distributed Simulation, Proc. of the (1991) SCS Multiconference*, 33–37.

Preiss, B. R., I. D. MacIntyre, and W. M. Loucks (1992). On the trade-off between time and space in optimistic parallel discrete-event simulation. In *Proc. of the Workshop on Parallel and Distributed Simulation*, 33–42.

Protić, J., M. Tomašević, and V. Milutinović (1995). A survey of distributed shared memory systems. In *Proc. of the Hawaii International Conference on System Sciences*, 74–84.

Rabin, M., and D. Lehmann (1981). On the advantages of free choice: a symmetric and fully distributed solution to the dining philosophers problem. In *Proc. of the Annual ACM Symposium on Principles of Programming Languages*, 133–138.

Rajsbaum, S., and M. Sidi (1994). On the performance of synchronized programs in distributed networks with random processing times and transmission delays. *IEEE Trans. on Parallel and Distributed Systems* **5**, 939–950.

Ramachandran, V., M. Solomon, and M. Vernon (1987). Hardware support for interprocess communication. In *Proc. of the Annual International Symposium on Computer Architecture*, 178–188.

Ramanathan, P., and K. G. Shin (1993). Use of common time base for checkpointing and rollback recovery in a distributed system. *IEEE Trans. on Software Engineering* **19**, 571–583.

Ramarao, K. V. S., and K. Brahmadathan (1990). Divide and conquer for distributed mutual exclusion. In *Proc. of the IEEE Symposium on Parallel and Distributed Processing*, 113–120.

Ramarao, K. V. S., and S. Venkatesan (1993). The lower bounds on distributed shortest paths. *Information Processing Letters* **48**, 145–149.

Ravi, T. M., and D. R. Jefferson (1988). A basic protocol for routing messages to migrating processes. In *Proc. of the International Conference on Parallel Processing*, 188–196.

Raymond, K. (1989). A tree-based algorithm for distributed mutual exclusion. *ACM Trans. on Computer Systems* **7**, 61–77.

Raynal, M. (1986). *Algorithms for Mutual Exclusion*. The MIT Press, Cambridge, MA.

Raynal, M. (1988). *Distributed Algorithms and Protocols*. Wiley, Chichester, UK.

Raynal, M. (1991). A simple taxonomy for distributed mutual exclusion algorithms. *Operating Systems Review* **25**, 47–50.

Reinhardt, S. K., J. R. Larus, and D. A. Wood (1994). Tempest and Typhoon: user-level shared-memory. In *Proc. of the Annual International Symposium on Computer Architecture*, 325–336.

Ricart, G., and A. K. Agrawala (1981). An optimal algorithm for mutual exclusion in computer networks. *Comm. of the ACM* **24**, 9–17.

Ronn, S., and H. Saikkonen (1990). Distributed termination detection with counters. *Information Processing Letters* **34**, 223–227.

Saleh, K., H. Ural, and A. Agarwal (1994). Modified distributed snapshots algorithm for protocol stabilization. *Computer Communications* **17**, 863–870.

Satyanarayanan, R., and D. R. Muthukrishnan (1992). A note on Raymond's tree based algorithm for distributed mutual exclusion. *Information Processing Letters* **43**, 249–255.

Schneider, M. (1993). Self-stabilization. *ACM Computing Surveys* **25**, 45–67.

Segall, A. (1983). Distributed network protocols. *IEEE Trans. on Information Theory* **29**, 23–35.

Seitz, C. L. (1985). The cosmic cube. *Comm. of the ACM* **28**, 22–33.

Selvakumar, S., and C. Siva Ram Murthy (1994). Static task allocation of concurrent programs for distributed computing systems with processor and resource heterogeneity. *Parallel Computing* **20**, 835–851.

Shabtay, L., and A. Segall (1992). Message delaying synchronizers. In *Proc. of the (1991) International Workshop on Distributed Algorithms*, 309–318.

Shen, C.-C., and W.-H. Tsai (1985). A graph matching approach to optimal task assignment in distributed computing systems using a minimax criterion. *IEEE Trans. on Computers* **34**, 197–203.

Sheth, B., and D. M. Dhamdhere (1991). Two-level scheme for distributed termination detection. In *Proc. of the Supercomputing Symposium*, 343–352.

Shiloach, Y., and U. Vishkin (1982). An $O(n^2 \log n)$ parallel max-flow algorithm. *J. of Algorithms* **3**, 128–146.

Silberschatz, A., J. L. Peterson, and P. B. Galvin (1994). *Operating System Concepts*. Addison-Wesley, Reading, MA.

Sinclair, J. B. (1987). Efficient computation of optimal assignments for distributed tasks. *J. of Parallel and Distributed Computing* **4**, 342–362.

Singh, G. (1992). Leader election in complete networks. In *Proc. of the Annual ACM Symposium on Principles of Distributed Computing*, 179–190.

Singh, S., and J. F. Kurose (1994). Electing "good" leaders. *J. of Parallel and Distributed Computing* **21**, 184–201.

Singhal, M. (1989a). A heuristically-aided algorithm for mutual exclusion in distributed systems. *IEEE Trans. on Computers* **38**, 651–662.

Singhal, M. (1989b). Deadlock detection in distributed systems. *Computer* **22**(11), 37–48.

Singhal, M. (1991). A class of deadlock-free Maekawa-type algorithms for mutual exclusion in distributed systems. *Distributed Computing* **4**, 131–138.

Singhal, M. (1993). A taxonomy of distributed mutual exclusion. *J. of Parallel and Distributed Computing* **18**, 94–101.

Sokol, L. M., D. P. Briscoe, and A. P. Wieland (1988). MTW: a strategy for scheduling discrete event simulation events for concurrent execution. In *Distributed Simulation, Proc. of the SCS Multiconference*, 34–42.

Sokol, L. M., and B. K. Stucky (1990). MTW: experimental results for a constrained optimistic scheduling paradigm. In *Distributed Simulation, Proc. of the SCS Multiconference*, 169–173.

Sokol, L. M., B. K. Stucky, and V. S. Hwang (1989). MTW: a control mechanism for parallel discrete simulation. In *Proc. of the International Conference on Parallel Processing*, III-250–254.

Sokol, L. M., J. B. Weissman, and P. A. Mutchler (1991). MTW: an empirical performance study. In *Proc. of the Winter Simulation Conference*, 557–563.

Spencer, J. (1986). Balancing vectors in the max norm. *Combinatorica* **6**, 55–65.

Spezialetti, M. (1991). An approach to reducing delays in recognizing distributed event occurrences. In *Proc. of the ACM Workshop on Parallel and Distributed Debugging*, 155–166.

Spezialetti, M., and J. P. Kearns (1989). Simultaneous regions: a framework for the consistent monitoring of distributed systems. In *Proc. of the Ninth International Conference on Distributed Computing Systems*, 61–68.

Srinivasan, S., and P. F. Reynolds, Jr. (1993). Non-interfering GVT computation via asynchronous global reductions. In *Proc. of the Winter Simulation Conference*, 740–749.

Stahl, S. (1976). *n*-tuple colorings and associated graphs. *J. of Combinatorial Theory, Series B* **20**, 185–203.

Stahl, S. (1979). Fractional edge colorings. *Cahiers du C.E.R.O.* **21**, 127–131.

Stamoulis, G. D., M. E. Anagnostou, and A. D. Georgantas (1994). Traffic source models for ATM networks: a survey. *Computer Communications* **17**, 428–438.

Sur, S., and P. K. Srimani (1992). A self-stabilizing distributed algorithm to construct BFS spanning trees of a symmetric graph. *Parallel Processing Letters* **2**, 171–179.

Sur, S., and P. K. Srimani (1993). A self-stabilizing algorithm for coloring bipartite graphs. *Information Sciences* **69**, 219–227.

Sysło, M. M., N. Deo, and J. S. Kowalik (1983). *Discrete Optimization Algorithms*. Prentice-Hall, Englewood Cliffs, NJ.

Tanenbaum, A. S. (1988). *Computer Networks*. Prentice-Hall, Englewood Cliffs, NJ.

Tanenbaum, A. S. (1992). *Modern Operating Systems*. Prentice-Hall, Englewood Cliffs, NJ.

Tel, G. (1994a). Maximal matching stabilizes in quadratic time. *Information Processing Letters* **49**, 271–272.

Tel, G. (1994b). *Introduction to Distributed Algorithms*. Cambridge University Press, Cambridge, UK.

Teo, Y. M., and S. C. Tay (1994). Efficient algorithms for conservative parallel simulation of interconnection networks. In *Proc. of the International Symposium on Parallel Architectures, Algorithms and Networks*, 286–293.

Theimer, M., K. Lantz, and D. Cheriton (1985). Preemptable remote execution facilities for the V-System. In *Proc. of the ACM Symposium on Operating System Principles*, 2–12.

Tsaan Huang, S. (1993). Leader election in uniform rings. *ACM Trans. on Programming Languages and Systems* **15**, 563–573.

Tsai, M.-S., and S.-T. Huang (1994). A self-stabilizing algorithm for the shortest paths problem with a fully distributed demon. *Parallel Processing Letters* **4**, 65–72.

Tucker, L. W., and A. Mainwaring (1994). CMMD: active messages on the CM-5. *Parallel Computing* **20**, 481–496.

van der Meyden, R. (1994). Axioms for knowledge and time in distributed systems with perfect recall. In *Proc. of the Symposium on Logic in Computer Science*, 448–457.

von Eicken, T., D. E. Culler, S. C. Goldstein, and K. E. Schauser (1992). Active messages: a mechanism for integrated communication and computation. In *Proc. of the Annual International Symposium on Computer Architecture*, 256–266.

von Neumann, J. (1966). *Theory of Self-Reproducing Automata*, A. W. Burks (Ed.). University of Illinois Press, Urbana, IL.

Wedemann, R. S., V. C. Barbosa, and R. J. Donangelo (1995). Defeasible time-stepping. In preparation.

Welch, J. L., L. Lamport, and N. A. Lynch (1988). A lattice-structured proof technique applied to a minimum spanning tree algorithm. In *Proc. of the Annual ACM Symposium on Principles of Distributed Computing*, 28–43.

Wilson, R. J. (1979). *Introduction to Graph Theory*. Longman, London, England.

Wolfram, S. (Ed.) (1986). *Theory and Applications of Cellular Automata*. World Scientific, Singapore.

Woo, T.-K., and R. Newman-Wolfe (1992). Huffman trees as a basis for a dynamic mutual exclusion algorithm for distributed systems. In *Proc. of the International Conference on Distributed Computing Systems*, 126–133.

Wood, K. R., and S. J. Turner (1994). A generalized carrier-null method for conservative parallel simulation. In *Proc. of the Workshop on Parallel and Distributed Simulation*, 50–57.

Wylie, C. R. (1975). *Advanced Engineering Mathematics*. McGraw-Hill, Tokyo, Japan.

Xu, J., and R. H. B. Netzer (1993). Adaptive independent checkpointing for reducing rollback propagation. In *Proc. of the IEEE Symposium on Parallel and Distributed Processing*, 754–761.

Yang, Z., and T. A. Marsland (1992). Global snapshots for distributed debugging. In *Proc. of the International Conference on Computing and Information*, 436–440.

Yang, Z., and T. A. Marsland (1993). Annotated bibliography on global states and times in distributed systems. *Operating Systems Review* **27**, 55–74.

Yu, M.-L., S. Ghosh, and E. DeBenedictis (1990). A non-deadlocking conservative asynchronous distributed discrete event simulation algorithm. In *Advances in Parallel and Distributed Simulation, Proc. of the (1991) SCS Multiconference*, 39–43.

Zhonghua, Y., and T. A. Marsland (Eds.) (1994). *Global States and Time in Distributed Systems*. IEEE Computer Society Press, Los Alamitos, CA.

Author Index

Subject Index